扬州大学出版基金资助

美 国 梦
——教育因·学术果

The American Dream
— From Education Commitment to Academic Excellence

田德新 著

西北工业大学出版社

【内容简介】 作为一本关于美国教育本质和西方学术特性的研究论著,本书分为两部分,第1~12章用中文撰写,内容涉及美国基础教育和大学的办学理念、特色与改革,私立学校和常春藤高校的办学特色,创新人才培养机制,学术自由和学术诚信,外语教学的最新动态,大学教育理念和课程大纲的重要性,以及人际传播学理论与研究评述等。第13~23章用英文撰写,内容包括评析美国与北约炸我驻南使馆事件的所谓道歉与空中撞机事件的霸权式回应,讨论中国森林环保的传播模式与转变性质,比照中美女性领导风格与中西家教文化差异,论述面向21世纪的中美大国交流途径与汉语常用术语的文化渊源,分析作为演讲课基石的经典阅读与课程改革以及测评《经济人》等西方媒体对新疆暴乱事件的失真报道等。

本书以英语专业高年级学生、研究生及预备赴国外深造人员为读者对象,可使其事半功倍地了解美国教育的本质,快捷高效地掌握国际学术研究的命门。

图书在版编目(CIP)数据

美国梦:教育因·学术果:汉、英/田德新著. —西安:西北工业大学出版社,2015.12
ISBN 978-7-5612-4686-3

Ⅰ.①美… Ⅱ.①田… Ⅲ.①教育研究—美国—汉、英 Ⅳ.①G571.2

中国版本图书馆 CIP 数据核字(2016)第 007387 号

出版发行:西北工业大学出版社
通信地址:西安市友谊西路 127 号　邮编:710072
电　　话:(029)88493844　88491757
网　　址:www.nwpup.com
印 刷 者:兴平市博闻印务有限公司
开　　本:787 mm×1 092 mm　1/16
印　　张:16.75
字　　数:409 千字
版　　次:2016 年 3 月第 1 版　2016 年 3 月第 1 次印刷
定　　价:48.00 元

前　言

《美国梦——教育因·学术果》(*The American Dream — From Education Commitment to Academic Excellence*)是一本关于美国教育本质和西方学术特性的研究论著,是一本帮助千万读者圆梦的学术著作。据美国国际教育协会2014年统计,2013—2014学年在美就读的国际留学生总数为886 052人,其中中国留学生的人数占总人数的31%。实际上,中国赴美留学生的人数自2010年超过印度后,逐年呈上升趋势,从2009—2010学年到2013—2014学年分别为127 628人、157 558人、194 029人、235 597人和274 439人。为什么成千上万的学子向往美国的大学教育?怎样才能深入地了解美国教育,有效地完成梦想学业?本书为您指点迷津,帮您圆梦!

笔者曾任职西安外国语大学英文学院主管科研和研究生教育的副院长、英语教授。2005—2008年在美国鲍林格林州立大学攻读媒体与传播学博士学位,获取2008年优秀研究生奖学金(Harold Fisher Scholarship Award)和毕业论文大奖(Non-Service Dissertation Award)。2009—2014年,先后任美国路易斯安那亚利桑那州立大学助理教授、萨凡纳艺术设计学院文科教授。本书基于笔者担任教育领事期间的实地教育调研、读博期间的深造经历,以及在美国两所大学任教过程中的教学和科研成果,由笔者精心整理、更新和撰写已经发表和即将付梓的论文组成,目的是向中国读者介绍笔者对美国教育特色与本质的感受与领会,同时分享和传授如何学习并掌握国际学术话语权,即必要的学术理论与研究方法,在诸如社会科学引文索引来源(SSCI)刊物和国际顶级学术会议等平台与场合发表研究成果,交流中国语言文化,畅谈华夏赤子的心声和愿景。

本书包括23篇论文,篇篇独立成章,内容前后衔接。全书分为上、下两部分,前12章用中文撰写,内容涉及美国基础教育的现状、特点、问题与改革,私立学校的管理体制与常春藤私立大学的办学理念和特色,创新人才培养机制与学术自由和学术诚信,外语教学的最新动态与美国明德学院的中文教学特色,大学课程大纲与教育理念和实践研究,以及人际传播学理论与研究评述。后11章用英文撰写,内容包括评析美国与北约炸我驻南使馆事件的所谓道歉与空中撞机事件的霸权式回应,讨论中国森林环保的传播模式与性质转变,比照中美女性领导风格与中西家教文化差异,论述面向21世纪的中美大国交流途径与汉语常用术语的文化渊源,分析作为演讲课基石的经典阅读与课程改革,以及测评《经济人》等西方媒体对新疆暴乱事件的失真报道。

本书主要有下述特点。

(一)高屋建瓴:以教育领事的视角,通过实地考察、走访有关专家学者和总结前人研究成果,全面、具体、生动地介绍美国教育、课程设置和课堂教学的独特之处。

（二）深入浅出：本书两部分的23章全部出自笔者和笔者与他人合作的已经发表和即将出版的学术论文。它们篇篇经过精心挑选和更新加工，用实例让读者省时省力地把握美国及西方相关国家的学习者在学术研究方面所必备的理论素养和研究方法功底。

（三）经济实用：所选章节对美国教育特色的介绍，正中命门；对西方学术水平的展示，点到为止。无论是准备到美国求学，还是想深入了解美国教育的读者，一方面可以省时高效地把握美国教育特色的关键，另一方面可以对学术研究的整个过程一目了然，并在日常实践中举一反三。

本书适用于英语专业高年级和研究生教学以及预备赴国外深造人员自学参考。

本书为"扬州大学出版基金资助"成果，特此衷心感谢扬州大学的资助，感谢扬州大学和外国语学院各级领导的支持和关怀，感谢同事们的帮助和鼓励！由于水平有限，书中错漏之处在所难免，恳请读者朋友批评指正。

著 者

2015年11月

目 录

上部 教 育 因

第一章　美国基础教育的现状、特点、问题与改革 …………………………………… 1
第二章　深入发展的美国基础教育改革 ………………………………………………… 7
第三章　美国私立学校的管理体制 ……………………………………………………… 12
第四章　美国私立高等教育中常春藤联盟院校的办学理念与特色 …………………… 16
第五章　美国创新人才培养机制 ………………………………………………………… 24
第六章　美国高校的学术自由与学术诚信 ……………………………………………… 29
第七章　美国外语教学最新动态研究 …………………………………………………… 34
第八章　美国明德学院的中文教学特色与启示 ………………………………………… 41
第九章　基于民族志方法的美国大学课程大纲研究与借鉴 …………………………… 45
第十章　美国高等教育理念的发展和大学教学实践特色研究与借鉴 ………………… 52
第十一章　美国人际传播理论与研究述评（上） ……………………………………… 60
第十二章　美国人际传播理论与研究述评（下） ……………………………………… 66

下部 学 术 果

Chapter 13　U.S. and NATO Apologies for the Chinese Embassy Bombing:
　　　　　　A Categorical Analysis ……………………………………………………… 81
Chapter 14　The American Hegemonic Responses to the U.S.-China Mid-air Plane
　　　　　　Collision ……………………………………………………………………… 99
Chapter 15　The Communication Model and the Nature of Change in Terms
　　　　　　of Deforestation in China since 1949 ……………………………………… 116
Chapter 16　Like Tiger Mother, Like Tiger Daughter: A Content Analysis
　　　　　　of the Impact of Cultural Differences on Eastern and Western

		Parenting Styles ………………………………………………… 127
Chapter 17		Keeping Relationships Positive or Doing Things Right: Bridging Women Leaders' Conflict Management Strategies in Non-profit Organizations in Taiwan and the United States ……………………………… 138
Chapter 18		Culturally Universal or Culturally Specific: A Comparative Study of Anticipated Female Leadership Styles in Taiwan and the United States ……………………………………………………………… 157
Chapter 19		Chimerica: U. S.-China Communication in the 21st Century ……… 185
Chapter 20		Prominent Chinese Terms and Their Profound Cultural Roots ……… 196
Chapter 21		Border Institutions—What Is Lacking in the Diaoyu/Senkaku Islands Dispute …………………………………………………… 209
Chapter 22		Laying the Cornerstone: Transforming the Public Speaking Course with Themed Classics ……………………………………………… 234
Chapter 23		Testing News Trustworthiness in an Online Public Sphere: A Case Study of *The Economist*'s News Report Covering the Riots in Xinjiang, China ………………………………………………… 241

上部 教育因

第一章
美国基础教育的现状、特点、问题与改革

一、现状

早在 17 世纪初,自从首批欧洲移民定居北美大陆,各种启蒙教育活动应运而生。1647 年,定居美国东北部的马萨诸塞州移民,就通过州议会颁布了著名的"祛魔法案",即要战胜魔鬼,就必须兴教兴学。该法案明确规定,50 户以上的乡镇必需建立小学,100 户以上的必需建立拉丁文法学校,学校的维持费用和教师的薪俸由州税收支付。同时,该法案责令家长和雇主也要担负起儿童教育的责任,否则课以罚款,从而开启了美国公立教育的先河(Omstein, & Levine,1981)。

当今的美国基础教育属于义务教育,一般学生在 18 岁时应完成基础教育。基础阶段的中小学校有公立和私立两种:公立学校的办学经费由政府税收支付,学生免费入学;私立学校多由教会支持和赞助。美国的义务教育普及率较高,大约有 90% 以上的适龄儿童接受高中教育,高中毕业率约为 90%,其中约 60% 的高中毕业生可以进入大学接受高等教育。

根据美国全国教育统计中心(National Center for Education Statistics)2013 年的统计数据,截至 2011—2012 学年,美国基础教育中,拥有公立学校 98 328 所,私立学校 30 861 所。其中公立学校包括小学 66 689 所、中学 24 357 所、中小学兼有的学校 6 311 所,以及其他诸如特许学校和家庭学校的基础教育机构 971 所。总体而言,美国的教育可分为 4 个阶段:学前教育、初等教育、中等教育和高等教育。美国的学前教育、初等教育和中等教育统称为基础教育。其中学前教育包括保育院(nursery school/day care center)和幼稚园(kindergarten),面向 2~6 岁学龄前儿童;小学(elementary school)一般实行六年制,招收 6~12 岁适龄小学生;初中(middle school)三年制和高中(high school)三年制,招收 12~18 岁适龄初高中学生(见表 1.1)。

从表1.1可以看出,美国的基础教育阶段从小学到高中毕业共12年,因而也常被称为K-12教育阶段。由于教育的管理和实施权归属各州,因此,表1.1所列出的小学六年、初中三年和高中三年的学制在全美并非整齐划一,而是各州之间有所不同。除了上述的"六三三制度",还有"四四制""五三四制"以及"六六制"。

表1.1 美国基础教育的学制阶段与年龄分布

阶 段	年 级	年 龄
学前	保育院	2～3岁
	幼稚园	3～6岁
小学	1年级	6～7岁
	2年级	7～8岁
	3年级	8～9岁
	4年级	9～10岁
	5年级	10～11岁
	6年级	11～12岁
初中	7年级	12～13岁
	8年级	13～14岁
	9年级	14～15岁
高中	10年级	15～16岁
	11年级	16～17岁
	12年级	17～18岁

二、特点

中国改革开放以来,国内学者(段素菊,2010;王定华,2008;赵中建,2001;张家勇,2003;张巍,2005;曾德琪,1999)对美国教育的研究和引荐,成果显著。作为美国历史、社会与文化的产物,美国基础教育特点鲜明,不乏可取之处,其中主要的有下述两方面。

(一)办学的灵活性和多样性

美国的基础教育由联邦、州和学区三级管理。由于美国是联邦制国家,其教育行政实行中央和地方分权。联邦教育部主要通过立法和拨款发挥规划、指导和协调作用。教育的管理和实施以州为主体,州政府的立法机构制定教育的法律和政策。地方学区委员会负责中小学的具体事务和管理,拥有征收教育税、人事、学校财产管理以及教学和课程安排等决策权力。由于联邦和州政府责权分明,加之地方学区和各个学校具备办学的主动性和积极性,美国的基础教育在办学体制上体现出较大的灵活性和多样性。

因此,美国的中小学除了公立学校外,还有各式各样的民办私立学校,其中有宗教性质的、公校私营的、家庭性质的、教育券(voucher)计划性质的(即学生家长可以选择让孩子不去公立学校,而上私立学校,并从政府领取有价教育券),还有国外组织为其职员或侨民子女承办的各种学校。另外,学校和教师在分班、开课、选教材以及教学评估各个方面有很大的自主权。学校可以根据其办学目标和学生的需求开设数十门课程,学校没有统一的分数标准将学生分为优等生和差等生,也没有按升学考试将任何课程分为主科与副科,教学评估也多为实际操作、研究项目报告以及课堂讨论表现等需要动手和动脑的测评形式。

(二)尊重和满足学生的个性需求,注重培养人的全方位发展

美国的基础教育深受以杜威为代表的进步主义教育思想的影响,在教学的培养目标上注重"全儿童"(whole child)的培养,使学生的身心得到全面发展。同时,通过"从做中学"的课内外教学活动,让学生学习生活,研究生活,在满足和开发其兴趣的同时,培养其解决实际问题的能力。美国小学的教育宗旨:①增进儿童的健康和发展儿童的体格;②增进儿童的心理健康和发展儿童的人格;③发展儿童对社会和科学世界的认识;④发展儿童有效地参与民主社会的技能;⑤发展儿童的民主生活价值观;⑥发展儿童的创造性技能。美国中学的教育宗旨:①作为学术目标,学生要学会通过听、说、读、写,获取和表达思想;②作为职业目标,学生要学会选择个人满意又适合本人兴趣和技能的职业;③作为社会、公民和文化目标,学生要熟悉和了解不同价值系统及其对个人和社会的影响;④作为个人目标,学生要学会在追求自我目标的同时,尊重他人的情感。

具体而言,美国的基础教育注重培养学生的学习兴趣,鼓励学生大胆地去想、去做、去交流,因此学生大多表现主动、灵活和快乐。美国人不崇拜权威,学生也不盲目崇拜老师,师生之间还有父母与孩子之间讲究平等,追求相互尊重的朋友关系。交谈时,父母往往席地而坐,与子女平等沟通;教师常常在书桌旁半跪下来,和学生交流。美国的中小学生每天多为上午九点上课,下午三点放学,年平均上课时间为1 000小时左右。这样,上学时间短,课业负担轻,学生有大量的时间做自己感兴趣的事情,诸如读书、实地参观与访问、动手实验与完成各种研究项目。笔头考试多为开卷,有些考试学生只要在一周内交卷即可。考试成绩属于学生的隐私,教师和学校若没有得到考生本人的许可,不能向任何人公开学生的成绩,包括向学生的父母或监护人,以避免学生承受不必要的心理压力。

三、问题

然而,美国基础教育也存在问题。譬如,美国中小学生学业水平持续低下的现状成为长期困扰其基础教育的一个老大难问题。概括起来,美国基础教育的主要问题有以下几方面。

(一)缺乏有效的宏观调控

如上所述,美国的基础教育分权而治,各州、各学区以及各学校都有较高的自主权。这种制度有其优点,但其最大的负面作用是不利于全国性统一的宏观调控。虽然美国联邦政府通过立法和拨款力图改变这一局面,以便制定和实施统一的教育改革法案。战后历次教育改革的结果证明,联邦,甚至有些州政府的宏观调控不灵,高标准和统一的改革方案很难落到实处。这种教育体制上的固有弱点,在一定程度上阻碍了美国基础教育质量的整体迅速提高和美国学生国际竞争力的快速全面攀升。

(二)让人汗颜的低下教育质量

根据美国教育部的统计数字,美国12年级学生的平均成绩持续下降,1996年有3%的12年级学生达到高级水平,19%达到熟练水平,36%达到基本水平,43%低于基本要求;而2000年的相关比例分别为2%,16%,34%和47%。2009年,美国教育考查所对全美140万名9～17岁的中小学生进行了几项基本技能的调查。结果是在阅读方面,有58%的17岁学生看不懂所学课文和报刊文章;在数学方面,有49%的17岁学生不知道"10的85%"是大于还是小于10;在科学方面,有56%的17岁学生不会运用所学知识去解决教科书中的问题。可见,美国的基础教育质量远远落后于其他发达的工业化国家。人们也不难理解,为什么美国学生在各类国际竞赛中表现平平。

(三)不敢恭维的恶劣校园环境

美国全国教育中心报道,2000年约380万名青少年辍学,占美国16～24周岁青少年人数的10.9%。其中,西班牙裔青少年辍学率为27.8%,非洲裔的为13.1%,白人孩子为6.9%。另据报道,近年来青少年学生旷课比例已经攀升至38%;每年无家可归者中,25%是儿童;未婚少女当妈妈的比例也从1996年的38%上升到2000年的55%。1999年,Henry J. Kaiser家庭基础研究所调查发现,美国2/3的高中毕业生有过性交的经历,50%的在校高中生有过性交的经历。其中15%的青少年染有生殖器尖锐湿疣病症,在所有的HIV病例中有25%是21岁以下的青少年。美国学生酗酒、吸毒、盗窃、抢劫和强奸等时有发生。

四、改革

由于上述有关美国基础教育的问题与美国的国计民生和长治久安有直接的关联性,因而引发了一次次有关中小学教育的大辩论,引起了包括美国总统在内的各方面人士的关注,导致了一次次基础教育改革的浪潮。例如,第一次大辩论发生在以冷战为背景的20世纪50年代。美国学者通过与当时欧洲和苏联的教育的比较,认为美国的中小学教育质量远远低于欧洲的许多国家,美国12年级学生的水平只相当于苏联10年级学生的水平。20世纪80年代,对美国基础教育质量的批评更加严厉。批评家们发现,美国学生在各种国际学业竞赛中几乎总是最后几名,许多中学毕业生缺乏最起码的读写和运算能力,大学入学考试的表现每况愈下。

美国独立战争(1775—1783年)的胜利,不但为美国赢得国家的独立,也为独立后的美国走向资本主义,实现国家的工业化开辟了道路。但是,当时的美国教育体制仍然带有浓厚的殖民性和宗教色彩。于是,美国历史上掀起了以建立世俗化公立教育体系为目标的第一次教育改革。改革的具体内容包括以下几方面:①教育内容世俗化,公立学校开始接收所有儿童入学,教学内容不再是纯粹的宗教传道;②基础教育公立化,它标志着美国资产阶级开始掌握教育的控制权,也为日后美国的教育体系打下了坚实的基础;③学校体制体系化,教育与宗教分离,并以法律的名义得到确立。从此,州政府依据其州宪法的规定,开始统管全州的所有学区及其学校。

从19世纪末到20世纪20年代,美国历史上兴起了进步主义思潮,其代言人是著名的美国实用主义哲学家和教育家约翰·杜威(John Dewey,1859—1952年)。进步主义要对当时的公立教育制度进行改革,使其更为开明和实用,成为美国历史上的第二次教育改革。杜威的教育哲学思想从进步主义的开端到20世纪50年代,对美国基础教育的改革产生了巨大的影响。杜威教育哲学思想主要包括以下几方面:①教育性质论,即"教育即生活"和"教育即生长";②教育活动论,即"从做中学"和"学校即社会";③教育价值论,即注重在学业、道德和职业各个方面培养身心全面发展的"全儿童"(whole child)式学生。

1957年,苏联卫星SPUTNIK发射成功。1958年美国总统艾森豪威尔签署通过了具有重大战略意义的《国防教育法》,从而开始了美国基础教育的第三次改革。此次改革以数学、自然科学和外语为重点,重视科学教学内容的现代化,注重现代化技术在教学过程中的运用,强调天才教育和科学精英团队的培养。这次改革不但扭转了美国基础教育中过分强调实用化的倾向,而且还适应了当时美国急需培养高级人才、发展尖端科技以及增强国家综合实力的战略需求。指导这一时期美国基础教育改革的是布鲁纳的认知结构学习理论。该理论认为学习的目的在于发现学习方法,使学科的基本结构转变为学生头脑中的认知结构。在学习观上,该理论强调:①学习的实质是主动地形成认知结构;②学习包括知识的获得、转化和评估三个过程。在教学观上,该理论人为教学的目的首先在于理解学科的基本结构,因此,学习一门学科的关键是理解和掌握基本的概念、原理和方法及其相互之间的意义联系。其次在于掌握学科基本结构的教学原则,即动机原则、结构原则、程序原则和强化原则。该理论虽然忽视了影响教育的社会因素,但是它推动了教育从行为主义向认知心理学的转变,从实验室研究向课堂研究的转变,从学习研究向教学研究的转变。它不但对美国,而且对世界许多国家的教育改革都产生了广泛而深远的影响。

1983年,里根总统授权成立的高质量委员会发表《国家处于危机之中:教育改革势在必行》的报告,开始了美国基础教育的第四次改革。该报告指出,美国有13%的17岁青年在实际能力上是文盲,大学需要给新生开设越来越多的补习课程。报告将美国在商业、工业和科学技术等方面落后于其他发达国家的现状归咎于美国基础教育质量的低下,明确了"危险"的含义和标志,指出了美国基础教育目标、内容和师资等方面的问题和改革建议。该报告列举了大量的事实和数据,让美国人震惊地发现其教育质量的低劣已经危及美国前途和民族精神。因此,建立全国统一标准和提高教育质量成为此次改革的主旋律。各州州政府、学区和学校一起振作了起来,为提高教育质量做出了巨大的努力,使此次改革的浪潮高过此前任何一次,《国家处于危机之中:教育改革势在必行》起到了振聋发聩的效应,成为美国基础教育改革史上里程碑的报告。

20世纪80年代以来,美国相继出台了不少基础教育改革法案和实施措施。譬如,1991年布什总统签发了《美国2000年:教育战略》的纲领性文件,提出了美国教育的主要战略和国家教育目标。1993年,克林顿政府制定了《2000年的目标:美国教育法》,试图建立全国性的课程标准和全国性的学业评估制度。2002年,美国总统小布什签署了《不让一个孩子掉队法》,确立了全美每一个孩子都应受到良好教育的总目标。2009年,美国总统奥巴马签署《力争上游计划》,将美国的基础教育改革又向前推进了一步。

五、结论

本章概述了美国基础教育的现状。从1620年欧洲先民定居美洲,教育也同时在美洲大陆扎根。自从1647年"祛魔法案"颁布以来,正规教育便应运而生,与美国一起生长繁荣。当今的美国基础教育,联邦、州政府、学区和学校责权分明,教育的管理和实施权归属各州,无论是私立还是公立学校拥有相当的自主和自治的权利。基础阶段从幼稚园到高中毕业12个年级,全部实现免费义务教学。

美国基础教育特点明显、众多,而本章仅细说了其中的两方面。一是办学的灵活性和多样性;二是尊重和满足学生的个性需求,同时注重培养学生作为人的全面发展。美国基础教育最可取的是,发展学生健康体格的同时,增进其健全的心理和人格;培养学生具备认识社会和世界科学知识的同时,鼓励其积极参与社区活动,从而不断丰富适应社会现实的技能;通过积极、主动、快乐和有趣的学习,拓展学生的学习兴趣、创造性和交际能力。

当然,美国基础教育中也存在许多问题,本章对缺乏有效的宏观调控、让人汗颜的低下教育质量以及不敢恭维的恶劣校园环境三点进行了描述。美国基础教育管理中,宏观调控不力,主要原因是来自国家的体制,同时某些富可敌国的利益集团从中作梗也是重要因素之一。美国校园环境恶化,许多公立学校教学质量长期不尽人意,致使越来越多的美国家长宁愿支付双重教育税收,将子女送到教育质量和校园环境较好的私立学校,或父母一方牺牲工作让孩子干脆在家就读家庭学校。

最后,本章探讨了美国基础教育的历次改革。首先,值得赞赏的是美国人的勇气,无论是官方还是学界,敢于挖掘、厘清和暴露自身教育各个环节中的缺陷,并通过改革促其不断完善。可以说,美国有关基础教育质量的辩论一轮接着一轮,改革一浪高过一浪。一系列的改革计划为美国基础教育质量的提高做出了巨大的贡献,但是由于美国的国体和国情,其基础教育固有的许多棘手问题仍然存在,需要持续不断的改进和改革。

参 考 文 献

[1] National Center for Education Statistics. (2013). Digest of Education Statistics,(NCES 2015-011). Available at: http://nces.ed.gov/fastfacts/display.asp?id=84.

[2] Omstein, A. C., & Levine, D. L. (1981). An introduction to the foundations of education [M]. Boston, MA: Houghton Mifflin Company.

[3] 段素菊.(2010).美国基础教育改革的路径与特征[J].教育发展研究,9,58-62.

[4] 王定华.(2008).美国基础教育改革与发展若干动向[J].河南教育(基础版).

[5] 张家勇.(2003).美国基础教育存在的问题与根源[J].当代教育论坛:宏观教育研究,9,104-106.

[6] 张巍.(2005).美国基础教育改革的政策与观点简述[J].上海教育科研,2,55-56.

[7] 赵中建.(2001).美国基础教育课程改革的动向与启示[J].全球教育展望,4,11-16.

[8] 曾德琪.(1999).美国基础教育的特点、问题与改革[J].四川师范大学学报(社会科学版),26(2),28-35.

第二章
深入发展的美国基础教育改革

一、美国基础教育改革的发展情况

第一章提到美国基础教育中由于宏观调控不力、教育质量相对低下以及校园环境恶化,致使其中小学教育质量长期不尽如人意。近年来,美国基础教育改革围绕着责任和提供选择,不断向纵深发展。

(一)落实责任

1. 高标准、严要求

美国基础教育理事会(Council for Basic Education)2004年的民意测验表明,美国中小学的学生、家长和教师、行政长官及企业家普遍支持学校确定更高更严格的教学标准。学生们说:"对我们要求得越高,我们就学得越多。"家长、教师和公众也表示:"希望孩子们在学校里有更高的标准和更好的成绩。"

美国学生多次在国际竞赛中失利,使得美国人注重研究别国的教育政策。研究发现,在教育方面超过美国的国家,几乎全都有统一的国家标准、全国教学大纲和全国考试。为了学习别国的经验,美国基础教育界近几年来从国家到各州,从学区到各学校都在通过制定统一的教学大纲,出台相应的教学标准。据美国《教育周刊》统计,截至1999年,已有40个州对主要课程制定了统一的标准和大纲;有48个州要求对学生进行全州统考;有23个州资助现任教师达标,并对新聘教师严格把关。

2. 定期评估、科学管理

评估涉及评估对象和评估内容及方式。定期评估的对象除学生外,还有教师和学校。评估的内容和方式多种多样。对学生的评估,包括课堂出勤、自由问答、论说题和社会实践,以及各州的统考等。教师评估,一看是否有教师执照,二看是否胜任所教课程,三看是否使每个学生都在其起点上按标准有所提高;四看所教学生的整体表现。学校评估,除了学生家长的日常监督,越来越多的州和学区开始实行"学校报告卡"考核制度。

"学校报告卡"是各州对学校实行评估的结果报告卡片。报告的内容包括各校学生的全州统考成绩、上课出勤率、参加快班学习人数,以及校园犯罪统计数字等。报告卡除了直接发往各有关学校,还寄给所有学生家长。截至2000年,已有36个州实行"学校报告卡"制度,2001年又有4个州实行这一制度。

据《教育周刊》1999年的统计,加利福尼亚州、特拉华州、南卡罗来纳州和威斯康星州已通过法律将学生的升留级与全州统考联系起来。另有26个州已经准备,或者正在准备高中毕业统考。例如,2000年1月进行的纽约州英语统考,及格分为55分,全州92%的12年级学生通过了该门毕业考试所要求的标准。另据美国国家教育统计中心(National Center for Education Statistics,NCES)报告,近年来,要求教师通过专业考试的学区从23.5%增加到39.3%,要求通过基本技能考试的学区从34.9%增加到49%,要求通过国家教师考试的学区从21.4%增加到38.8%。在过去的几年里,美国中小学的生师比下降了22%,而获得硕士以上学位的教师人数却增加了50%。

3. 坚持标准、赏罚分明

赏罚分明一改美国教育固有的自由与松散。时下的美国,学生考试多门或多次不及格,不许升级或毕业。例如,1999年,纽约州和加利福尼亚州的全州统考中,各有平均50%的学生考试不及格,这两州均没有降分迁就的做法。学生缺课,有校纪堂规;学生逃学,将由警察直接遣送回校。教师不合格,或送去进修,或解聘下岗。例如,1999年马萨诸塞州举办的新教师考试,就有59%未能通过,需要再次进修。学校不达标准,先亮黄牌,限期整顿,到时还达不到标准,将被关闭。

《教育周刊》1999年统计,全美已有19个州对表现良好的学校进行名誉奖励,有14个州对其进行物质奖励,有19个州令表现欠佳的学校写出或修订学习改进计划,有16个州已通过立法,将对"失败"的学校进行关闭、接管或重组。纽约、俄克拉荷马和得克萨斯3个州已采取措施,对特别差的学校进行了相应的制裁。

(二)提供选择

美国基础教育改革所提供的选择,主要有以下5个方面。

1. 学校自主管理与教师专业化

美国基础教育按照基于现场管理(Site-Based Management,SBM)的模式,使学校和教师拥有更多的权利参与教育管理的决策。基于现场管理实际上是一种学校自主管理机制。针对各州及学区的官僚作风,美国许多中小学采用SBM,使基础教育改革的决策权从上层转移到每一所学校。学校依据SBM产生特别校董会,特别校董会再将教师、管理人员、学生及家长联合起来,通过现场自主裁决,对学校进行改革。根据资料反馈(data retrieval),现在已经有73%的美国学校是按SBM运行的,比1977年增加了36%。

教师专业化是指在美国基础教育改革中,为增强教师的责任心和权威性而推行的一系列改革政策和措施,使教师在给学生评分、掌握评估方式、参与学校决策,以及个人发展等方面拥有更多的权力。教师专业化提高了教师的地位,也增加了他们的收入,让从教人员越来越多地体验到一种置身"职业"生涯的感觉。

2. 特许学校与教育维护组织

特许学校(charter school)给学生提供公立学校的学习环境,而不受各州传统管理体制的约束。据教育改革中心的统计,目前特许学校在美国37个州具有合法地位。1994年美国只有108所特许学校,到1999年已有1 205所特许学校了。其中,50%为小学,20%为中学,22%为两者兼顾。特许学校在校生总计25万~30万人,每所特许学校在校生平均为250人。由于在校生相对较少,特许学校在提高办学效益方面存在一定的困难。

于是,有些学校为了减轻教学管理方面的负担,与一些私营公司签订合同。这些公司通称为教育维护组织(Education Maintenance Organization,EMO)。EMO 是一种以营利为目的的教育实体。他们在学校自主权逐渐得到加强的背景下,与一些学区或单个特许学校签约,参与学校的教学管理,并在一定程度上提高了特许学校的办学效益和办学质量。现在,美国大约有 10% 的特许学校是由 EMO 管理的。特许学校的存在与发展,已使当地的公立学校感受到挑战和竞争的压力。

3. 税单学校

税单学校(voucher school)是另一种形式的选择。学生家长手持纳税凭单,既可以为孩子选择公立学校,也可以选择私立学校。1999 年的民意测验显示,如果政府按政策提供学费,51% 的家长将仍然让孩子待在原来的学校,5% 的家长会为孩子选择另一所公立学校,39% 选择私立学校或教会学校。税单学校的存在同样对公立学校构成一种竞争和挑战。

4. 小班化

虽然小班化会带来补充教师、添置校舍,以及教学设备等一系列问题,1996—1997 年的研究表明,小班至少在幼儿园至小学 3 年级意味着更好的教学效果。克林顿总统 1998 年提议的小班化计划出台后,全美大部分地区幼儿园至小学 3 年级每班的平均人数已经降到 18 人。目前,小班化小到什么程度,尚无定论。当然,小班化的根本前提是资金,美国 1999 年和 2000 年两个财政年度的小班化基金数额分别为 12 亿美元和 13 亿美元。

5. 家庭学校

尽管美国在基础教育改革中做出了很大的努力,但是,还有一小部分家长认为,现行的小学教育不适合他们的孩子。于是,家庭学校(home school)应运而生,并由少到多。以前,家庭学校在美国曾被视为不合法,现在家庭学校已经遍布全美,并受到法律保护。据家庭学校法律保护协会统计,美国家庭学校的学生人数 1988 年为 22.5 万人,1998 年已达到 150 万人,是 10 年前的 6 倍。

所谓家庭学校,就是家长将自己的家作为学校对孩子进行教育。这些家长,一部分由于不满意现行的美国小学教育,另一部分由于宗教或其他原因,为孩子选择了家庭学校的教育方式。家庭学校的教育内容和方法,一般由家长参照本学区的有关条文自定,若家长不能胜任某门课程,可以借助其他家长的协助,也可以让孩子到学校补齐所缺课程。按规定,所有家庭学校的学生必须定期参加学区的考评。由于家庭学校能够对学生因材施教,加之国际互联网和社区环境的有效利用,因此,这种办学方式在美国已经得到普遍认可。

二、美国基础教育改革中存在的主要问题

基础教育改革是一个庞大而复杂的系统工程。多年来,虽然美国上上下下、方方面面对教改的酝酿、推行和投资都给予了极大的重视和支持,但是,在美国基础教育改革中还存在以下几个方面的主要矛盾和问题。

(一)传统与革新的矛盾

长期以来,美国基础教育没有统一的教学大纲和统一考试,各州、学区,乃至学校在教学的标准上差异很大。杜威所倡导的机会均等和注重实践的教育思想已经使美国中小学习惯了松散、自由的办学方式。因此,尽管近年来各州都在陆续制定或修订统一的教学大纲,实行学区乃至全州统考,开始执行严格的教学管理。但是,各方面所遇到的阻力很大,所制定的标准也很难完全落到实处。

(二)教师工会与教学改革的矛盾

美国的教师工会除了各地的教师协会以外,还有全国性的国家教育协会和美国教师联合会。教师工会权力很大,一般以论资排辈的方式极力维护各位会员的利益,以致校长通常也很难罢免一个教学成绩欠佳而有工会会员身份的教师。因此,《网上政策研究》(Policy.com) 1999年研究表明,教师工会是美国基础教育改革中最大的障碍之一。《教育周刊》也表示,在教改中,只有工会的运作和学校的管理相互协调,才能双双持久生存。

(三)英语国家移民与非英语国家移民的矛盾

美国是个移民国家。由于语言和文化背景的关系,从非英语国家来的移民子女很难一下子适应美国的英语教学环境。加之,美国的非英语国家移民数量猛增。根据美国移民局1999年的统计,到2050年,整个美国的白人将不再是多数人种。因此,人口比例的变化也是阻碍美国基础教育改革速见成效的另一重要因素。

(四)单一智能理论与多种智能理论的矛盾

传统的美国教育将智能解释为人们对不断变化的外部世界作用与反作用的单一性集合能力。因此,法国心理学家阿尔弗雷德·比尼特所设计的智商测验(IQ Test)几乎成了美国人长期测验儿童智力,以发展其弱智领域的国家标准。由此演变而来的学习能力倾向测验(Scholastic Aptitude Test,SAT)也成为美国大学入学的主要依据(Fletcher,2009)。然而,更多研究表明,该考试只能显示考生的标准化试题成绩,并不能测出学生具有的全部潜能。教育的目的就是开发每个学生的潜能,因此,测试学生,不应只测试其不能做什么,更应测试其能做什么。

多种智能理论对智能的解释是,智能是由若干种不同属性的能量和心理素质组合而成的综合体。每个人都有多种智能。它们可以单独运作,也可彼此协作。美国哈佛大学心理学家霍华德·加德纳(Howard Gardner)提出,人有6种智能:语言能力、逻辑数学能力、音乐能力、空间能力、身体能力和个人自处能力。多种智能理论的推出,使越来越多的美国人认识到,现行美国教育制度下的中小学若要完全有效运作,尚需更新观念,持续创新,使基础教育改革不断向纵深发展。

(原载于《基础教育参考》,2004(11):20-21)

参 考 文 献

[1] Council for Basic Education. http://www.edweek.org/ew/articles/2004/07/14/42cbe.h23.html.
[2] Fletcher, D. (2009). Brief history of standardized testing[J]. Time. http://content.time.com/time/nation/article/0,8599,1947019,00.html.
[3] 霍华德·加德纳.(2012).多元智能新视野[M].沈致隆,译,北京:中国人民大学出版社.

第三章
美国私立学校的管理体制

私立教育在美国具有悠久的历史。早在17世纪初期,美国建立的第一批学校皆为私立学校。美国宪法明文规定,父母拥有为其子女选择教育的基本权利。私立学校作为美国教育体系不可分割的一部分,在美国50个州享有与公立学校同等的合法地位。近年来,美国基础教育中的私立学校呈现发展趋势,其科学的管理体制、日益成熟的办学模式以及显著的教学效果已经得到普遍认可。

一、概况

1. 起源与宗教

美国私立学校的起源打下了浓厚宗教色彩的烙印。据 Naomi 和 Peter（2002）的研究,1618年,基督教圣公会在美国南部的詹姆斯城设立了一所名为亨利克（Henricus School）的私立学校,从而拉开了在美洲大陆创办私立学校的帷幕,也奠定了美国的私立教育与宗教之间的密切关系。若按宗教和非宗教划分,美国的私立中小学主要属于天主教、其他教派和非宗教组织,分别占全美私立学校的49%、28%和23%；若按宗教派别划分,美国的私立学校主要属于天主教、路德教和保守基督教,分别拥有学生250万人、22万人和82万人,占全美私立学校学生总数的4.7%、0.4%和1.6%。另外,在全美的私立幼儿园中,也有33%属于教会性质。

2. 政教分离与政府资助

相关研究（陈立和刘华,2012；傅松涛和刘亮亮,2006；关学增和宋朝丽,2008）表明,1791年美国宪法规定,为确保美国公民的宗教自由,必须实行政治与宗教的彻底分离。因此,无论是联邦政府还是州政府,一方面不能插手宗教组织的事务,对其存在和发展进行任何限制或阻碍；另一方面,也不能给予其支持和赞助,包括各宗教派别创立和维持的私立教育事业。

到了19世纪后期,随着美国教育整体迈向现代化的发展阶段,"政教分离"才被注入切合时代发展的新内涵。美国人普遍认为私立学校已经成为美国国民教育不可分割的重要组成部分。因此,上至联邦政府最高法院,下至各州州议会纷纷出台相关法案,重新明确各级政府对私立学校应该承担的责任和义务。其中主要有：①政府应遵守义务教育的成本补偿原则,对私立学校教育的义务教育部分提供公共资助；②为避免不必要的政治与宗教的纠缠,政府以间接和中立的方式资助私立学校；③政府对私立学校运营和发展的任何管制必须以联邦法律、州宪法以及教育法为准绳。

3. 规模与管理机构

根据美国国家教育统计中心 2001 年 9 月的统计,1999—2000 学年,美国共有私立幼儿园 6 622 所,共有学生 98 413 名,教师 15 398 名。私立中小学 27 223 所,占全美中小学总数的 24%。在校学生人数为 5 300 000 人,占全美中小学生的 11%;在编教师人数为 425 406 人,其中 48% 为私立小学教师,16% 为中学教师,37% 为中小学混合学校教师。

美国联邦政府内与私立教育有关的管理机构有 10 多家,其中隶属美国教育部的非公立教育办公室(Office of Non-Public Education,ONPE)最有代表性。ONPE 成立于 1971 年,其主要职责如下:

(1)最大限度地使非公立学校的学生参与适合他们的联邦教育项目;

(2)向教育部长建议修改有关法规,尽可能多地向非公立学校学生提供服务;

(3)审核联邦政府和其他全国性机构向非公立学校学生开放的教育项目的合法性。

美国全国非官方私立教育协会有 30 多家。其中,较大的非营利性组织有 10 多家,最有代表性的是美国私立教育理事会(Council for American Private Education,CAPE)。CAPE 成立于 1971 年,是美国各地私立教育组织的一个全国性联合会。其宗旨是代表全美私立学校的利益,与公立学校及其管理层沟通,以提高美国教育的整体质量。最有代表的营利私立教育组织是职业院校协会(Career College Association)。

二、管理体制

1. 各州地方性私立教育管理体制

美国法律规定,州政府及其教育管理部门不直接干预私立教育的管理,其责任主要体现在监管和确保本州所有适龄儿童在非公立学校和公立学校一样,能够平等地接受基本相等水平的教育。州政府一般通过州教育厅及其教育董事会对私立教育进行宏观指导。州教育厅设立有非公立教育办公室和州非公立学校督学的职位。该办公室及督学依据本州教育法对私立学校进行审批注册、颁发许可证书,并确保其办学手续齐全、合法。由于美国各州教育法规不同,现仅以纽约州为例说明情况。

纽约州 2000 年 6 月颁布的非公立学校法规共有 10 多条,主要包括以下内容。

(1)注册登记:非公立学校可自愿注册登记,但只有经注册登记的非公立高中才有资格颁发高中毕业证书,有资格参加州教育董事会统考。

(2)学生档案管理:所有非公立学校必须按照州教育法第 104 条对学生档案进行管理,以确保州政府对学生情况的追踪和统计。

(3)学年与日学时:公立学校一年为 180 天,1～6 年级每天 5 小时,7～12 年级每天 5 小时 30 分钟。州教育厅要求私立学校的学年长短与日学时与前者相似或保持一致。

(4)语言:教科书和课堂语言必须使用英语。

(5)教师资格:法规没有明文要求非公立学校的教师必须具备资格证书,但纽约州教育厅要求任课教师必须具备应有的能力。

(6)教学大纲:非公立学校不必使用与公立学校相同的教学大纲,但是 1～6 年级必须教授算术、英语、科学、音乐、体育、美国历史等 13 门课程,7～12 年级必须教授英语、社科、科学、数学、音乐、体育、健康教育等13门课程。同时,要达到"基本相等水平"的教学要求,非公立学校还必须向学生开设爱国主义、公民职责与权利、人权问题、美国宪法及独立宣言等课程。

2. 私立学校内部管理体制

美国私立学校分为营利和非营利两种。例如,纽约州共有2 400多所私立学校,其中10%为营利性质,90%为非营利性质。营利性私立学校有残疾儿童学前班、3~5岁儿童幼儿园,以及小学和中学等不同级别和种类。学校运营前,须向纽约州州务卿申请企业法人许可证,按照纽约州企业法规办学,并像其他公司一样如期向地方、州和联邦政府纳税。

非营利私立学校首先须向纽约州教育厅董事会申请临时办学许可证,经州教育厅非公立学校办公室定期或不定期现场视察和审核达标后,换取长期办学许可证。非营利性私立学校自领取临时办学许可证之日起,可免缴地方、本州和联邦税及财产税,但必须成立不少于5人和不多于25人的校董事会。

校董事会主要有以下权限:
(1)选举不少于5人的学校管理层;
(2)制定学校规章制度;
(3)管理人事和工资;
(4)管理校产和设备;
(5)按照许可范围,授予学位和颁发证书。

非营利性私立学校管理层在校长的领导下,除了处理学校日常事务外,主要有以下职责:
(1)确定学校办学宗旨和办学方针;
(2)制定教学计划和实施方案;
(3)管理学校财务;
(4)确保校舍安全和设备运转正常;
(5)保障教学正常进行和教员定期进修;
(6)定期与校董事会和学生家长联系;
(7)保持与公立学校和学校所在社区的联络;
(8)参与社区、专业组织和相关协会的活动。

无论是营利性还是非营利性私立学校,其学校规模、班级人数和师生比例都小于或少于公立学校。而私立学校的教师在教学上则表现出更大的自主性,在学校教学决策方面也有更多的发言权。在教学上,私立学校的教师基本自定教材、辅助材料和教学方法,自我命题和自定评分标准。在诸如确定教学大纲与学习标准,制定课堂纪律与评估教师教学效果等教学决策上,68%的私立学校教师认为他们的意见受到重视,而公立学校持相同观点的教师人数仅为44%。

三、结论

综上所述,占全美中小学24%的私立学校已经构成美国整体教育体系中不可分割的一部分。私立学校学生在国内测试和国际数学与科学竞赛上的优异成绩,与其小班化、较小的生师比以及教师较大的自主权等特点密切相关。这些特点已在美国基础教育改革中得到认可与体现。另外,通过高标准、严要求来追求卓越学业成绩的私立学校教育传统,也在美国各地的公立学校中得到广泛赞许和不同形式的效仿。

从管理的角度看,州政府"基本相等水平"的教育法规等,对私立教育从宏观指导到实际操作上进行了有效的调控。各州的企业法明确地规范着营利性私立学校的正常经营。注册登记、审批特许以及从法律上明确校董事会的权限等措施,使约占90%的非营利性私立学校实施着"基本相等水平"的教学。

美国私立学校在追求各自办学宗旨的同时,基本都能主动地与当地社区、政府部门非公立学校主管及相关公立学校建立良好的沟通关系,同时也不失时机地参与和享受法律许可的政府教育项目和社会福利。

(原载于《基础教育参考》,2003(5):14-16)

参 考 文 献

[1] Naomi, A. M., Peter, K. (2002). Findings from the condition of education 2002: Private school—A brief portrait [Z]. National Center for Education Statistics. http://nces.ed.gov/pubsearch/pubsinfo.asp? pubid=2002013.

[2] National Center for Education Statistics. (2009). Characteristics of private schools in the United States: Results from the 2007-2008 private school universe survey [Z]. http://nces.ed.gov/pubs2009/2009313.pdf.

[3] National Center for Education Statistics. (2001). Private school universe survey [Z]. http://nces.ed.gov/pubs2001/2001330.pdf.

[4] The Education Department of New York. (2001). Guidelines for determining equivalency of instruction in non-public schools [Z]. http://www.emsc.nysed.gov/rscs/nonpub/guldelinesequivofinstruction.htm. 2001.

[5] The Education Department of New York. (2002). Selected sections of the education law relating to education corporations (Section 210, Sections 214-219) [Z]. http://www.counsel.nysed.gov/pamphlet9/appenda210.

[6] 陈立,刘华. (2012). 美国政府对私立学校的责任述评[J]. 宁波大学学报(教育科学版),34(4),48-53.

[7] 傅松涛,刘亮亮. (2006). 美国私立学校与公立学校的比较研究[J]. 外国中小学教育,10,27-29.

[8] 关学增,宋朝丽. (2008). 论美国政府职能在教育管理中的彰显[J]. 郑州大学学报(哲学社会科学版),41(3),119-122.

[9] 刘琳娜,张彦通. (2011). 美国私立学校办学经验对我国民办教育的启示[J]. 教育探索,6,150-152.

[10] 刘兆璟. (1996). 简论美国私立学校的功能[J]. 教育科学,1,61-63.

[11] 邵金荣,张文,张晓东. (1994). 美国私立教育:历史、现状及启示[J]. 教育研究,6,71-75.

第四章
美国私立高等教育中常春藤联盟院校的办学理念与特色

美国的高等教育质量在国际范围首屈一指,众多美国大学堪称世界一流,美国的世界一流大学多为私立大学,而常春藤联盟(Ivy League)堪称美国私立大学中的佼佼者。常春藤联盟包括以下8所大学:哈佛大学、耶鲁大学、宾夕法尼亚大学、普林斯顿大学、哥伦比亚大学、布朗大学、达特茅斯学院以及康奈尔大学。这8所大学历史悠久、治学严谨,历年毕业生中世界级顶尖人才层出不穷。许多世界闻名的科学家、政治要人和商贾巨子都曾在此深造。作为众多美国学生和世界各国学子梦想进入的高等学府,常春藤联盟院校历来只看报考学生的能力和潜质。因此,只要考取,出身贫寒的子弟不必为缴不起学费而担忧;没有考取,纵使家有万贯也无济于事。针对国内现有文献的薄弱环节,本章从常春藤联盟院校的起源、发展历程、办学理念以及专业特色与世界排名四个方面进行讨论,以便使读者对美国私立高等教育有更加具体和深刻的认识。

一、起源

根据蓝劲松(2005)的研究,大学一词来源于拉丁文"universitas",指"行会""社团"和"公会"的意思。虽然古代埃及、印度、中国等地都是高等教育的发源地,古希腊、罗马、拜占庭等也具备了相当发达的高等教育体系,但是,公认的第一所正规大学是于欧洲中世纪的1087年在意大利建立的博罗尼亚大学。此后,世界著名大学的传承可图示如下(见图4.1)。

博罗尼亚大学(1087)→巴黎大学(1150)→剑桥大学(1209)→ 哈佛大学(1636)→耶鲁大学(1701)→普林斯顿大学(1746)等

来源:蓝劲松(2005,58)

图4.1 世界著名大学的传承线索

图4.1中的哈佛大学(Harvard University)于1636年在美国波士顿的剑桥市创建,由移居美洲的英国清教徒仿效英国的剑桥大学模式而建,因而起先命名为剑桥学院,后于1639年更名为哈佛大学,以纪念学校的创始人和主要捐赠者、英国剑桥大学毕业生约翰·哈佛。第一批欧洲移民是大约100多人的英国清教徒,他们乘坐"五月花"号轮船,于1620年在美国马萨诸塞州的普利茅斯登陆,在时间上距哈佛建校的1636年仅有16年。美国的国庆日是1776年7月4日,这就是为什么人们常说"先有哈佛,后有美国"。

耶鲁大学(Yale University)于1701年创立于美国康涅狄格州的吉灵伍斯市,最初命名为大学学院(Collegiate School),1716年学校迁至该州的纽黑文市,1718年更名为耶鲁学院,即今天耶鲁大学的前身,以纪念英国东印度公司高级官员伊莱斯·耶鲁先生向学校捐物捐书的义举。根据耶鲁大学校长理查德·莱文(2004)的描述,耶鲁大学的毕业生在常春藤联盟的普林斯顿大学、哥伦比亚大学和康奈尔大学以及威廉姆斯学院、霍普金斯大学、芝加哥大学、乔治亚大学、密西西比大学、密苏里大学、威斯康星大学和加利福尼亚大学担任过第一任校长。因此,耶鲁大学享有"学院之母"的赞誉。

实际上,常春藤联盟最早指的是起源于1900年非正式的大学美式足球赛事。1937年纽约《先驱论坛报》的一名记者Caswell Adams看到参赛球队的校园里古老的建筑物上大多爬满了常春藤,于是就首次将常春藤来比喻参赛球队历史悠久而誉满全球的学校。据说,一开始常春藤联盟是由哈佛、耶鲁、哥伦比亚和普林斯顿4所大学组成,其英文"Four League"被写为"IV League",其中的"IV"后来演变为"Ivy"。1945年常春藤联盟的8所大学的体育教练签署了有关学术、财政和运动标准的常春藤协议,标志着常春藤联盟正式问世。1954年,常春藤盟校成立常春藤盟校校长董事会(The Council of Ivy Group Presidents)。

在8所常春藤盟校中,除康奈尔大学是于1865年建立以外,其他7所全部创建于美国建国(1776年)前的殖民地时期,迄今已有300多年的历史。在其发展过程之中,各常春藤盟校都具有了自己独特的办学理念和远大目标。他们在保持各自特色的同时,将国内外其他大学,特别是联盟内的其他院校,既作为竞争的对手,又作为学习的榜样,在模仿、借鉴和消化别人长处同时,不断改革与创新,保持进步与发展。

二、发展历程

美国大学虽然种类较多,但大致可分为社区学院、文理学院和综合性大学。据美国卡内基教学促进基金会的高等教育机构分类(The Carnegie Classification of Institutions of Higher Education)2010年的统计,美国的大学总数为4 634所,其中公立院校1 704所,占总数的36.8%,私立院校2 930所,占总数的63.2%。其中的2 930所私立院校,由1 714所非营利性院校和1 216所营利性院校组成,各占总数的37%和26.2%。2009—2010学年,公立院校在校生为14 908 227人,而私立院校的在校生是5 819 433人。

国内研究(顾宝炎,1989;袁祖望,1997;王天一、夏之莲、朱美玉,1985;吴福光、张仕华,2000)表明,美国私立大学的发展与常春藤盟校的壮大,至少在两个历史阶段并行交织,齐头并进。

首先,在美国独立战争前的殖民地时期,美国一共创建了10所大学,常春藤联盟8所大学中的7所就在此期间相继问世。按时间顺序,这7所院校分别是马萨诸塞州的哈佛大学(1636年)、康涅狄格州的耶鲁大学(1701年)、宾夕法尼亚州的宾夕法尼亚大学(1740年)、新泽西州的普林斯顿大学(1746年)、纽约州的哥伦比亚大学(1754年)、罗得岛州的布朗大学(1754年),以及新罕布什尔州的达特茅斯学院(1769年)。另外,在这个时期创建的著名私立院校还有威廉和玛丽学院。上述院校全部是私立的,由教会掌控的,也基本是为教会和当时的上层社会服务的,因为,他们招收的是上层社会和有钱人的子弟,通过博雅教育的方式,培养传教士和对宗教虔诚信奉的政府官吏。

其次,在美国独立战争(1775—1783年)和南北内战(1861—1865年)期间,美国的私立大学从建国前的10所增加到内战结束时的247所,其中包括常春藤联盟的第8所院校,即1865

年在纽约州成立的康奈尔大学。在此期间,也出现了17所公立或州立大学。当时的美国高等教育从精英阶段走向大众阶段,大学的大门向社会各阶层的学子开放。然而,美国宪法第10修正案规定:"凡是宪法未曾给予联邦而又未曾限制给予各州的权利,都是保留给各州或人民的"(U. S. Constitution,1791)。由于教育的管理和实施权符合这一规定,因而确立了美国地方分权制的教育管理体制。在此值得指出的有两点:第一是美国联邦政府和州政府为了满足日益增长的教育需求,曾企图接收私立高校为州立或公立高校。达特茅斯学院就有这样的经历,只得通过上诉联邦最高法院,胜诉后保持继续独立。这一案例不但阻止了日后政府的类似动议,而且激励和增长了教会和其他社会力量办学的积极性。第二是康奈尔大学是一所私立的政府赠地高校。为了发展高等教育又同时克服经费匮乏的困难,美国国会于1862年通过了有名的《莫雷尔法案》,亦称"赠地法案"。该法案规定,各州凡有国会议员一名就拨联邦土地3万英亩,用其收益来资助和维持至少一所大学。无论公立或私立大学,皆可成为赠地大学,但赠地大学必须开设有关农业和机械技艺方面的专业,以培养工农业急需人才。康奈尔大学创立于1865年,当时美国南北战争刚刚结束,高等教育正在酝酿着一场大变革:有倡导民主、科学与实用的功利主义思潮,也有主张向当时的德国大学学习,强调学术研究的思想。康奈尔大学依据自身的办学理念,明确地提出了既传授实用知识,又进行学术研究的两大发展方向。董泽宇(2010)认为,"康奈尔大学的办学理念集中代表了当时美国大学崛起的发展方向和成功缩影"(91)。

三、办学理念

什么样的办学理念造就什么样的大学。蓝劲松(2002)认为,"理念"是"组织的最高指导原则","大学理念"是"大学发展远景与方向的指导原则……是对大学的精神、使命、宗旨、功能与价值观等发展基本思想的概括性论述"(52)。接着,蓝教授将西方大学的办学理念概括为以下几点:①合理求是:从实际出发,理性地寻求事物内在的规律或原则;②使命引导:西方大学大多都有使命陈述(mission statement),并将其作为大学发展战略的宏观先导;③学术自由:在各种合法的学术活动中,当事人不受任何外在力量的阻挠;④大学自治:大学教授及其他研究者研究并发表其研究成果的自由以及为了保障这些自由的自治;⑤积极应变:能够在变化着的世界中不断地站住和重新站住。在上述五种办学理念中,①和②属于核心层级,③和④属于中间层级,而⑤属于外围层级,其内在关系如图4.2所示。

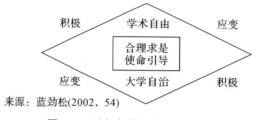

来源:蓝劲松(2002,54)

图4.2 西方大学办学理念系统

上述五种办学理念及其相互之间的关系,并非完全适用美国的私立大学和常春藤盟校各自的独特情形。但是,研究(董泽宇,2010;蓝劲松,2002;刘宝存,2003;徐文,2000;吴福光、张

第 四 章
美国私立高等教育中常春藤联盟院校的办学理念与特色

仕华,2000;张鲁宁,2009;朱鹏举和李文英,2013)表明,它们在很大程度上具有令人信服的代表性。限于篇幅,我们在此仅以哈佛大学和康奈尔大学为例,来说明问题。卡尔·亚斯贝尔斯(2007)在其《大学之理念》一书开宗明义,认为"大学是一个人们可以在这里自由地探索真理、传授真理的地方,也是一个人们可以为了这个目的而蔑视任何想剥夺这种自由的人的地方"(20)。哈佛大学的校训是"以柏拉图为友,以亚里士多德为友,更需要以真理为友"。虽然哈佛大学没有使命陈述,但是哈佛学院的使命陈述是,"我们的使命是为社会教育市民和培养市民领袖。我们承诺通过人文和科学教育的转化力量,来实现这一目标"(Harvard College Mission,1650)。很显然,哈佛大学是要将追求真理作为办学的指导原则。370多年来,哈佛人一直固守这一办学理念,"只是在不同的时期表述与侧重点不同"(刘宝存,2003,38)。刘宝存(2003)发现,1869年,哈佛大学迎来年仅35岁的新任校长查尔斯·艾略特(Charles W. Eliot)。此人在位40年,他坚持大学是真理的寻求者,因而他根据时代的需求,倡导学习当时的德国,在哈佛首先推行选课制,发展研究生教育,强调大学要教学与学术研究并举,从而奠定了哈佛大学的研究型大学地位。在日后的发展过程中,哈佛大学始终坚持通过务实和创新的教学和科研去寻求真理的办学理念,并根据时代的变化和需求,将教学、科研和社会服务确定为哈佛大学的三大职能。这三大职能已经成为当今无论是公立还是私立大学的共同奋斗目标。

在人才培养的理念上,哈佛大学至少在以下三个方面成为榜样:①因地制宜、因材施教:随着时间的推移、时代的变化,哈佛的人才培养理念也随之适时而变。起初的哈佛主要面向宗教界和上层社会,因此以培养品格和虔诚为中心。到了艾略特做校长时,哈佛重点培养的不再是现实生活的旁观者和批评家,而是实干家和成功者,再后来是智力、能力和伦理各方面都有教养的人。为了培养这种通专兼备、品学兼优的人才,哈佛大学启用"集中与分配制"(concentration and distribution)引导学生选课,以确保其在专业领域的知识深度,以及自然科学、社会科学与人文科学三个领域的知识面,同时,学校还积极引导学生理性地设计甚至创造适合自己的专业,以挖掘和培养不同学生的兴趣和潜能。②博专并重、独立成才:经过多年的实验,哈佛大学针对学校人才培养的目标,形成了"核心课程+专业课程+选修课程"的课程设置体系,力图达到博雅教育与专业教育的最佳平衡。在实际教学中,不再强调教师对固定知识的传授,转而倡导培养学生不断自我获取知识、独立理解知识、积极创新知识的能力。因此,教学中更多见的是以学生为中心的互动式问答、小组或课堂讨论、案例分析、角色扮演以及现代多媒体、数字化、远距离或虚拟空间教学设备的广泛应用。③宽松自由与自律自强:首先,学术自由既适用于学校和教师,也适用于学生。对哈佛大学而言,学校全面执行选课制和学分制,以便为学生创造一个自由发展的学习环境。对教师而言,他们有权制定教学大纲,选择课程教材和教辅材料、教学方法以及课程的测评模式。对学生而言,学术自由意味着他们可以根据自己的兴趣以及兴趣的变化,而合法地申请转系和调换专业,可以在开学听完第一周的课后再确定是否注册某门课程。但是,紧随自由选择而来的是永恒的挑战和责任。哈佛要保持世界领先,教师要履行教学、科研和服务的软性和硬性指标,学生要争取在每门课上拿A的前提下,通过助教、助研或实习来丰满自己的履历。

讨论完常春藤联盟中最古老的哈佛大学后,我们再来介绍一下最晚加入常春藤联盟的康奈尔大学。根据研究资料(Bylaws of Cornell University,2007;董泽宇,2010;Rogers,1942;朱章华,2010),康奈尔大学的办学理念首先体现在其创始人埃兹拉·康奈尔的办学初衷和康奈尔大学的校训上:"我要建立一所大学,让任何人都能在这里学到想学的科目。"在当时的社会环境里,与其他大学只面向某些人群的传统做法相比,康奈尔大学不论性别、种族、国籍、宗教信仰以及经济能力,面向所有合格的学生开放,这本身就是一件破天荒的创举。同时,《康奈尔大学章程》规定:"为了促进工业阶层的自由教育和实用教育,以适应他们的追求和职业生活,大学的主要目标应当是教授有关农业、机械技术,包括军事战术的学科知识。"学者李硕豪和王丹丹(2011)将康奈尔大学的上述追求总结为"平等、公正和学科综合的办学理念"(60)。董泽宇(2010)将其归纳为两点:"一是注重实用教育,通过实用知识的传授为社会大众服务;二是注重学术研究,强调科学研究的重要性。"(92)由于其坚持平等和公正的指导原则,倡导传授实用知识的同时,开展学术创新研究的办学理念,康奈尔大学被美国教育历史学家Rudolph(1977)赞誉为"美国第一真正的大学"(116)。

根据Rogers(1942)的描述,康奈尔大学首任校长安德鲁·怀特1866年向校董事会提交《关于大学管理委员会的报告》,后被誉为"康奈尔计划",用以阐释和实施学校的办学理念。该计划有三大主要内容值得在此分享:①自由教育与实用教育紧密结合。自由教育的提出是为了突破传统以英才教育为主的观念,实施人人平等的招生策略。实用教育是为了适应美国工农业发展的需求,培养能够学以致用的实用人才。②推行核心课程体系和限制性选修制度。为了避免当时普遍存在的课程差别和学徒制度,怀特强调所有课程同等重要,同时设置多种职业课程供学生自由选择。③大学要开展科学研究,并主动为社会服务。怀特注重大学的科研功能,为此设置了研究生课程与研究生院,建立了农业试验站以及其他科学实验室,并鼓励将教学和科研成果向社会推广,有效地将教学、科研和服务融为一体。

由此可见,哈佛大学和康奈尔大学的办学指导思想和原则,与上述五种西方大学的办学理念基本匹配,也在很大程度上体现了其内在的相互关系。

四、专业特色与世界排名

在各自的历史演变和求新发展中,8所私立常春藤盟校,个个励精图治,在整体严谨治学的同时,成功打造鲜明的专业特色。在专业设置和学科建设方面,8所常春藤盟校都具有可与世界级强手匹敌的专业领域和学院建制(见表4.1)。表4.2所示为《泰晤士报》和《美国新闻与世界报道》2015年分别对8所常春藤盟校的世界大学综合排名和美国大学综合排名。

表 4.1 常春藤盟校的著名学院

盟校名称	著名学院
哈佛大学	商学院、法学院、医学院和肯尼迪政府管理学院
耶鲁大学	法学院、文学院、音乐学院和医学院
宾夕法尼亚大学	沃顿商学院、医学院、护理学院和工程学院
普林斯顿大学	数理学院、伍德鲁·威尔逊公共与国际事务学院
哥伦比亚大学	商学院、教育学院和新闻学院
布朗大学	国际关系学院、历史学院和经济学院
达特茅斯学院	文学院和塔克商学院
康奈尔大学	酒店管理学院和工程学院

来源:U. S. News and World Report, 2015.

表 4.2　2014—2015 学年常春藤盟校的世界和美国排名

盟校名称	《泰晤士报》世界大学综合排名	《美国新闻与世界报道》美国大学综合排名
哈佛大学	2	2
耶鲁大学	9	3
宾夕法尼亚大学	16	8
普林斯顿大学	7	1
哥伦比亚大学	14	4
布朗大学	54	16
达特茅斯学院	125	11
康奈尔大学	19	15

来源：Times Higher Education，2015；U.S. News and World Report，2015.

表 4.1 罗列了常春藤盟校各自的著名学院，从学院的名称可以看出其著名的专业领域。8 所常春藤盟校以各自著名的专业设置和学院建制为荣，每年世界各地也有数以万计的学子冲着这些专业而来。但是根据笔者在美国的求学和教学经历，常春藤盟校之中不会有任何一所大学会对各自学校的其他专业和学院有所轻视或偏废。一旦是学校教学大纲确认的课程，一旦学生注册，就没有必修、选修或主课、副课的主次之分。表 4.2 显示了 8 所常春藤盟校的最新世界和美国国内综合排名名次。他们虽然名次有别，但是个个榜上有名，除布朗大学和达特茅斯学院的世界综合排名较后外，其余 6 所常春藤盟校全部进入世界大学综合排名和美国大学综合排名的前 20 名。

五、结论

本章有选择性地探讨了美国常春藤盟校的起源、发展历程、办学理念、专业特色与世界排名，旨在帮助读者从一个侧面更加深刻地认识和理解美国私立高等教育的办学特色。从起源上讲，美国的私立高校为美国日后的整体高等教育打下了基础，开创了局面。作为美国私立高校的佼佼者，8 所常春藤盟校中，7 所在美国建国前的殖民地时期创立，1 所在美国南北战争结束时的教育大变革中诞生。他们根据时代的变迁和社会的需求，适时更新各自的办学理念，打造自身的品牌与特色。从发展历程来看，美国的私立大学占美国大学总数的 63.2%，几乎是公立大学的两倍，但在校学生总数还不及公立大学人数的一半。美国的私立大学首先在师生比上就占了优势，再加上其他方面的优势，特别是特色的办学理念，才能保持其领先的地位。从哈佛大学和康奈尔大学办学理念的分析来看，美国常春藤盟校完全具备文中叙述的 5 种西方大学办学理念，即合理求是、使命引导、学术自由、大学自治和积极应变。最后讨论的专业特色和世界排名，使我们清楚地看到美国的常春藤盟校具有一个共同的特点，在保持整体水平提高的同时，发展特色专业和品牌院系。

在此有三点值得总结：一是独立性。美国的私立高校始终追求独立办学，虽然美国的私立院校多为宗教团体创办和维持，但是，各校通过校董事会体制基本可以在办学方向、教学与科研内容以及师生的招聘等方面进行独立和自主的管理。二是竞争意识。美国的常春藤盟校乃至其他许多著名高校，之所以能不断发展壮大，就是因为他们永不自满，不甘人后的竞争意识使其能够随时将其他院校既作为竞争的对手,又作为学习的榜样。三是品牌观念。美国的常春藤盟校具有很强的品牌意识,为此,他们找准了各自的优势,发展出了独具特色的办学理念和专业方向。也正是因为他们独一无二的办学特点和享誉世界的品牌,才使他们能够代表美国的私立高等院校,长期雄踞世界名牌大学的高位。

参 考 文 献

[1] Bylaws of Cornell University. (2007). http://theuniversityfaculty. cornell. edu/pdfs/cornellbylaws. pdf,2007.

[2] Harvard College Mission. (1650). http://www. harvard. edu/faqs/mission-statement.

[3] Rogers, W. P. (1942). Andrew D. White and the modern university [M]. Ithaca, NY: Cornell University Press.

[4] Rudolph, F. (1977). A history of the American undergraduate course of study since 1636 [M]. San Francisco: Jossey Bass, Inc. , Publishers.

[5] U. S. Constitution. (1791). Amendment 10: Powers of the state and people [Z]. http://www. usconstitution. net/xconst_Am10. html.

[6] U. S. News and World Report. (2015). National universities rankings [Z]. http://colleges. usnews. rankingsandreviews. com/best-colleges/rankings/national-universities.

[7] The Carnegie Classification of Institutions of Higher Education. (2010). IPEDS institutional characteristics [Z]. http://carnegieclassifications. iu. edu/summary/enrollment_profile. php.

[8] Times Higher Education. (2015). World university rankings 2014－2015 [Z]. https://www. timeshighereducation. co. uk/world-university-rankings/2015/world-ranking#/sort/0/direction/asc.

[9] 董泽宇. (2010). 美国康奈尔大学办学理念形成与启示[J]. 国家教育行政学院学报,3,91－95.

[10] 顾宝炎. (1989). 美国大学管理[M]. 武汉:武汉大学出版社.

[11] 蓝劲松. (2005). 略论大学的起源[J]. 科学文化评论,2(6),55－68.

[12] 蓝劲松. (2002). 大学办学理念:东西方文化的比较[J]. 清华大学学报(哲学社会科学版),6(17),52－58.

[13] 李硕豪,王丹丹. (2011). 康奈尔大学章程对我国大学章程建设的启示[J]. 教育与教学研究,25(8),60－63.

[14] 刘宝存. (2003). 哈佛大学办学理念探析[J]. 外国教育研究,30(1),48－53.

[15] 卡尔·亚斯贝尔斯. (2007). 大学理念[M]. 邱立波,译. 上海:上海世纪出版社.

[16] 理查德·莱文. (2004). 大学工作[M]. 北京:外文出版社.

[17] 徐文. (2000). 美国私立高等教育管理的特点及启示[J]. 教育与职业,8,55－57.

[18] 袁祖望. (1997). 美国名牌大学的成长道路及其借鉴意义[J]. 汕头大学学报,13,104－109.

[19] 王天一,夏之莲,朱美玉. (1985). 外国教育史[M]. 北京:北京师范大学出版社.

[20] 吴福光,张仕华. (2000). 美国私立大学发展的历史、进程、贡献及启示[J]. 广州大学学

报,14(5),10-15.

[21] 张鲁宁.(2009).大学:一个寻求真理的地方——亚斯贝尔斯《大学之理念》的解读[J].理工高教研究,28(1),103-106.

[22] 朱鹏举,李文英.(2013).康奈尔计划对美国高等教育的影响[J].河北学刊,33(4),255-258.

[23] 朱章华.(2010).美国一流大学对中国高等教育的启示——以康奈尔大学为例[J].语文学刊(外语教育研究),6,115-118.

第五章
美国创新人才培养机制

知识经济的兴起,使得知识创新的速度和现代科学技术的占有量,不仅成为一个人、一个组织、一个企业竞争力强弱的首要标志,而且成为衡量一个国家国力的重要尺度。出于其称霸全球的战略需要,美国从20世纪60年代起,就开始关注创新理论的研究,对教育进行全面改革,强调学校教育在培养学生全面发展的同时,应注重开发其个性、原创精神和创新能力。

一、开展创新理论研究,增强国民竞争意识

20世纪40年代,美国广告商亚历克斯·奥斯本在其公司发起创新研讨,成为运用集体讨论解决问题(brainstorm)的发起人和完善者。1954年,奥斯本先生作为布法罗大学(现名布法罗州立大学)的校董之一,促成了该校创新教育基金会的成立。60年代,创新作为一门学科在美国开始得到重视和认真研究。1985年,布法罗大学创新教育基金会更名为创新研究中心,并逐步开设本科与硕士研究生课程。

目前,在美国像布法罗州立大学创新研究中心这样就创新建科、设系、授学位的例子尚不多见。但是,根据自身需求对创新进行不同方面研究的学会、协会、咨询机构、培训项目及网络服务商已有50多家,例如,美国创新协会、哈佛大学肯尼迪政府学院的美国政府创新研究中心和雅各布·贾维茨天才学生教育项目。

那么,创新和创新人才对美国人意味着什么呢?根据美国布法罗州立大学创新研究中心主任杰拉德·普希欧博士的解释,每个人都可以创造性地思维,都可以通过培训而具备创新的能力。美国《创新杂志》给创新所下的定义是,运用已有的知识想出新办法、建立新工艺、创造新产品。创新的特点如下:①创新必须经过人的努力才能产生;②创新需要战胜社会成见的挑战;③创新需要付出艰辛的劳动并承担一定的风险;④创新来自原创力、责任感和坚强的毅力;⑤人们可以对创新加以识别、学习和应用。

所谓创新人才,是指能够孕育出新观念,并能将其付诸实施,取得新成果的人。创新人才通常表现出灵活、开放、好奇、精力充沛、坚持不懈、注意力集中、想象力丰富以及富于冒险精神等特点。一个人的创新能力不仅表现为对已有知识的获取、改组和运用,对新思想、新技术、新产品的研究与发明,而且也表现为一种追求创新的意识,一种发现问题并积极探求的心理取向,一种善于把握机会的敏锐性,一种积极改变自己并改变环境的应变能力。

从历史的眼光看,美国人在不同的历史时期对创新有不同的解读。20世纪50年代,苏联人造卫星上天,美国人将创新定位在物理和工程两门学科,欲在太空竞赛中与当时的苏联人抗衡。在冷战结束后的经济发展时期,美国人将创新的焦点移位到国内外经济市场,力求在开发

新产品、生产流程和企业管理等经贸领域寻求发明专利、创新成果和生产效率。目前,高科技产品,特别是电脑自动化设备,遍及人类日常生活的各个角落,创新对美国人来说已成为保持心理健康和维护自我尊严的独特需求。

二、实行全面教育改革,用多种形式培养创新人才

针对创新和创新人才的培养,美国制订了著名的"2061"计划(2061年是哈雷彗星下一次回归地球附近的年份),旨在用一代人的时间根本改变美国的教育体制,造就新一代具有高度科学素养的国民。实际上,美国联邦政府早在1958年就出台了《国防教育》法案,拨出大笔经费改善美国中小学的数学和科学教学状况,力图以此提高中小学整体教学水平。2002年1月8日,乔治·布什总统签发《不让一个孩子掉队》法案。据统计,在该法案实施的7年中,美国国会为教育拨款544亿美元,用于完善美国教育体系,培养优秀有用之才。2009年,奥巴马总统签署《力争上游计划》,当年就向教育拨款43.5亿美元,截至2012年,为该项教育计划的拨款预算已达到680亿美元,成为美国教育史上单项教育计划拨款的最高纪录。《力争上游计划》的实施,旨在激励优质学校的教育创新,鼓励优秀学生的个人进步和成功,努力成为全校、全国乃至全世界的上游(周满生,2012)。

为达上述目标,美国教育在教学内容、学校种类和学校管理等方面做了重大改革。目前,美国公立中小学大多采用统一大纲,实行统一考试。在教育改革中通过高标准、严要求达到高质量的做法已经得到普遍认可。在此基础上,以统一教学大纲为指导的学校网在全美各地逐渐兴起。多数学校网都设有一个对学校教学进行监督并为其提供必要技术服务的监管组织。例如,1984年成立的基础学校联合体是美国最大的一个学校网,成员包括32个州约1 000所K-12学校。该联合体的宗旨是以教育改革家西奥多·赛泽先生的理论为指导,使所有联合体学校取长补短,共同提高教学质量。

除了一般的公立和私立学校外,美国为学生和家长提供了特许学校、学校选择和家庭学校等多种就学途径,为学生选择适当的学习场所,开发其潜力和创造力准备了必要条件。据美国教育改革中心2002年的统计,美国已有37个州通过了特许学校的立法。截至2001年春季学期,美国37个州共有2 431所特许学校,培养着约580 000名学生,秋季学期还将新增374所特许学校。据《纽约时报》2000年5月24日报道,在全美5 300万名适龄儿童中,家庭学校的学生数量约占3%,约为170万人,而且每年以7%的速度在增长。美国大学数量大,种类多,可为不同需要的高中毕业生或成年人提供学习和再学习的机会。美国教育部在提供有关高等教育信息时,提醒希望进入大学的申请人争取进入一所最适合自己的、能让自己愉快的、丰富而有意义的学校。

三、理论联系实际,学校成为创新人才培养基地

早在1938年,美国著名教育家杜威就已经提出"所有真正的教育来自经验"的论断。1995年,美国颁布的国家科学教育标准确定"重点应是教育学生掌握人们每天使用的多种技能,比如创造性地解决问题、批判性地思维和在工作中具有合作精神"。美国教育历来强调学生独立思考,大胆实验,不断进取,有所创新。教育工作者在培养创新人才的过程中,达成了一个广泛

的共识。这就是学习基础知识,反对死记硬背,反对为了应试去"死读书",强调理解基础上的全面掌握;培养技能避免机械照搬,注重保护学生的好奇心和想象力,允许质疑和批评,鼓励学生挖掘潜力,努力创新。多年来,美国注重创新教育,各级各类学校在加强基础知识和基本理论教学的同时,高度重视学生创新能力的培养。

(一)学前教育创新模式

据国家教育统计中心2014年统计,2012—2013学年,美国每天有787.8万名学龄前儿童接受不同形式的学龄前正规教育。各种幼儿园或学前班除了给孩子们提供一个安全的娱乐场所外,还要依照各州所规定的标准实施教学。现在已有45个州颁布了学前教育标准。美国国会已通过法令,要求所有的学前教育机构的正式教师必须获得幼师学位,以保证学前教育的质量。

从实地考察看,美国学前教育非常重视创新在日常课堂教学的融入。其具体做法如下:①时间。给孩子提供时间,紧迫逼不出创新,孩子们需要较长而自己可以控制的时间,完成其最理想的作品。②空间。一个能够激发孩子动手创作的空间,一个第二天能够继续其未完成作品的场所。③材料。老师通过购买、收集、循环积攒等方式,为孩子提供各种所需教具。④氛围。学习氛围尽量鼓励挑战、接受错误、容忍孩子的随意举动(包括噪音)等。⑤机会。创造各种户内外机会,激发孩子内在和对外界的想象力和创造力。

例如,纽约长岛勒克斯特谷幼儿园的教学内容在遵循纽约州标准的同时,根据学生的特点和需求,教师又增添了许多生动有趣的读本和教具。小小的教室被布置得温馨如家,有上课、读书、游戏、老师办公的固定空间。学生的桌椅三两个一组,散放在室内,并不刻意摆放得多么整齐,只要教师和学生活动方便、交谈自由即可。教室内外包括走廊贴满了学生的优秀作文、图画和手工作品。该班学生用数字"100"组成多达20余种的图画和造型,挂满了横穿整个教室的一条长线。

(二)中小学教育创新模式

在基础教育中,美国的中小学除了将创新能力的培养贯穿在整个教学活动之中,使所有学生都有机会提高其创新能力外,还设立专门的天才班级和天才学校。美国的中小学共12个年级,2000—2001学年共有在校生4 700万人。中小学教育在创新人才培养方面的具体做法和特点如下:①教学内容丰富,重视培养学生的实际动手能力;②学校与社区密切联系,强调学生的社会责任感;③师生平等交流,鼓励学生的参与意识;④课堂教学活动除教师以外,还有同学互教、小组讨论或团队协作等形式;⑤教师通常作为协调人和协作人的角色出现在课堂;⑥学生不仅是为了教师而且是为了教师以外的现实社会而完成作业;⑦课内外活动丰富多彩,为激发学生开发和发挥其想象力和创造力提供机会;⑧强调理解并掌握新知识,坚持重温所学内容;⑨实行定期或不定期测试与评估。

例如,纽约长岛古西堡小学,每个教室都有一个读书角。读书角数目可观的读物,适合该班学生的程度和需求,学生可随时借阅并带回家中阅读。学校的图书馆采用电脑自动化管理,与社会上的公共图书馆管理一般无二,目的是让学生从小就学会利用图书馆摄取新知识。该校二年级的数学课因材施教地分为三组:主讲教师负责全班,辅助教师帮助差生,尖子学生被集中到另外一个教室特别辅导。三年级地理课教师在教学生查阅地图时,先带学生到附近观察一处地理概貌,回来后和学生用泥土做出模型,让学生将所看到的地形按模型画到纸上,最后参照真实地图,逐步真正学会使用地图。四年级的英语教师课堂上在讲解着数学课的内容,但教师是从理解语言的重要性的角度去讲解的。

美国的中学更是教学内容丰富,注重学生社会实践。例如,西得威尔中学的《基础物理》1 050页,《化学》1 200页,《微积分》900页,《英文文学集》2 800多页。教师课堂除选课本部分章节外,还要增加许多散页。除课堂教学内容外,学生还积极参与丰富多彩的课外、校外活动,如学生刊物、学生"政府"、演讲队、兴趣小组、体育俱乐部等。纽约史蒂文森高中就有100个俱乐部、30种刊物和26个体育运动队。另外,许多中学要求,学生参加社会活动的时间每年不得少于50小时。这些活动对提高学生的动手能力、组织能力及团队合作精神都大有益处。

(三)大学教育创新模式

美国的大学教育经历了三个阶段。第一阶段,殖民地大学,主要通过品德教育培养行政和宗教官员。第二阶段主要培养国家建设所需的各种实用人才。第三阶段集中培养具有国际竞争实力的研究和创新型人才。第一和第二阶段的教育培养模式是,教师讲授知识,学生被动记忆,最后通过考试学生之间彼此竞争。第三阶段是,教师引导学生有效获取已有知识,鼓励学生通过与教师或同学的合作,积极创建新的知识,努力开发创新能力。具体做法和特点如下:①在教师的指导下,学生自己发现、重组和创造知识;②教师的作用是开发学生的能力和天赋;③大学教育是一种人际交往过程,是一种学生之间和师生之间的交流过程,因此,良好的人际关系在这种学习环境非常重要;④创新人才的成长需要一个合作的学习环境,因为激烈竞争的学习环境不利于发展良好的人际关系,对相互合作和积极创新都有负面影响;⑤教学是一个应用理论和研究的复杂过程,它需要教师具备足够的训练,不断更新知识和改进教学技巧。

据美国卡内基教学促进基金会的高等教育机构在2010年的统计,美国的大学总数为4 634所,美国在校大学生人数为207.277万人。在美国,大约有2/3的高中生能够升入大学,他们多数根据自己的不同素质和经济能力,选择适合自己的大学。许多大学本科期间,学生一、二年级进校不进系,全面接受基础教育。三、四年级学生可以选择主专业和辅修专业或两个主专业,并且可以申请改变专业。无论学生所选专业是文科还是理工科,他们都必须按照学分管理要求,修够文理兼顾的必修课和选修课若干。例如,佛蒙特州明德学院的中国语言文学专业的学生必须选修包括高等数学在内的数门理科课程。

美国大学的研究生教育,特别是研究型大学的研究生教育,已成为美国国内外学生、教师和研究人员渴望提高和测试其创新能力的理想教育模式。首先,美国大学的科研与教学不分家,二者互为补充,相互提高。换句话说,好的大学教授必须是好的科研能手。研究生既是获得研究经验和技能的学生,也是国家未来的科学家和工程师。美国联邦政府和其他要害部门对此有清醒的认识,也给予了足够的重视。大学终身教授制度的确立,保证了大学校园的学术自由。1980年颁布的《贝·杜法案》,又从法律上保障了大学科研成果的转换和知识产权的保护。2000年,联邦政府为大学提供的科研基金高达175亿美元,约占大学研究总经费的58%,其余经费来自企业界、州政府、地方政府和私人捐款。美国大学承担了全美44%的基础研究,为众多领域的研究、发明与创造打下了坚实的基础。据经济效益测试权威埃德温·曼斯菲尔德博士的统计,美国大学科学研究的社会回报率为28%。

另外,大学教师的聘用与管理制度对创新人才的培养起着关键作用。例如,马萨诸塞州的波士顿大学招聘新教员时,必要的条件是应聘者具有博士学位,且不能是本校毕业生,具有一定的研究工作经历,且5～6年后有望位于国内本研究领域的前沿,10年后有望成为本领域世界级领袖。在学术研究上,助理教授、副教授和教授之间没有领导和被领导的关系,既相互协作,又相互监督。例如,一个助理教授只要具备所需资格,完全有可能成为一个副教授或教授申请科研基金的同行评估专家。教授在教学和科研上,除了与本校同事合作外,还积极寻求校外合作。例如,波士顿大学将研究生导师看作树干,其研究生看作树干上的树枝。就像树枝最终肯定超过树干一样,每一个研究生必须在其研究领域超过自己的导师。美国研究生教育中的跨学科现象十分普遍,物理学教授的研究生有可能是搞物理的,也有可能是搞化学、医学或其他学科的。因此,波士顿大学的研究生导师与校内外不同领域的相关教授和学者建立了导师联合小组制度,定期或不定期地集中或分头指导彼此的研究生。

美国大学校园师生成分的多样性,也为创新人才的快速成长提供了得天独厚的沃土。据美国国际教育研究所《门户开放》(Opendoors)2014年的统计,美国的大学校园2013—2014学年共招收有国际学生212.16万人,其中274 439人为中国留学生,占国际学生总数的31%。该研究所的总结报告指出,美国校园师生成分的多样性为学生了解各种文化,扩大视野,尽快提高其创新能力提供了一个难得的机会。

(原载于《基础教育参考》2003(5)和《教育参考资料》2002(19-20))

参 考 文 献

[1] Center for Collaborative Education. (2001). Success in school:Education ideas that count [M]. Casey Connects & InSites.

[2] Fox,M.,Roni,J.,& Fox,L. (2000). Exploring the nature of creativity[M]. Duuque:Kendall Hunt Publishing Company.

[3] Lombardi,J. (2001). The strategic principles for competitive universities in the 21st century [J]. Francisco de Miranda,2001(15).

[4] National Center for Education Statistics. (2014). Enrollment of 3-, 4-, and 5-year-old children in preprimary programs, by age of child, level of program, control of program [Z]. http://nces.ed.gov/programs/digest/d14/tables/dt14_202.10.asp.

[5] Opendoors 2014 Fast Facts. (2014). International students in the U.S. [Z]. http://opendoors.iienetwork.org/.

[6] Sternberg,R. (1996). How to develop student creativity [M]. New York:Association for Supervision and Curriculum Development.

[7] Stuart,N. (2001). Encouraging academic creativity in research [J]. The Innovation Journal,1,20-27.

[8] The Carnegie Classification of Institutions of Higher Education. (2010). IPEDS institutional characteristics [Z]. http://carnegieclassifications.iu.edu/summary/enrollment_profile.php.

[9] 周满生. (2012). 奥巴马政府任内的教育政策[J]. 华中师范大学学报(人文社会科学版),4,140-145.

第六章
美国高校的学术自由与学术诚信

美国的大学总体可分为教学型、教学研究型和研究型三大种类。学术研究在后两类院校极受重视。据美国国家科学基金会2014年的统计,美国高校的研究开发经费近年来历年呈上升趋势。2010年,美国高校的研究开发经费是61 257 398美元,2011年为65 282 162美元,2012年为65 744 254美元,2013年为67 041 154美元。美国高校所完成的基础研究项目,占全国基础研究项目总量的44%。多年来,其研究硕果累累,令世人注目。20世纪初,可拉克大学研发的火箭基本原理与技术为太空探索奠定了基础;1938—1949年,哥伦比亚大学、哈佛大学和麻省理工学院三所大学的基础研究成果,使卫星定位系统(Global Position System,GPS)的诞生成为可能;1974年,斯坦福大学与加州大学的脱氧核糖核酸(Deoxyribo Nucleic Acid,DNA)重组技术,给生物学领域带来一场革命,并孵化出现代生物技术工业。美国高校在培养世界顶尖级人才方面所取得的成就,在科学研究上所取得的丰硕成果和重大发现,与其历来强调的学术自由与学术诚信具有直接关系。

一、学术自由与责任

早在17世纪美国高校陆续诞生之时,学术自由概念的雏形就已经形成。长期以来,美国各界人士对学术自由的正确理解与有效落实,使大学正常的教学活动和学术研究得到了根本的保障。与其配套而相继出台的美国大学教授协会的声明与各校相关规定和制度,使美国高校的教学与研究以及科研成果的转让既有充分的自由,又有明确的责任。

(一)学术自由的界定

1850年,学术自由的合法性首先在德国得到确立。根据当时的普鲁士宪法,科学与科学教育不受任何外力干扰。教师可以教授任何科目,学生可以选择任何课程。由于美国的联邦宪法没有提及教育,学术自由虽早已在美国高校扎根,但其合法性迟迟没有得到确认。1915年,美国大学教授协会首次发表了有关学术自由的报告。1940年,美国大学教授协会与美国大学协会共同发表了《学术自由与终身制原则声明》。该声明对学术自由的表述,尽管不具法律效应,但被美国最高法院确认为学术自由的标准和专业定义,并很快得到240多所学术与专业机构的认可。现在,多数美国大学是根据上述声明,来制定各自教师和学生手册中有关学术自由的表态和相关规定。

上述声明对学术自由的表述主要包括三点:①在完成其教学任务的前提下,教师在研究和研究成果的发表上享有完全自由,但是研究所获金钱收入须与校方协商解决。②教师在课堂上可以自由讨论所教课程,但是必须谨慎处理与本课程无关且有争议的内容。校方由于宗教或其他原因对学术自由的限制,必须在聘用合同中明确表述。③大学教师是公民、知识阶层的成员和教育机构的官员。他们在作为公民而发表言论或著书立说时,不应受到校方的审查或约束,但是他们在社区的特殊地位使其肩负着特殊的责任。作为学者和教育官员,他们应牢记公众会以其言论判断其职业和所代表的院校。因此,他们在任何时候,都应言辞准确,适当克制,尊重他人意见,并尽量使人感到其言论并不代表校方。

(二)对学术自由的理解

如前文所述,学术自由包含两层含义。第一层含义指个人学术自由。大学教师根据其与校方所签订的合同,在教学和研究以及研究成果的转让上享有充分的自由。在教学上,教师自己可以选择教材、选择教学方法以及确定学生学习成绩。在研究上,教师可以自己确定研究课题、申请研究经费、组建研究队伍,并将研究成果商业化或申请专利。第二层含义指院校学术自由。首先,院校学术自由可以让大学教师不因当权者或政客的指责而被除名。其次,大学可根据教学和科研的需求,拥有确定谁来教、教什么、怎么教和给谁教的自主权。最后,大学还有权根据在职教师的表现,决定晋升哪些教师、提升哪些教师的薪水、授予哪些教师终身职位,以及终止与哪些教师的合同。由于多数美国高校能对学术自由抱以正确的看法,因此其师生多年来可以自由交流思想、传播知识并创造新知识。

然而,学术自由在美国的推广并非一帆风顺。早在1917年,由于美国参加第一次世界大战,哥伦比亚大学不得不关闭其刚刚成立的德国语言文化中心,该中心于1929年才重新开放。1947年至1954年,麦卡锡主义泛滥,被各州和全国"忠诚委员会"提审的人员中,20%为大学教师和研究生。美国"9.11"事件后,部分大学师生的言论受到监控,16个敏感专业领域禁止外籍学生选修课程。不过,学术自由在美国大学的规则和制度早已健全,且行之有效。例如,代表大学教师心声的美国大学教授协会对"9.11"后的学术状况发表了声明,重申了大学校园言论自由的重要性。另外,大学教授终身制(tenure system)和"拜-杜法案"(Bayh-Dole Act),也早已使美国大学的学术自由制度化。

(三)学术自由的责任

从前文美国大学教授协会对学术自由的三点表述中可以看出,学术自由一方面给大学和大学教师带来自由,另一方面也使二者肩负起任重而道远的责任。大学,特别是名牌私立大学必须全力以赴地在学术自由的大氛围里,在由此而引发的激烈竞争中,招来最有潜力的学生并留住最有能力的教师,来培养杰出人才和创造重大科技成果。对大学教师而言,三点表述中的"在……前提下"和"但是"后的内容全是其必须履行的责任,而且这些责任基本都以书面的形式出现在他们与校方所签订的合同之中。

作为学术自由制度化产物的大学教授终身制,实际成了为大学教师而确立的奋斗目标。在美国,从助理教授到副教授,再到教授,一般各需5~7年时间。期间,除年度考评外,每3年或每5年要全面评估。考评或评估时,学生、同行以及主管领导对每位教师的教学效果、科研水平和社区服务表现进行打分,供校方最终决定晋升哪些人或告知哪些人准备离开。在多数大学,晋升为副教授即可享受终身教授待遇,但像哈佛这样的重点名牌大学,只有晋升为教授才能享受终身教授的待遇。有了终身教授的待遇,并不意味着可以松懈不前而高枕无忧。终身教授后评估(post-tenure evaluation)已在美国约一半高校推行。美国大学教授协会和美国大学协会表示,终身教授后评估可以使大学教授终身制得到进一步完善。

笔者在康奈尔大学实地调研时,该校著名动物生理学专家罗伯特·H.福特教授介绍说,学校聘用他时,校长明确表示:"你在这个领域比我知道得多,你就按你的想法去做吧,但要把工作做好。"福特教授在康奈尔大学工作了30多年。其体会是学校在教学和科研上给他的自由越多,他的责任就越大。他本人现已退休,但仍潜心研究。据在场的其他教授介绍,福特教授退休后还写了100篇论文,其中99篇已公开发表。康奈尔大学给学术自由的注解是"为了使命,追求自由,不忘责任"(Freedom with responsibility for a mission)。

二、学术诚信与创新

奉行学术自由使美国大学校园有了宽松的氛围,使在校师生有了使命感和责任感。追求学术诚信让美国大学注重教学质量,强调知识创新。在几乎所有美国大学的教师和学生手册中,都有关于学术诚信的具体注释和相关规定。不少大学还专门制定了"学术信誉规范"条例。而信息网络时代的到来,使社会各界对学术诚信的保障措施不断翻新。

(一)学术诚信的必要性与重要性

由于种种原因,美国某些社会机构和高校师生的所作所为,给大学校园带来了学术诚信危机。根据美国学术诚信研究中心2002年的调查结果,在多数美国大学校园,75%的学生承认他们有过作弊行为,学生参与互联网作弊的比例,从1999年的10%增加到2001年的41%。网络论文作坊(专为顾客撰写或提供论文而牟利的非法公司)已从1999年35家增加到2002年的250家。美国政府曾通过司法程序截获了多家向学生出售论文的邮件,并责令其停止营业。另外,部分大学教授以自己的名义发表别人的作品,研究生导师用自己的名义发表学生论文等现象,让大学学术诚信的不良状况雪上加霜。

当然,这种导致学术诚信的不良行径并未遍及全美大学校园。在美国,多数大学仍将追求学术诚信视作治校的根本,作为校园学术生命赖以生存和繁荣的基础。美国名牌大学多,知名度高,很大程度上归功于在培养人才和创造科研成果过程中对学术诚信的重视。2002年底,当北卡罗来纳州和马萨诸塞州有些大学查出其业已毕业的学生中,有人在毕业前的电脑软件设计过程中有作弊行为时,当即通过媒体向社会公开其行径,并宣布取消有关人员的学位资格。再如,美国大学教授协会在其职业规范5点声明中,每一点都从不同方面给大学教师提出了诚信的要求。《美国新闻与世界报道》历年的全美大学排行榜,都将"学术声望"作为第一指标,权重一直为25%,是确定学校排名的最重要的因素。

(二)学术诚信的概念与内涵

学术诚信(academic integrity)是一个复杂而不易界定的概念。虽然美国各大学对其重要性认识基本一致,但对其表述或简单解释为学术诚实(academic honesty),或在强调完重要性后直接列出遵守和违背学术诚信的注意事项和惩罚条款。根据美国学术诚信研究中心2002年的表述,学术诚信是指即使在逆境中也须对5种基本价值观做出的一种承诺,即诚实、信任、公平、尊敬与责任。第一,学生只有诚实地对己、对人,对待已知和未知,才能学到真知,才能增长才干。教师只有坚持诚实的原则,才能与学生进行有效的双向交流,在科研上取得创新,为学生树立榜样。第二,信任孕育于诚实,只有在相互信任的学术环境中,彼此方可自由交流思想,相互鼓励,挑战极限。第三,公平竞争,准确评价。赏罚分明的激励机制是学术诚信在大学校园的根本保障和最好体现,也是重点名牌大学地位牢固的根本所在。第四,无论是学生还是教师,都要尊重他人的劳动,必须在作业或作品中对他人的成果的引用——注明出处。最后,维护大学的学术诚信,需要全校每个学生、教师和管理人员的共同努力和相互监督,其责任重大,但责无旁贷。

(三)学术诚信的保障措施与知识创新

为了在人才培养和知识创新方面领先世界,美国在学术诚信的保障方面,形成了一套行之有效的机制。

首先,建立有效的社会诚信机制和学术诚信环境。例如,美国的社会安全号码系统使每个人对自己的言行和信誉,不得不随时随地给予足够的重视。中小学的"诚实周"等活动,让学生从小懂得诚实的重要性。像卫斯理女子学院这样所有考试无人监考的大学,在美国也为数不少,其目的就是要培养学生既在学业上又在做人上学会诚信。

其次,违背学术诚信的人在美国大学和社会较难容身。据报道,普林斯顿大学一个四年级本科生,在其为西班牙语课准备的12页论文中,多次引用同一本书的原文和大意,但没有注明足够的出处。此事经核实后,校方推迟一年为该生发放毕业证书。另一位申请在马萨诸塞州开业行医的医学博士,未能获准领取执照,因为该州医药注册委员会查实,此人在读博士期间发表的4篇论文中皆有作弊行为,因而不具备行医所需的品德素质。

再次,美国联邦政府、州政府主管部门以及各基金会在审批科研经费和项目基金时,除考查学术能力外,重点把关的是申请人的学术信誉。因此,欲在学术研究上成就一番事业的人士,都将学术诚信视为第一生命,放在职业道德规范的首位。

另外,各大学对学术诚信十分重视,对此皆有明文规定和详尽的操作程序说明。例如,康奈尔大学要求所有师生在其进行的一切学术活动中必须绝对遵循学术诚信的准则。该校除大学本身外,各学院、各系、各教师对学术诚信都有进一步的书面要求和具体规定。违背学术诚信规定的当事人要经过起诉、听证、答辩和裁决等程序而得到应有的惩处。哈佛大学对其师生在学习和研究中的抄袭剽窃行为给予最严厉的惩罚。

最后,为了在大学校园有效地预防、核查和杜绝各种抄袭和剽窃等作弊行为,多数美国大学教师采用的主要措施包括以下几方面:①一开学,教师就在其课程描述中让学生明白如何做到学术诚信,一旦作弊将受到怎样的惩罚。②布置学生作业要具体明确,学期论文,特别是毕业论文的选题宜与学生的知识结构和学术水平相吻合。值得一提的是,许多美国大学的本科生并非人人都得撰写毕业论文,只有各方面表现优秀的学生才有撰写毕业论文的资格,写好经过答辩后,他们可带着荣誉毕业。③学生撰写论文或研究项目报告时,教师注重过程,要求学生上交写作提纲、第一稿和所有修改稿及最后的成品。④教师若对某篇论文发生怀疑,可根据经验边看边找出证据,或到诸如 Termpapers.com 和 Internet Paper Mills 等有关互联网址搜寻线索,还可利用诸如 Turnitin、Plagiarism.com 或 Wordcheck 等网络平台获取所需信息。

(原载于《中国高等教育》,2003(18))

参 考 文 献

[1] Association of American University Professors. (1940). Statement of principles on academic freedom and tenure [Z]. http://www.aaup.org/file/1940%20Statement.pdf.

[2] Cornell University. (2012). Cornell university faculty handbook [Z]. http://www.cornell.edu/search/? q = faculty + handbook&submit = go&q = %2Bsite%253Atheuniversityfaculty.cornell.edu&target=unit.

[3] National Science Foundation. (2014). Rankings of total R&D expenditures of American academic institutions [Z]. http://ncsesdata.nsf.gov/profiles/site;jsessionid = CF04C8E6E96F867188D6CF256EEAE3AC.prodas2? method = rankingBySource&ds=herd.

[4] Princeton University. (2012). Princeton university students handbook [Z].

[5] Standler, R. B. (2000). Plagiarism in colleges in the USA [J/OL]. http://www.rbs2.com/plag.htm.

[6] The Center for Academic Integrity. (2002; 2003). CIA research [J/OL]. http://www.academicintegrity.org/cai_research.asp.

第七章
美国外语教学最新动态研究

作为当今世界的超级大国,美国上下达成了重视外语教学的共识。对个人而言,多掌握一门外语可拓宽与人交往的途径,增多获取信息的渠道,提高就业竞争力。对学校而言,有利于开发学生智力和发挥创造性,带动学生学好其他功课。1997年,美国教育统计专家比亚里斯·托克博士对134名4~5岁的美国儿童进行抽样调查的结果表明,学习双语儿童的理解力优于仅学习一种语言的儿童。在路易斯安那州进行的另一项调查结果显示,接受外语教育的学生在该州英语统考中的成绩普遍高于未接受外语教育的学生。美国大学入学考试董事会1992年的统计表明,学生学习外语的时间越长,他们在诸如学术潜能测试(SAT)和美国研究生入学考试(GRE)等考试中,语言测试部分的成绩就越高,在英语和数学等课堂上的表现也越好。对美国社会而言,鼓励国民学习并掌握外语,有利于促进国内不同种族之间的相互谅解与和睦相处,有利于加强美国经济在海外的竞争力,也有利于维护美国的国家利益和国防安全。美国一直渴望在政治、军事、科技、经贸及文教各领域,将其控制他人的触角伸向世界的各个角落。为了保证其对外政策得到有效落实,对外语人才和外语复合人才的需求也就越来越迫切。2000年9月,美国前教育部长理查德·赖利在参议院国际安全会议上表示,加强全国外语教学,将会使美国的劳动大军更加出色,国家安全得到更好的保障,教育的其他领域也将随之改善。这正是美国重视外语教学原因的精辟概括。因此,其远见和思路值得我们关注和研究。美国小学注册学习外语的人数是400万人(当时的小学生人数为2 710万人)。

一、尺有所短,寸有所长

美国外语教学的现状,客观地说在世界还是名列前茅的。据美国应用语言学中心2008年委托Rhodes和Pufahl统计,从1997—2008年,美国开设外语的小学从31%降到25%,中学从75%降到58%。西班牙语仍是首选外语,且开设该语种的学校数字呈上升趋势,小学从1997年的79%增加到2008年88%,中学保持在93%。同期开设法语和德语的中小学皆有所下降。开设法语的小学从27%降至11%,中学从64%降至46%;开设德语的小学从5%降至2%,中学从24%降至14%。相比之下,同期开设汉语和阿拉伯语的中小学有所增加。2008年,美国有3%的小学和4%的中学开设汉语,有1%的小学和0.6%的中学开设阿拉伯语。值得一提的是开设外语的中小学,有越来越多的学校具备正规的外语教学大纲,具体数字是从1997年的64%增加到2008年的78%。

根据美国现代语言协会委托Goldberg,Looney和Lusin 2015年刚做的统计报告,在2003年秋季学期,美国大学注册学习外语的人数是1 562 179人,比2009年的1 673 543人减少了6.7%。减少的原因与美国大学在校总人数的减少有关。在所学外语中,西班牙语和法语仍然遥遥领先。紧随其后的是意大利语、日语、汉语、阿拉伯语、拉丁语和俄语。2013年,西班牙语的注册人数为790 756人,比2009年降低了8.2%;法语、德语、意大利语和日语分别为197 757人、86 700人、71 285人和66 740人,与2009年相比分别减少了8.1%、9.3%、11.3%和7.8%。在此期间,注册人数有所增加的是美国手势语和汉语,分别从2009年的92 072人和59 876人增加到109 577人和61 055人,分别增长了19%和2%。

随着经济全球化的迅速发展,美国急需大批能直接用目的语与别国交流的外语人才,而目前的外语教学现状显然不能满足这一要求。因此,美国政府在大力加强培养各领域所需外语人才的同时,开始重视借鉴别国外语教学经验。联邦教育部为此成立了国际教育信息工作组,进行国际教育信息比较,推广先进的教学经验和改善美国的教育研究手段。美国应用语言学中心则承担着国际外语教育信息比较的任务。2000年10月,联邦教育部委托该中心对世界其他国家的外语教学情况进行调研。经过与44个国家有关专家的有效接触,应用语言学中心认为,澳大利亚、奥地利、巴西、加拿大、智利、捷克、丹麦、芬兰、德国、意大利、以色列、哈萨克斯坦、卢森堡、摩洛哥、荷兰、新西兰、秘鲁、西班牙和泰国等19个国家的外语教育可资借鉴。2001年9月,该中心的Pufahl, Rhodes和Christian提交了一份题为《外语教学:美国可向别国学习些什么》的综合报告。

该报告称:在过去的20多年里,与其他国家相比,美国的外语教育状况相对落后。在上述19个可资借鉴的对象国中,多数国家基础教育外语普及率已经到达80%左右,而美国1997年仅有15%的小学生、36%的初中生和52%的高中生学习外语。另据美国教育资源信息中心2000年2月的报道,美国学生从小学到大学,学习外语的经历缺少连贯性,而且,多数州仅要求学生考入大学前学过2~3年外语即可。大学培养出来的外语人才,不仅数量不够,而且质量较差,就连美国总统的某些翻译人员素质也不尽如人意。造成这种状况,一是由于英语在世界应用广泛,而且美国经济发达,科技先进,许多美国人缺乏学习别国语言的外部动力。二是美国政府对外语教育缺乏有力的指导和支持。外语教学的软硬件设施不够完善,许多学者和专家对此状况提出了严厉的批评。

二、他山之石,可以攻玉

应用语言学中心将上述国家外语教学的成功经验归纳为7个特点,并对改善美国的外语教学提出了相应建议。

(一)外语学习低龄化

从学龄期或小学就开始教授外语,在上述对象国较为普遍。其中有7个国家将外语作为必修课向8岁以下儿童开设,他们中又有2个国家同时开设2门外语必修课。有12个国家将外语作为必修课向12岁以下儿童开设,他们中有4个国家同时开设2门外语必修课。美国虽也有小学开设外语课,但多数学生从14岁才开始接受外语教育,而且并非必修课。欧盟的研究显示,儿童提早开始学习外语,有利于更好地接受此种语言,懂得尊重其他语言和文化。因此,美国也应大力开发资源,创造条件,使更多的儿童尽早开始学习外语。

(二)行之有效的教学大纲

大多数对象国认识到,完整、系统和具体的外语教学大纲,对外语教育的连贯性和协调性都起着重要的指导作用。他们普遍制定了全国性的外语教学大纲,一些欧洲国家甚至将其外语教学大纲纳入到欧共体的大框架之内。1996年,欧洲议会推出了旨在促进各成员国使用多种语言的《现代语言:学习、教授与评估》的欧盟参考框架。该框架对欧盟各国确定外语教学大纲、目标、教材、教法、测试以及师资培训等提供了一个共同的指导标准。美国宪法规定,教育的权利在地方,因此,美国没有全国统一性的外语教学大纲。自1993年联邦政府推出《外语学习标准:准备迎接21世纪》以来,各州参考联邦标准,规范其教学实践的外语教师占56%,但是,仍有46%的外语教师有待将其教学活动纳入到联邦政府或州政府规定的外语教学标准之内。

(三)严格把关的教师队伍,切实有效的教师培训

不少对象国向外语教师提供相对优厚的福利、较好的工作保障和较高的薪金,同时严格规定外语师资的岗前和在岗培训。岗前培训一般从大学本科生录取时开始。例如,芬兰、摩洛哥、德国和英国均从应届高中毕业生中选择佼佼者作为未来外语教师的培养对象。在大学4年里,这些学生除了学习所选外语课程外,还必须掌握相应的外语教育理论和教学方法,并且要完成至少半年到一年的教学实习。有些国家甚至将学生送往国外学习或实习一年。对象国外语教师的在岗培训,一般包括在当地、异地或到国外以脱产、半脱产和不脱产等形式进行选课、研讨和出席学术会议等进修活动。目前,美国从事外语师资培训的大学和学院有100多所。同时,《福布莱特-海斯法案》每年拨出专款,资助中小学外语教师进修。大学外语教师可以通过年度创新教育改革项目获得专项基金,并依据各校实际情况享受定期学术休假。据美国应用语言学中心1999年的统计,在美国开设外语课程的中小学,有67%的小学和76%的中学外语教师,在1997年前接受过在职或脱产培训。该中心认为,在外语师资队伍的建设方面,美国必须向芬兰和摩洛哥等国学习。一方面选拔优秀高中毕业生作为未来外语教师的培训对象;另一方面,创造条件使所有外语教师能够定期接受高质量的岗前与在职培训。

(四)广泛应用现代信息和媒体技术

上述调研的许多对象国在其外语教学中充分利用信息技术,特别是联网计算机,获取所需信息和资料,加强使用外语进行交流,改善外语教学课堂环境。加拿大、丹麦和泰国重视通过国际互联网和专业资料库来获取信息,并以此推动其国民学习获取信息所必需的外国语言。丹麦、芬兰和以色列等国播放大量外文电视和广播节目,外文影片不译制,而通过打字幕用原文播放。加拿大、泰国和多数欧洲国家还利用电子邮件、布告板、聊天室等网络途径,使学生用外语与教师和同学进行交流,甚至同所学语言的本族人沟通。德国、法国、丹麦和卢森堡等国开发了供课堂外语教学使用的计算机软件、模拟写作过程与编辑口语表达。对美国来说,在外语教学中应用现代技术处于相对优势地位,但怎样发挥其应有的作用,值得进一步探讨。

(五)成功的教学方法

对象国行之有效的教学方法有以下几种:①将外语课程与其他课程融为一体;②按学生的外语程度而非年龄编班;③在已掌握一门外语的基础上,学习更多门外语;④使用外语完成各

种教学项目;⑤强调目的性和得体性的交际教学方法等。最值得一提的是第一种。这种方法将外语作为交流媒体,进行部分课程的教学,或使用外语进行全部教学活动。如奥地利、德国、法国、丹麦、荷兰等通常使用英语进行地理、历史、音乐和体育课教学,其酒店管理等专业课程也用相应的外语授课。使用外语进行全部教学活动的沉浸式教学方法,主要见于加拿大的法语教学和奥地利、荷兰及德国的英语教学。美国的外语教学方法自由度高,灵活性大。如何在保持已有特色的同时,充实授课内容和提高教学效果,是美国需要向别国学习的地方。

(六)强有力的外语政策

多数对象国都强调国际外语政策的重要性。澳大利亚、加拿大、以色列、泰国及欧洲国家都将外语与数学等其他课程同等对待,并制定相应的国家政策。例如,澳大利亚的《国家语言政策》为全国的外语教学提供了宏观的指导框架。其《亚洲语言研究》政策又为汉语、日语、印度尼西亚语和韩语教育提供专项基金。以色列教育部为全国的外语教学规定了3+X的政策,即国内的犹太人和阿拉伯人必须在掌握希伯来语、英语和阿拉伯语的同时,学习另一门外语。在德国的中学毕业考试中,外语是必考科目。德国大学录取的新生,都必须学习过9年英语和至少5年法语或其他语种。美国联邦政府对外语教学已经制定了《国家安全教育法案》《2000年目标:美国教育法案》及《外语学习标准:准备迎接21世纪》等一系列宏观性的政策,但各州的配套政策与执行细则还须在系统性、连贯性和协调性上做更大的努力。

(七)强调测试评估的作用

在大部分对象国中,外语评估基本分为课堂测试和地区或全国统考两种形式。课堂测试由任课教师掌控,对学生每一阶段的学习成绩做出小结。地区和全国外语统考一般在学生高中毕业时举行,一是对中学外语教学情况进行评估,二是为大学录取新生提供参考。应用语言学中心强调,虽然多数对象国未明确指出,在其成功的外语教学中,外语测试发挥了多大的作用,但美国专家应予以足够的重视,并配合联邦政府新出台的《全国外语教育评估方案》,研究出一套有效且适合美国国情的外语教育评估标准。

自应用语言学中心的调研报告问世以来,很快引起了美国联邦教育部、教育研究办公室及国家教育图书馆的重视,3家共同资助将其发布于网上,向世人公布。《现代语言》和《语言教学》等杂志也纷纷部分转载或登文摘。作者通过与应用语言学中心教育处主任、调研报告作者之一的南希·C.罗兹联系得知,联邦教育部对这份报告非常满意,也十分重视,决定组织专家认真研究,并将其作为日后美国外语教学进一步改革的重要参考文献。

三、落实加强外语教学的政策措施,努力实现外语教学的新气象

(一)制定外语学习标准

依据联邦政府制定的外语学习标准,各州相继出台本州的外语教学标准。美国宪法规定,教育的权利在地方。联邦政府对教育一般不制定统一的官方政策,但针对外语教学制定了一系列的法案:如1961年的《福布莱特-海斯法案》、1988年的《外语资助项目》、1992年的《国家安全教育法案》,以及1994年的《2000年目标:美国教育法案》。特别值得一提的是,为了提高

美国学生的外语能力,以适应美国全球战略目标的需要,美国教育部牵头,多个外语教育协会参加研制的美国国家外语课程标准,即《外语学习标准:准备迎接21世纪》(以下简称《标准》)于1996年出版,对美国外语教学的发展起到了"催化剂"的作用。《标准》规定,美国所有学生必须在掌握英语的同时,至少掌握一门外语。1999年,《标准》修订版发行,增添了对各种不同语言学习的具体标准。两个版本都围绕交际、文化、联系、比较和社区5个领域,对美国的中小学提出了11条标准。每条标准下又分别对4年级、8年级和12年级的外语教学提出了相应指标。这为美国中小学外语教学大纲的制定和课堂教学实践,提供了不可或缺的依据。该《标准》具体目标和标准见表7.1。

表 7.1 美国《21世纪外语学习标准》

目 标 Goals	1 沟通 Communication	2 文化 Culture	3 关系 Connections	4 比较 Comparisons	5 社区 Community
标 准 Standards	人际交流 Interpersonal Communication	2.1 文化习俗 Practice of Culture	3.1 建立关系 Making Connections	4.1 语言比较 Language Comparisons	5.1 学以致用 School and Community
	诠释交流 Interpretive Communication	2.2 文化产品 Product of Culture	3.2 获取信息 Acquiring Information	4.2 文化比较 Cultural Comparisons	5.2 终生学习 Life-long Learning
	演示交流 Presentational Communication				

来源:National Standards in Foreign Language Education Project,1999.

为了推进《标准》的执行,联邦政府还通过各州和地区教育机构,为外语教学提供专项基金。例如,联邦政府教育部资助外语教师培训,并向全国7个外语研究中心提供基金,以改善和发展全美的外语教学。教育部每年给各州教育机构的外语教育拨款,至少占各州此项拨款的50%。教育部对外语教学的拨款数额,1999年为600万美元,2000年为200万美元,2001年为600万美元。此外,美国情报和国防部门也向外语教育大量投资。

为了落实《标准》,14个州随即从本州的实际出发,制定了各自的外语教学标准。40个州为此立法,要求州立学校必须向所有学生开设至少3年的外语课程。康涅狄格州格拉斯顿伯利学区是一个普通的中产阶级社区,有28 000人口,6所小学,初中和高中各1所,学生总人数为5 000人。根据《标准》和本学区的实际情况,全学区1至8年级,100%的学生学习外语,9至12年级,86%的学生学习外语。所有外语教师都有上岗证书。该学区中小学生在州外语统考中基本全部通过,许多毕业生考入大学时,其外语程度已经达到大学二年级水平。

(二)注重发挥民间学术团体的作用

美国学术团体林立,仅外语研究和指导组织就有100多个,其中外语研究机构20多家,如美国应用语言学中心、语言教育与研究中心等。在外语指导性组织中,有全国范围的,如美国外语教学指导委员会,有联络各州各学区的,如美国外语教学地区督学学会,也有针对某一外语的,如美国汉语教师协会,还有网络技术应用方面的,如国际语言学习技术协会。外语研究和指导组织的职能,大到制定美国外语学习标准,组织不同语种的年度研讨会,小到网上向新任外语教师提供教学建议,甚至回答诸如外语班级规模应该多大合适等问题。例如,本文所列举的教育部资助应用语言学中心,对世界19国成功的外语教学经验进行的调查和报告。

(三)广泛应用计算机网络技术

据美国国家教育统计中心(National Center for Education Statistics)2010年的统计,2009年,97%的美国公立学校教师可以每天使用安装在教室的电脑,54%的教师人手配备一台笔记本电脑,可以随时用于课堂教学。教室电脑和教师随身携带的笔记本电脑联网率分别为93%和96%。学生平均每5.3人一台电脑。美国私立学校和大学虽然没有有关统计数字,但根据笔者的了解和亲身体验,其现代化教学设施的应用只能大大优于公立学校的状况。计算机网络技术的广泛应用,使美国的外语教学得到了最经济和最直接的效果。

目前,应用比较广泛的计算机网络途径主要有以下几种:①电子邮件。外语教师通过电子邮件开展部分教学活动,使学生与教师,特别是与目的语国家的人士进行书面、画面和有声交流。②电子论坛。外语学习者通过外语兴趣论坛网址,向他人提问,并与其讨论,最终得到满意的答案。他们还可以通过诸如"网上你我相见"和"网上接力聊天"等途径,与世界任何地点的人士单独或集体聊天,进行交流。③电子期刊。美国的外语电子期刊一般仅在网上发行,多数是免费供读者阅读的,如《外语学习与技术》和《电子版第二外语教学》等。④网上图书馆和数据库。越来越多的网上图书馆与数据库向外语学习者免费或注册开放,例如 Retanet,Erie 和 Rosetta Stone。⑤网上授课。作为远程教育的一部分,网上外语授课已在美国逐步展开,已经面世的相关软件有 WebCT,PC Globe 和 WebSTAR 等,现在诸如有名的 MIT OpenCourseWare 的网上课程真可谓俯拾皆是。

(四)课堂外语教学新动态

美国的外语教学,听说读写不分家,所学内容紧扣现实生活。课堂上,教师自主性很强,教学模式与教学方法因人而异,灵活多样,教材丰富多彩,各具特色。其主要教学模式可归纳如下:①传统式。外语作为一门单独课程,每周3~5节,每节20~50分钟不等,学生集中学习某门外语的听、说、读、写的技能,并初步了解其文化背景。美国大多数小学采用此种模式。②探索式。每周1~2节,每节20~30分钟不等,目的是让学生对某种语言和文化有一个大概的了解。语言水平的提高和交际能力的培养已不是教学重点。③沉浸式。分完全沉浸和部分沉浸两种,前一种让学生用外语学习所有课程,后一种用外语学习部分课程。后者比前者更为常见,但前者有非常成功的范例。例如,佛蒙特州明德学院的暑期外语强化班让学生在6~9周的时间内,强化学习西班牙语、汉语和法语等8种外国语言。在外语强化学习期间,师生同吃同住,利用一切活动时间,完全学习和使用外语进行交流,除非特殊情况,一般不允许讲母语,为外语人才的培养开辟了一条独特之路。④技术辅助式。外语学者利用影视音像、电子邮件、国际互联网及交互式多媒体软件,在仿真语言环境中学习并掌握实际语言交际能力。

美国外语教学的方法更是灵活多样,主要有以下几种:①轻松自由式。外语教师根据学生的水平、兴趣和需要,选择自己认为有效的方法进行教学;学生在一种轻松自在与活泼有趣的课堂气氛里学习语言。例如,纽约大学的汉语教学就没有固定的教学方法,课堂教学完全由教师根据学生情况灵活掌握。②理论指导式。教师根据外语教学理论,按照一定套路安排课堂教学。交际法是美国外语教学中应用最广泛的教学理论。从20世纪80年代开始,美国外语教学从注重语法、词汇和语音的教学,转向重视培养应用语言交际的能力。交际法主张,语言能力是积极的、动态的,而不是机械的、静态的;掌握一门语言,是从直觉上掌握语言形式和语言形式表达的语言、认知、情感以及社会文化方面的意义;在最大限度地注意交际,最小限度地注意形式的情况下运用语言,进行思想交流与沟通。交际法在外语教学中的应用,使课堂教学以学生为中心,注重特定情景中的口头或书面含义。师生在课堂上尽量使用目的语,教材大多使用原文,而非简写本。交际法并不排斥语法教学,但强调语法的作用是为了实现交际的目的。正如海姆斯(Hymes)1971年所言,交际语言能力由四部分组成,语法知识(形式上的可能)、心理语言知识(操作上的可行)、社会文化知识(语境中合适)和实际存在的知识(实际运用)。③团队强化式。教研室或教研组教师集体备课,确定教材,讨论教法,以及命题改卷等,典型的例子有普林斯顿大学和佛蒙特州明德学院的外语教学实践。④丰富多彩、各具特色的教材。美国的外语教学材料主要有四类,一是教师自编或自选材料,二是视听材料,三是课本及辅助材料,四是原文文学作品和阅读材料。目前,美国大学外语教材的使用从实地考察得知,也基本属于上述四种情况,使用率最高的是教师自编或自选的教材,针对性强,特色鲜明,也很受学生欢迎。

(原载于《外语教学》2002(1),田德新,张喜荣)

参考文献

[1] Center for Applied Linguistics. (1999). Foreign language instructions in the United States: A national survey of elementary and secondary schools [Z]. www. cal. org.

[2] Goldberg, D., Looney, D., & Lusin, N. (2015). Enrollment in languages other than English in United States Institutions of Higher Education [Z]. Modern Language Association. http://www. mla. org/pdf/2013_enrollment_survey. pdf.

[3] Hymes, D. H. (1971). On communicative competence [M]. Philadelphia: University of Philadelphia Press.

[4] National Center for Education Statistics. (2010). Teachers' use of educational technology in U. S. public schools: 2009 (NCES 2010 - 040) [Z]. http://nces. ed. gov/fastfacts/display. asp? id=46.

[5] National Standards in Foreign Language Education Project. (1999). Standards for foreign language learning in the 21st century: Including Chinese, classical languages, French, German, Italian, Japanese, Portuguese, Russian, and Spanish [M]. Kansas: Allen Press, Inc.

[6] Pufahl, I., Rhodes, N. C., & Christian, D. (2001). What we can learn from foreign language teaching inother countries [Z]. Center for Applied Linguistics. http://www. cal. org/content/search? SearchText = Foreign + Language + Teaching%3A + What+the+United+States+can+learn+from+other+countries.

[7] Rhodes, N. C., & Pufahl, I. (2008). Foreign language teaching in U. S. schools: Results of a national survey [Z]. Center for Applied Linguistics. http://www. cal. org/resource-center/publications/foreign-language-instruction-in-the-united-states-a-national-survey-of-elementary-and-secondary-schools.

第八章
美国明德学院的中文教学特色与启示

一、明德学院的基本情况

(一)办学规模与教学重点

美国佛蒙特州的明德学院(Middlebury College)创建于1800年,是一所私立本科文理学院。根据《美国新闻与世界报道》(US News and World Report)2015年的排名,明德学院在全美200多所本科文理学院中,排名第7位。该校有本科在校学生2 495人,学杂费46 044美元,新生录取率为17.51%。该校主校园实施本科教育,师生比为1:12。该校开设有文学、艺术、哲学与宗教研究、历史、物理与生命科学、逻辑、社会学及外文8个专业方向,另开设所有学生必修的文化与文明课程。每年6~8月份,明德学院开办8个7~9周的暑期外语语言学校,1个英语语言学校和1个作家研修班,供校内外学生和成人选修。

美国虽然没有专门的外国语言学院,但十分重视外语语言专家和专门人才的培养。明德学院即为培养外语专门人才的理想场所之一。该校前任校长黎天睦(Timothy Light)就是一位外国语言教育学家,能讲标准的汉语普通话。明德学院对语言教学和外语语言培训项目的高度重视,与当年的办学方针及日后的影响不无关系。

(二)外语语言教学与暑期语言学校

明德学院的外语专业分为中文、法文等7个系。每个系分别承担英语、目的语(学生所学外语)以及目的语国家的社会与文化背景知识等教学任务。其中学生在英语方面须掌握的技能包括听、说、读、写、译。目的语教学强调以学生为中心的交际教学法,所有合格毕业生可获得学士学位,部分学生可通过本系或暑期语言学校获得硕士甚至博士学位。明德学院注重语言与文化的紧密联系,因此开设与目的语相关的社会与文化背景课程。

在明德学院,中文独立成系,可授予中文专业学士学位。在职教师5人,专业学生60名。学生在选修中文专业的同时,全部另外主修或辅修另一门专业。课堂上,教师以学生为中心,尽力创造真实的语言环境,通过灵活多样的方式反复操练,直至学生学懂用会。课外活动更加强调语言的实际应用,学习外语的学生必须遵守"语言誓约",在不同场合尽可能使用目的语。例如,明德学院的外语系有中午师生共进午餐的传统,中文餐桌上只能使用中文,从上菜、报菜名、讲解食谱到品尝、说笑以及讨论中国饮食文化等,都在教师的现场参与和指导下,在真实的语言环境中使学生在课堂上或自学的知识点得到实际应用和反复巩固。

为了更好地检验教学效果,使学生在真实语言环境中学到更多有用的东西,明德学院长期为学生提供到校外和目的语国家学习和实践的机会。一般情况下,学生在目的语国家不纯粹是进修语言,而是通过学习技艺或选修专业课程来实现学习语言和了解文化的双重目的。明德学院约2/3的学生有一个学期或一学年是在校外或国外度过的。中文系每年安排三年级学生到中国昆明、北京或杭州学习,因为明德学院分别于2004年9月、2009年9月和2010年3月在上述三地建立了明德学院中文分校。去中国之前,多半学生都在暑期中文学校学习过。

二、明德学院的暑期中文学校

(一)办学规模与管理模式

每年6～8月份,明德学院利用暑假,开设6个语种的暑期语言学校,即阿拉伯文、中文、德文、意大利文、日文和西班牙文。暑期课程相当于一个学年的语言教学内容,硕士或博士课程相当于一个学期的教学内容,其学分在国内外得到普遍认可。

明德学院第一所语言学校是德语学校,创办于1915年,中文学校创办于1966年。现在,暑期语言学校每年招聘教师200余名,招生1 200名左右,师生比为1:6。教师聘自全美高校,还有一些直接聘自学生所学语言的母语国。学生来自全美,除了在校生外,还有一些来自企业、机构和国家机关。中文学校历来的学生中,包括国务院雇员、联邦调查局和中央情报局人员,以及国防部军职官员。驻华使领馆的美方官员,有相当一部分曾经就学于明德学院,前驻华大使李洁明就是其中之一。每年暑假,明德学院平均授予150个文学硕士学位和3个现代语言学博士学位。在其开办暑期语言学校90多年的历史中,有38 000名学生来此学习,11 000名学生获得硕士学位。

在管理上,明德学院为暑期学校提供食宿条件、教学场所和教学秘书等后勤保障,校图书馆、语言实验室及游泳池等设施照常供所有师生免费使用。而在教学管理方面,各种语言学校自成体系,学校校长从明德学院校外聘请,任期3年,可连任3年。校长有财权和人事权,可左右暑校的整体办学方向。据现场采访得知,明德学院暑期中文学校的校长人选多年来一直由来自台湾的教授把持,但近20年来情况有所变化,特别随着简体中文字的推广,来自中国大陆的教授逐渐替代了台湾教授一统明德的局面。

(二)教学安排与办学特色

明德学院暑期中文学校每期9周,聘请教师15人左右,招收学生100多名,分5个年级,1～4年级为基础汉语语言课程,难度逐级加大,5年级为文言文。整个暑期学习期间,教师与学生共进三餐,同住一栋宿舍楼,学生依照"语言誓约",除非紧急或特殊情况,全天只能使用中文。

语言誓约(Language Pledge)已成为明德学院的注册商标。它要求暑期语言学校的学生自进校之日起,庄严发誓,只用所学语言进行听、说、读、写等全部交际活动。语言誓约的表述是:"签此语言誓约,我同意在暑期中文学校,只用中文作为唯一的交际语言。我懂得若违反此约,将被开除,既无学分,又无退款。"所有学生都知道,明德学院确有学生因违反语言誓约而被除名的先例。此誓约仅对意外紧急情况和初学者进校的前几日例外。其他诸如课外读书、看报、看电视以及交谈等,必须使用所学语言,以反复巩固课堂所学内容。

严格的语言誓约必须与紧张有序的教学安排相配套。暑期中文学校每天上午4课时,两节大班(20人左右)导读,两小节小班(5人左右)练习课。下午教师与学生个别谈话,每人20分钟。晚上学生自习、讨论或举办各种知识竞赛和演讲活动,教师除答疑或集体备课外,其余时间均参与学生活动。在暑期中文学校,教学进度快,9周时间里须完成1个学年的教学量。教师工作量大,除了备课、上课和休息,教师其他时间皆与学生打成一片,实行封闭式、全天候教学。教师之间,强调团队精神,提倡协同合作,定期集体备课,对新来教师或年轻教师的教学全程录像,并进行集体评议,以帮助其不断改进。中文学校校长随时进班听课,获取第一手资料,确保课堂教学正常进行。

在总结长期教学经验的基础上,明德学院暑期中文学校已形成了自己独特的教学理念和教学方法:①学以致用,注重学生的实际需求;②情景教学,注意使语言教学活起来;③授人以渔,想方设法教会学生怎样学;④真实语料,教科书及课内外不使用人造的不自然的语言材料;⑤实际运用,强调学生随时随地使用所学语言;⑥以学生为中心,用学生的学习成绩检验教学效果;⑦定期严格测试,保质保量完成教学计划。明德学院暑期中文教学的理念和方法可以归结为"全面沉浸式",即在暑期9周的中文强化学习期间,师生同吃同住,利用一切活动时间,完全学习和使用中文进行交流。根据原明德中文暑期学校校长周质平的说法,明德的中文课堂,强调在教师引导下以学生为中心反复操练的教学方法。这种方法,教师只针对学生的实际需求,不断进行校正和操练。由于上述教学理念切合实际,实用性强,教学方法省时高效,针对性强,明德学院暑期中文学校的学生一般经过9周的严格训练,基本可以用汉语进行日常交谈,汉语程度可达到中级或中高级以上水平。来此任教的教师也在这里得到全面的锻炼,其敬业精神、工作责任心和教学方法都在不同程度上更上一层楼。

三、明德现象及其启示

近年来,美国大学利用暑期在中国大陆开办了为数不少的汉语学习班,其中较大的项目有"普林斯顿在北京""哥伦比亚在清华"以及"美国国际教育交流协会(Council on International Education and Exchange,CIEE)在北大"等。另外,还有哈佛大学的HBA(北京语言大学)和美国各大学联合汉语中心在ACC(中央民族大学)和IES(北京外国语大学)(汲传波,2006)。除此而外,中国国内大学还吸引许多美国留学生前来学习汉语。即使在这样一个激烈竞争的态势下,明德学院暑期中文学校每期仍保持百人以上的规模,长盛不衰。实际上,其他不少暑期中文教学班却因生源不足而纷纷下马。明德学院暑期中文学校的人均学费高达6 000美元,比去中国留学(含往返国际旅费)还要昂贵,但其生源始终充足。这一是归功于明德学院暑期中文学校的名气和信誉,二是由于美国一些政府和情报机构的人员不便去中国留学,不便长期脱产,因此明德便成为他们学习汉语的首选。

明德学院暑期中文学校高年级学生中,来自美国政府、情报机构及军方的学生比例相当高。在明德,中国老师通过言传身教,通过中国语言文化的教学,对他们产生了很大的正面影响。普通学生在接受中国语言文化熏陶后,多数人在价值观念,甚至行为举止上发生许多变化,自身对中国亲善,其言行亦影响家人和周围朋友对中国的好感。例如,有一名学生去明德学习汉语之前,母子关系紧张,儿子长期不怎么理睬母亲。当这个儿子学习并领会到中国古诗

《游子吟·慈母手中线》的含义时,幡然悔悟。回家后,他主动地将该诗的意思用英文讲给母亲听,并从此开始对母亲孝敬起来。激动的母亲将此诗的中英文抄本随身携带,逢人便说,是中国老师教"好"了她的儿子,是中国诗歌让其母子和好。

明德学院暑期中文学校通过它的学生和教师将其教学经验带到全美各地,也带到中国大陆。其影响力越来越大。前文提到的规模较大的"普林斯顿在北京"等汉语学习班,其教学管理和教学方法完全如同明德。可以说,明德学院在语言教学界颇有影响力,而随着它在全美一枝独秀局面的形成,及其学生成分的日渐社会化,其影响力将超出学术圈而进一步扩大。

(原载于《世界汉语教学》2004(1),张喜荣,田德新。笔者对当时在明德学院暑期中文学校任教的李铠教授的大力支持和帮助,表示由衷的感谢!)

参 考 文 献

[1] About Middlebury College. (2015). http://facstaff. middlebury. edu/stories/index. 2015.
[2] 汲传波. (2006).论对外汉语教学模式的构建——由美国明德学院汉语教学谈起[J]. 汉语学习,65-69.
[3] US News and World Report. (2015). Ranking of best colleges in the United States [Z]. http://colleges. usnews. rankingsandreviews. com/best-colleges/middlebury-college-3691.

第九章
基于民族志方法的美国大学课程大纲研究与借鉴

据美国国际教育协会(2014)统计,2013—2014学年在美国际留学生的总数为886 052人,其中中国留学的人数占总人数的31%。实际上,中国赴美留学生的人数自2010年超过印度后,呈逐年上升趋势,从2009—2010到2013—2014学年分别为127 628人,157 558人,194 029人,235 597人和274 439人。为什么成千上万的学子向往美国的大学教育?从身临其境的求学和教学经历中,笔者发现美国大学教育的吸引力固然有诸如美国的自然环境、社会制度以及办学条件等因素,但根本的原因还是其教育质量。保障美国高等教育质量的因素很多,其中能让不同学科的各个专业将其教育宗旨和教学目标落到实处,在教学效果上得以显现,使众多的学生既在学校又在社会长期受益的一个关键因素是美国大学的课程大纲制度。作为师生之间的一份合约,课程大纲一方面是教师教学的依据,另一方面是学生学习的指南。正如Diamond(2008)所言:"课程大纲是一份合法的契约,受到学生、大学和法庭的关注。完整确切的课程大纲可以让教师避免学生的抱怨、委屈,甚至对教师的诉讼。"(285)同时,国内学者叶信治(2011)认为美国大学的课程大纲"是保证教学质量的成本低廉却效果很好的重要课程文件"(60)。本文基于民族志的田野研究方法,从理论依据、相关概念界定、内容、格式与功能,以及管理作用与管理制度方面,探讨美国大学的课程大纲,以资国内相关人士借鉴。

一、民族志的田野研究方法

民族志是英文"ethnography"的意译,源自于希腊文"etnnos"(民族)和"graphein"(记述),合起来意思是对一个民族的记述,而作为研究方法,国人将其译为民族志。根据常燕荣和蔡骐(2005)的研究,民族志在20世纪初期首先由文化人类学家所创立。研究者主要通过田野调查,深入到某些特殊的人群之中,从其内部着手,观察、整理和提供相关其行为和意义的整体描述与分析。其中参与和观察是民族志研究方法体系的核心内容。樊秀丽(2008)进一步指出,研究者将人类学的民族志方法运用到教育领域,从而形成教育民族志,从宏观到微观描述和解释教育现象和教育问题。研究者一般通过三个步骤进行研究:"第一,通过田野调查,获取某一群体的相关资料;第二,对相关资料进行整理、分析和解释,并从中提炼出观察研究的精华;第三,撰写民族志,并继而完成定性理论证明"(81)。

笔者从1999—2003年在驻纽约总领馆做教育领事,期间曾访问过美国东北部数十所大学,进班听课,走访专家,撰写调研报告,试图探寻美国大学的整体成功办学之道。2005—2008年,笔者在美攻读博士;2009—2014年在美两所大学任教期间,笔者身在其中,仔细观察和领会各位导师和教师同行成功教学的秘诀,并通过近十门课程的亲身历练,终于发现,在众多因素之中,美国大学课程大纲的制定具有明确的理论指导依据,其内容和格式相对固定,审批和管理制度规范科学,从而对大学教育整体质量的保障发挥了根本性的作用,是美国高等教育多年来保持世界先进水平的秘诀之所在。

二、理论依据

如果说大学课程是实现大学理想不可或缺的中介,那么大学课程大纲就是落实大学目标的关键环节。著名课程研究专家 Taylor 和 Richards(1985)认为,社会变革、科技经济进步和教育思想是影响课程发展的三大主要因素。在教育思想方面,美国大学经历了一个从传统大学观向现代大学观转变的过程。首先,纽曼(2001)认为,大学的教育目的是通过传授博雅教育和从事智力训练,培养社会所需的牧师、律师和官员。纽曼通过古典人文学科来进行教育的主张对美国早期殖民地时期的教育产生了深远的影响。19世纪,美国留学生将德国洪堡的大学理念引进到美国,从而使自然科学在美国的大学登堂入室,同时推崇大学学术自由、教师讲课自由和学生选课自由(贺国庆,1998)。20世纪,Flexner(1986)强调大学的研究功能,并主张在大学课程的目标中,增添培养学生研究能力的内容。科尔(1993)则认为现代大学应该成为"公众的服务站,努力满足学生和社会的各种需求"(3)。落实到课程大纲的设计上,俄克拉荷马大学课程发展中心主任 Fink(2003)提出,大学课程应该传授重要学问(significant learning),每门课程都必须通过严密的课程大纲为学生提供可供其终生享用的以下6种综合技能(见图9.1)。

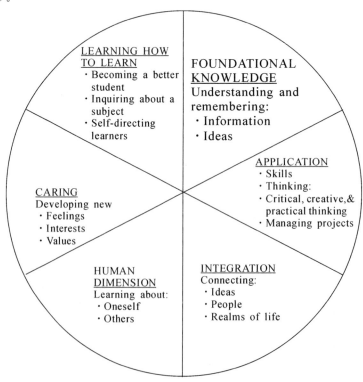

图 9.1 大学课程应为学生提供的 6 种综合技能

(1)基础知识:理解和记忆课程的主要信息和关键内容;
(2)应用目标:培养学生的批判、创造和应用性思维能力,学习技能和完成复杂研究项目的能力;
(3)综合目标:培养学生理论联系实际,将所学知识与思想、人以及不同生活范畴相互联系的能力;
(4)人文情愫:让学生养成不断了解自己和理解他人的习惯;
(5)关爱情怀:培养学生不断产生新的情感、兴趣和价值观;
(6)自学能力:培养学生争先恐后、勤学好问和自我掌控学习方向的良好习惯与自学能力。

虽然美国现有 4 000 多所大学,且其特色各异,层次多样,质量不一,但是上述教育观念及其发展过程或多或少涉及和影响着每所大学的日常教学活动和未来发展方向,特别是决定大学理想目标能否最终实现的课程大纲的设计与实施环节。

三、相关概念的界定

在详细讨论课程大纲之前,有必要对专业设置(program)、专业(major)、所有课程(curriculum)和课程大纲(syllabus)几个相关概念进行界定。根据 Lynch(1996)的界定,美国大学里的专业设置是指"为了实现某种教育目标而设置的一系列不同层次、不同学科方向的所有课程的总称",而专业是指"为了实现该教育目标而确定的不同学科方向及其主修和辅修课程"(2)。例如,笔者所就读的美国鲍林格林州立大学媒体与传播学院的专业设置是媒体与传播学,包括本科和研究生两个层次,有权授予学士、硕士及博士学位。其专业方向包括传播、新闻与公共关系及技术传播,各方向要求修完 20 多门必修和选修课程。学校鼓励资源共享,学生可以跨系跨专业选课,各专业方向都有明确的必修和选修课程、学分总数以及各科成绩的平均积分点(GPA)要求。

所有课程和课程大纲的区别在于前者是一个涉及专业设置规划,包括哲学、社会和管理因素在内的总体概念,而后者是指某专业设置里各专业方向下每门课程的教学计划书。Richards,Platt 和 Platt(2000)指出:"顾名思义,所有课程指一所大学所有学科专业的全部课程。作为一个总体概念,它除了表明该校所有专业设置的总体教育目标外,还说明要达到上述教育目标所设置的学科和专业方向及其所规定的教学内容、教学过程和学习体验。"(118)根据 Snyder(2002—2010)的研究,英文课程大纲 syllabus 起源于希腊语 sittyba 一词,起初用作羊皮纸手稿的标签。17 世纪,syllabus 在英文中用作书本的索引。18 世纪末,该词进入学术界,表示系列讲座的名称。20 世纪初,该词获得现代词义,用作教师和学生之间类似合同的教学文件。在国内,有的将 syllabus 翻译为"课程大纲",也有的将其译为"课程纲要""授课计划""课程教学计划""课程教学大纲"以及"课程实施大纲"等。现采用"课程大纲"的译文,以区别于国内读者熟悉的由教育部组织专家学者编写来指导学科教学内容的"教学大纲"。Ur(2000)指出,课程大纲既是教师教学的根本依据,也是学生进行该门课程学习的重要指南。因为一份合格的课程教学大纲应该详尽而明细地列举该门课程的教学目标、教学研究任务、具体进度安排、作业与论文要求、考试评分标准,以及学生预习、复习课文和参与课堂讨论的表现等行为规范。

四、内容、格式与功能

尽管美国大学并没有统一的课程大纲规定,但是从社区学院到教学型大学,再到研究型大学,无论是本科课程还是研究生课程,不管是必修课还是选修课,都必须具备基本大同小异的课程大纲。

首先,在内容上,课程大纲一般包括以下几项:①课程名称、上课时间与地点。②教师姓名、答疑时间与联系方式。③课程描述。④课程目的。⑤课程目标。⑥教学日程。⑦评分规则与程序。⑧政策与期望,其中包括 a. 出勤奖惩办法;b. 缺课补习与作业迟交规定;c. 课堂行为和课堂礼仪要求;d. 学术诚信规定与要求;e. 方便残障学生的声明与校园安全注意事项;⑨课程必备教材、参考读物以及相关资源;⑩该课程所需的研究和学习工具。除此而外,有些教师会在课程大纲中添加诸如"我思故我在""通过做而学"或"授人以鱼不如授人以渔"等勉励性的座右铭,而另一些教师会在其中添加自己的教学哲学陈述。

其次,在格式上,不同的美国高校对其课程大纲会有不同的体例要求。许多大学对其教师提供编写课程大纲的模板,然后教师再根据自己的教学理念、课程要求以及学生的实际需求编写出各具特色的课程大纲。这样,课程大纲的质量不会因其格式或体例的不同而大相径庭。一般说来,能得到普遍认可并受多数学生欢迎的课程大纲会展现出一些相同的优点。譬如,Snyder(2002—2010)研究发现,获得1997年全美卡内基年度奖优秀教师的课程大纲具有以下共同的特点:① 课程目标表述清晰;② 课程进度一目了然;③ 课程预习量大且期限紧迫;④ 课堂参与和表现,指令明确,责任到人;⑤作业、考试和论文或课题均衡地分布于整个学期,大纲对其内容、范围、体例、最后期限以及评分标准都有准确无误的描述和成绩记录。

最后,对课程大纲的功能,学者们各具慧眼,表述不一。例如,Matejka 和 Kurke(1994)言道:"课程大纲是一份合同、一种沟通工具、一项计划和一幅认知地图。"(3)Parkers 和 Harris (2002)认为,课程大纲的功能一是作为师生之间的合同,分别规定了彼此的权力和职责;二可作为长期记录,记载某门课程的教学内容和教学目标;三是作为学生学习的工具,帮助其预习、复习和成功地完成该课程的学习。而 Grunert(1997)列举了 16 项有关课程大纲的功能:①尽早建立师生接触和联络的方式;②确定该门课程教学的基调;③帮助教师阐明其教育理念和教学目标;④使学生明了课程进度与组织安排;⑤规划和按时发放课程辅助材料;⑥明确学生成功完成该课程而应承担的责任;⑦指导学生如何积极学习;⑧帮助学生评判自己的课程准备状况;⑨描述与该课程相关的学科领域及其发展前景;⑩点明该课程的关键内容和实用社会价值;⑪提供与课程相关的参考资料和学习资源;⑫强调现代技术在该课程中的重要作用;⑬提供与课程相关的紧缺材料的获取途径;⑭提高学生课堂笔记和课后记忆的效率;⑮扩充学生课外学习的兴趣与途径;⑯充当师生相互协作和监督的合同。

除此而外,笔者发现由于每门课程的课程大纲都将教学重点和难点均匀分散,测试手段和评分标准明确公开,学生的课堂表现评价和测试成绩也可随时上网浏览与掌握,几乎所有学生都能以最好的成绩尽力修完所选课程。由于所有课程大纲标准统一,管理严明,学生只要选了某门课,无论是必修课还是选修课,他们都得将其如必修课一样对待。由于师生将教学大纲视若合约,学生又随时知晓合约进展情况,只要是大纲规定的,即使阅读量大了一些,测试和作业频繁了一些,教师的标准和要求也苛刻了一些,学生们多能欣然接受,并乐在其中。

五、管理作用与管理制度

根据 Eberly,Newton 和 Wiggins(2001)的研究结果,除了上述教学功能外,课程大纲在管理方面的作用表现在:①有助于教务管理部门及时掌握各门课程教师的备课状况以及相关部门所需筹备的教材和教辅材料信息;②提供学校各个学科和专业中各门课程的详尽描述;③用作应对各级监督和评估教学质量的关键教学文件;④用作解决评分纠纷和学生可能在校内外申诉的重要依据;⑤提供学生转学时对其跨校学分是否认可的根本凭证。由于这些不可替代的重要作用,美国多数高校对课程大纲都制定有严格的管理制度。

作者曾在美国大学任教,亲身经历相关管理制度如下:第一,学校为所有教师提供编写课程大纲的模板,其中诸如学校使命陈述、相关校纪校规、课程进度日期、学术诚信要求、课堂行为标准等内容以及整体格式都已设置到位。第二,各位教师应在每个学期开学前三周将编写好的课程教学大纲通过校园网上交院系主管领导审批;若有问题会被打回,须认真修改后重新上交审批。第三,教师应在开学前将审批过的课程大纲上传到学校教学管理平台,供选课学生参考,购买所需教材并备齐其他教辅材料。第四,开学第一堂课的主要内容之一是任课教师确保学生人手一份课程教学大纲,并宣讲其中关键内容和注意事项。第五,在接下来的整个学期,教师将其作为教学的依据,学生将其作为学习的指南。除非特殊情况,一般教师不再对课程大纲中的内容进行改动。第六,所有学生的作业、考试、论文或课题以及课堂表现的评分标准应以课程大纲对各个项目的具体要求为根本依据。最后,在学期结束前,每位教师按要求需要将其各门课程的课程大纲,学生成绩单以及主要作业,考试和论文的优、良、差三份代表作,一起上交教学秘书处存档。这样,每个学期的每门课程都能按要求和期望善始善终,存档教学材料足以应对校内外随时抽查,确保定期与不定期的教学评估可以真正在原生态状态下进行。

六、结论

综上所述,虽然美国大学对课程大纲的规格和标准没有统一的要求,但是,所有高校教师或按照学校提供的模板,或遵循约定俗成的传统,编写出各具特色的课程大纲。从笔者在就读大学和任教院校的亲身体验和广泛观察来看,多数教师在编写其各门课程大纲时,都能自觉自愿和认真负责地在内容上与校内外同课程同行保持一致,以便向学生传授本学科最有代表性和最新的前沿内容。其中一个典型的例证是,各份课程大纲所规定的必备教材(经常不止一本)基本是当年出版或最新的版本。在格式或体例上,即使学校没有统一的要求,年轻教师或新来的教师也在创新和保持特色的同时,尽量仿照富有经验的同事们的样式。至于功能,无论是学校管理部门,还是教师本人,也都尽可能地使其课程大纲的功效发挥到极致。一方面,各个学校和所有教师都希望通过课程大纲来体现其教育理念,以便使上述六种综合技能的培养目标得以实现。另一方面,在当今教育资源激烈竞争的美国,各个大学欲靠良好的教育质量保障尽可能丰富而理想的生源,各位大学教师也深知其声誉、晋级与收入直接与其课程大纲的质量和实施效果紧密相关。

本研究成果对国内各级教学管理者和一线广大教师皆具有理论和实际的启发意义。在理论上或教育观念方面,我们必须认识到现在的师生关系早已冲破师道尊严和传道、授业、解惑的师徒关系。韩愈当年所描写的"无贵无贱,无长无少,道之所存,师之所存"的师生关系在现今的数字化、信息化和市场经济社会已经成为现实。教师的作用从以往的知识传授转向现今的教学相长,教学引导。国家对大学生虽有一定程度的补贴,但学生家长要掏腰包为子女付学费的现实,学生毕业后要面对竞争激烈的就业市场的现状以及当代大学生对教师有效引导的期盼,使中国这样具有数千年传统的权威性教育模式将逐渐向合约式的、专业性的和具有法律保障的道路迈进。

另外,对美国大学课程大纲的引进,可以在实际教学中彻底扭转应试教育的负面影响。多数学生,包括美国学生在内,平时只关心考试考什么,他们就学什么。但是,完整有效的课程大纲将学习重点化整为零,把用来评估教学的作业、测试、论文或实验均匀地分散在整个学期的各个阶段。这样虽然学生的阅读量成倍增加,但是由于其随时掌握合约的进展状况,几乎所有学生都能信守完成课程大纲所规定内容的诺言,将所选课程以最好成绩尽力修完。实践证明,通过合约式的、专业性的和具有法律保障的课程大纲,美国大学教育整体质量才能得到根本性的保障,美国高校才能长久享誉全球,并像磁石般地吸引着来自世界各国的优秀学生和顶尖人才。

参 考 文 献

[1] Diamond, M. Robert. (2008). Designing and assessing courses and curricula: A practical guide (3rd ed.) [M]. San Francisco: Jossey-Bass.

[2] Eberly, M. B., Newton, S. E., & Wiggins, R. A. (2001). The syllabus as a tool for student-centered learning [J]. The Journal of General Education, 50(1).

[3] Fink, L. D. (2003). Creating significant learning experiences: An integrated approach to designing college courses [M]. San Francisco: Jossey-Bass.

[4] Flexner, A. (1986). Universities: American, English, German [M]. New York: Oxford University Press.

[5] Grunert, J. (1997). The Course syllabus: A learning-centered approach [M]. Bolton, MA: Anker Publishing Company, Inc.

[6] Institute of International Education. (2014). Open doors report on international educational exchange. Retrieved from http://www.iie.org/opendoors.

[7] Lynch, B. K. (1996). Language programs evaluation [M]. Cambridge: Cambridge University Press.

[8] Matejka, K., & Kurke, L. B. (1994). Designing a great syllabus [J]. College Teaching, 42.

[9] Parkers, J., & Harris, M. B. (2002). The purposes of a syllabus [J]. College Teaching, 50.

[10] Richards, J. C., Platt, J. & Platt, H. (2000). Longman dictionary of language teaching and applied linguistics [M]. Beijing: Foreign Language Teaching and Research Press.

[11] Snyder, J. A. (2011). Brief history of the syllabus with examples, 2002 - 2010.

Available at http://isites.harvard.edu/fs/html/icb.topic58495/syllabushistory.html.

[12] Ur, P. A. (2000). Course in language teaching: Practice and theory [M]. Beijing: Foreign Language Teaching and Research Press.

[13] 常燕荣,蔡骐. (2005). 民族志方法与传播研究[J]. 湖南大众传媒职业技术学院学报, 5(2), 22-25.

[14] 樊秀丽. (2008). 教育民族志方法的探讨[J]. 教育学报, 4(3), 80-84.

[15] 韩愈. 师说. 古诗文网. 选自: http://www.gushiwen.org/GuShiWen_de14d6f28c.aspx.

[16] 科尔(Clark Kerr). (1993). 大学的功能[M]. 陈学飞,等,译. 南昌:江西教育出版社.

[17] 贺国庆. (1998). 德国和美国大学发达史[M]. 北京:人民教育出版社.

[18] 纽曼(John Henry Newman). (2001). 大学的理想[M]. 徐辉,等,译. 杭州:浙江大学出版社.

[19] 叶信治. (2011). 美国大学课程质量保证机制研究[J]. 西南交通大学学报(社会科学版),12(6),58-64.

第十章 美国高等教育理念的发展和大学教学实践特色研究与借鉴

美国高等教育以其规模、质量和成就,享誉全球,令世人瞩目。美国大学对美国的科技进步和国家富强发挥着举足轻重的作用。有数据表明,在二战后的西方发达国家,60%的重大技术革新首先在美国研制成功,其中25%首先在美国投入使用。在20世纪诺贝尔奖得主中,美国人占1/3,其中多数来自大学的教学和研究部门。[1]根据美国国家教育统计中心(National Center for Education Statistics)统计,2011—2012学年美国共有4 706所授予学位的高等院校,其中两年制社区学院1 738所,四年制高等院校2 968所,公立院校1 649所,私立院校3 057所。[2]另据美国国际教育协会统计,2013—2014学年在美国高校就读的国际留学生总数是886 052人,其中中国留学生占总人数的31%;2014—2015学年,美国高校在校学生总数预计为21 266万,约占美国总人口的35.15%,应届高中毕业生的75%。[3]以上数字从一个侧面显示出美国高等教育的勃勃生机和对包括中国学子在内的各国留学生的强大吸引力。研究显示,当今的美国"已经拥有了世界上最庞大的高等教育体系之一",它为"美国科技、经济和社会的飞速发展奠定了重要的基础"。[4]下面,笔者依据自身在美国高校学习和任教的经历,汲取前人研究成果的精华,归纳对相关学者和专家的访谈记录,系统而深入地探讨美国高等教育理念的发展和大学教学实践,希望对国内广大教师和各级教学管理人员有所启迪。

一、理念、教育理念和大学理念的界定

"理念"一词起源于古希腊文(eidos),表示"形象"或"观点"。在西方,古希腊哲学家苏格拉底认为理念是存在于自然之中的一种模型,是我们心中的一个想法。[5]《辞海》将"理念"解释为"看法、思想或观念",其中理念是根本,观念是形式。尽管理念与观念相互关联,但是先有意念,正确的意念可以转换为观念,观念经过观察和深思可升华为理念。[6]在综合了中西学者对"理念"的不同理解和定义后,韩延明给理念所下的定义是,"人们对某一事物或现象的理性认识、理想追求及其所形成的观念体系"。他将教育理念界定为"教育主体在教育实践、思维活动及文化积淀和交流中所形成的教育价值取向与追求"。他对大学理念的解释是,"人们对那些综合性、多学科、全日制普通高等学校的理解认识、理想追求及其所形成的教育思想观念和教育哲学观点"。[7]

潘懋元教授指出,从"理念"切入,既可以把握高等教育的本质、功能和规律,又可以理解高等教育规律是怎样影响人们对高等教育的认识和追求的。教育理念具有民族性、国际性、导向性、前瞻性和规范性的特征。对潘懋元教授来说,大学理念"是一个上位性、综合性的高等教育哲学概念。它是发展的,随着时代的进步和认识的加深,新的大学理念会不断出现"[8]。由此

可见,教育理念是基于教育规律基础之上的教育理想追求。虽然教育理念并不等于教育现实,但是它能够指明教育前进的方向,引导人们遵循教育规律,科学而高效地实现教育目标。因为教育理念指导和制约教育实践,所以说有什么样的教育理念,就有什么样的教育制度和教育实践。

二、美国高等教育理念的发展

作为一种教育哲学观点,美国的高等教育理念几经变革,最后形成独具特色且受广泛推崇的教育思想观念,主要包括以下几个方面。

1. 追求公平而平等的教育

从1636年哈佛大学创建至今,美国高等教育一共经历了近380年的历史。起初,美国大学仿照英国牛津大学和剑桥大学的办学模式,通过以古典语言和古典文学为主的博雅教育,为当时的美国社会培养绅士和牧师。根据英国教育名家纽曼(Newman)的解释,所谓博雅教育(liberal education),是相对于某种实用知识或技能为目标的职业教育(professional education)而言的,其目标是为了知识本身的价值而追求知识,而不是为了诸如利益、财富、权力或荣誉等知识之外的目的。纽曼认为,"知识的本质是真正的、无可否认的善。知识可以提高人的精神情操,使人达到绅士的境界,形成一种可以终身受用的心智的习惯"[9]。作为英国殖民地的美国,当时的教育崇欧亲英,执行的是贵族哲学的理念,接受高等教育的多为出身名门、付得起学费的绅士阶层。

1776年7月4日,美国独立战争结束,新的美利坚合众国诞生。饱受政治压迫、宗教迫害和被剥夺教育权利的美国大众渴望教育公平和教育机会均等的理想。尽管理想和现实出入较大,追求理想的道路布满荆棘、坎坷崎岖,但是,《美国独立宣言》开篇的"人人生而平等,造物主赋予他们若干不可剥夺的权利,其中包括生存权、自由权和追求幸福的权利"[10]的主张让平等、自由和个人追求的种子植根于每个美国人的心田,同时也深深地扎根于美国的教育体制之中。美国还于1866年和1871年制定《重建民权法案》,于1964年和1991年又修订和增补了《民权法案》,确保美国公民人人平等,均有接受教育的权利,任何公立学校不能"基于种族、肤色、宗教信仰或民族的原因"[11]将学生和教师拒之门外。此外,联邦政府成立了公平就业委员会(Equal Employment Opportunity Commission),监督和处罚美国公民在就业中可能遭受的不公平待遇。

2. 推行学术自由和实用主义

到了19世纪,美国通过向当时欧洲高等教育最发达的德国派遣大批留学生,引进了德国教育家洪堡(William van Humboldt)教育与研究相结合、学术自由与独立创新的新理念。从1850年至1914年,美国向欧洲,特别是德国选派了成千上万的留学生。学成回国的留学生带回了从德国学到的学以致用的授课模式、讨论式授课方法、博士学位制度和实验室操作规则等,使学生除了学习知识外,还要从事研究和创造知识。更重要的是他们在模仿中改造,同时也在引进时创新。美国不但引进了德国的研究院体制和教育与研究相结合的制度,也自身独创了职业训练性质的硕士制度,并将专业学院引入大学体系。[12]最值得一提的是,美国将德国的学术自由、教学自由和学习自由发扬光大,使其成为美国学术自由的三原则,即学术自由、学术自治和学术自立。

根据美国大学教授协会(American Association of University Professors, AAUP)的界定,学术自由包括三个方面:第一,教师完成教学任务后,可以自由从事研究并发表其研究成果,若有收入,可与校方协商解决。第二,课堂上,教师可以自由教学,但要谨慎处理与本课程无关的内容或有争议的地方。校方由于宗教或其他原因对学术自由的限制,须在合同中明确表述。第三,校方不应审查或约束教师的公开言论或著述,但是教师作为知识分子和学校职员,应谨言慎行,言责自负。[12]张国骥指出,学术自由催生了"美国教育中独立思考、质疑一切的精神,已经被全社会接受为美国教育的灵魂"[13]。

1861—1865年的美国内战废除了美国南方的奴隶制度后,国家百废待兴,教育需求剧增。实际上,1862年美国国会就通过了《莫雷尔法案》,用赠地的方式发展教育,鼓励受惠院校在不排除科学、经典学科及军事战术课程的前提下,教授与农业和工业有关的学科。《莫雷尔法案》不但加快了美国高等教育的发展,而且在教育理念上,让重视古典学科的博雅教育失去了昔日的支配地位,使实用主义主导的专业教育和可以学以致用的实用学科大放光彩。杜威是美国实用主义教育思想的创始人,其"教育即生活""学校即社会"以及"从做中学"的教育理念和教学方法,对美国教育产生了深远的影响。作为教育理念,杜威的"教育即生活"指的是"生活就是发展,而不断发展,不断生长,就是教育",反过来说,"没有教育就不能生活";其"学校即社会"指的是学校应该"成为一个小型的社会,以反映大社会生活的各种类型的作业进行活动"。[14]威斯康星首位大学校长约翰·贝斯康是该教育理念的支持者之一。他强调道德和价值的观念,认为个人有责任和义务参与社会实践活动。该校第10任校长查尔斯·范海斯更加明确地主张:大学应当是为本州全体人民服务的机构。他们的主张和威斯康星大学的实践催生了有名的"威斯康星思想",即"在教学和科研基础上通过培养人才和输送知识两条途径,发挥高等教育直接为社会服务的职能"。[15]

3. 培养个体化与本土国际化人才

美国多年来以欧洲移民为主,因而其欧洲文化渊源深厚,文艺复兴时期的"人本主义"思想在美国开花结果,不但全民个人主义盛行,而且从家庭到学校再到社会都给个性主体的成长与进步给予充分的肯定和特别的尊重。周光礼教授指出,"盎格鲁-撒克逊传统的高等教育体系基于这样一种逻辑:在高等教育中没有整合一切的统一目标,只有个人的目标和地域性的目标"[16]。美国大学鼓励学生独立思考、质疑一切,并将其作为原创之魂。落实到教育理念上,美国高等教育在4个方面强调学生个性主体的培育:第一,大学教育的宗旨是培养人才;第二,肯定学生在教学中怀疑权威、独立思考和批判性思维的学风;第三,调动学生自主学习、动手实践、敢想敢干的自信心;最后,采用讨论式、互动性教学,使学生养成表达观点、交流思想、运用知识和创造知识的习惯。[17]正如张伯苓先生的观察:"无论世界中哪一个大学都没有像美国大学那样尊敬天性的。美国大学教育是以助长及启发琢磨个人的天才为其存在条件的。"[18]

两次世界大战使美国告别严守中立、不结盟的外交政策而转向谋求世界霸主和按照美国的构想塑造世界的对外策略。加之一波又一波的国际化浪潮使美国与世界其他国家接触和交涉的频率急剧增长。但是,美国人发现,语言和文化的障碍已成为影响其通畅跨文化交际的主要因素,在很大程度上甚至制约其国际战略图谋的预期实现。另外,经济全球化迫使高等教育国际化。美国为此于1958年通过了《国防教育法》,希望加快高等教育发展,培养国家所需人才,接着还陆续于1966年颁布了发展国际教育的《国际教育法》,1990年制定了推广全球观念的《2000年目标:美国教育法》,2002年推行了强调教育与国家政治、经济、军事等整体利益关系的《美国教育部2002—2007年战略规划》。于是,"在大学教育中培养学生的国际化思维与视野,成为美国高等教育一个坚定不移的目标"[19]。奈特将国际化定义为"将国际的、跨文化的或者全球维度融入院校或国家层面的高等教育目标、功能的过程"[20]。本土国际化(glocalization)是由本土化(localization)和全球化(globalization)组合而成的,由罗兰德·罗伯逊首先提出,表示某种同时面向国内和国际的产品或服务。后来在教育界被引申为培养具有全球意识和本土才干的人才(think globally and act locally),培养他们的过程实际上就是国际人才本土化和本土人才国际化的过程。[21]

三、美国大学教学实践

前文提到有什么样的教育理念,就有什么样的教育制度和教育实践。美国大学在教育和教学实践中的特色主要表现在以下几个方面。

1. 公平而平等的教育和教学实践

首先,自美国内战以来,美国高等教育先是实行英才教育,即在学习成绩面前人人平等,大学按学生成绩择优录取。接着推行高等教育是美国公民的权利的主张,并通过建立奖学金、助学金和贷学金的制度,逐年大幅度地提高全国适龄人口的大学入学率。比如,1947—1948学年,美国高校在校人数是262万人,占18~24岁同龄人口的16%;到1997—1998学年,统计数字分别是1 460万人和57%;到2009—2010学年,数字分别增至1 750万人和60%。[22]

其次,美国大学包括大学、学院和社区学院,构成三级高等教育人才的培养结构。美国大学又分为研究型、教学研究型和教学型,向不同层次的人才提供副学士、学士、硕士和博士学位的不同教育需求。同时,美国大学实行的学分制度和学分互认制度,使学生可以跨专业、跨系甚至跨校选课和更换专业。笔者曾经任教的一所美国大学拥有在世界不同国家的4所校园,学校允许学生跨系跨校选课,同时鼓励学生利用不同学期前往不同校园修课,以便在学习专业的同时,开阔视野,增长知识才干。

第三,最重要的是美国大学在招聘教师时,为了保证录取到最佳人选,一般面向全世界公开招聘,招聘委员会由同行教师3~5人组成,包括电话或视频初试、筛选后的2~4人现场面试、教学演示和/或研究课题演示等环节。由于有《民权法案》的相关规定和联邦政府成立的公平就业委员会的监督机制,没有哪个高校会因国籍、种族、肤色、年龄、性别或残障等因素将任何候选人拒之门外。笔者在美国求学和求职的经历中,也没有遇到因为是中国人,或性别和年龄而不予录取。

2. 学术自由和实用主义的教育和教学实践

在实践中,学术自由包含两层含义:个人学术自由和院校学术自由。根据个人学术自由并依据合同,美国的大学教师在教学上,可以自选教材、教学方法和考试模式;在研究上,教师可以自拟课题、申请经费、组建研究团队,并将研究成果商业化或申请专利。院校学术自由首先可以让教师不因当权者或政客的指责而被除名。其次,根据需求,大学拥有确定谁来教、教什么、怎么教和给谁教的自主权。最后,大学也可根据教师的表现确定晋升哪些教师、提升哪些教师的薪水、授予哪些教师终身职位,以及终止与哪些教师的合同。[23]因此学术自由既给大学和大学教师带来自由,又让二者肩负起任重道远的责任,谁能说这不正是实用主义的最好体现呢!

大学要培养出经得起现实社会和市场考验的人才,否则生源和经费就会受到影响;教师须在规定的年限内在教学、科研和服务上达到校内外同行专家公认的标准,否则就得下岗另谋生路。尽管大学教授终身制度使某些教师有些许安全感,实际上终身教授后评估(Post-tenure Evaluation)早已在美国多数高校推行,最主要的是美国大学教师清楚,作为大学教授,学术自由中的自由和责任将伴随他们终生。

有一位华裔美籍教授,在美国大学从事教学和研究数十载,在接受笔者访问时表示,他最推崇"作为美国大学教授所享受的学术自由、学术责任以及学术成就"[24]。其言语重心长,同时代表许多其他受访者和美国众多大学教授的心声。再譬如,康奈尔大学对学术自由的理解,"为了使命,追求自由,不忘责任"(Freedom with responsibilities for a mission),可谓学术自由在美国高等教育实践中的最好注脚。另外,学术自由给予学生自由和责任,不妨以布朗大学为例。该校的教纲精神是,"在布朗大学,不会有人告诉你该上什么课或怎么做。但是,学生必须在毕业前以某个学科为中心,修完30门课程"[25]。其实,学术自由和实用主义对美国大学生具有同样重要的指导意义。首先,自由的代价无论是在选课上还是对待课业的态度与行为上,失误和失败就意味着时间和金钱的流逝。虽然多数课堂以互动式的讨论形式为主,但是每堂课课前学生都要完成大量的阅读或实验作业,否则他们在课堂上不但会因为回答不上来问题或在讨论中无话可说而丢人现眼,还会因课堂表现消极影响最终成绩。所以,"蛮拼"是美国大学生,特别是研究生的普遍表现行为。

3.个体化和本土国际化的教育和教学实践

美国大学教育以学生为中心,课堂教学多采用以学生为中心的授课方式,其中包括两人或多人小组讨论、苏格拉底式问答、角色扮演、现场模拟、案例分析、成果演示、演讲和辩论。同时,大学的课堂学习与课外学习、学生的知识接受与知识创造以及他们的学习和研究是合二为一的整体。根据笔者对10名在美国大学任教的美籍华人教授的访谈结果,课堂学习和课外学习二者的比例约为1∶5,1∶4和1∶3不等。他们有教本科生数学的、文学的、写作的、演讲的,也有教研究生跨文化交际的、社会科学研究方法的、服装设计的以及市场营销。无论本科还是研究生,文科还是理科生,课外都要完成比课内多3倍以上的阅读或动手实验作业。另外,美国大学教育积极鼓励学生批判性思维,十分注重开发学生原创性。在知识创新和学术研究方面的体现有课堂内容讨论、作业过程分享、影视作品评论、理论应用课题、实地考察调研、辩论性短文写作、学术论文写作及其学术会议演示和刊物发表。正如耶鲁大学校长所言,学生要对任何事情都提出质疑;要多读书,多提问;学会独立思考,学会发表思考成果。[26]

为了培养本土国际化人才,美国大学一般采用专业设置和课程内容国际化、教师国际互访与学术交流、学生赴国外学习和实践、留学生来校学习与交流、校际姐妹关系与交流项目、国际研究与外语培训、国际俱乐部以及国际文化节。在此我们以最后两项为例,美国的国际研究仅其智库就有1 828家,占全世界智库总数6 826家的26.77%,在全球顶级智库的前10名中,美国智库就有6家,占60%。[27]美国的外语教育自1994年《2000年目标:美国教育法案》颁布以来,外语与数学、科学和社会学的科目被并列为法定基础教育核心课程。大学外语教育以沟通、文化、联系、比较和社区为目标。外语授课的主要方法有以下几种:①将外语与其他课程融为一体;②按学生的外语程度而非年龄分班;③在已掌握一门外语的基础上,学习更多门外语;

④使用外语完成各种项目;⑤强调目的性和得体性的交际教学法。[28]

美国大学校园的国际俱乐部是美国学生对某个国家或地区及其社会文化感兴趣而成立的俱乐部,也有来自国外的留学生为了将自己国人集结到一起联络感情的俱乐部。他们除了组织俱乐部成员内部活动外,还时常邀请相关学生、教师或专家举办讲座或其他学术性活动。笔者就被两三个团体邀请讲过中国的文化大革命、中国领导人(毛泽东、邓小平和江泽民)以及中国神话故事。

国际文化节是美国大学一年一度的国际文化庆典。届时,校方提供专门场地,搭舞台请乐队、支帐篷飘彩旗、列展台布展品,展品主要是国际学生从家乡带来的能代表自己文化的物品,展台后的学生身着民族服装,向其他学生和观众讲解展品,并提供民族饮食。一般情况下,饮食是收费的,收入用作学生俱乐部活动经费。除此以外,身边国际同学的存在,课堂国际话题的讨论以及跨学科、跨国度和跨文化课题的承担以及国际互联网的频繁使用,都构成美国大学生迅速成材过程中得天独厚的有利条件。

四、结论

综上所述,从美国殖民地时期的博雅教育,到南北战争后的职业教育,再到当今的知识学习和知识创造并举、教学与科研结合以及教育个性化、社会化和国际化,美国的高等教育理念随着时代的变革而发展,学习先进的同时有创新。美国的高等教育和教学实践在其教育理念的指导下,灵活而有效地履行了相对公平而平等的高等教育,在校师生享受充分的学术自由,并按照社会的需求和自身的愿望,努力成为具有全球意识和本土才干的人才。美国的高等教育理念和教育实践对我们至少具有三方面的启示。

第一,从实际出发,教育理念在继承和借鉴中不断发展、不断创新。美国的高等教育之所以能在短时间内领先世界,就在于它敢于扬弃殖民地时期接受教育就是进入学术象牙塔的过时思想和填鸭式的教学方法,敢于到当时教育最发达的德国学习并发扬光大学术自由、批判性思维和创新型研究的教育理念和互动、讨论和动手的课堂教学模式,同时严格依法消除各种歧视行为,使学生享受均等的教育机会,教师获得宽松自由的学术氛围。

第二,以实效为目的,教育模式的改进为的是培养市场所需的人才。美国高等教育理念强调学术自由,因为学术自由包含自由和责任。学生有选课的自由,教师有授课的自由,但同时学生有学分制的要求,教师有教学、科研和服务的标准。在学术自由的氛围里,每个人都可以将自己的学术潜能发挥到极致。美国高等教育理念强调实用主义,教学实践中以市场为导向,淘汰不受市场欢迎的院校和专业,同时增设市场需求的专业和课程。各大教育评估机构对大学办学效益的评估标准之一是其毕业生在离校一年内在所学专业的就业率。在此应该指出的是,虽然基础知识的学习和理论课题的研究并不能在短时间内见效,但是大学有必修课和选修课的机制,研究资助从联邦政府,到州政府,到基金会,再到学校都有用于基础和理论研究的专项基金。

最后,培养本土国际化人才是美国高等教育一个坚定不移的目标。为了这个目标,美国大学靠的是宽松自由的氛围和明确严格的管理机制,美国大学教师靠的是评价优良的教学效果、校内外同行公认的学术成就以及分内和分外的社会服务,大学生靠的是拼命地大量阅读、通常是通宵达旦地动手制作或研究实验,以及无比积极的课堂表现和学术成果。

参 考 文 献

[1] 曲辉.(1996).英美教育比较及其对现代化的影响[J].云南民族学院学报,4,87-92.

[2] 美国国家教育统计中心.(2014).2011-2-12全国高等院校统计数字[N].http://nces.ed.gov/programs/digest/d13/tables/dt13_105.50.asp.

[3] [22] Institute of International Education. (2014). Open doors report on international educational exchange [N]. Retrieved from http://www.iie.org/opendoors and http://nces.ed.gov/programs/digest/d13/tables/d13_303.10.asp.

[4] 胡寿平,梅红.(2015).21世纪美国高等教育面临的挑战[J].新疆师范大学学报,2:124.

[5] 颜一.(1997).流变、理念和实体—希腊本体论的三个方向[M].北京:中国人民大学出版社.

[6] 舒新城,陈望道.(1989).辞海[M].上海:中华书局香港有限公司合作出版.

[7] 韩延明.(2003).理念、教育理念及大学理念探析[J].教育研究,9:53-55.

[8] 潘懋元.(2001).多学科观点的高等教育研究[M].上海:上海教育出版社.

[9] 纽曼(John Henry Cardinal Newman).(1947). The idea of a university [M]. London: Longman.

[10] 美国独立宣言[A].(1776).第二段.来源:http://wenku.baidu.com/view/b7ccf648e518964bcf847c31.html.

[11] 美国第88届国会.(1962).1964年美国民权法案[L].http://www.doc88.com/p-691303274718.html.

[12] American Association of University Professors. (1940). Statement of principles on academic freedom and tenure, 1940. http://www.aaup.org/statements/Redbook/1940stat.htm.

[13] [27] 张国骥.(2015).美国教育理念之分析[J].湖南师范大学教育科学学报,4(3):61.

[14] 约翰·杜威.(1990).民主主义与教育[M].北京:人民教育出版社.

[15] 李翠莲.(2004).美国教育理念对近代中国教学的影响——以南开经济研究所为研究个案[J].河北大学学报(哲学社会科学版),29(5):48.

[16] 周光礼.(2010).走向高等教育强国:发达国家教育理念的传承与创新[J].高等工程教育研究,2010(3):70.

[17] 肖向东.(2007).美国高等教育的理念与人才培养方式[J].江南大学学报(教育科学版),27(3):28.

[18] 孙彦民.(1971).张伯苓先生传[M].台湾:中华书局.

[19] 肖向东.(2007).美国高等教育的理念与人才培养方式[J].江南大学学报(教育科学版),27(3):30.

[20] Knight, J. (1994). Internationalization: Elements and checkpoints [J/OL]. CBIE Research, 3.

[21] Joachim Blatter. (n. d.). Glocalization. Encylopedia Britannica. http://global.britannica.com/EBchecked/topic/1927789/glocalization.

[23] 田德新.(2003).美国高校的学术自由与学术诚信[J].外语教学,24(7):94.

[24] 陈国明.美国罗得岛大学传播学教授.本项目受访者.

[25] 曹绪中.(2014)."常春藤"盟校:开拓新知的青青长藤[J].创新人才教育,4:74.

[26] 蔡律.(2014).全球智库报告[N].美国宾夕法尼亚大学.

[28] 田德新,张喜荣.(2002).美国外语教学最新动态研究[J].外语教学,23(1):67.

第十一章
美国人际传播理论与研究述评（上）

自从人类诞生以后，人际传播便随即产生。无论是最初两人之间的肢体语言运用，还是后来几人当中的口头交谈，还是再往后他们彼此之间的书面交流，一直到今天流行的各种电子社交或电脑媒介沟通，都标志着人类在不同的历史阶段在人际传播方面所取得的捷足发展与辉煌成就。起初，学者们对人类的传播活动仅集中在公开演讲、修辞风格及信息传达等方面。只是到了20世纪初叶，传播学才作为一门学科进入萌芽孕育阶段，在接下来的整个20世纪，一直到21世纪初的今天，传播学如沐春风，集腋成裘，在第二次世界大战后美国这片得天独厚的环境里，稳健地走完了初步开创、基本成型、迅猛发展和确立显学地位的历程。在这一章里，我们首先对人际传播做一个严格而详细的界定。其次，我们对人际传播学的历史、主要发展过程和阶段以及各个阶段的特点与目前现状进行详尽的描述。再次，我们对人际传播学的具体研究内容、主要理论、研究方法，以及代表学者及其代表作、学术观点和关注议题，包括一些具体的案例展开分析和评述。最后，我们对人际传播学领域还存在的问题、争议和不足，及其发展动向和趋势加以评说。

1. 人际传播之界定

自从人际传播学问世以来，由于关注的角度和重点不同，学术界关于传播的界定众说纷纭，各种定义不胜枚举。有将其界定为两人之间面对面的交谈，也有将其理解为除面谈外的传统式书信与电话交流，以及当今流行的数据广播、交互电视与互联网多媒体多渠道沟通，还有将日常发生在各种人际关系之间的信息传播活动统统纳入人际传播的范畴之内。根据Burleson即将付梓出版的最新研究，我们可以把学术界对人际传播的界定划分为下述三类。

（1）情境视角。持情境视角的学者（如：Miller，1978；Trenholm，1986）认为，传播情境是区分各种传播种类的依据。传播情境包括参与交际的人数、交际者身体之间的距离、非语言交际途径以及交际者彼此之间反馈的快慢。因此，人际传播指发生在两人之间，借助语言和非语言符号彼此交流并随即得到对方反馈的传播行为。这一定义的特征是人际传播等于双人传播（dyadic communication）。其另一典型定义是，"人际传播发生在两人之间，彼此扮演信息传递和信息接收的角色，并通过相互协作而传情达意"（Trenholm & Jensen，2008，p.29）。但是，情境视角存在两大缺陷：一是过分强调交际人数和场景环境的次要因素，而轻视相对重要的交际者之间的关系和彼此交流的内容；二是除了建议研究者通过控制不同场景因素来观察其对传播过程的影响之外，别无其他重大建树。这使邮递员与顾客之间的谈话和戍边将士给家人的信函变得同等重要，就其定义而言，甚至前者比后者更应成为人际传播的例证。另外，这也使有人关心像"多少人参与交流后该交际行为就不是人际传播了"的一些细枝末节的问题。

(2)发展视角。为了纠正情境视角的缺陷,一些学者(如:Miller,1976,1978,1990;Miller & Steinberg,1975;Stewart,1973)从发展的视角来界定人际传播。他们首先对非人际传播(impersonal communication)和人际传播加以区分。前者指交际者双方都以社会角色而非个人身份参与交流,因此他们彼此以常理和常识以及共有的人情世故来判断交流信息的深浅。相比之下,后者却常常以独特的个体积极参与交流,并以彼此特有的心理特征不断调整出得体的对应姿态。将二者加以区分,并不是要对二者加以隔离。正确的理解是将二者作为一个连续体,并将非人际传播和人际传播置于该连续体的两端。陌生人刚见面时的交谈通常为非人际传播,而当他们逐渐熟识,交谈内容由浅入深,由一般到具体,由他人到彼此,传播的标尺就不断从非人际传播向人际传播的方向移动。总之,发展视角"将亲密关系变成了人际传播学的重要议题"(Roloff & Anastasiou,2001,p.53)。该视角对人际传播另一代表性定义为,"人际传播属于典型的人类之间的沟通。对其界定不应该以交流人数为前提,而应该以交流的质量为标准。质量存在与否,不取决于交谈双方肤浅的搭讪,而取决于彼此之间都将对方作为一个活生生的人而进行有意义的沟通"(Beebe,Beebe,& Redmond,2002)。同样,发展视角对人际传播的界定也存在重大欠缺:一是亲密关系并非人类生活中唯一的重要因素,各种不同角色的人际交流行为都应成为人际传播学研究的范畴;二是该视角虽然探明人际传播过程中亲密关系的特征与重要性,但是它对传播本身并未进行应有的探究。这使得无论交际双方有多么熟识,他们在交流时到底在做些什么,很难给出明确的理论阐释。

(3)互动视角。与前两种视角不同,互动视角将大多数社会交往行为统称为人际传播。该视角强调探究人际交往的本质与影响。因此,Cappella(1987)认为"所有互动的相会都是人际传播",因为"只有交际双方对彼此的行为模式产生某种影响,人际传播才算发生"(p.189)。该视角对人际传播的另一代表性定义是,"人际传播包含从社会到日常到亲密的各种人际关系之间的信息交换与情感互动"(Guerrero,Andersen & Afifi,2007)。然而,对互动视角的批评也有两点。第一,将互动作为判断人际传播的标准本身就存在逻辑上的缺陷。因为传播可以是互动的,但并非所有互动的人际交往都可以算作人际传播的行为。例如,人们在马路上对其他行人的点头问候或在其他公共场合的寒暄谦让,当然不能算作人际传播。第二,互动视角在界定人际传播时,没有将信息这一重要因素考虑其中。而信息却包含了可供传达内心状态、创建共享意义和完成交际目的的符号系统。

虽然以上三种视角都有助于理解人际传播的本质,但鉴于其各自的缺陷,Burleson结晶其毕生所学(Burleson,1992;Burleson et al.,2000),并在前人(Delia,et al.,1982;Swanson & Delia,1976)的研究基础上,提出了界定人际传播的信息中心论。Burleson认为,人际传播是以产生和阐释信息为主的社会交往行为。他将人际传播定义为"一个建立有交际关系的人们之间交换信息,以求获得共享意义并完成各种社会目标的复杂且受情境限制的社会过程"。其中,交际双方之间建立一定的交际关系是人际传播的前提。在此关系之中,表达一方有欲望描述自己内心的某种状态或观点、思想、感情等,而接受的一方也有意听取和理解对方的心声。信息是用来表达行为的一套共享符号,包括有声的语言文字和无声的动作表情。意义为内心状态,包括有思想、观点、信念,感情等。双方交流时,一方试图清晰地表达其内心状态,而另一方则尽可能准确地理解对方所传递的信息或情感,以获得双方都能感同身受的共享意义。社会目标是指交际双方需通力合作才能获取的交际意图,如一同消遣时光、交换某种重要信息或获取彼此的感情谅解与支持。另外,人际传播之所以是一个复杂的过程,这是因为当人们进行人际交流时,他们所涉及的不是一个简单过程,而是几组需要相互协作的关联过程。这些过程中包括有信息的产生、传递与接受,交流时的彼此协作、相互认同与社会支持等环节。至于说人际传播是一个受情境限制的过程,这是因为人际传播所发生的场所绝非是虚拟抽象的空间,而是具体实在的环境,而且交流双方的态度、交流内容以及交流结果都会左右整个情境过程的不断变化。最后,人际传播是一个社会过程,这是因为参与这一过程的双方至少由两人或多人组成,他们彼此所代表的社会,必然对各自所从事的交流过程产生相互影响。

2. 人际传播学的历史、主要发展过程和阶段,以及各个阶段的特点与目前现状

根据相关学者(如:Burleson, in press; Knapp & Daly, 2011, Roloff & Anastasiou, 2001)的最新研究成果,人际传播学作为一门学科于20世纪初叶进入萌芽孕育阶段,20至30年代为初步开创阶段,40至50年代为基本成型阶段,60至80年代为迅猛发展阶段,90年代以来迈向成熟,确立显学地位,在向纵深发展的同时,迎接全球化与技术革新所带来的新挑战。下面,我们就对人际传播学在各个阶段的发展过程与突出特点及其目前现状进行详尽的述评。

(1) 萌芽孕育阶段。20世纪初期,人类学、心理学、社会学、社会心理学、精神病学等学科的学术成果为人际传播学的诞生提供了必备的条件。学者们开始关注有关人际传播的一些重要概念,其代表是被誉为"社会学之父"的Georg Simmel。Simmel(1950)观察到社会分化给人们的物质层面和精神层面都带来极大的变化。他通过对现代都市人际关系的变化进行分析,揭示人际交流的动机、内容和形式,并提出了诸如"交互知识""二人交际特点""交流仪式""谎言与事实"以及"社会关系的种类"等概念。其研究成果对人际传播学在美国的诞生与发展奠定了必要的基础,并对今天的人际传播学研究仍有一定的借鉴意义。

(2) 初步开创阶段。20至30年代,众多学者在其他领域的研究为日后硕果累累的人际传播研究播种下了珍贵的种子。首先,哈佛商学院的Eton Mayo教授和他的同事们在霍桑西电公司的研究,涉及监工与工人纠葛,同事关系对生产的影响开创了"人际关系"研究的先河,并对日后的关怀传播研究带来许多启示作用。其次,芝加哥学派的George Herbert Meed, Robert E. Park和Charles Horton Cooley等人把人际传播看成是一切社会实体产生的原创力。当时,美国正处在激烈的社会都市化时代,芝加哥学派将急剧变革的都市作为"天然实验室"来研究社会现实问题。他们对都市化过程中出现的移民现象、贫民阶层、舞女流浪汉以及市民报刊等问题做了大量的调研,极大地推动了人际传播学关注社会现实,并开创了运用实地考察研究方法的风范。同时,其他领域的学者们对团队机制的研究也对人际传播学带来较大影响。这些学者探讨的话题,诸如合作与竞争、反馈、冲突、交流顺序以及社会关系网等,也成为人际传播学所关注的研究对象。最后,20世纪30年代还孕育了符号互动论(symbolic interactionism)和语义学研究运动(semantics movement)的形成。譬如,Mead(1934)的研究揭示了理解个体需要与他人交往的道理。Korzybski(1933)在《科学与理智》(*Science and Sanity*)一书中介绍了语义学的概况,而Hayakawa(1941)的《行动中的语言》(*Language in Action*)一书则使语义学在普通大众之中得到广泛推广,甚至当今人际传播教材中通过日常实例来启发和提高人际交流技巧的做法,也是延续上述理论的具体实例。

(3)基本成型阶段。20世纪40至50年代,人际传播学继续吸纳其他领域的研究成果,并使自身作为一个学科基本成型。这一时期,好几个领域都有重大成就问世。

首先,人类学家(Gregory Bateson)根据其对新几内亚和巴厘岛岛民所进行的民族志研究,提出了"关系传播"的重要观点,并将人际传播信息区分为"内容信息"与"关系信息"。内容信息指传播的内容,关系信息指传播者之间的关系,而后者在实际交流过程中比前者更能影响交流的效果。正如 Jurgen Ruesch(1951)所强调的,人际传播的作用是为了建立、维持和改变关系,而不仅仅是传递交谈的内容。其他人类学家,诸如 Ray Birdwhistell(1952)与 Edward T. Hall(1959)的研究,涉及人类交流的整个过程,但其对身体动作、手势、姿势以及时间与空间的考察和描述为非语言交际学的研究奠定了坚实的基础。

其次,精神病理学专家 Sullivan 认为童年和成年时期在人际关系中的种种问题是导致精神分裂症的主要根源。在其影响之下,Ruesch(1951),Ruesch 和 Kees(1956)著书探讨人际交流对精神病以及各种社会组织问题的影响。其作品《非语言交际》和《实用人类交际学》(*Nonverbal Communication*;*Pragmatics of Human Communication*)成为人际传播学研究中的力作。同时,Eliot Chapple(1953;1970)的研究发现,交谈节奏的适当把握会带来和谐交流的印象。因此,交谈内容的密度、时间选择以及谈话模式等时控手段成为学者们关心的热点,掌握 Chapple 所强调的交谈节奏,也成为提高日常人际交流能力的一个关键。社会心理学家 Fritz Heider(1958)所著的《人际关系心理学》(*The Psychology of Interpersonal Relations*)一书带动了对人际传播学对归因理论(attribution theory)的重视和研究。Charles Osgood 等(1957)开始通过"语义差别"(semantic differential)研究人际交流中的不同意义并带动了大批学者开始对态度、意义和社会交流等方面的广泛研究。

最后,社会学家 Erving Goffman(1959)所著的《个体在日常生活中的表现》(*The Presentation of Self in Everyday Life*)一书对社会行为的组织性和日常行为的重要作用都进行了精辟的阐述。因此,其作品对人际传播学影响颇深,多年来一直在研究生必读书目之列。作为耶鲁学派的代表,Goffman 的研究涉及信息来源的可信度、传播过程中团体的作用与诉诸恐惧等方面。他发现,人际传播的质量对说服他人的成败起着关键的作用。直到今天,说服实验仍是人际传播研究的一项重要内容。

(4)迅猛发展阶段。20世纪60至80年代,美国的人权运动,如火如荼;反战浪潮,席卷全美。冰冷的社会现实,使大众和社会团体体察到大众媒体多年来对舆论导向的操弄,也逐渐意识到大众媒体的欺骗性与社会权力斗争的负面影响。然而,残酷的社会现状却推进了人际传播学的迅猛发展与壮大,并最终成为众多社会科学领域中的一门显学。学者们开始更多地关注在人际传播中个体的成长和个人觉悟的提高,并强调人际传播中真诚交流的重要性。他们指出,生活质量取决于人际关系的纯正性,而不是来自广告和媒体中各种诱人上当的伎俩。于是,Watzlawick 等(1967)的论著《人类交际语用学》(*Pragmatics of Human Communication*)应运而生,鼓励人们主动积极地参与各种社交活动,介绍改善诸如家庭、朋友、同事以及生意伙伴之间人际关系和交流质量的宝贵经验与途径。其许多理论观点,表现出长久的生命力。譬如"你不可能不交流"的公理,还有人际交往中的相同与互补关系等,对今天的许多学者来说仍然那么耳熟能详。几乎同时,Barnlund(1968)与 Argyle(1969)也分别编撰和评述了一系列人际传播方面的伦理和实证性学术论文,集中介绍了有关人际关系的开始、发展与维系,以及社会交往与社交技巧等方面的论著。其最大贡献是引发了许多大学及其研究人员对传播学专业产生日益浓厚的兴趣。于是,开始梳理诸如语言、风格、意图、反馈以及上下文等相关学科概念的举措,调整与增添诸如两人交流环境、社会交换理论、个人感知与相互吸引等教学内容的现象,屡见不鲜,蔚然成风。以至于 Jesse Delia(1987)感慨道,人际传播学在这一时期的发展为该学科奠定了核心的研究范围。

到了 20 世纪 70 年代,人际传播学在教学方法、理论指导、研究发展以及学术组建等各个方面都得到确立与认可。各大院校纷纷开设相关课程,不同版本的教材(如:Giffin & Patton 1971;Keltner 1970;McCroskey, Larson, & Knapp, 1971)相继问世。美国全国传播协会和国际传播协会开始下设人际传播分支协会,人际传播学成为硕士和博士研究生的专业,同时也成为上述两大学术协会和其他不同学术协会年会研讨的主要议题。同时,有关人际传播学的理论相继诞生,例如,Berger 与 Calabrese(1975)创建了不确定性减少理论(uncertainly reduction theory),Barnett Pearce 和 Vernon Cronen(1980)创建了意义协调管理理论(coordinated management of meaning)。此外,其他学者(如 Burgoon,1978;Knapp,1972;Knapp & Comadena,1979;Miller & Rogers,1976;Wiemann, 1977)也相继推出了非语言交际、欺骗、关系控制、交际能力以及相互影响等人际传播学的理论概念。

20 世纪 80 年代的人际传播学除了拓展 70 年代已经确立的相关理论以外,新的学术理论层出不穷,将人际传播学的研究进一步推向了巅峰。譬如,Delia 等(1982)创立了人际传播建构主义理论(constructivism),强调认知对交流过程的影响。Burgoon(1983)提出了期望违背理论(expectancy violation theory),Baxter(1988)也推出其辩证理论(dialectical theory)。有一些学者(如:Bell & Daly, 1984;Hopper, Knapp, & Scott, 1981;Miller et al. 1977;Sillars, 1980)开始关注交流中的信息,并将其分成不同的种类,包括诸如冲突策略、顺从策略、寻求共同途径和表达赞美之辞等各种信息。而另一些学者(如:Burgoon & Hale, 1988;Cappella & Green, 1982;Giles et al., 1987;Patterson, 1982)对整个传播过程,特别是传播过程中的相互影响和人际关系,进行了拓展性的研究。在此,特别值得一提的是 Michael E. Roloff 的突出贡献。在其连续出版的《说服——理论与研究的新方向》《人际传播——社会交换对策》和《社会认知与传播》论著中,Roloff 对各种相关理论进行整合,不但使人际传播学的理论更加系统化与科学化,而且也为日后在新技术环境下人际传播学的研究打下了坚实的理论基础。

(5)确立显学地位和迎接新挑战阶段。自 20 世纪 90 年代以来,全球化趋势,狂飙突进,势不可挡。信息与传播技术进步,日新月异,令人目不暇接,使日常生活节奏不断加快。一方面人际交往变得频繁而多样,而另一方面人际冲突也变得普遍而激烈。人际传播学在不断吸纳更多研究方法和理论与日益细化的研究分支机构的同时,也在迎接更多更新的各种挑战。首先,人际传播学加强了对诸如家庭关系、工作关系、友谊关系和浪漫关系等各种人际关系的全面研究,并对面试、会谈以及谈判等场合的人际传播技巧进行了深入细致的探讨。

其次,人际传播学的研究方法与理论中多了量化与质化的区别与争论、宏观与微观的运用与比较。新的人际传播学理论层出不穷,其中包括 Burgoon, Stern 和 Dillman(1995)进一步完善的非语言行为理论,Baxter 和 Montgomery(1996)拓展的辩证法理论,Berger(1997)创始的认知理论,Petronio(2000)创立的隐私管理理论,Berger(2007)提出的计划理论以及 Dillard(2008)创立的目标计划行动理论。同时,人际传播学的学术分支中也增加了自我传播、家庭传播、小组传播、社会传播、Bochner 和 Ellis(1992)强调的自传性叙事故事,以及 Gudykunst 等(1996)所拓展的跨文化交际等全新或翻新种类。

特别是 Walther(1992)阐述的计算机中介传播已经成为现今人际传播研究的关键显题。Thompson(1995)区分了网络时代新技术环境下人际传播的 3 种互动形态:一是传统的面对面的互动,二是中介式互动,三是准中介式互动("face-to-face interaction, mediated interaction, and mediated quasi-interaction")。由于以因特网为核心的传播技术不断革新当今的社会生活面貌,彻底打破了人们习以为常的时空观感,并使人际交往变得越来越缺乏任何共同在场形式。那么,这种新型的人际关系、交往环境以及传播的信息、动机、性质、形式与效果等就成为当今人际传播学所要面临的新课题与新挑战。

第十二章
美国人际传播理论与研究述评(下)

3.人际传播学的研究内容、理论、方法,代表学者、代表作及其学术观点和关注议题

根据学者们(如:Burleson, in press; Knapp & Daly, 2011; Salhab, 2011; Smith & Wilson, 2010; Wood, 2010)的最新研究,人际传播学的研究内容可谓包罗万象,主要理论与研究方法也是名目繁多,主要代表学者及其代表作更是繁星浩瀚,汗牛充栋。下面,我们尽可能将其中的结晶进行全面而详尽的评述。

(1)具体研究内容。在界定人际传播时,Burleson认为人际传播是以产生和阐释信息为主的社会交往行为,并提出了界定人际传播的信息中心论。根据这一界定取向,人际传播的具体研究内容包括人际传播的过程、结构、功能和场景。首先,人际传播是由信息生成、信息处理、相互协调以及社会认知等相互联系的复杂过程而组成的。信息生成指产生表达内心状态的语言和非语言行为,以便完成各种社交目的。信息处理就是对他人的交际行为进行解释,并对其意义,特别是隐含意义加以理解的过程。相互协调是在交际过程中对信息生成和信息处理不断进行调整,以保证整个交集过程的顺畅。社会认知指认识世界,其中包括我们自己、其他人、社会关系及社会机构等的过程。那么,针对人际传播过程的研究,就应力图解决以下问题:①确定传播过程的组成部分;②表述不同的运作模式与影响这些模式的因素;③详述整个过程中各组成部分运作结果的主要特点;④确认在整个过程中影响运作和结果的不同因素。

人际传播的结构是通过无数认知、语言、社会和行为模式所构成的。语言学家和社会学家研究交际信息在词汇、句法、词义以及语用层次的结构形式,因为正是这些结构形式才使交际可以传递信息,信息可以得到理解,且满足语用要求。传播学者关注交际者是如何运用不同策略来达到预期交际目的。研究者和教育家不断识别和探究用来达到各种目的的交际策略。同时,社会心理学家也在不断发现和研究用来阐释自我、他人、社会行为与社会关系的人际结构。话语分析家也在细究不同的行为结构是如何产生出连贯和顺畅的话语。总之,一套相互关联的行为结构实际上控制着我们日常的人际交往与言谈举止。这些结构,如同行为规范一样,确定谁与谁在何时何地可以交谈些什么内容。

讨论完人际传播的过程与结构,下面,我们再来探讨一下人际传播的功能和场景。在人际传播的过程中,信息的产生与阐释是为了完成某种社会目标或功能。此功能可分为互动管理功能、关系管理功能和工具功能。互动管理功能表示开始和维持连贯的交谈,其中包括开始与结束交谈;保持交谈内容适度、容易理解,且合乎场合;明确社会身份和交谈场景;把握谈话分寸,相互照顾面情;监控感情流露适当等。关系管理功能指发展、维持和修正交谈者的相互关系,其中包括获取所需的隐私和亲密度、控制紧张情绪以及维持交谈者双方的健全人格。工具功能指确定交谈主题,以区分不同的话题种类,一般包括坚持己见还是顺从退让、索取还是提

第十二章
美国人际传播理论与研究述评（下）

供信息、求援还是援助以及取乐还是逗乐等。学者们（如：Burleson，2003；Dillard，2003；Rowan，2003）对人际传播功能的研究业已包括情绪支持、信息提供与说服。

Applegate 与 Delia（1980）二位学者将人际传播的场景分为五类：物理场景（如空间、氛围和媒介）、社会/关系场景（如亲友、同事和邻居）、机构场景（如家庭、学校和教堂）、功能场景（如提供信息、说服和支持）以及文化场景（如种族、国籍和社会阶层）。场景的重要性一方面表现在它直接影响着人际传播所包含的过程、结构、功能和规律四个部分的运作及其结果。另一方面，场景又是可变的和不稳定的，因为创造、维护和改变场景的每个细节都是由参与传播活动的人所掌控的。因此，学者们（如：Baxter & Brainthwaite，2007；O'Keefe，1998；Tracy，2002）对场景的关注比较多地集中在影响场景的交谈范围、话语调整以及信息结构等方面。

（2）主要理论、研究方法，以及代表学者及其代表作、学术观点和关注议题。时代在发展，特别是势不可挡的全球化和日新月异的信息传播技术，已经在很大程度上改变了我们所处的社会结构与人际传播模式。随着时代的发展变化，人际传播理论与研究方法也在不断地推陈出新，相关代表学者、作品、观点和议题名目繁多，难以一一列举。在参考有关学者（如：Burleson，in press；Knapp & Daly，2011；Salhab，2011；Smith & Wilson，2010）；Wood，2010)研究成果的基础上，现对其中的 8 个典型代表的学术观点作以下评述。

1）过程。人际传播被认为是一个不断发展和变化的过程。因此，我们有了过程视角下的人际传播理论。该理论认为所有的人际关系都是处在某种特定的过程之中。换言之，过程可以说是关系总和的存在。研究者可以通过观察该过程中的某一个时间点或几个时间点来理解人际传播的性质。譬如，Kendon（1970）通过观察一段胶卷，对其中录制的交谈片段逐段进行描述，包括动作变化、眼光接触以及各种言语交替等。Gottman（1979）对快乐和不快乐的夫妻之间的连续交谈进行了细致的分析并取得较大发现。Cappella 和 Planalp（1981）对一段对话录音从头到尾进行分析，研究双方在谈话时对其声音和停顿的不同运用。将人际传播作为一个过程来研究，重要的是要知道被研究的交际行为在某一时刻所发生的频率，该行为发生的顺序特征和发生时所延续的时间，以及该行为与其他一起发生的行为之间的节奏、速度及时间点。所有这些时间特征也都应该放在某一个人具体的交际行为、某一次具体的交谈、某一段人际关系或某个研究对象的整个人生中去加以考究与评判。

过程视角下的人际传播理论主要包括社会渗透理论（social penetration theory）、关系发展模式（relationship development model）和不确定性减少理论（uncertainty reduction theory）。社会渗透理论认为，随着人际关系的发展，人际传播会由浅入深，向更亲密、更个人化的层次发展。该理论的代表学者是 Irwin Altman 与 Dalmas Taylor，他们于 1973 年出版专著《社会渗透：人际关系的发展》。该理论通过交际双方如层层剥洋葱一样的自我坦露，来判断人际传播的进程与人际关系的发展。关系发展模式由 Mark Knapp 在 1984 年发表的《人际传播和人类关系》一书中首先提出。该模式通过人际关系亲密程度的层级变化来识别和理解人际传播的个人经历。其描述性的功能大于预见性的功能，因为该模式更精于描写和解释已经发生的人际传播片段，而对传播过程和人际关系将要发展的层级只能起到雾里看花的作用。不确定性减少理论于 1975 年由 Charles R. Berger 和 Richard J. Calabrese 两位学者提出。该理论将人际传播的过程分为建立关系、人际交往和退出交往三个阶段。该理论主要针对第一阶段，认为两个陌生人之间起初的交往一般通过不断询问对方的相关信息而逐渐减少彼此之间的不确定感。换句话说，随着自我坦露、相互熟识以及身体语言的热络不断升级，不确定性随之逐步减少。由于该理论具备预测和解释陌生人初步交往阶段彼此关系的发展,因此,它被广泛地运用于各种研究之中。但是,也有学者对该理论的复杂性和不可否证性(falsifiability)提出质疑。

2)行为。将人际传播作为交际行为来研究,由来已久。其中的代表学者(如 Birdwhistell, 1952;Goffman, 1963;Ruesch & Bateson, 1951)通过系统的观察,并结合被研究者对某些具体场景和亲身经历的描述报告,来研究人际传播行为。这种方法已经成为一种传统,一种切实可行的良方。其研究的内容起初多少涉及明显的语言和非语言性交际行为,后来更强调对隐含的语言和非语言交际行为进行探讨。譬如,交际者的期待、想象和计划等更可能成为其做出相应反馈的依据。交际一方在交际时没有发出的动作也会刺激对方做出相应的反应。交际者在之前的交流中所表现的行为,也会成为对方(即使对方当时不在现场)做出相应反应。因此,大批学者开始关注显而易见以外的人际传播行为。

同样,研究两人的交际行为,也已超出仅仅这两个人的范围。其他诸如二人各自的社交圈、社交规范以及关系史都会成为影响二人交际行为的因素。对非语言交际行为的研究也从单一的非语言研究,走向语言和非语言研究相结合的道路,以揭示诸如话语交替和撒谎行为等复杂的人际传播行为的实质。同时,研究人际传播行为也从人控的实验室转向传播行为自然发生的现实社会。这一趋势为更多学者注重交际环境或情境的研究埋下了伏笔。

3)情境。情境视角下的人际传播理论强调人际传播的特定背景。正如 Bateson(1978)指出,"如果脱离上下文环境,语言和行为的意义将无从谈起"。Geertz(1973)也强调信息环境对解释交际行为的深层含义至关重要。也就是说,若要深刻理解人际传播行为的真实含义,就要对该行为发生时,及其前前后后的环境进行仔细的考察。传播情境通常包括:①整个传播学界或人际传播学界;②各种社交场合;③各种人际关系和角色;④不同物体或环境特色;⑤语言风格与感情流露等。

情境视角下代表性的人际传播理论包括传播适应理论(communication accommodation theory)与社会比较理论(social comparison theory)。前者于 20 世纪 70 年代由 Howard Giles 提出。该理论常被用来预测和解释人们在实际交往中不断调整交谈时彼此之间距离的现象、技巧、原因及结果。它植根于语言风格研究,其应用范围已经远远超出人际传播学,而被广泛地应用于涉及社会族群、社会环境和不同媒体等方面的研究。社会比较理论是由 Leon Festinger(1954)在其发表的"社会比较过程理论"一文中提出的。该理论认为,每个人都有将自己与其他人进行比较,来确定自我价值的倾向。因此,我们随时随地都在诸如吸引力、财富、智力以及成功等方面与其他人进行比较。当比较的目的是见贤思齐时,那就是积极向上的比较;相反,当比较的目的是用贬低别人来抬高自己,那就是消极退步的比较。由于人们比较的目的不同,因此他们描述比较对象的相同与不同点时,常常带有片面和偏激的现象。这也正是采用社会比较理论所得出的研究结果有时受到质疑的原因。

另外,由于学者们对各种交际环境的本质理解不同,因而他们用来研究传播情境的方法也大相径庭。譬如,对认知图式学者们来说,研究信息情境就是考究语言构成以及可以组成具体认知图式的各种语言线索。而对热衷不确定减少理论的学者们而言,传播情境就是信息之源或不确定的物体。同样,主张期望违背理论的学者认为,交际环境可以提高信息,供其准确评判各种人际交际行为。总之,研究人际传播学的学者们应该探明情境是怎样影响传播的,其中原因何在。正如 Rawlins(1987)所言,交际者与交际信息既在改变情境,也在被情境所改变。

4) 能力。人际传播能力理论认为,传播能力是指在一定的情境中选择得体而有效的交际行为的能力。这种能力使交际者双方既可以满足彼此的交际意图,又不使对方感到有任何栽面的地方。该理论由 Brian H. Spitzberg 与 William R. Cupach 于 1984 年在其《人际传播能力》一书中提出。该理论包括三个组成部分:①知识,即知道在某一情境中选择最合适的交际行为;②技能,即具备在某一情境中运用最恰当交际行为的能力;③动机,即拥有与他人得体而有效交流的愿望。另外,该理论强调,得体而有效的传播活动需要交际者双方都应具备上述三个条件。交际者可以通过基于该理论而创建的"人际传播能力自评表"自测自己的人际传播指数。然后以此为参考,为实现理想的人际传播效果而进行必要的准备和训练。

虽然人际传播能力理论自问世以来,在包括传播学在内的许多学科领域得到广泛应用和普遍好评,但是,它还不能算是一个传播学的理论。它只是为人们提供一个让彼此的交流变得相对得体而有效的指导模式。

5) 辩证关系。人际传播就是信息发送者和信息接受者相互交换信息的过程。在这一过程中,交际双方都在经历着来自内在和外部的冲突力量,使双方的关系始终处于一种辩证紧张的状态。由紧张而产生的压力如波涛一样,一浪接着一浪,循环往复,无休无止。辩证关系理论揭示,交际者之间的关系越紧密,将其分开的冲突力量也就越大。这一理论是由 Leslie A. Baxter 和 Barbara M. Montgomery 于 1996 年提出的。

该理论有三组主要的辩证关系:①联系与分开,尽管所有亲人都想让彼此的关系亲密无间,直到永远,但是,如果双方没有任何属于自己的空间,过度的联系反而会使双方由于感到失去自我而分道扬镳。②确定性与不确定性,亲密伙伴之间需要存在一定的预期性,这样双方才能对彼此感到放心。但是,如果这种稳定的预期感不被偶尔的新鲜感、惊喜波和随意性所打破,那么亲密伙伴之间的关系就会因一成不变而索然无味。③开放与保密,在人际交往中,双方多大程度开诚布公,多大程度保守隐私,才能使彼此既感到对方的信任,又捍卫自己的尊严。这对辩证关系表明任何亲密关系,都不会一亲到底,密而不断。

辩证关系理论被广泛地应用于各种质化研究的人文领域。它在指导和阐释具体案例方面,功绩卓著。然而,正因为其针对性强这一特性,该理论不适宜用作指导全面而概括性较强的研究课题。

6) 文化。在人际传播的实践中,人们通常会对双方交际的结果或效果做出预期性的判断。除了交际情境的因素外,另一因素就是文化或交际双方所代表的诸如行为规范、交际模式与价值观念等的生活方式。人际传播文化理论的代表学者们(如 Carbaugh, 1988, 1990; Fitch, 1998; Leeds-Hurwitz, 1995; Monaghan & Goodman, 2006; Philipsen, 1992; Stewart, 2002)认为人们的交往过程和交往特征是由其所代表的文化所确定的。例如,Monaghan & Goodman(2006)强调,我们与他人交往的模式是与我们的文化知识和社会期待密切相关的。

在人际传播文化理论当中,礼貌理论是其中的一个代表。该理论的创始人是 Brown 和 Levinson。他们以 Goffman 的研究为基础,先后在 1978 年和 1987 年发表了《语言应用共同点:礼貌现象》和《礼貌:语言应用的共同之处》两本专著。礼貌理论认为,人们在日常交往中懂得维护双方的身份和面子对保持良好的人际关系起着关键性的作用。该理论假定:①每个人都在意自己的正面形象或面子;②人类对维护面子一般都比较理性化;③然而,有些行为对维护面子具有根本的威胁性,即面子威胁行为(Face Threatening Act)。面子威胁行为涉及交际双方之间的三个因素,即权利关系、社会距离和威胁行为的强迫程度,而威胁行为的强迫程度受交际双方归属文化的直接影响。

根据上述理论,维护面子的途径有:①防御,采取可以避免威胁交际双方面子的举措;②修正,一旦有威胁交际双方面子的举动发生,迅速通过恰当言语或行为进行补救;③回避,即在某些场合有意避免说出或做出使对方难堪的话语或举动;④提醒,必要时对某些可能威胁面子的话题发出暗示,以便回避;⑤主动,在某些场合尽力维护对方的面子需求。自问世以来,礼貌理论在人际传播学各领域都得到广泛应用,且收效甚佳。学者们在其提供的理论框架下,探究如何更有效、更得体地树立自我正面形象、维护和支持伙伴的合理面子需求,同时迎战并挫败不怀好意的各种面子威胁行为。

7)社会认知。思维与行为之间的相互关系一直是学者们,特别是传播学和社会心理学界的学者们所关注的研究课题。社会认知理论的代表学者是 Bandura(2001)和 Glanz(2002)。该理论主张每个人的行为主要是通过观察他人,并在其所生活的环境中通过与他人交往而逐渐习得的。因此,它要力图解释人们为什么会获取并保持某些行为模式,然后为所需者提供相应的辅助或控制手段。环境、人和行为是该理论用来鉴别行为变化的三个要素,而三个要素之间彼此相互影响。健康传播学的学者们成功地将该理论与调查和试验的方法相结合,探究医患以及其他医疗提供者与医疗接受者之间的人际传播课题。

总体而言,上述研究大致可分为两类:①对社会认知和社会行为之间相互关系的理解;②思维对行为的抽象和具体影响。研究者通常选择认知活动的某一单元进行探讨与分析。譬如,对其他人的研究集中在印象构成、归因理论和视角选择方面,而对交际认知的研究则集中在个体觉悟、个体监督、假设交谈与交际恐惧等方面。随着对思维与行为之间相互关系研究的不断深入,学者们发现思维影响行为,而行为反过来也在影响思想记忆与后续思维。同时,学者们也发现对人们如何能够将相关信息转化为人际交流行为的过程,还需做进一步的探究。这一过程包括态度、期望、推测、图式、幻觉、规则以及返想等环节。因此,研究社会思维的形成过程非常重视不同层次行为信号意义的阐释,而这里所谓的不同层次包括:①字面内容;②对交谈者相互反映的解释;③交谈者对某一信息应有反映的提示;④交谈者对自身和对方的感觉迹象;⑤是否需要进一步的交谈。

学界对该理论的批评是它将先天基因的差异与后天学习能力的区别混为一谈。另外,该理论的复杂性也只能使其相对容易的部分,譬如自我效能(self-efficacy)得到实际检验与广泛运用。

8)意识和意向。意识和意向一直受到学者们的关注和争论。以 Michael Motley 为代表的一些学者认为有意向或有意图的行为才算交际行为,而一个没有任何意向的动作,如一个人累时打的哈欠,就不能算作交际行为。而以 Paul Watzlawick 为代表的学者们却坚持,人不可能不交流。因此,无论是有还是没有意向,人类的所有行为都是交际行为。也就是说,意向标志着所有意识行为的特点。多年来,有关意识和意向的研究不但来自各个领域,而且来自传播学界的各个方面。首先,在界定传播学的分支学科时,意向性对许多学者来说是必不可少的决定因素。他们要确定的一个中心问题是交际双方到底在多大程度知道他们在做些什么或做了什么。而意识是发生交流的前提。纵观对说服和服从所进行的研究,不难看出多数学者认为交际双方之所以确定目标、分析对方和环境,然后选择交流策略,都是为了最大化地取得预设目的。相比之下,不同仪式程序、感情自然流露、交谈管控动作,以及熟人之间的习惯性交流却很少掺杂特别意识与精心设计的成分。

第十二章

美国人际传播理论与研究述评（下）

虽然相关学者（如 Brentano，1874；Gillet & McMillan，2001；Husserl，1962；Lycan，1996；Motley，1986；Stamp & Knapp，1990；Tye，1995，2000）来自不同领域，但是他们在理论层面，对意识和意向的研究表现出以下几方面的共识：①交流涉及多种层次和程度上的意识成分；②每一交流行为都包含至少两种意向；③意识和意向在交流之中可能变化；④交流双方可能明白总体目标，但彼此对要达到这一目标各自所流露的一些具体意念，并不一定都能体会得到。

因此，任何单一的理论框架或研究方法都不足以完成上述所列的研究任务。我们只有从不同的视角入手，才能全面深刻地理解意识和意向的内涵。同样，我们只有综合几种相关理论框架，取其所长，才能为人际传播在意识和意向方面的课题提供具体而有用的理论指导。

4.人际传播学研究的问题、争议、不足及发展动向与趋势

(1)问题。美国人际传播理论研究总体存在以下几个问题：首先，以认知心理学为主要理论支撑，以自然科学研究方法为主的量化分析方法（如人际传播构建主义理论研究）盛行，而质性研究方法（如民族志方法）呈现弱势，文化批评方法受到排挤和打压，不同学派并没有处在平等竞争的状态，导致理论和研究成果的信度和效度在全球范围内相对低迷。虽然社会科学研究界正兴起量质混合的研究方法（Ragin，1987；2000），以期提高理论和研究成果的信度和效度，但混合法的运用在人际传播研究领域仍然罕见。其次，量化分析法本身也没有得到合理的使用。像心理学研究的老问题一样，美国人际传播理论研究量化方法采集的数据大多来自研究者所在大学的学生，甚至研究者自己的学生。众所周知，一国的大学生不仅代表不了这一国的所有国民，更不用说代表全人类了。运用这种方便和价格低廉或免费的，来自单一社会群体、单一国家和单一文化的取样法所创建的理论，其普世性有多高就可想而知了。最后，一方面人际传播理论色彩纷呈，另一方面碎片化严重。大多学者专门研究人际传播的一个或几个面，如幽默传播（DiCioccio，2012）、性别传播（Tannen，2007）、健康传播（Schiavo，2007）、嫉妒传播（Bevan，2013）和社交媒体式人际传播（Konijn et al，2008）等，并试图构建相关的具体理论，却忽视了整合性理论研究和对该学科的全貌性理论构建。

(2)争议。当代人际传播研究领域存在两大争议。

第一是以认知心理学为理论基础的人际传播构建主义理论（constructivism）和以实用主义（pragmatism）为哲学基础的人际传播构建、重建主义理论与意义协调管理理论（Coordinated Management of Meaning，CMM）的争议。人际传播构建主义理论认为，虽然每个人的人际传播行为起源于社会，但是每个人的认知过程、认知心理结构和其相应的人际传播能力，随着年龄的增长和教育程度的提高会变得更加复杂和成熟，并相对稳定。而 CMM 认为人际传播过程本质是社会性的，不承认认知心理的独立存在；所谓认知心理不过是社会传播的结果，也可以通过传播性干预得到重构；人际传播过程不包含所谓固化的相对独立的个体心理认知结构。人际传播构建主义理论认为意义世界是相对一元的，CMM 却认为意义世界原本是多元的也应保持多元。人际传播构建主义理论注重个人交际传播能力的评估、提高和个人主义理想的实现。CMM 注重提升置身多元意义世界人际传播者保护多元，促进多元文化和谐相处的能力。

第二是以 Donal Carbaugh（1991）为代表的强调"文化即是通过人际传播达到的共识"人际传播理论人类文化学/民族学派和以 John Fiske(1991)为代表的强调"文化的性质乃是冲突和斗争"的新马克思主义学派的争议。与 Fiske 相呼应的是人际传播学者 John Lannamann

(1991)。他一针见血地指出,人际传播研究不过是不同研究者不同意识形态观点的实践和阐发而已。也就是说,不同的人际传播理论反映了不同的价值观,没有客观性、普世性可言。这一争议虽然发生在二十多年前,但在人际传播界引发了不大不小的骚动:一方面产生了"共识"和"斗争"折中派,如 Dwight Conquergood(1991)创造了批评民族志方法论;另一方面至今两派大多更加坚守己见。

3)不足。基于以上综述,我们能够看出,美国人际传播理论研究看似百花齐放,百家争鸣,但却受限于其特定的历史文化环境及其主流价值观。例如,至今没有类似马克思主义政治经济学性质的人际传播理论进入人际传播研究领域。美国畅销的传播理论教材如 Em Griffin 的 *A First Look at Communication Theory*(2011)和 Steven Littlejohn 的 *Theories of Human Communication*(1989)都几乎排除或轻描淡写马克思主义批判学派的视角。另一个不足是美国主流人际传播理论研究以个人为观察和分析单位,使以其他诸如家庭或家族等为观察和分析单位的研究边缘化。再一个不足是忽略了世界其他主流哲学、文化和宗教的人际传播视角。例如伊斯兰宗教信仰文化、拉丁美洲和非洲文化等人际传播理论资源没能够得到充分挖掘。近几十年来,以亚太文化,尤其包括中国、韩国和日本为主的东亚文化所包含的丰富的人际传播哲学理论资源,受到了活跃在英美相关的学术界相当规模的亚裔学者群比较深刻的挖掘,产生了大量正式出版的英语学术文献,原创了多个基于东亚文化普世概念的人际传播理论(Jia, Lu, & Heisey, 2002; Jia, 2006)。然而,至今只有基于中国文化脸面观的"面子谈判理论"已成为一个英美人际传播学界广泛接收的普世理论。而中国文化脸面观从初次介绍到西方(Smith, 1894/2003)至丁冬梅(Ting-Toomey, 2005)创造出成熟的面子谈判理论经历了长达111年的时间!笔者认为,博大精深的中国文化具备了远远超过创造或启发一个或几个人际传播理论的丰富资源。最后,美国主流人际传播理论大都是线下理论。新媒体和全球化有待催生多元的线上理论。线下理论,例如 Joe Walther 的"Social Information Processing Theory"(2008)也有待和稀有的线上理论融合。但愿从互联网和全球化第一代里崛起的人际传播学者群在不久的将来对线上线下、多元思想和多种文化视角的人际传播理论发展做出他们应有的贡献。以上几点均是美国主流人际传播理论普世化的努力有待克服的瓶颈。

4)动向和趋势。美国人际传播理论研究领域正在走向多元和分支化,甚至碎片化,似乎呈现以下几个动向和趋势:①健康传播是过去几十年来美国人际传播理论研究领域衍生出的一大分支。②人际传播社交媒体化研究(包括电讯如以手机为媒介的人际传播,电脑为媒介的人际传播研究)也是过去十多年来美国人际传播理论研究领域衍生出的又一大分支。③在美国人际传播理论研究领域,基于非西方文化视角尤其是东亚文化视角的人际传播理论和研究在过去二十多年有了长足的发展。④分支化和专题化诸如幽默传播、谣言传播、嫉妒传播、家庭传播、关系传播、浪漫传播、性别传播、跨族裔传播、跨文化交际,以及全球传播(尤其是跨文化传播和全球公民身份和全球公民社会的构建关系研究)等研究也是过去几十年来陆续呈现的几大经久不消的动向和趋势。

结束语

中国文化甚至东亚儒家文化圈乃是举世闻名的人际关系学文化,但却不是人际传播学文化。以中国文化为代表的古典人际关系学是以关注现世的儒家伦理学为哲学基础的,目的是修身、齐家、治国、平天下。它是一种圆润的处世哲学,强调说教、实践和自省,注重品德修炼。相反,以美国文化为代表的人际传播学注重描绘和阐释人际传播本质、微观过程、结构和规律,注重提高人际传播者个体的技巧和能力。当代中国文化的人际关系学延续了儒家模式,但是笔者认为,仅仅依靠儒家人际关系模式很难维系当代中国文化和社会的秩序。这是因为当代中国文化正在演变成为既重集体又关照个人,既强调个人竞争又强调人际社会和谐的中西合璧的新文化。本文着重介绍美国当代人际传播理论研究现状,正是作者为了促进中式人际关系学和美式人际传播学的交流、嫁接或联姻,为最终打造更普世的人际传播/关系理论,促进中、美和其他人类社会的和谐而做的一个努力。希望我们的努力对读者能够起到抛砖引玉的作用。

(原载于《传播学新趋势》,清华大学出版社,贾文山,田德新,2014)

参 考 文 献

[1] Altman, I., & Taylor, D. (1973). Social penetration: The development of interpersonal relationships. New York, NY: Holt, Rinehart and Winston.

[2] Applegate, J. L., & Delia, J. G. (1980). Person-centered speech, psychological development, and the contexts of language usage. In R. S. Clair & H. Giles (Eds.), The social and psychological contexts of language usage (pp. 245 – 282). Hillsdale, NJ: Lawrence Erlbaum.

[3] Argyle, M. (1969). Social interaction. New York: Liber-Atherton.

[4] Bandura, A. (2001). Social cognitive theory: An agentive perspective. Annual Review of Psychology, 52, 1 – 26.

[5] Barnlund, D. C. (1968). Interpersonal communication: Survey and studies. Boston: Houghton Mifflin.

[6] Bateson, G. (1978). Mind and nature: A necessary unity. New York: E. P. Dutton.

[7] Baxter, L. A. (1988). A dialectical perspective on communication strategies in relationship development. In S. Duck (Ed.), Handbook of personal relationships. New York, NY: Wiley and Sons.

[8] Baxter, L. A., & Braithwaite, D. O. (2007). Social dialectics: The contradictions of relating. In B. B. Whaley & W. Samter (Eds.), Explaining communication: Contemporary theories and exemplars (pp. 275 – 292). Mahwah, NJ: Lawrence Erlbaum.

[9] Baxter, L. A., & Montgomery, B. M. (1996). Relating: Dialogues and dialectics. New York: Guilford Press.

[10] Beebe, S. A., Beebe, S. J., & Redmond, M. V. (2002). Interpersonal communication: Relating to others. Boston: Allyn & Bacon.

[11] Bell, R. A., & Daly, J. A. (1984). The affinity-seeking function of communication. Monographs, 51, 91 – 115.

[12] Berger, C. R. (2007). Plans, planning, and communication effectiveness. In B. B. Whaley

& W. Samter (Eds.), Explaining communication: Contemporary theories and exemplars (pp. 149 - 164). Mahwah, NJ: Lawrence Erlbaum

[13] Berger, C. R. (1997). Interpersonal communication: Theory and research. In B. D. Ruben (Ed.), Communication yearbook 1 (pp. 217 - 228). New Brunswick, NJ: Transaction Publishers.

[14] Berger, C., & Calabrese, R. (1975). Some explorations in initial interaction and beyond: Toward a developmental theory of interpersonal communication. Human Communication Research, 1, 99 - 112.

[15] Bevan, J. L. (2013). The communication of jealousy. New York, NY: Peter Lang.

[16] Birdwhistell, R. L. L. (1952). Introduction to kinetics: An annotation system for analysis of body motion and gesture. Ann Arbor, MI: U. S. Department of State, Foreign Service Institute/University Microfilms.

[17] Bochner, A. P., & Ellis, C. (1992). Personal narrative as a social approach to interpersonal communication. Communication Theory, 2, 65 - 72.

[18] Brentano, F. (1874). Psychologie vom emprisschen standpunte (Psychology from an Empirical Standpoint). Leipzig, Duncker & Humblot.

[19] Brown, P., & Levinson, S. (1978). Universals in language usage: Politeness phenomenon. In E. Goody (Ed.), Questions and politeness: Strategies in social interaction. Cambridge, UK: Cambridge University Press.

[20] Brown, P., & Levinson, S. (1987). Politeness: Some universals in language. Cambridge, UK: Cambridge University Press.

[21] Burgoon, J. K. (1978). A communication model of personal space violations: Explication and an initial test. Human Communication Research, 4, 129 - 142.

[22] Burgoon, J. K. (1983). Nonverbal violations of expectations. In J. M. Wiemann & R. P. Harrison (Eds.), Nonverbal interaction (pp. 77 - 111), Beverly Hills, CA: Sage.

[23] Burgoon, J. K., & Hale, J. L. (1988). Nonverbal expectancy violations: Model elaboration and application to immediacy behaviors. Communication Monographs, 55, 58 - 79.

[24] Burgoon, J. K., Stern, L. A., & Dillman, L. (1995). Interpersonal adaptation: Dyadic interaction patterns. New York: Cambridge University Press.

[25] Burleson, B. R. (in press). The nature of interpersonal communication: A message-centered approach. In C. Berger, M. Roloff, & D. R. Roskos-Ewoldsen (Eds.), Handbook of communication science (2nd ed.). Thousand Oaks, CA: Sage. Retrieved March 16, 2013 from http://www.corwin.com/upm-data/29757_9.pdf

[26] Burleson, B. R. (2003). Emotional support skills. In J. O. Greene & B. R. Burleson (Eds.), Handbook of communication and social interaction skills (pp. 551 - 594). Mahwah, NJ: Lawrence Erlbaum

[27] Burleson, B. R. (1992). Taking communication seriously. Communication Monograph, 59, 79 - 86.

[28] Burleson, B. R. Metts, S., & Kirch, M. W. (2000). Communication in close relationship. In C. Hendrick & S. S. Hendrick (Eds.), Close relationships: A sourcebook (pp. 244 – 258). Thousand Oaks, CA: Sage.

[29] Cappella, J. N., & Greene, J. O. (1982). A discrepancy-arousal explanation of mutual influence in expressive behavior for adult and infant-adult interaction. Communication Monographs, 49, 89 – 114.

[30] Cappella, J. N. (1987). Interpersonal communication: Definition and fundamental questions. In C. R. Berger & S. H. Chaffee (Eds.), Handbook of communication science (pp. 184 – 238). Newbury Park, CA: Sage.

[31] Cappella, J. N., & Planalp. S. (1981). Talk and silence sequences in informal conversations III: Inter-speaker influence. Human Communication Research, 7, 117 – 132.

[32] Chapple, E. D. (1953). The standard experimental interview as used in interaction chronograph investigations. Human Organizations, 12, 23 – 32.

[33] Chapple, E. E. (1970). Culture and biological man: Explorations in behavioral anthropology. New York, Holt, Rinchart & Winston.

[34] Carbaugh, D. (1988). Talking American: Cultural discourses on Donahue. Norwood, NJ: Ablex.

[35] Carbaugh, D. (1990). Cultural communication and intercultural contact. Hillsdale, NJ: Lawrence Erlbaum Associates.

[36] Conquergood, D. (1991). Rethinking ethnography: Towards a critical cultural politics. Communication Monographs, 58, pp. 179 – 194.

[37] Delia, J. G. (1987). Communication research: A history. In C. R. Berger & S. H. Chaffee (Eds.), Handbook of communication science (pp. 20 – 98). Newbury Park, CA: Sage.

[38] Delia, J. G., O'Keefe, B. J., & O'Keefe, D. J. (1982). The constructivist approach to communication. In F. E. X. Dance (Ed.), Human communication theory: Comparative essays (pp. 147 – 191). New York, Harper & Row.

[39] DiCioccio, R. L. (2012). Humor communication: Theory, impact, and outcomes. Dubuque, IA: Kendall Hunt.

[40] Dillard, J. P. (2003). Persuasion as a social skill. In J. O. Greene & B. R. Burleson (Eds.), Handbook of communication and social interaction skills (pp. 479 – 514). Mahwah, NJ: Lawrence Erlbaum.

[41] Dillard, J. P. (2008). Goals-plan-action theory of message production. In L. A. Baxter & D. O. Braithwaite (Eds.), Engaging theories in interpersonal communication: Multiple perspectives (pp. 65 – 76). Thousand Oaks, CA: Sage

[42] Festinger, L. (1954). A theory of social comparison processes. Human Relations, 7(2), 117 – 140.

[43] Fiske, J., Carbaugh, D. (1991). Forum: Writing ethnographies. Quarterly Journal of Speech, 77, 327 – 42.

[44] Fitch, K. (1998). Speaking relationally: Culture, communication and interpersonal connections. New York: Guilford Press.

[45] Geertz, C. (1973). The interpretation of cultures: Selected essays. New York: Basic Books.

[46] Giffin, K., & Patton, B. R. (1971). Fundamentals of interpersonal communication. New York: Harper & Row.

[47] Giles, H., Mulac, A., Bradac, J. J., & Johnson, P. (1987). Speech accommodation theory: The next decade and beyond. In M. McLaughlin (Ed.), Communication Yearbook 11 (pp. 13-48). Newbury Park, CA: Sage.

[48] Gillet, G. R., & McMillan, J. (2001). Consciousness and intentionality. Philadelphia, PA: John Benjamins Publishing.

[49] Glanz, K., Rimer, B. K. & Lewis, F. M. (2002). Health behavior and health education: Theory, research and practice. San Francisco, CA: Wiley & Sons.

[50] Goffman, E. (1959). The presentation of self in everyday life. Garden City, NY: Anchor.

[51] Goffman, E. (1963). Behavior in public places: Notes on the social organization of gatherings. New York: Free Press.

[52] Gottman, J. M. (1979). Marital interaction: Experimental investigations. New York: Academic Press.

[53] Griffin, E. (2011). A first look at communication theory (the 8th Ed.). Ohio, USA: McGraw-Hill.

[54] Gudykunst, W., Matsumoto, YU., Ting-Toomey, S., Nishida, T., Kim, K. S., & Heymans, S. (1996). The influence of cultural individualism-collectivism, self construals, and individual values on communication styles across cultures. Human Communication Research, 22, 510-543.

[55] Guerrero, L. A., Andersen, P. A., & Afifi, W. A. (2007). Close encounters: Communication in relationships (2nd ed.). Thousand Oaks, CA: Sage.

[56] Hall, E. T. (1959). The silent language. Garden City, NY: Doubleday.

[57] Hayakawa, S. I. (1941). Language in action. New York: Harcourt Brace Jovanovich.

[58] Heider, F. (1958). The psychology of interpersonal relations. New York: Wiley.

[59] Hopper, R., Knapp, M. L., & Scott, L. (1981). Couples' personal idioms: An exploration of intimate talk. Journal of Communication, 31, 23-33.

[60] Husserl, E. (1962). Ideas: General introduction to pure phenomenology. Collier Books.

[61] Jia, W., Lu, X., & Heisey, D. R. (Eds., 2002). Chinese Communication Theory and

[62] Research: Reflections, New Frontiers and New Directions. Westport, CT: Ablex/Greenwood.

[63] Jia, W. (2006). Wei (positioning)-ming (naming)-lianmian (face)-guanxi (relationship)-renqing (humanized feelings). In Peter Hershock & Roger Ames (Eds.) Cultures of Authority: China (pp.49-64). Albany, NY: SUNY Press

[64] Keltner, J. W. (1970). Interpersonal speech-communication: Elements and structures.

Belmont, CA: Wadsworth.

[65] Kendon, A. (1970). Movement coordination in social interaction: Some examples described. Acta Pyschologica, 32, 100–125.

[66] Knapp, M. L. (1984). Interpersonal communication and human relationships. Boston, MA: Allyn & Bacon.

[67] Knapp, M. L. (1972). Nonverbal communication in human interaction. New York: Holt, Rinchart & Winston.

[68] Knapp, M. L., & Comadena, M. E. (1979). Telling it like it isn't: A review of theory and research on deceptive communication. Human Communication Research, 5, 270–285.

[69] Knapp, M. L., & Daly, J. A. (2011). The Sage handbook of interpersonal communication (4th ed.). Thousand Oaks, CA: Sage.

[70] Konijn, E. A., Utz, S., Tanis, M., & Barnes, S. B. (2008). Mediated interpersonal communication (Eds.). London, UK: Routledge.

[71] Korzybski, A. (1933). Science and sanity: An introduction to non-Aristotelian systems and general semantics. Lancaster, PA: Science Press.

[72] Lannamann, J. W. (1991). Interpersonal communication research as ideological practice. Communication Theory, 1(3), pp. 179–203.

[73] Leeds-Hurwitz, W. (1995). Social approaches to communication. New York: The Guilford Press.

[74] Littlejohn, S. (1989). Theories of human communication (3rd ed.). Belmont, CA: Wadsworth.

[75] Lycan, W. G. (1996). Consciousness and experience. Boston, MA: MIT Press.

[76] McCroskey, J. C., Larson, C., & Knapp, M. L. (1971). An introduction to interpersonal communication. Englewood Cliffs, NJ: Prentice Hall.

[77] Mead, G. H. (1934). Mind, self, and society. Chicago: University of Chicago Press.

[78] Millar, F. E., & Rogers, L. E. (1976). A relational approach to interpersonal communication. In G. R. Miller (Ed.), Explorations in interpersonal communication (pp. 87–103). Beverly Hills, CA: Sage.

[79] Miller, G. R. (1976). Foreword. In G. R. Miller (Ed.), Explorations in interpersonal communication (pp. 9–16). Beverly Hills, CA: Sage.

[80] Miller, G. R. (1978). The current status of theory and research in interpersonal communication. Human Communication Research, 4, 164–178.

[81] Miller, G. R. (1990). Interpersonal communication. In G. L. Dahnke & G. W. Clatterbuck (Eds.), Human communication: Theory and research (pp. 91–122). Belmont, CA: Wadsworth.

[82] Miller, G. R., Boster, F. J., Roloff, M. E., & Seibold, D. R. (1977). Compliance-gaining message strategies: A typology and some findings concerning effects of situational differences. Communication Monograph, 44, 37–51.

[83] Miller, G. R., & Steinberg, M. (1975). Between people: A new analysis of interpersonal

[84] Monaghan, L, & Goodman, J. (Eds.). (2006). A cultural approach to interpersonal communication: Essential readings. Malden, MA: Blackwell Publishing.

[85] Motley, M. T. (1986). Consciousness and intentionality in communication: A preliminary model and methodological approaches. The Western Journal of Speech Communication, 50, 3–23.

[86] O'Keefe, B. J. (1988). The logic of message design: Individual differences in reasoning about communication. Communication Monographs, 55, 80–103.

[87] Osgood, C. E., Suci, G. C., & Tannenbaum, P. H. (1957). The measurement of meaning. Urbana: University of Illinois Press.

[88] Patterson, M. L. (1982). A sequential functional model of nonverbal behavior. Psychological Review, 89, 231–249.

[89] Pearce, W. B., & Cronen, E. V. (1980). Communication, action, and meaning: the creation of social realities. Westport, CT: Praeger.

[90] Petronio, S. (Ed.). (2000). Balancing the secrets of private disclosures. Mahwah, NJ: Lawrence Erlbaum.

[91] Philipsen, G. (1992). Speaking culturally: Explorations in social communication. Albany, NY: SUNY Press.

[92] Ragin, C. C. (1987). The Comparative Method: Moving Beyond Qualitative and Quantitative Strategies. San Francisco, CA: University of California Press.

[93] Ragin, C. C. (2000). Fuzzy-Set Social Science. Chicago, IL: University of Chicago Press.

[94] Rawlins, W. K. (1987). Gregory Bateson and the composition of human communication. Research in Language and Social interaction, 20, 53–77.

[95] Roloff, M. E. & Anastasiou, L. (2001). Interpersonal communication research: An overview. In W. B. Gudykunst (Ed.), Communication Yearbook 24 (pp. 57–71). Thousand Oaks, CA: Sage.

[96] Rowan, K. E. (2003). Informing and explaining skills: Theory and research on informative communication. In J. O. Greene & B. R. Burleson (Eds.), Handbook o [97] f communication and social interaction skills (pp. 403–438). Mahwah, NJ: Lawrence Erlbaum

[98] Ruesch, J. (1951). Communication and the social matric of society. New York, NY: Norton.

[99] Ruesch, J., &Bateson, G. (1951). Communication: The social matrix of psychiatry. New York: W. W. Norton.

[100] Ruesch, J., & Kees, W. (1956). Nonverbal communication: Notes on the visual perception of human relations. Los Angeles: University of California Press.

[101] Salhab, J. (2011). Explaining theories of interpersonal communication. In M. Dainton & E. D. Zelley, (Eds.), Applying communication theory for professional life: A practical introduction (2nd ed.). Thousand Oaks, CA: Sage.

[102] Schiavo, R. (2007). Health communication: From theory to practice. US: Jossey-Bass.
[103] Sillars, A. L. (1980). Attributions and communication in roommate conflicts. Communication Monographs, 47, 180-200.
[104] Simmel, G. (1950). The sociology of Georg Simmel (K. H. Wolff, Ed. & Trans.). New York: Free Press.
[105] Smith, H. A. (1894/2003). The Chinese characteristics. New York, NY: Eastbridge.
[106] Smith, S. W., & Wilson, S. R. (2010). Evolving trends in interpersonal communication research. In S. W. Smith & S. R. Wilson (Eds.), New directions in interpersonal communication research. Thousand Oaks, CA: Sage.
[107] Spitzberg, B. H., & Cupach, W. R. (1984). Interpersonal communication competence. Beverly Hills, CA: Sage.
[108] Stamp, G. H., & Knapp, M. L. (1990). The construct of intent in interpersonal communication. Quarterly Journal of Speech, 76, 282-299.
[109] Stewart, J. (2002). (Ed.). Bridges not walls: A book on interpersonal communication (8th ed.). New York: McGraw Hill.
[110] Stewart, J. (1973). Introduction: Bridges not walls. In J. Stewart (Ed.), Bridge not walls: A book about interpersonal communication (pp. 2-26). Reading, MA: Addison-Wesley.
[111] Swanson, D. L. & Delia, J. G. (1976). The nature of human communication. Chicago, IL: Science Research Associates.
[112] Tannen, D. (2007). You just don't understand: Women and men in conversation. US: William Morrow.
[113] Thompson, J. B. (1995). The media and modernity: A social theory of the media. Stanford, CA: Stanford University Press.
[114] Ting-Toomey, S. (2005) The matrix of face: An updated face-negotiation theory. In W. B. Gudykunst (Ed.), Theorizing About Intercultural Communication (pp. 71-92). Thousand Oaks, CA: Sage.
[115] Tracy, K. (2002). Everyday talk: Building and reflecting identities. New York: Guilford.
[116] Trenholm, S. (1986). Human communication theory. Englewood Cliff, NJ: Prentice Hall.
[117] Trenholm, S., & Jensen, A. (2008). Interpersonal communication (6th ed.). New York: Oxford University Press.
[118] Tye, M. (1995). Ten problems of consciousness: A representational theory of the phenomenal mind. Boston, MA: MIT Press.
[119] Tye, M. (2000). Consciousness, color, and content. Boston, MA: MIT Press.
[120] Walther, J. B. (1992). Interpersonal effects in computer-mediated interaction: A relational perspective. Communication Research, 19, 52-90.
[121] Walther, J. B. (2008). Social information processing theory-impressions and relationship development online. In L. A. Baxter & D. O. Braithwaite (Eds.) Engaging theories in

interpersonal communication: Multiple perspectives (pp. 391 - 404). North America: SAGE.

[122] Watzlawick, P. , Beavin, J. H. , & Jackson, D. D. (1967). Pragmatics of human communication: A study of interaction patterns, pathologies, and paradoxes. New York: W. W. Norton.

[123] Wiemann, J. M. (1977). Explication and test of a model of communicative competence. Human Communication Research, 3, 195 - 213.

[124] Wood, J. T. (2010). Interpersonal communication: Everyday encounters (6th ed.). Boston, MA: Wadsworth.

下部 学术果

Chapter 13
U. S. and NATO Apologies for the Chinese Embassy Bombing: A Categorical Analysis

In 1999, North Atlantic Treaty Organization (NATO) forces were carrying on an airstrike campaign to stop the Milosevic regime from killing Kosovar Albanians in the then Federal Republic of Yugoslavia (FRY). On May 7, a U. S. B-2 bomber dropped five GPS-guided bombs on the Chinese Embassy in Belgrade of the FRY. The bombs fell onto the embassy from different directions and killed three Chinese journalists with more than twenty other personnel injured. Following the incident, both the NATO headquarters and the U. S. government publicized statements of regret. Responding to the Chinese government's condemning statements and solemn requests for public apologies coupled with angry Chinese demonstrators stoning U. S. embassy windows in Beijing and damaging U. S. consulate property in Guangzhou, Shanghai, and Chengdu, NATO and U. S. officials made repeated statements of regret and apologies for the world-shocking bombing of the Chinese Embassy in the former FRY.

The purpose of this paper is to examine the U. S. and NATO statements of regret and apologies for the Chinese Embassy bombing through the theoretical lens of categorical apology and via the method of close textual analysis of the U. S. and NATO official statements, public speeches, and diplomatic notes following the Chinese Embassy bombing. Through a close reading of the transcripts of these written records or rhetorical artifacts and by testing them critically against the nine standards of categorical apology, I intend to search for answers to the following two research questions.

RQ 1: How much do the U. S. and NATO official statements, public speeches, and diplomatic notes fit in with the categorical apology standards?

RQ 2: What can we draw from the U. S. and NATO official statements, public speeches, and diplomatic notes?

Literature Review

In everyday interactions, apologies have been offered and received due to their communicative functions. Just as Lazare (2004) pointed out, "apologies have the power to heal humiliations and grudges, remove the desire for vengeance, and generate forgiveness on the part of the offended parties" (p. 1). In fact, apology making, as an important rhetorical tool, has become a fashion in the last decade of the 20th century. There were so many notable figures apologizing for what people had done in the past that this particular decade was called "the current age of apology" (Shapiro, 1997, p. 18) and "the decade of group apology" (Leo, 1997, p. 17). While the notable figures were mostly apologizing for what had happened in the distant past, the U.S. and NATO officials were expressing regret and apologies for their overnight bombing of the Chinese Embassy.

In recent years there has been burgeoning popular and scholarly literature on the importance of apologies. Popular attention has been witnessed in newspapers and magazines (Lazare, 1995; Shapiro, 1997; Ching, 1998; Krauze, 1998; Tannen, 1999). Scholarly work has flourished in books and journals (Tavuchis, 1991; Benoit, 1997; Murata, 1998; Yamazaki, 2004). However, besides some popular attention (Carroll, 1999; Goldstein, 1999; Israel, 2000), there has been little scholarly work directly addressing the U.S. and NATO apologies to the Chinese Embassy bombing. As for popular attention, Carroll (1999) contended in a newspaper article that NATO's apologies are insincere because "before apologizing, we must stop the war" (p. 2). There is more criticism in on-line articles. For instance, Goldstein (1999) sharply pointed out that "almost as provocative as the bombing were the so-called 'apologies' issued by the U.S. and NATO...[which] amounted to an insult" (p. 1). Israel (1999) stated, "power breeds arrogance and arrogance breeds [power]. So [it is] with the Chinese Embassy bombing" (p. 1). As these newspaper and on-line articles came out shortly after the Chinese Embassy bombing, the opinions may be simply personal or somewhat biased. Now that dust has settled over the bombing of the Chinese Embassy, which occurred seven years ago, it is necessary to conduct a thorough study of the U.S. and NATO apologies.

According to Tavuchis (1991), an apology is a speech act, in which the speaker expresses sorrow and regret so as to seek forgiveness from the person wronged. He says to the one he wronged that he is sorry, indicating that he morally regrets doing what he did and wishes to restore his relationship (pp. 22–32). Lazare (2004) further conceptualized apology as "an encounter between two parties in which one party, the offender, acknowledges responsibility for an offense or grievance and expresses regret or remorse to a second party, the aggrieved" (p. 23). Actually, the speech act in Tavuchis's definition of apology entails verbal and nonverbal, private and public human interactions. The two parties in Lazare's conception of apology encounter can be individuals or groups such as families, businesses,

Chapter 13

U.S. and NATO Apologies for the Chinese Embassy Bombing: A Categorical Analysis

ethnic groups, or nation states.

In their article entitled "The Promise and Pitfalls of Apology". Govier and Verwoerd (2002) listed three types of meanings associated with the term "apology". The first one is a defense as in Socrates' Apologia, the second an excuse or account (e. g., "Sorry. I'm late."), and the third a moral apology. A moral apology is concerned with significant wrongdoing and usually implies a request for forgiveness and reconciliation (p. 67). Since significant wrongs affect the wide social web connecting the wrongdoer and the victim, it usually takes a public apology to express the sorrow for moral wrongdoing. The attack of an embassy with bombs is definitely a significant wrong, so the apologies for such act fall into the category of moral apology and/or public apology. Govier and Verwoerd (2002) stated:

> A public apology is one that is expressed in the public domain on the assumption that it is relevant to the public at large and not solely to the victims of the wrongdoing. Public apologies may be issued by individuals purely as individuals, or by individuals acting as spokespersons for groups or institutions. (pp. 67 - 68)

Thus, apologies for significant wrongdoing need to reach the ears of the relevant public. If an institution has been instrumental in the wrongdoing, an institutional apology is needed. Govier and Verwoerd (2002) further pointed out, emotion tends to be diminished in the institutional case because the spokesperson that issues the apology may not himself or herself have been involved directly in any wrongdoing. Therefore, what is crucial is that the apology-maker sincerely acknowledges the wrongdoing of the offender and human dignity of the victims by legitimating their feelings (p. 74).

While Govier and Verwoerd emphasized the acknowledgement of wrongdoing, human dignity, and legitimate feelings in public or institutional apologies, Jason Edwards (2005) focused on remembrance, reconciliation, mortification, and atonement in community-focused apologies (p. 321). According to Edwards (2005), a community-focused apology, also labeled as a political apology, is a speech act from one community to another, and the actors involved are broadly defined as communities, including nation-states, organizations, racial, ethnic, and religious groups or individuals speaking on behalf of those groups. Such apologies help to mend and resolve old wounds, strengthen communal bonds, and even deepen relationships among varying actors. It is also possible that they can reaffirm communal values between those communities at both the national and international levels (p. 320).

The success of an apology lies in the match between the apology and its audience (Hoover, 1989, pp. 235 - 236). In this regard, Tavuchis (1991) contended that, while sorrow is the cornerstone of interpersonal apologies, documentation lies at the core of collective apologies, which consists of public acknowledgement, acceptance of responsibility, and an implicit or explicit promise that the behavior in question will not occur again (pp. 98 - 105). In addition, Meier (2004) pointed out that there have been two approaches to addressing the quality of apologies. One approach involves experiments designed to judge perceptions and effectiveness of contextualized apologies, and the other approach uses actual or elicited apologies to evaluate their success or expected results (p. 6). By taking the second approach, the present paper studies the success or results of the U. S. and NATO official statements, public speeches, and diplomatic notes as public, institutional, and political apologies.

Theoretical Framework

By critiquing the theories of social scientists, Aaron Lazare and Nicolas Tavuchis, Nick Smith has developed his theory of categorical apology. Smith (2005) stated:

> While the leading social science accounts by Lazare and Tavuchis aptly demonstrate how apologies lubricate reciprocally egoist relationships, such theories ultimately prove unsatisfying because apologies achieve their highest meaning as morally rich acts. (p. 473)

To Smith, both Lazare and Tavuchis offer only descriptive accounts, but a prescriptive argument is necessary for deciphering the full meaning of apologies. Believing that apologies fall within a spectrum of meaning, Smith (2005) defined his theory of the categorical apology as representing "the maximally meaningful apology" (p. 473). Confessing that "a categorical apology is a rare and burdensome act, and under certain circumstances full apologies may not be possible no matter how badly we may desire them," Smith has developed his theory to protect the "full meaning of apologies" (p. 473).

There are altogether nine "rigorous and precise" (Smith, 2005, p. 473) standards in the categorical apology theory. The first standard is corroborated factual record. According to Smith (2005), "contested facts often lie at the heart of moral injuries, and in order to apologize categorically the offender must confess to the facts surrounding the offense and establish a record to which the parties agree" (p. 476). To meet this standard, all parties involved agree on a material fact to the offense. The offender should not conceal any facts, and the victim should not exaggerate the offense, either. When new material facts come to light after an apology has been made, a revised apology should account for them (p. 476).

The second standard is acceptance of causal responsibility rather than mere expression of sympathy. For this, Smith (2005) stated: "The offender must not only admit that certain events transpired but must also accept causal responsibility for the harm" (p. 477). Instead of simply saying, "I am sorry that something occurred," the offender need to confess that he or she is the cause for the occurrence and will take the causal responsibility. Otherwise, the offender is not apologizing but merely expressing condolences. To treat an offense as an accident is to deny intentionality and avoid moral culpability. Categorical apologies are unconditional, and the "but" in the form of "I'm sorry, but …" actually degrades the apology (pp. 477–479).

Identification of each moral wrong is the third standard. As Smith (2005) remarked, "having secured the historical record and taken causal responsibility for the harm, an

Chapter 13

U.S. and NATO Apologies for the Chinese Embassy Bombing: A Categorical Analysis

offender must now recognize the wrongdoing ... [and] pair the harm the victim suffered with the moral principle underlying that harm" (p. 479). Requiring the offender to identify each offense and explain the reason for the apology, this standard guards against conflating several wrongs into one apology. In addition, by isolating precisely what the offender is responsible for, the parties involved can disentangle the causal chain and match the transgression with the moral principle transgressed (pp. 479 – 480).

The fourth standard is shared commitment to violated moral principles. Smith (2005) noted: "With the historical record agreed upon and the violated principles made explicit, a categorically apologetic offender will commit to the values at issue" (p. 480). Willing to share moral values, the offender will understand the victim's claim as legitimate, his or her behavior wrong, and say: "I was wrong." Only when the offender recognizes the victim as someone who shares common deep beliefs, will the victim believe that the offender is intrinsically motivated and likely to reform (p. 480).

Categorical regret is the fifth standard. In the words of Smith (2005), "categorical regret recognizes and declares a transgression as wrong and wishes it could be undone. It entails a promise that the offender will not repeat the offense even under the same conditions and with the same incentives" (p. 483). A categorical apology is more than the expression of sympathy, sorrow, or guilt. To regret can mean several things that are not consistent with apologizing. First, it may imply that one has not done anything wrong if one just regrets for something that he or she wishes done otherwise. Second, an informal use of regret may also refer to the displeasure for unintended consequences. Third, there is also a distinction between guilt and regret. For instance, one may feel a sense of guilt for some privilege, but it does not necessarily indicate that he or she regrets for such privilege (pp. 482 – 483).

The next standard is performance of the apology. Although the utterance of an apology is necessary, simply saying "I'm sorry" may do little of the work required for realizing the meaning of an apology; therefore, Smith (2005) explicated:

> Ideally, the offender would speak the apology and provide a written record of it. ... A full apology is a potentially technical undertaking as it identifies moral norms and parses causal responsibility, and a written version allows the offender to craft a precise statement. (pp. 484 – 485)

With this standard, Smith emphasizes the necessity that the offender should appear before the victim with a written statement of apology. Such apology creates emotional and ceremonial meaning.

The seventh standard is reform and reparations. This standard has two requirements. As Smith (2005) explained:

> Categorical apologies promise to never repeat the offense because they denounce transgression as morally wrong. ... Categorical apologies can require the offender to provide what are often called reparations, implying that such responses make a victim "whole" by returning what the offense has taken away. (pp. 485 – 486)

To meet this standard, the offender has to make a promise of moral reform and take the practical responsibility for the harm to the victim.

Standing is the eighth standard. According to Smith (2005), "in order to issue a categorical apology, one must possess what is understood in legal terms as standing ... [which means that] only legitimate disputants adjudicate claims" (p. 489). With this standard, Smith emphasizes the significance that much of an apology's meaning can only be provided by the offender. Although a third party can represent the offender, only the offender can promise never to offend again because he or she recognizes that it is wrong (pp. 489 - 490).

The last standard is intentions. In Smith's (2005) words, "even if the offender satisfied all of the previous elements, it matters why [he or] she apologizes.... We should not underestimate the significance of the offender's motivations and mental states" (490). To Smith, categorical apologies entail a commitment to not only a shared value and prospect of a future free from harms due to breaches of this principle but also a shared sense of goodness, justice, and the meaning of life (p. 491).

Having introduced Nick Smith's theory of categorical apology, I need to make one point clear before applying it in the analysis of the particular case of the U. S. -NATO bombing of the Chinese embassy. As we can see from the above definition of apology by Tavuchis, the apology-making process comprises the apology from the offender's end and the forgiveness from the end of the offended party. Tavuchis (1991) further elucidated this by saying that, "a proper and successful apology is the middle term in a moral syllogism that commences with a call [from the offender] and ends with forgiveness [from the offended]" (p. 21). However, Smith's (2005) theory has "not considered the crucial relationship between apologies and forgiveness" because "forgiveness is also a subtle and complex moral act and considerable additional argument would be required to determine when we should accept categorical apologies" (p. 493). Since the present paper focuses on the U. S. and NATO apology-making process and results, Smith's theory of categorical apology well applies to the present study.

Research Method

The Chinese Embassy in Belgrade of the former FRY was bombed on May 7, 1999. Since then both sides have taken some important measures. On July 30, 1999, the U. S. government agreed to pay $4.5 million to the people who were injured and the families of those killed in the bombing. The U. S. government also agreed on December 16, 1999 to provide $28 million in compensation for the Chinese Embassy bombing. Meanwhile, the Chinese government agreed to pay $2.87 million for the damage done to the U. S. diplomatic facilities in China (Statement by U. S. State Department, 1999). On April 9, 2000, the Central Intelligence Agency (CIA) of the United States fired one officer and reprimanded six others "for their roles in mistakes that led to the accidental bombing of the Chinese Embassy in Belgrade" (Cable Network News [CNN], 2000, p. 1). During the

Chapter 13

U.S. and NATO Apologies for the Chinese Embassy Bombing: A Categorical Analysis

whole process, a series of official statements, public speeches, and diplomatic notes or letters as well as press conference briefings from both the offender and the victim sides have been made public. Since the purpose of this study is to examine the quality and results of the U.S. and NATO apologies for the Chinese Embassy bombing, I have made a purposive selection of NATO's Official Statement, the U.S. State Department Statement, the U.S. Defense Department and CIA Joint Statement, President Clinton's Apologetic Speech, and Albright's Letter of Apology for analysis. These documents are preserved as transcripts in several websites. Except for NATO's Official Statement, which I have downloaded from the website of the Online News Hour of the Public Broadcasting Service [PBS], I have downloaded the rest of the selected written records from the website of the U.S. Consulate General in Hong Kong; therefore, the authenticity of the written documents can be guaranteed.

Apart from this authenticity, there are three main reasons for selecting the above written documents of apologies as rhetorical artifacts for this study. First, the Chinese Embassy bombing is a significant offense and requires public and institutional apologies. The selected artifacts fall into this category. Second, the selections are representative because the first two official statements express the responses of NATO and the United States as two institutions. As the United States played a leading role in the NATO's air-strike campaign in that war and it was the U.S. plane that dropped the bombs onto the Chinese Embassy, the Joint Statement of the Defense Department and CIA should have sent the very message China required. President Clinton was the head of the United States at that time, and his speech should have represented the most authoritative apology. As the Secretary of State then, Albright could also have addressed the most practical demands from both the U.S. and Chinese sides. Finally, the selection of the above documents instead of others such as the Oral Presentation by Under Secretary of State Thomas Pickering on June 17 to the Chinese Government and the written responses of the Chinese side are determined by the purpose of this study and the space of the present paper.

To analyze the artifacts, I will use the rhetorical method of close textual analysis to locate evidence from the texts and match them in accordance with the nine standards of categorical apologies in a critical manner. A close textual analysis or close reading, as Sigler pointed out (2006) "offers a detailed interpretation of a passage of prose, showing how the details of a text relate to the central themes of the story or novel" (p.1). This method is appropriate for the present research because it "studies the relationship between the inner workings of public discourse and its historical context in order to discover what makes a particular text function persuasively" (Burgchardt, 2005, p.563).

Critical Analysis

To critically analyze the selected rhetorical artifacts, I will first explicate the context within which the artifacts were produced and then analyze the artifacts while evaluating the analytical results at the same time.

Context

As for the context within which the U. S. and NATO official statements, public speeches, and diplomatic letters were produced, there are two situations for explication. The first one is what actually happened. On June 17, 1999 U. S. Under Secretary of State Thomas Pickering went to Beijing, P. R. China as the personal envoy of President Clinton to present the official report of investigation into the accidental bombing. His oral presentation was released on July 6, 1999. In this "Oral Presentation" (U. S. Department of State, 1999a, pp. 1 – 11), Pickering first emphasized that, "the report has been prepared by senior U. S. governmental officials from the intelligence and military organizations" (p. 2). Then he pointed out that "multiple factors and errors in several parts of the U. S. government were responsible for the mistaken bombing" (p. 2). The mistaken bombing resulted from three basic failures:

> First, the technique used to locate the intended target —the headquarters of the Yugoslav Federal Directorate for Supply and Procurement (FDSP) —was severely flawed.
> Second, none of the military or intelligence databases used to verify target information contained the correct location of the Chinese Embassy.
> Third, nowhere in the target review process was either of the first two mistakes detected. (p. 2)

Because of these crucial errors, according to Pickering, about midnight local time in Belgrade on May 7, 1999, a U. S. B-2 bomber from Whitman Air Force Base in Missouridropped five joint direct attack munitions 2000 lb. GPS-guided bombs onto the Chinese Embassy, which killed three Chinese journalists and over 20 other personnel.

The second situation for explication is the responses from all sides after the bombing and the subsequent responses. On the second day of the Chinese Embassy bombing, the NATO headquarters issued an official statement expressing its "deep regret for the tragic mistake" (PBS, 1999, p. 1). On the same day, the U. S. State Department publicized its official statement regretting "the loss of life and injuries of Chinese citizens and damage to property caused by NATO's accidental bombing," and expressing "sincere condolences and remorse to the Chinese people andgovernment" (U. S. Department of State, 1999b, p. 1). The U. S. Secretary of Defense William Cohen and CIA Director George Tenet also issued a joint statement, "deeply regretting the loss of life and injuries from the bombing" (U. S. Department of Defense, 1999, p. 1). In addition, the U. S. Secretary of State Madeleine Albright sent a letter to China's Minister of Foreign Affairs Tang Jiaxuan, expressing both personal "sorrow for the loss of life, injuries, and damage" and "governmental apologies and condolences" (U. S. Department of State, 1999c, p. 1).

Following the U. S. and NATO official gestures, governments and media from all over the world expressed their different responses. For instance, the United Nations Security

Council agreed to issue a statement expressing "profound regret and distress at NATO's bombing of the Chinese Embassy in Belgrade" (British Broadcasting Corporation [BBC], 1999a, p. 1). On May 8, Boris Yeltsin, Russian President at that time, signed a statement, stating that "this was pure tyranny," and condemning the bombing as "the barbarian action of NATO" (*People's Daily*, 1999, p. 1). As for media responses, *The London Observer*, *China Daily*, and *Philippine Star* respectively reported the bombing and the U.S. and NATO's explanations as "a war crime of plotted attack," "a deliberate government conspiracy," and a "ridiculous excuse" (Northeast Asia Peace and Security Network, 1999, pp. 1–16).

The Chinese government responded with "a gross violation of Chinese sovereignty and a random violation of the *Vienna Conventions on Diplomatic Relations* and the norms of international relations," (PBS, 1999, p. 1) "an utmost barbarous act, and a gross violation of Chinese sovereignty, which is rare in the diplomatic history," (BBC, 1999, p. 1) and "a brazen contempt and serious violation of the *UN Charter* and the basic norms governing international relations" (University of California at Los Angeles [UCLA] Center for East Asian Studies, 1999, pp. 1 – 2). Besides, due to complicated reasons (that need further research), the Chinese "state-run media delayed by several crucial days publishing reports of U.S. official apologies and explanations" and there was inexplicable delay in Jiang Zemin's willingness to accept the phone call from President Clinton (Testimony, 1999, p. 2). Consequently, "the U.S. Embassy in Beijing was besieged by Chinese protestors. Embassy facilities were significantly damaged. Other U.S. posts in China were also targets of demonstrators" (p. 2).

In addition, Chinese Foreign Minister Tang Jiaxuan sent a formal note on May 10 to the United States and NATO, presenting four "solemn and just demands" as follows:

1. To make a public and official apology to the government and people of China and the families of the Chinese victims;
2. To conduct a comprehensive and thorough investigation into the NATO's missile attack against the Chinese Embassy in the Federal Republic of Yugoslavia;
3. To publicize a detailed report of the investigation as soon as possible;
4. To severely punish the perpetrators. (UCLA Center for East Asian Studies, 1999, pp. 1 – 2)

On the same day, U.S. President Bill Clinton made a second (the first one was made in an informal manner on a golf course, see Israel, 2000, p. 2) formal public speech, apologizing again to Jiang Zemin and to the Chinese people and expressing his "commitment to strengthen our relationship with China" (President Clinton Again Apologizes, 1999, p. 1).

Analysis and Evaluation

Against the nine standards of Smith's categorical apology, a close textual analysis of the selected artifacts reveals the following findings. When I list each of the analytical findings, I will also present an evaluative judgment.

The first standard of categorical apology is corroborated factual record, which requires the offender to confess to the facts concerning the offense and to establish an agreed-upon record by all parties. Except for President Clinton's Apologetic Speech, all the other written records were made public on the second day of the Chinese Embassy bombing. It is true that there are records of the statements and the letter as they were all made public and archived in various traditional or on-line sources; however, there is no indication from the records that efforts had been made for any possible corroboration before these official statements and the diplomatic letter were issued.

Since modern technology has already made all-season communication possible, it is really either negligent or arrogant of both the United States and NATO to fail to contact the Chinese government. Furthermore, it is also an inconsiderate rush job for the North Atlantic Council and the U. S. Department of State to jump respectively at the conclusions of a "tragic mistake of the bombing of the Chinese Embassy in Belgrade," (PBS, 1999, p. 1) and an "accidental bombing of the Chinese Embassy in Belgrade yesterday" (U. S. Department of State, 1999b, p. 1). Such conclusions were made public within hours after the bombing before any real facts could be released without a thorough investigation. Consequently, the Chinese side responded with extremely indignant and diplomatic terms and even cut off high-level and military contacts with United States.

Lazare (2004) pointed out: "The most essential part of an effective apology is acknowledging the offense" (p. 75). To do so, the offender needs to correctly identify the party or parties responsible to the victims for the grievance, acknowledge the offending behaviors in adequate detail, recognize the impact these behaviors had on the victims, and confirm that the grievance was a violation of the social or moral contract between the parties (p. 75). The acknowledgement requirements for an effective apology overlap the first standard of categorical apology with higher and more detailed requirements. Close readings of the selected artifacts reveal little efforts made by neither the United States nor NATO to reach such requirements.

The second standard of categorical apology is acceptance of causal responsibility rather than mere expression of sympathy. A close reading of all the written artifacts finds no such words as "responsibility" or "repay". After expressing "deep regret for the tragic mistake" and "sincere sympathy and condolences," the NATO headquarters turned to say that it "never has, and never will, intentionally target civilians" and it will continue with its "air strikes" (PBS, 1999, p. 1). The U. S. State Department expressed its "sincere condolences and remorse" and then conveyed a message that it will "maintain order and safety at our mission sites" in China together with the Chinese government (U. S. Department of State, 1999b, p. 1). After a "joint examination of the mistake over the intervening hours," the Defense Department and CIA "deeply regret the loss of life and injuries" but added that "NATO has conducted thousands of strikes… with a degree of precision and professionalism unparalleled in military history" and "we are determined to strike military and related targets" (U. S. Department of Defense, 1999, p. 1). In her letter to the Chinese Foreign Minister, Albright wanted to express personally her "sincere sorrow for the loss of life, injuries, and damage" and extend "sincere apologies and condolences" on behalf of the U. S. government and as a member of NATO. Then she emphasized that "there was absolutely no intention to hit your embassy," and "it is also important to remember why NATO undertook the mission." Finally, she made clear the U. S. concern about "the large-scale demonstrations at our Embassy and Consulates in China" and asked, "the Chinese government provide as soon as possible substantial security reinforcements around the Embassy and Consulate buildings" (U. S. Department of State, 1999c, p. 1). Two days later, President Clinton made a public speech, reiterating:

> I have already expressed our apology and our condolences.... But again, I want to say to the Chinese people and to the leaders of China, I apologize; I regret. But I think it is very important to draw a clear distinction between a tragic mistake and a deliberate act of ethnic cleansing. And the United States will continue to make that distinction. (President Clinton Again Apologizes, 1999, p. 1)

From the above, it is clear that neither the institutions nor the high officials of the offender made clear their intention to shoulder any "responsibility". They all followed the patterns as pointed out by Smith "I am sorry that something occurred," and "I'm sorry, but...." Meanwhile, they all stressed that the bombing was an accidental and unintentional mistake without providing any convincing evidence.

As for the apology President Clinton reiterated, the President started with "I have already expressed", which may impress the Chinese audience that President Clinton was doing something that he was really reluctant to do since he had done it already. Although it was a sign of sincerity for him to say straightforward "I apologize; I regret" in the middle of his speech, the President turned to instruct the Chinese leaders and people to "draw a clear distinction between a tragic mistake and a deliberate act of ethnic cleansing". Such condescending instruction to the Chinese as victims definitely discounts the sincerity of the speaker as the offender. By stating that "the United States will continue to make that distinction", President Clinton was sending the message that the continuation with the air-strike campaign was more important than any recognition of or commitment to the responsibility associated with the Chinese Embassy bombing.

With regard to the acceptance of causal responsibility, Smith (2005) emphasized that "when accepting responsibility, the offender must parse precisely what [he or] she is responsible for" (478). He made clear the significance of moral responsibility for a meaningful or categorical apology. Tavuchis (1991) also remarked, "the attribution and nomination of an offense can be negotiated not by an account or appeal to reason, but only through the faculty of forgiving" (p. 20). This means that the action of the offender must be "semantically and symbolically transformed into 'apologizable' discourse" (p. 20). When the USA and NATO downplayed their bombing of the Chinese Embassy and declared it to be a mistake or an accident, they were not targeting categorical apologies, which are unconditional. Furthermore, the excuses and reasons the USA and NATO were stressing after the word "but" in their statements "will likely degrade the apology" in the words of Smith (2005, p. 479). Even if the USA and NATO had bombed the Chinese Embassy by mistake, they should have at least made clear, in the written statements, their willingness to accept the causal responsibility for the bombing and the moral responsibility for failing to take necessary measures to prevent the occurrence of the bombing.

The third standard is identification of each moral wrong. As Smith (2005) pointed out, to meet this standard, the offender needs to identify each offense and explain the reason for the apology so as to avoid conflating several wrongs into one apology (pp. 479 – 480). Among the written artifacts, only the Defense Department and CIA Joint Statement was attempting to clarify each moral wrong, which reads:

> We have been jointly examining this mistake over the intervening hours. It was the result of neither pilot nor mechanical error. Clearly, faulty information led to a mistake in the initial targeting of this facility. In addition, the extensive process in place used to select and validate targets did not correct this original error. A review of our procedures has convinced us that this was an anomaly that is unlikely to occur again. Therefore, NATO authorities intend to continue and intensify the air campaign. (U. S. Department of Defense, 1999, p. 1)

Instead of "conflating several wrongs into one apology," the Joint Statement has identified three faulty steps that led to the bombing. This conclusion coincides with the three failures in the Oral Presentation by Pickering.

There are two things to comment upon here. First, if the coincidence holds water, it means that the United States and NATO were able to detect the complicated mistakes that led to the bombing of an embassy within several "intervening hours." The argument here is: how could they have failed to correct any of the three failures or errors in the first place? Second, the purpose of identifying each moral wrong is to apologize more convincingly; however, the Joint Statement concluded that NATO would "continue and intensify the air campaign" (U. S. Department of Defense, 1999, p. 1). Instead of "isolating precisely what the offender is responsible for," (Smith, 2005, p. 480), the United States was producing a self-defense.

The fourth standard is shared commitment to violated moral principles. By this standard, Smith (2005) meant that the offender was willing to share moral values, understand the victim's claim as legitimate, his or her behavior wrong, and say: "I was wrong." Apologies that fail to meet this standard often take the pattern of "I am sorry that X bothers you" (p. 480). First of all, in no place in the five selected written artifacts can sentences like "I was wrong" or "we were wrong" be found. Instead, we do read sentences following the above pattern in the U. S. statements of apology. For instance, the State

Department Statement (1999) begins with "the United States deeply regrets the loss of life and injuries of Chinese citizens and the damage to property caused by NATO's accidental bombing of the Chinese Embassy in Belgrade yesterday" (p. 1). Similarly, the U. S. Defense Department and CIA Joint Statement also starts with "we deeply regret the loss of life and injuries from the bombing of the Chinese Embassy in Belgrade last night. The bombing was an error," which then reiterates the argument in the middle of the statement by "we regret any loss of civilian life or other unintended damage, but there is no such thing as risk free military operations" (p. 1).

Such statements just express regret, and the regret is expressed in a way that downplays the offense of an Embassy bombing as a minor mistake or error. What is more serious is that, by following the pattern of "I am sorry that X bothers you," the offender was trying to make the offense sound as if it had been committed by somebody else. In another word, simply by expressing sympathy with words like "regret" and "condolences" and emphasizing words like "mistake" and "accident," neither the United States nor NATO offered "the most meaningful sentence 'I was wrong' in an apology" and was not "intrinsically motivated and likely to reform" (Smith, 2005, p. 480).

The fifth standard is categorical regret. By categorical regret, Smith (2005) meant that the offender recognizes and declares a transgression as wrong and wishes it could be undone. It entails a promise that the offense will not be repeated under the same circumstances (p. 483). Although we have found no such sentences as "we were wrong" in the written artifacts, we do find somewhat responsible sentences and promises in the written records. For instance, we read in NATO's Statement, "NATO never has, and never will intentionally target civilians" (PBS, 1999, p. 1). In the Defense Department and CIA Joint Statement, there is "a review of our procedures has convinced us that this was an anomaly that is unlikely to occur again" (U. S. Department of Defense, 1999, p. 1). Thus, we may say that the fifth standard of categorical regret is partially satisfied in the selected artifacts.

The sixth standard is performance of the apology. To meet this standard, the offender should appear before the victim with a written statement of apology to create emotional and ceremonial meanings. Although no one with regard to the selected written artifacts of apology really appeared before the Chinese victims, we did have the U. S. Under Secretary Thomas Pickering going to Beijing as President Clinton's personal envoy. Besides presenting the investigation report, he represented the President and the United States and expressed "the heartfelt condolences of the American people and government to the families of the three Chinese journalists who died in the bombing of your [the Chinese] embassy in Belgrade on May 7" (U. S. Department of State, 1999a, p. 2). The investigation report was in written form and the Oral Presentation by Pickering was also made public as a record; therefore, we can say that the standard of the performance of the apology is met in a diplomatic and praiseworthy way.

The seventh standard is reform and reparations. This standard requires that the offender promise to never repeat the offense and offer to provide reparations for the victim. From what has been mentioned in the discussion about the fifth standard of categorical regret, we find that both the United States and NATO promise never to repeat the offense. In addition, there have been the U. S. government's repayment of $4. 5 million to the people who were injured and the families of those killed in the bombing and $28 million in compensation for the Chinese Embassy bombing (Statement by U. S. State Department, 1999). Thus, Standard Seven is fully satisfied.

As for the eighth standard of standing, both the United States and NATO are legally represented in their respective official statements, public speech, and diplomatic letter. Under Secretary of State Thomas Pickering also went to Beijing as the personal envoy of President Clinton. He presented the official report of investigation into the accidental bombing to the Chinese Government and expressed "the heartfelt condolences of the American people and government" (U. S. Department of State, 1999a, p. 2). As Smith (2005) pointed out, "third parties can corroborate the victim's account of the event, apportion responsibility, vindicate [his or] her moral principles, legitimate [his or] her suffering, and provide reparations" (p. 489); hence, we can say that Standard Eight is also fully satisfied.

The last standard is intentions. As Smith (2005) stated, "even if the offender satisfied all of the previous elements, it matters why [he or] she apologizes.... We should not underestimate the significance of the offender's motivations and mental states" (490). A close reading of the selected artifacts reveals three intentions. First, as discussed earlier, both the United States and NATO did express sympathy, condolences, and remorse for the loss of lives and injuries in the Chinese Embassy bombing, but they did so without the intention to admit that they have done something wrong.

Second, since they assumed that they had not done anything wrong intentionally, the USA and NATO planned to continue with their air strike campaign. For instance, in the NATO Statement, there is "NATO will continue to pursue its goals" (PBS, 1999, p. 1). In the Defense Department and CIA Joint Statement, we read, "NATO authorities intend to continue and intensify the air campaign" (U. S. Department of Defense, 1999, p. 1). Albright expressed the same intention in her letter, saying "NATO cannot allow Milosevic's 'ethnic cleansing' to go unchecked, and its mission will continue until an acceptable resolution is reached" (U. S. Department of State, 1999c, p. 1). In his speech, President Clinton also made clear: "Until NATO's simple conditions are met, the military campaign will continue" (President Clinton Again Apologizes, 1999, p. 1).

Finally, the U. S. and NATO intended to continue their relationships with China. NATO promised to "continue to review the circumstances surrounding the incident and we will make available any further information as soon as possible" (PBS, 1999, p. 1). The U. S. State Department (1991) made clear to "remain committed to our developing relationship with China and will... build a constructive strategic partnership for the twenty-

Chapter 13

U.S. and NATO Apologies for the Chinese Embassy Bombing: A Categorical Analysis

first century" (p. 1). Albright stated in her letter that, "it is more important than ever for us to remember our President's —and our —commitment to work together to build a constructive strategic partnership" (U. S. Department of State, 1999c, p. 2). Briefly, we can say it was the second and third intentions that motivated the United States and NATO to carry out their first intention of sympathy and apology.

Summary and Conclusion

The purpose of this paper was to look into the results of the U. S. and NATO apologies for the Chinese Embassy bombing, which occurred on May 7, 1999. Adopting the theoretical lens of Nick Smith's categorical apology with reference to the relevant works of Tavuchis and Lazare and employing the rhetorical method of close textual analysis, this study has analyzed NATO's Official Statement, the U. S. State Department Statement, the U. S. Defense Department and CIA Joint Statement, President Clinton's Apologetic Speech, and Albright's Letter of Apology following the Chinese Embassy bombing. A close reading of the transcripts of these 5 selected rhetorical artifacts against the 9 standards of categorical apology reveals the following findings.

Positively, the United States and NATO as the offender in this case have fully met the sixth standard of performance of apology in a diplomatic and praiseworthy way by sending Under Secretary of State Thomas Pickering to Beijing, the seventh standard of reform and reparations in their promise never to repeat the offense and offer to provide reparations for the victim, and the eighth stand of standing in their legal representation of the written documents and sending Under Secretary of State Thomas Pickering to Beijing as the personal envoy of President Clinton. They have also partially satisfied the fifth standard of categorical regret by recognizing the bombing as a mistake but refusing to admit it as their wrong.

Negatively, the United States and NATO in their apologies have not met the first standard of corroborated factual record in their failure to contact the victim for an agreed-upon record, neither have they satisfied the second standard of acceptance of causal responsibility rather than mere expression of sympathy because their written records were filled with the latter instead of the former. In addition, they have not reached the third standard of identification of each moral wrong because they were more anxious to justify their air-strike campaign than to make their apologies more convincing. The fourth standard of shared commitment to violated moral principle was also too high for them because they did not want to say in their apologies the simple but most meaningful sentence of "we are wrong." Finally, as for the last standard of intentions, the United States and NATO had the most motivation to continue with their air-strike campaign and the least motivation to present a full categorical apology.

Even though they were challenged with the humanitarian necessity and the intention to maintain their relationships with China, the United States and NATO, in the last analysis, failed to produce meaningful or categorical apologies for an unexcused missile attack upon an embassy. For future research, the responses of the Chinese side to the U. S. and NATO apologies and the U. S. and NATO declarations of the bombing as an accident need to be further explored.

(Tian, D. X. (2001) U. S. and NATO apologies for the Chinese embassy bombing: A categorical analysis. *International Journal of Communication*, 1, 360 – 376.)

References

[1] BBC. (1999a, May 15). UN 'regret' embassy attack. Retrieved Nov. 20, 2006, from http://news. bbc. co. uk/2/hi/world/monitoring/339866. stm.

[2] BBC. (1999b, May 10). Jiang statement-Nato's barbarous act. Retrieved Nov. 20, 2006, from http://news. bbc. co. uk/2/hi/world/monitoring/339863. stm.

[3] Benoit, W. L. (1997). Huge grant's image restoration discourse: An actor apologizes. Communication Quarterly, 45, 251 – 267.

[4] Burgchardt, C. R. (Ed.) (2005). Readings in rhetorical criticism, 3rd ed. State College, PA: Strata Publishing, Inc.

[5] Carroll, J. (1999, May 18). NATO's insincere apologies. Boston Globe, A19. Retrieved Oct. 19, 2006, from http://members. tripod. com/sarant_2/ks22apol. html.

[6] Ching, F. (1998). World leaders vie to say sorry. Far Eastern Economic Review, 12, 34.

[7] CNN. (2000, April 9). CIA punishes seven staffers linked to accidental bombing of Chinese Embassy in Belgrade. Retrieved Oct. 21, 2006, from http://tanscripts. cnn. com/TRANSCRIPTS/0004/09/sm. 07. html.

[8] Edwards, J. A. (2005). Community-focused apologia in international affairs: Japanese Prime Minister Tomiichi Murayama's apology. The Howard Journal of Communication, 16, 317 – 336.

[9] Goldstein, F. (1999, May 20). Bombing of Chinese Embassy was not an accident: Two imperialist tendencies in the war. Workers World.

[10] Govier, T., & Verwoerd, W. (2002). The promise and pitfalls of apology. Journal of social philosophy, 33(1), 67 – 82.

[11] Hoover, J. D. (1989). Big boys don't cry: The values constrain in apologia. The Southern Communication Journal, 54, 235 – 252.

[12] Israel, J. (2000). The arrogance of Rome. Retrieved Nov. 20, 2006, from http://globalresistance. com/aticles/jared/arrogance. htm.

[13] Krauze, A. (1998, May 29). Never apologize, never explain. New Statesman, 4.

[14] Lazare, A. (1995). Go ahead, say you're sorry. Psychology Today, 28, 40 – 45.

[15] Lazare, A. (2004). On apology. New York, NY: Oxford University Press.

[16] Leo, J. (1997, June 30). So who's sorry now? U. S. News & World Report,

122, 17.

[17] Meier, A. J. (2004). Conflicts and the power of apologies. Retrieved Nov. 27, 2006, from http://web.fu-berlin.de/phin/phin30/p30t1.htm.

[18] Murata, K. (1998). Has he apologized nor not?: A cross-cultural misunderstanding between the UK and Japan on the occasion of the 50th anniversary of VJ Day in Britain. Pragmatics, 8, 501–513.

[19] NATO. (1999). NATO's official statement on the accidental bombing of the Chinese Embassy in Belgrade. Retrieved Nov. 20, 2006, from http://www.pbs.org/newshour/bb/europe/jan-june99/nato_statement_5-8.html.

[20] Northeast Asia Peace and Security Network. (1999, May 17). Special report. Retrieved Oct. 19, 2006, from http://www.nautilus.org/archives/pub/ftp/napsnet/special_reports.

[21] PBS. (1999, May 8). China responds. Retrieved Oct. 19, 2006, from http://www.pbs.org/newshour/bb/europe/jan-june99/china_statement_5-8.

[22] People's Daily. (1999, May 10). NATO's bombing of Chinese Embassy strongly condemned. Retrieved Nov. 21, 2006, from http://english.people.com.cn/1999/26/eng199926_286979.html.

[23] President Clinton Again Apologizes. (1999). Retrieved Nov. 21, 2006, from http://hongkong.usembassy.gov/uscn/state/1999/0510.htm

[24] Shapiro, W. (1997, June 30). Mama Mia, that's mea culpa. Time, 18.

[25] Sigler, C. (2006). Close textual analysis. Retrieved Nov. 30, 2006, from http://www.d.umn.edu/~csigler/3906_close-analysis.html.

[26] Smith, N. (2005). The categorical apology. Journal of Social Philosophy, 36(4), 473–496.

[27] Statement by U.S. State Department. (1999). State Department legal advisor on China embassy bombing. Retrieved Nov. 21, 2006, from http://www.hongkong.usembassy.gov/uscn/state/1999/0730.htm.

[28] Tannen, D. (Ed.) (1999). A sorry state of affairs. Civilization, 4, 63–73.

[29] Tavuchis, N. (1991). Mea culpa: A sociology of apology and reconciliation. Stanford, CA: Stanford University Press.

[30] Testimony of Stanley O. Roth. (1999, May 27). The effects on U.S.-China relations of the accidental bombing of the Chinese Embassy in Belgrade. Retrieved Nov. 21, 2006, from http://hongkong.usembassy.gov/uscn/state/1999/0527.htm.

[32] The London Observer. (1999, Oct. 19). Chinese Embassy attack: Deliberate. Retrieved Nov. 20, 2006, from http://www.globalresearch.ca.

[33] UCLA Center for East Asian Studies. (2001, Jan. 21). A payment to China for U.S. bomb error. Retrieved Nov. 20, 2006, from http://www.isop.ucla.edu/eas/newsfile/bombing05-99/010121-ap.htm.

[34] UCLA Center for East Asian Studies. (1999, May 10). Formal note of 10 May to the

U. S. by Foreign Minister Tang Jiaxuan on the embassy bombing. Retrieved Nov. 20, 2006, from http://www.isop.ucla.edu/eas/newsfile/bombing05 - 99/990510 - cmfa4.htm.

[35] U. S. Department of Defense. (1999). Joint statement by Secretary of Defense William S. Cohen and CIA Director George J. Tenet. Retrieved Nov. 21, 2006, from http://hongkong.usembassy.gov/uscn/uscn/others/1999/0508.htm.

[36] U. S. Department of State. (1999a). Oral presentation by Under Secretary of State Thomas Pickering on June 17 to the Chinese Government regarding the accidental bombing of the PRC embassy in Belgrade. Retrieved Oct. 19, 2006, from http://www.usconsulate.org.hk/uscn/state/1999/0706.htm.

[37] U. S. Department of State. (1999b). State spokesman on bombing of China embassy in Belgrade. Retrieved Nov. 21, 2006, from http://hongkong.usembassy.gov/uscn/state/1999/0508a.htm.

[38] U. S. Department of State. (1999c). Alright apologizes for accidental bombing of China embassy. Retrieved Nov. 21, 2006, from http://hongkong.usembassy.gov/uscn/state/1999/0508b.htm.

[39] Yamazaki, J. W. (2004). The failure of Japanese apologies for World War II. In G. M. Chen & J. S. Williams (Eds.), Dialogue among diversities: International and intercultural communication annual NCA, 27, 169 - 190.

Chapter 14
The American Hegemonic Responses to the U. S. -China Mid-air Plane Collision

On April 1, 2001, a U. S. EP-3 navy surveillance plane collided with a Chinese F-8 fighter jet "about 70 miles off the Chinese Island of Hainan in international airspace" ("Navy Admiral...", 2001, p. 1). Admiral Blair, Commander in Chief of the U. S. Pacific Command, made public the accident of the mid-air plane collision when he was addressing the media during a press conference. He accounted that the U. S. surveillance plane was on a routine operation in the South China Sea when two Chinese fighters intercepted the EP-3 aircraft, and one of them flew into the wing of the aircraft. Due to sufficient damage, the pilot of the EP-3 declared a mayday in-flight emergency and landed safely at Lingshui Military Airport on Hainan Island of P. R. China without the Chinese authorization (pp. 1 - 2). Twenty-four military personnel were on board the EP-3 surveillance aircraft, and they "were removed from the aircraft by the Chinese military personnel and detained in an undisclosed location" (Senate Resolution 66, 2001, p. 2).

Immediately following the accident, both the U. S. and Chinese governments blamed each other for the collision. U. S. Pacific Command in Chief Blair (2001) stated, "Chinese fighters intercepted the aircraft, and one of them bumped into the wing of the EP-3 aircraft" ("Navy Admiral...", 2001, p. 1). Zhu Bangzao, the spokesman of the Chinese Foreign Ministry then, announced, "by veering and ramming the Chinese jet at a wide angle, against flight rules, the U. S. surveillance plane caused the crash of the Chinese jet" (Chinese Foreign Ministry, 2001, p. 2). Besides blaming each other for causing the accident itself, the two governments also accused each other of violating international laws of air and sea and of infringing upon each other's sovereignty of territory. To the Chinese, the U. S. aircraft "violated the United Nations Convention on the Law of the Sea, which stipulates that any flight in airspace above another nation's exclusive economic zone should respect the rights of the country concerned" (Chinese Foreign Ministry, 2001, p. 2). To the Americans, it was "in contravention of international norms" that "Chinese officials have boarded the [EP-3] aircraft and may have removed portions of the equipment" (Senate Resolution 66, 2001, p. 2).

From the plane collision on April 1, to the release of the U. S. crew on April 12, and to the return of the U. S. EP - 3 aircraft [in pieces] on July 3, 2001, a tug-of-war was launched over the responsibility for the collision. Several rounds of intense negotiations were conducted over the Chinese requests for an apology and reparations and the U. S. demands for the release of the 24 military personnel and the return of the EP – 3 aircraft to the United States. Meanwhile, quite a number of official statements and diplomatic notes were exchanged between the two sides, made public, and reserved as transcripts available in several websites. Having downloaded all the relevant transcripts as artifacts for this study from the websites of the U. S. Department of State and other major news agencies, we intend to look into the major documents of the American side concerning the mid-air plane collision from April 1 to April 12, 2001. Before examining the artifacts through the hegemonic theoretical lens of Robert Cox's frame of action and via the research method of hermeneutics, we will seek the gap for our enquiries based on the existent literature.

Literature Review

In general, there have been four major categories of existing literature.

The first category compares and contrasts media coverage of the incident in the two countries. For example, Zhang (2005) wrote his master thesis by using news framing and found that mainstream Chinese and American media covered the plane collision incident in a similar time-series slope, depicting their own country as morally superior, blaming the opponent's country as the wrongdoer, and deliberately withholding unfavorable reporting. The major difference, however, is that U. S. media quoted from more sources while the Chinese media relied more on governmental sources (pp. 47 – 48). In addition, Slingerland, Blanchard and Boyd-Judson (2007) used grounded theory to interpret the importance of conceptual metaphors used in media accounts from *The New York Times* and the *Washington Post* in the United States and the *People's Daily*, *Jiangnan Times*, and *Tianjin Daily* in China. Their analysis of the discourse surrounding the 2001 collision reveals "a surprisingly high degree of similarity in conceptual metaphors used across the two cultures" (p. 53).

The second category of literature studies the plane collision incident from the linguistic point of view. In his article entitled "Semantic Ambiguity and Joint Deflections in the Hainan Negotiations," Yee (2004) noted the significance of semantics and translations in facilitating the resolution of the Hainan incident. While the Chinese have six different levels of apology, the Americans could say "sorry" for either something they have done wrong or any loss of life. It is the semantic ambiguity and linguistic flexibility of the languages and translations that facilitated successful shifts in the two-level negotiations over the Hainan plane collision crisis (1 – 19). By the same token, Cheng (2002) explored the stances, intentions, and ideologies of the United States and China by analyzing the if-clause utterances in nearly one hundred news stories covering the spy plane incident. He concluded by saying that "news leaves many things unsaid as in diplomatic discourse or political discourse" (p. 309).

The third category of literature takes the legal and real-political perspective. For instance, in his article entitled "The United States-China EP-3 Incident: Legality and

Realpolitik," Donnelly (2004) found that both countries' interpretations of the international law and responses to the incident were "frequently founded on realpolitik rather than by any regard for a strict adherence to the international law" (p. 1) after he had examined the arguments of both China and the United States over the incident against the United Nations Convention on the Law of the Sea.

The last category of literature analyzes the incident from the perspective of bilateral or international relationship. For example, Sheng (2001) remarked that it was dangerous for the United States to treat China "as a 'strategic competitor' and corner China by repeated pushes, as the Bush Administration has so far been doing" (p. 27). For another example, Yang (2001) stated that it was within expectation for the Bush Administration to reset China as a strategic competitor rather than a strategic partner, but "the mid-air collision between a US EP-3 surveillance plane and a Chinese interceptor surely caught the world by surprise" (p. 14). He concluded by saying that U.S.-China relations are marked by exquisite complexity and the two countries could be military rivals despite the fact that they are major trading partners with breathtaking potentials (p. 17).

Having summarized the relevant literature, we find it necessary and meaningful to further the research on the U.S.-China mid-air plane collision incident from a different perspective—the perspective of looking into the nature of the doctrine that the Bush Administration has been pursuing and the ramifications of such a pursuit. As Mailloux (1985) emphasized, it is important to make our "acts of persuasion always take place against an ever-changing background of shared and disputed assumptions, questions, assertions, and so forth" (p. 631). By putting the analysis of the plane-collision incident into a larger dynamic historical background, we intend to explicate the motivation behind the American responses to this particular incident with the hope to elucidate the pattern that the United States has been following on similar occasions and the possible consequences for the parties involved. Given that we are now living in a post-9/11 climate, our study of the U.S. responses to an international standoff due to the mid-air plane collision incident four months before 9/11 will not only shed light on the understanding of the incident itself but also provide insightful implications for the involved parties to take necessary precautions against the occurrence of and appropriate steps to handle such international conflicts in the future.

Theoretical Framework

With regard to the doctrine the Bush Administration has been implementing in terms of the U.S.-China bilateral relations, there has been burgeoning scholarship. In fact, during his 2000 presidential campaigns, Bush was advised to advocate "the use of American power to advance its national interests, the building and strengthening of alliances, and firmness in dealing with potential U.S. foes" (Yuan, 2003, p. 53). Upon coming into office, the Bush Administration prioritized the establishment of "strengthening its relationships with key allies in Asia" while seeking to adopt "a China policy that characterizes the rising power of

East Asia, if not a 'strategic competitor' across the board, then certainly a 'military competitor with a formidable resource base'" (Yuan, 2003, p. 39). According to Amin (2006), one of the five objectives of the project of the American ruling class is "to break up China, to ensure the subordination of other major states, and to prevent the constitution of any regional blocs that might renegotiate the terms of globalization" (p. 10). Layne and Thayer (2007) also pointed out very clearly that the Bush Administration "has embraced containment of China as an alternative to engagement" which is "unsurprising given the influence of neoconservative foreign policy intellectuals on the administration's grand strategy" (p. 72).

Then, what exactly is the Bush Doctrine? And what can we draw from it? According to Jervis (2003), there are four components in the Bush Doctrine:

> A strong belief in the importance of a state's domestic regime in determining its foreign policy, and the related judgment that this is a time of great opportunity to transform international politics; the perception of great threats that can be defeated only by new and vigorous policies (mostly notably preventive war); a willingness to act unilaterally when necessary; and, as both a cause and a summary of these three elements, an overriding sense that peace and stability require the United States to assert its primacy in world politics. (p. 365)

In the opinion of Jervis, the Bush Doctrine is consistent with standard patterns of international politics and with much previous American behavior in the Cold War. Since the beginning of the Second World War, American leaders knew that the United States would emerge as the prime architect of a new world order. To Jervis, the essence of the Bush Doctrine is "the establishment of American hegemony, primacy, or empire" (p. 376). To this end, the United States is required "to act in ways that others cannot and must not" which is "not a double standard, but what world order requires" (p. 376). In the case of China, Washington does not think that China has any justifiable basis for regarding the American military presence in East Asia as threatening to its interests. In Pentagon's view, "China's military modernization remains ambitious" (Layne & Thayer, 2007, p. 72). Therefore, China is regarded as one of the three main potential adversaries for the United States due to its huge size and economic success, and the Bush Administration "has a strategic goal of dismembering the country" (Amin, 2006, p. 11).

Thus, we can see an apparent hegemonic feature in the Bush Doctrine and in the China policy of the Bush Administration. Now the point is: how do we conceptualize hegemony theoretically and how can we apply it to the analysis of the U.S. responses to the mid-air plane collision incident in the selected artifacts? The word "hegemony" originates from the Greek word "hegemonia" meaning "leader" and gradually gives place to the idea of dominance, especially the dominance of ideas (Standford, p. 1). Hegemony as a concept refers to "political leadership based on the consent of the led, a consent which is secured by the diffusion and popularization of the world view of the ruling class" (Bates, 1975, p. 352).

Chapter 14

The American Hegemonic Responses to the U.S.-China Mid-air Plane Collision

In international relations, hegemony is used to "connote the predominant position of the most powerful state in the international system or the dominant state in a particular given region" (Faiz, 2007, p. 1).

The modern usage of hegemony as a concept comes from the Italian Marxist and social theorist, Antonio Gramsci. As Strinati (1995) noted, Gramsci used "hegemony" to mean the ability of a dominant class to exercise power by winning the consent of its subjugators. Consent is produced and reproduced by the hegemony of the ruling class in society. In the context of the developed West, consent is maintained not merely via coercion but more importantly through "the negotiated construction of a political and ideological consensus which incorporates both dominant and dominated groups" (Strinati, 1995, p. 165). The consensus is achieved via the process by which the dominant classes propagate their values and ideology via social institutions such as mass media, religious organizations, schools and the family. The dominant values and ideology are so ingrained in people's minds that they not only limit people's vision but also enable it (Raphael, 2003, p. 2).

Based on Gramsci's idea of hegemony and in response to the crisis of Marxism, Laclau and Mouffe(2001) defined hegemony as a discursive strategy of combining principles from different systems of thought into one coherent ideology. To them, hegemony functions as a political logic of articulation, in which a particular social force such as a particular class, group, or political party represents or stands in for the whole. As a specific form of universality based on a tension between difference and equivalence, Laclau and Mouffe's notion of hegemony "provides an innovative way to interpret contemporary political struggles" with powerful analytical tools or concepts such as chains of equivalence, antagonism, and articulation (Newman, 2002, p. 4).

According to Faiz (2007), Robert Cox further developed the notion of hegemony by drawing upon Gramsci's notion of hegemony and put his thought of hegemony in the global context as follows:

> Successive dominant powers in the international system have shaped a world order that suits their interests, and have done so not only as a result of their coercive capabilities, but also because they have managed to generate broad consent for that order even among those who are disadvantaged by it. (p. 2)

To Cox, countries like the United States are dominant powers in the international system, which have successfully globalized their hegemonic ideas such as free trade all over the world including China. The idea of free trade or free market based on neo-liberalism is so widely accepted today in the world that even many adversely-affected countries treat the idea as common sense. Building upon the critical formulation of Robert Cox, Beeson and Higgott (2005) regarded hegemony as "the ability of some power or authority in a system to 'lay down the law' about external relations between states in the international system" (p. 1174). To them, the discussion of Cox about the interplay among ideas, material capabilities and institutionalization can be adopted to crystallize the dynamic process, in which the U.S.

interests and values are reflected in a rule-governed, normatively-informed post-war international order.

Then, let us see how Cox himself clarifies the changes in the world order. Cox (1981) proposed his idea of the "frame of action" based on historical materialism, which comprises ideas, material capabilities, and institutionalization. Ideas are those shared notions or thought patterns of the nature of social relations and those of collective images of social order held by different groups of people. As the ideas are historically conditioned, they can predict behaviors when conflicts arise between states such as negotiation, confrontation, or war. Material capabilities refer to material conditions composed of technological and organizational capabilities and natural resources, which can be productive and destructive potentials. Institutionalization is a means of stabilizing and perpetuating a particular order through human institutions. Such institutions reflect the power relations and the collective images that are consistent with these power relations. In a word, the institutions are a combination of ideas and material power, which in turn impact the development of ideas and material capabilities (p. 137).

Research Method

To analyze the selected artifacts, we adopt the qualitative research method of hermeneutics. According to Byrne (2001), the assumptions of hermeneutics are "human beings experience the world through language, and language provides both understanding and knowledge" (p. 1). He defined hermeneutics as the interpretation and understanding of texts derived from stories, interviews, participant observations, letters, speeches, or other relevant written documents and personal experiences. While interpreting the denotative and connotative meanings of the texts, hermeneutics also emphasizes the historical and socio-cultural influences on the interpretation. To this end, the texts are usually closely examined in connection to their relevant contexts for the generation of themes or patterns as research findings, which reflect the knowledge of the phenomenon under study. (p. 1).

A theme refers to a relevant issue, opinion, understanding, or experience. According to Owen (1984), three criteria are required for the generation of a theme. The first criterion is occurrence, which means that at least two parts of a report have the same thread of meaning even though the meaning was indicated by different wording. The second criterion is the repetition of key words, phrases, or sentences, which is an extension of the first criterion in that it is an explicit repeated use of the same wording. The third criterion is forcefulness, which refers to the underlining of words or phrases in a written report or vocal inflection, volume, or dramatic pauses in a recording. When generating the themes, the two authors separately read the transcriptions of the selected artifacts thoroughly and repeatedly to determine the common themes and patterns so as to achieve validated evidence for data analysis.

The texts or artifacts for analysis and interpretation in this study include the U. S. Navy

Chapter 14

The American Hegemonic Responses to the U.S.-China Mid-air Plane Collision

Admiral Description of the Aircraft Incident in South China on April 1, Statement by the President on American Plane and Crew in China on April 2 [Statement A], Statement by the President Calling for Prompt Release of Crew and Return of Plane on April 3 [Statement B], Powell April 3 Briefing on U.S.-China Aircraft Accident, Secretary of State Powell Expresses Regret over Loss of Chinese Pilot on April 4, Senate Resolution 66 Calling for Release of Plane and Crew on April 5, Remarks by Secretary of State Powell Expressing Regret over Loss of Chinese Pilot on April 4, Letter from Ambassador Prueher to China's Minister of Foreign Affairs on April 11, Powell at Contact Group Joint Press Conference on April 11, and Welcome Speech of the President for the U.S. Service Members on April 12, 2001.

We have made this purposive selection of the above artifacts for three reasons. First, the mid-air collision took place near the coast of China. To this day, there has been no definite answer to which side was responsible for the collision. As Donnelly (2004) pointed out, "it is almost impossible for any conclusions to be drawn from the widely differing accounts of the collision" (p. 29). How the United States, as represented by the President, Commander in Chief of the Pacific Command, Senate, and the Secretary of State in this case, responded to this incident attracted extensive attention across the world, thus providing a significant research topic for communication scholars. Second, President Bush, who "was facing the most complex crisis in his presidency of fewer than 100 days" (Cheng, 2002, p. 312), had to choose whether to handle China as a strategic competitor advocated by those neoconservative hardliners around him or a strategic partner from the legacy of the Clinton Administration. Since the United States had and still has the strongest military power in the world, whose "annual defense expenditure is more than the rest of the world combined" (Layne & Thayer, 2007, p. 61), the choice of President Bush and the responses of the Bush Administration regarding the incident offers a core issue of study in international communication, which refers to the communication that occurs across international borders (Thussu, 2006. p. 14). Finally, the decision to analyze the artifacts of just the American side is determined by the accessibility to the required documents or transcripts and the space of the present paper.

Critical Analysis

Having made clear the hegemonic theoretical framework and the research method of close reading, we can now analyze the selected artifacts through the hegemonic theoretical lens in terms of Cox's ideas, material capabilities, and institutionalization. While analyzing the transcripts of the official U.S. responses to the mid-air plane collision and subsequent U.S.-China negotiations, we will also refer to some relevant responses from the Chinese side and other parties from different parts of the world for the purpose of clarifying our argument.

Shared Notions. As discussed earlier, shared notions refer to those ideas or thought patterns in the nature of social relations and the collective images of social order held by different groups of people. Then, what are the shared notions of the United States toward China. Since the Communists came into power in 1949 in Mainland China, China has been on the radar screen of the U.S. foreign policy makers and political strategists. The U.S. policy toward China during all the three post-Cold War administrations has maintained an unwillingness to "countenance China's emergency as a peer competitor" on the one hand and a willingness to "give China the opportunity to integrate itself into the American-led international order on Washington's terms" (Layne & Thayer, 2007, p. 70) on the other hand. When the Bush Administration came into office in 2000, China was regarded as a strategic competitor as advocated by the neoconservative hardliners around President Bush. To the hardliners, there have been several indicators of the rising China as a revisionist power. First, China's economy has been growing at an average rate of nine percent for two decades. Second, China has become a serious challenge to the regional balance of power with its double-digit increases in defense expenditures, imports of advanced Russian weapons, and modernization of its army. Third, China has been affecting the American image by its assertiveness in handling international affairs. Thus, the best strategy for the United States is "to contain or constrain China before it becomes too powerful and therefore too costly to do so" (Yuan, 2003, p. 54 – 56).

With the above China policy, the United States has made clear its fundamental interests as "the prevention of the rise of any single power in the Asia Pacific that can challenge and even pose a threat to U.S. national security and access to the region's expanding markets" (Yuan, 2003, p. 45). To this end, the United States has been conducting annually about two hundred intelligence gathering missions by the U.S. Navy and Air Force ranging from undersea platforms to ground and satellite antenna systems. The purpose is to capture military and government communications along the Chinese coastline. The EP-3 plane that collided with the Chinese F-8 fighter jet is a U.S. Navy surveillance plane on a routine intelligence-gathering mission (Angelis, 2002, p. 2).

Against this background, the official U.S. responses in the selected artifacts reveal three major notions. First, we find the American officials demanding immediate release of the crew and the return of the plane and instructing the Chinese side the expected etiquette under such circumstances. Second, the Chinese have violated international norms by keeping the U.S. crew and plane, boarding the U.S. EP-3 aircraft, and removing portions of the equipment. Third, the American officials keep saying that they have done nothing wrong and there is no reason for the Chinese side to ask for an apology. To be specific, our thorough examination of the selected artifacts against the above historical background manifests the following findings.

First, as for demanding immediate release of the crew and return of the plane, President Bush clearly stated on April 2, "our priorities are the prompt and safe return of the crew, and the return of the aircraft without further damaging or tampering" ("Statement A",

Chapter 14

The American Hegemonic Responses to the U.S.-China Mid-air Plane Collision

2001, p. 1). Secretary Powell remarks on April 3, "we will continue to impress upon the Chinese that they need to move quickly to return the crew to its unit, the crew to its families and to return the plane to its United States base" ("Powell", 2001, p. 2). The U.S. Senate also calls for the release of the plane and crew on April 5:

> It is the sense of the Senate that the government of the People's Republic of China should immediately release the crew members of the EP-3 into the custody of the United States military or consular officials, and allow them to leave the country and return the EP-3 aircraft and all its equipment to the possession of the United States. ("Senate Resolution 66", 2001, p. 2 - 3)

With regard to instructing the Chinese side the expected etiquette under such circumstances, Commander in Chief Blair says to the press on April 1:

> If a Chinese aircraft had been 70 miles of f of Kaneohe here in Hawaii... we would have gotten the pilot right to a telephone, say here's a phone, call home, tell them you're okay and we would have been in contact with the Chinese government saying, 'What do you need to help?' And we would have stayed out of the aircraft and away from it, because we recognize that it is what international rules say. ("Navy Admiral", 2001, p. 2 - 4)

Second, the American side insists that the U.S. surveillance aircraft "was on a routine operation in the South China Sea. It was 70 miles off the Chinese Island of Hainan in international airspace.... The airplane itself, military aircraft of all countries in situations like this, has sovereign immunity" ("Navy Admiral", 2001, p. 1). Therefore, Secretary of State Powell says, "I have heard that they are investigating something. I don't know what there is to investigate. Our plane was flying over international water and international air space" ("Powell", 2001, p. 2). The U.S. Senate also warns the Chinese side not to infringe the U.S. sovereign immunity and violate the international law, which "recognizes both the right of the crew of an aircraft in distress to land safely on foreign soil and the inviolable sovereignty of an aircraft in distress that has landed on foreign soil" ("Senate Resolution 66", 2001, p. 2).

Third, it has been China's post-Cold War security policy to maintain a relatively "stable and peaceful environment for economic development and building comprehensive national strength, protecting territorial integrity and achieving reunification with Taiwan, and upholding regional security cooperation through dialogues and consultation" (Yuan, 2003, p. 45). Therefore, when the plane collision incident occurred, China clearly stated its primary principles that "the most urgent matter for the US side is not to table all manner of requests, but to make a thorough review on the incident, apologize to the Chinese side and respond to China's concerns and demands" ("Chinese Foreign Ministry", 2001, p. 4).

In response, Secretary of State Powell remarked on April 3, "I have heard some suggestion of an apology, but we have nothing to apologize for. We did not do anything wrong. Our airplane was in international airspace" ("Powell", 2001, p. 2). Then the Chinese side reiterated its request by Ambassador Yang Jiechi to the United States, "our side has said it very clearly that the U. S. side should share all the responsibility and apologize to the Chinese side" ("CNN", 2001, p. 2). The United States knows well that in diplomacy, apology means accepting responsibility, but expressing regret does not; therefore, we read all sorts of "regrets" instead of a single "apology" in the selected artifacts. For instance, Secretary of State Powell tells the press on April 3, "unfortunately it apparently was fatal for the pilot of the Chinese plane and I regret that," ("Powell," 2001, p. 2) and says again on April 4, "we regret that the Chinese plane did not get down safely, and we regret the loss of the life of the Chinese pilot" ("Secretary of State", 2001, p. 1). In addition, the U. S. Senate expresses "its regret at the damage and loss of life occasioned by the accidental collision of the two aircraft" ("Senate Resolution 66," 2001, p. 2). In the letter from Ambassador Prueher to China's Minister of Foreign Affairs on April 11, we still read words like "sincere regret" and "very sorry" instead of an apology:

> Both President Bush and Secretary of State Powell have expressed their sincere regret over your missing pilot and aircraft. Please convey to the Chinese people and to the family of pilot Wang Wei that we are very sorry for their loss. ("Letter from Ambassador Prueher", 2001, p. 1)

To analyze the shared notions in the American responses, we may first refer to a series of questions the Chinese Foreign Ministry spokesman Zhu Bangzao asked including:

> Why does the US side frequently send its military surveillance planes on spy flights over sea areas close to China? Why did the US warplane make an abrupt turn and ram the Chinese jet in violation of operation rules? Why did the US plane intrude into China's airspace and land at a Chinese airport without approval from the Chinese side? ("Chinese Foreign Ministry," 2001, p. 4)

We know from earlier discussions that, in line with its hegemonic grand strategy, the United States keeps sending its military surveillance planes on spy flights over sea areas close to China to capture military and government communications along the Chinese coastline in order to guard against the rise of China in the Asia Pacific. In specific legal terms, the mid-air plane collision occurred 70 miles southeast of China's Hainan Island, which is within China's 200-nautical-mile Exclusive Economic Zone (EEZ). Although the 1982 *United Nations Convention on the Law of the Sea* (UNCLOS) stipulates the freedom of over-flight in the EEZs of a country, it also clearly states that in the EEZs, "States shall have due regard to the rights and duties of the coastal State and shall comply with the laws and regulations adopted by the coastal State" (Donnelly, 2004, p. 29 – 32). Since the U. S. EP-3 plane was targeting at China in its surveillance in the airspace over China's EEZ instead of an ordinary "over-flight," it is an abuse of the principle of over-flight freedom. Furthermore, the Chinese side made public photos showing that the nose of the U. S. plane had been knocked off and the propeller on its left wing was damaged and the paint from the Chinese jet fighter was found on the front instead of at the back of the propeller of the U. S. plane and the antenna on the left wing of the U. S. plane had been knocked backwards instead of forward (Sheng, 2001, p. 3). Finally, although it was an emergency landing, the U. S. EP-

Chapter 14

The American Hegemonic Responses to the U.S.-China Mid-air Plane Collision

3 Navy surveillance plane "entered China's territorial space and landed at a Chinese airport without China's approval, so the US plane's action constituted an infringement upon China's sovereignty and territorial space" ("Chinese Foreign Ministry," 2001, p. 3).

Material Capabilities. As mentioned earlier, material capabilities refer to material conditions composed of technological and organizational capabilities and natural resources, which can be productive and destructive potentials. Being the only superpower in the world, the United States is in possession of and intends to maintain cultural, economic, and military dominance all over the world. As Monton (2005) pointed out:

> The Bush Doctrine follows a period of enormous material expansion.... The United States ended the 1990s at the top of a unipolar distribution of power, commanding a greater share of world capabilities than any state in modern international history. U. S. economic dominance is surpassed only by its own position immediately following World War II. U. S. military dominance is even more asymmetrical. (142)

Endowed with such favorable capitalist environment, bounty natural resources, and sufficient human talents, the United States raises the most powerful army and has its military presence all over the world. According to Posen (2003), "one pillar of the U. S. hegemony is the vast military power of the United States" (p. 5). The U. S. Navy plane involved in the mid-air collision is a sample that can showcase the U. S. material capabilities militarily. The U. S. EP-3 spy plane is equipped with a distinctive saucer-shaper antenna on its underbelly and packed with electronic devices. It is capable of monitoring Chinese military activities by intercepting, tracking, and recording a wide variety of communications such as telephone, radio, radar transmissions, and even electronic mail. Equipped with the electronic surveillance gear, it can also hear and see into Mainland China as a treasure trove of military intelligence (Sheng, 2001, p. 2).

It is now easy to understand why the U. S. side cared so much about the Chinese boarding the EP-3 plane and obtaining hardware and software information. For instance, Commander in Chief Blair shows his concern by saying, "the airplane itself, military aircraft of all countries, has sovereignty immunity. That is no other country can go aboard them or keep them. They are in sovereign-immune territory." ("Navy Admiral," 2001, p. 2). The U. S. Senate asks the Chinese side to "return the EP-3 aircraft and all its equipment to the possession of the United States without any further boarding or inspection, or removal of equipment" ("Senate Resolution 66," 2001, p. 3).

However, on September 4, 1976 a Soviet MIG-25 military plane was flown to Japan. On that occasion the United States believed that there was a right to examine the aircraft. Despite the Soviet protests, the American and Japanese intelligence officials disassembled the plane to study it for over two months before they returned the plane to the Soviet Union in packing crates because that type of military plane was a mystery to the West at that time (Donnelly, 2004, p. 40). If this cannot be considered double standards, the norm the United States is observing manifests at least that the right belongs to the side that has more power.

Now the point is whether the United States will use its power or material capabilities, especially military capabilities for productive or destructive potentials. Beeson and Higgott (2005) noted that the United States, under the Bush Administration is moving from a benign hegemon to a selfish one, thus attracting more enmity and resistance (p. 1185). Currently, the American strategy is to maintain the status quo in East Asia, but China as a rising power may clash with the American strategy of primacy. Unless the U. S. and Chinese interests can be accommodated, there is great potential for future tension between the two sides. Nevertheless, as Layne and Thayer (2007) pointed out, "whether Washington and Beijing actually come to blows depends largely on what strategy the United States chooses to adopt toward China" (p. 73).

Institutionalization. Institutionalization refers to a means of stabilizing and perpetuating a particular order through human institutions. Human institutions are a combination of ideas and material capabilities. Closely linked to Gramsci's notion of hegemony, institutions provide ways to deal with conflicts and anchor hegemonic strategies in the representation of diverse interests and universalization of policy (Cox, 1981, p. 137). Since the end of the Second World War, the United States took the lead in establishing the core institutions of the global capitalist and political system. The global capitalist system, according to Leatherman and Webber (2005), "rests on the outward projection of the national hegemony of the dominant social classes of the United States and their protection through national security strategies" (p. 9).

In Asia Pacific, the use of military force is the main instrument in the current U. S. drive for hegemony. To this end, the Bush Administration entitles itself the right to take preventive actions against any potential adversaries. China is on the list of the three major potential adversaries of the United States, and the Bush Administration has set "a strategic goal of dismembering the country" (Leatherman & Webber, 2005, p. 11). To implement such ideas or shared notions of primacy, the United States, as mentioned earlier, has been carrying out hundreds of intelligence gathering missions each year by its Navy and Air Force to capture military and government communications along the Chinese coastline.

When one of its Navy reconnaissance planes collided with one of the Chinese fighters on April 1, 2001, the Commander in Chief of the U. S. Pacific Command, Admiral Dennis C. Blair, expressed his expectation on the same day that the Chinese side should give back the U. S. spy plane so that "we can repair the plane, our people can return, and we can go on about our business"("Navy Admiral," 2001, p. 2). President Bush regarded the U. S. naval maritime patrol as "a routine surveillance mission in international airspace over the South China Sea" ("Statement A", 2001, p. 2). On April 3, Secretary of State Powell said that the safe landing of the U. S. plane after the collision at a Chinese military airport without authorization was "quite a feat of airmanship" ("Powell", 2001, p. 3).

After the 24 crew members were finally released on April 12, 2001, the Secretary commented on the same day at a press conference, "there was nothing to apologize for. To apologize would have suggested that we had done something wrong and were accepting responsibility" ("Secretary of State", 2001, p. 2). On the next day, President Bush praised the crew in his welcome speech by saying that "they represent the best of American patriotism and service to their country" and emphasized, "reconnaissance flights are part of a comprehensive national security strategy that helps maintain peace and stability in our world" ("Welcome Speech", 2001, p. 2). All this reveals that the U.S. side considers it a normal routine job to use military planes to spy on other countries and the United States will continue with such military operations because they are carried out for maintaining world peace and stability. Thus, barely two weeks after the plane collision standoff ended, the Bush Administration decided to offer Taiwan the largest arms package in a decade, including 4 Kidd-class destroyers, 12 P-3C Orion aircraft, and 8 diesel submarines, to name just a few. Furthermore, the United States resumed its military surveillance along the Chinese coastline (Yang, 2001, p. 14).

Besides the governmental role in the institutionalization of the U.S. notion of primacy, the crew members, the media, and a large portion of the general public in the United States have also demonstrated their roles in safeguarding the U.S. hegemonic ideology. For instance, when the crew members realized that they had to land their spy plane on a Chinese airport, they began implementing the classified destruction plan by erasing computer memory units that recorded the day's mission, shredding the computer floppy disks containing various encryption codes, and smashing various eavesdropping and cryptographic code machines (Thompson, 2001, p. 1). During the U.S.-China standoff as a result of the plane collision, the American media "functions as an arm of the U.S. national security apparatus," presenting the TV viewers and the newspaper readers that "American spy flights on the edge on the Chinese mainland as defensive, while the Chinese monitoring of these flights as aggressive and provocative" (Martin, 2001, p. 4). As for the general public, there are some relevant poll results during the U.S.-China standoff. For example, sixty-nine percent Americans thought the United States should continue with the U.S. military surveillance flights off the Chinese coast ("Newsweek Pool", 2001, p. 4). For another example, sixty-one percent of the Americans approved of the way George W. Bush was handling the mid-air collision situation ("Gallup Poll", 2001, p. 5). For still another example, fifty-four percent of the Americans thought the United States should not officially apologize to China ("Gallup Poll", 2001, p. 5).

Conclusion

The purpose of this study was to look into the major documents of the American side concerning the U.S.-China mid-air plane collision from April 1 to April 12, 2001. We have made a purposive selection of nine artifacts for this study from the U.S. official statements, Senate resolution, the President's welcome speech, and Secretary of State Powell's briefings and remarks at press conferences during the U.S.-China standoff. Via the hegemonic theoretical lens in terms of Cox's ideas, material capabilities, and institutionalization, we have analyzed the selected artifacts by using the rhetorical method of hermeneutics. Our findings are twofold as follows:

First, as a shared notion, the essence of the Bush Doctrine is to establish American hegemony, primacy, or empire all over the world. To this end, the United States will make use of its power to advance the U. S. national interests by means of building and strengthening alliances and taking firm stance in dealing with potential U. S. enemies. Washington does not allow Beijing to regard the American military presence in East Asia as a threat and, at the same time, intends to dismember China due to its huge size, steady economic growth, and military ambitions. Seeing China as a strategic competitor, the United States considers its mission to gather Chinese military and government information via military surveillance planes. Interpreting international laws in line with its hegemonic grand strategy, the Bush Administration contends that the United States is privileged and obliged to guard against the rise of China in the Asia Pacific in the name of maintaining world peace and regional stability.

Second, to maintain cultural, economic, and military dominance all over the world, the United States has both preserved the most resourceful material capabilities and established the necessary human institutions. An example of the material capabilities is its military presence in all parts of the world with an annual expense twice as much as that of the rest of the world combined. The human institutions have been manifested in the Bush Administration's grand strategy, the support of the Senate and other governmental organs, and the average sixty percent approval and consent of the U. S. notion of primacy in the public opinion poll.

Although the twelve-day U. S.-China standoff as a result of the mid-air plane collision came to an end in a peaceful manner, the U. S. side soon resumed its military surveillance along the Chinese coast. As discussed earlier, material capabilities can be used for either productive or destructive potentials. If the United States continues with its current grand strategy of hegemonic primacy, similar crisis may occur again in Asia Pacific and potential conflicts may arise elsewhere in the other parts of the world. Future research may either focus on the study of the Chinese responses or a comparative study of the responses of both sides.

(Tian, D. X., & Chao, C. C. (2008). The American hegemonic responses to the U. S.-China Mid-air plane collision. *International Journal of Communication*, 2, 1–19.)

References

[1] Amin, S. (2006). Beyond US hegemony? Assessing the prospects for a multipolar world. Trans. New York, NY: World Book Publishing.

[2] Angelis, J. (2002). The Hainan incident and the application of international regime

theory on Chinese foreign policy. Retrieved April 15, 2007, from http://www-mmd. eng. cam. ac. uk/people/jannis/Extended%.

[3] Bates, T. R. (1975). Gramsci and the theory of hegemony. Journal of the History of Ideas, 36(2), 351–366.

[4] Beeson, M., & Higgott, R. (2005). Hegemony, institutionalism and US foreign policy: Theory and practice in comparative historical perspective. Third World Quarterly, 26(7), 1173–1188.

[5] Byrne, M. (2001). Hermeneutics as a methodology for textual analysis—nursing applications. AORN Journal, 5, 1–4.

[6] Cheng, M. (2002). The standoff—What is unsaid? A pragmatic analysis of the conditional marker "if". Discourse & Society, 13, 309–317.

[7] Chinese Foreign Ministry. (2001). FM spokesman gives full account of air collision. Retrieved April 5, 2001, from http://english. people. com. cn/english/200104/print20010404_66760. html.

[8] CNN. (2001, April 5). Chinese have got to act. Retrieved March 17, 2007, from http://archives. cnn. com/2001/WORLD/asiapcf/east/04/05/china. aircollision. 04/index. html.

[9] Cox, R. (1981). Social forces, state and world orders: Beyond international relations theory. Millennium, 10(2), 126–155.

[10] Donnelly, E. (2004). The United States-China EP-3 incident: Legality and realpolitik. Journal of Conflict & Security Law, 9(1), 25–42.

[11] Faiz, P. M. (2001). Marxist theory of hegemony. Journal Hukum, 1, 1–10.

[12] Gallup Poll. (2001). China. Retrieved March 21, 2007, from http://www. pollingreport. com/china. htm.

[13] Jervis, R. (2003). Understanding the Bush doctrine. Political Science Quarterly, 118(3), 365–388.

[14] Laclau, E., & Mouffe, C. (2001). Hegemony and socialist strategy: Towards a radical democratic politics, (2nd ed.). London and New York: Verso.

[15] Layne, C., & Thayer, B. A. (2007). American empire: A debate. New York, NY: Routledge.

[16] Leatherman, J., & Webber, J. A. (Eds.). (2005). Charting transnational democracy: Beyond global arrogance. New York, NY: Palgrave Macmillan.

[17] Letter from ambassador Prueher to Chinese minister of foreign affairs Tang. (2001). Retrieved March 15, 2007, from http://www. whitehouse. gov/news/releases/2001/04/20010411-1. html.

[18] Mailloux, S. (1985). Rhetorical hermeneutics. Critical Inquiry, 11(4), 620–641.

[19] Martin, P. (2001). US adopting aggressive anti-China posture in aftermath of spy plane crisis. Retrieved April 15, 2007, from http://www. wsws. org/articles/2001/apr2001/chin-a15. shtml.

[20] Monten, J. (2005). The roots of the bush doctrine. International Security, 29(4), 112-156.

[21] Navy Admiral describes aircraft incident in South China Sea. (2002, April 1). Retrieved September 9, 2007, from http://www.fas.org/news/china/2001/china-010401zdb-e3.htm.

[22] Newman, S. (2002). On the future of radical politics. The Drawing Board: An Australian Review of Public Affairs, 7, 1-5.

[23] Newsweek Poll. (2001, March 21). Retrieved September 16, 2007, from http://www.pollingreport.com/china.htm.

[24] Owen, W. F. (1984). Interpretative themes in relational communication. Quarterly Journal of Speech, 70, 274-287.

[25] Posen, B. R. (2003). Command of the commons: The military foundation of the U.S. hegemony. International Security, 28(1), 5-46.

[26] Powell April 3 briefing on U.S.-China aircraft accident. (2001). Retrieved March 28, 2007, from http://www.fas.org/news/china/2001/china-010403zsb1.htm.

[27] Raphael, C. (2003). Theory of hegemony and ideology. Retrieved September 16, 2007, from http://codesign.scu.edu/chad/120/heg.html.

[28] Remarks by Secretary of State Powell expressing regret over loss of Chinese pilot. (2001). Retrieved March 28, 2007, from http://lists.state.gov/SCRIPTS/WA-UNIAINFO.EXE? A2=ind0104a&L=us-china&D=1&H=1&O=D&P=2987.

[29] Senate Resolution 66. (2001). Retrieved April 6, 2007, from http://lists.state.gov/SCRIPTS/WA-UNIAINFO.EXE? A2=ind0104a&L=us-china&D=1&H=1&O=D&P=4027.

[30] Sheng, L. J. (2001). A new U.S. Asia policy?: Air collision, arms sales and China-U.S. relations. Retrieved March 25, 2007, from http://www.iseas.edu.sg/pub.html.

[31] Slingerland, E. B., Blanchard, E. M., & Boyd-Judson, L. (2007). Collision with China: Conceptual metaphor analysis, somatic marking, and the EP-3 incident. International Studies Quarterly 51 (1), 53-77.

[32] Standford, M. (n.d.). Hegemony. New Perspectives 2, 1-3. Retrieved February 9, 2007, from http://www.history-ontheweb.co.uk/concepts/hegemony23.htm.

[33] Statement by the President on American lane and crew in China. (2001). Retrieved March 28, 2007, from http://www.whitehouse.gov/news/releases/2001/04/20010402-2.html.

[34] Statement by the President calling for prompt release of crew and return of plane on April 3. (2001). Retrieved Sept. 5, 2007, from http://www.whitehouse.gov/news/releases/2001/04/20010403-3.html.

[35] Strinati, D. (1995). An Introduction to Theories of Popular Culture. London: Routledge.

[36] Thompson, M. (2001). Spy plane's crew trained to destroy data and technology. Retrieved March 21, 2007, from http://www.time.com/time/world/article/0,8599,104853,00.html.

[37] Thussu, D. K. (2006). International communication: Continuity and change, (2nd ed.). London and New York: Oxford University Press.

[38] Tripattana, K. (2004). A neo-Gramscian approach to interpreting the role of the Thai State in globalization: A case study of the telecommunication section." Paper presented at the International Conference on Revising Globalization & Communication in the 2000s at Bangkok, Thailand. Retrieved February 16, 2007, http://www.commarts.chula.ac.th/revisiting/pdf/07_DR_KA.PDF.

[39] Welcome speech of the President for the U.S. service members. (2001). Retrieved March 28, 2007, from http://lists.state.gov/SCRIPTS/WA-UNIAINFO.EXE? A2=ind0104a&L=us-china&D=1&H=1&O=D&P=1674.

[40] Yee, A. S. (2004). Semantic ambiguity and joint deflections in the Hainan negotiations. China: An International Journal, 2(1), 1-19.

[41] Yang, J. (2001). US - China relations: More bumpy road ahead. New Zealand International Review, 26(4), 14-18.

[42] Yuan, J. D. (2003). Friend or foe? The Bush administration and U.S. China policy in Transition. East Asian Review, 15(3), 39-64.

[43] Zhang, X. L. (2005). News framing: A comparison of the New York Times and the People's Daily coverage of Sino - U.S. spy plane collision of April 1, 2001. A master thesis. University of Central Florida, 2005.

Chapter 15
The Communication Model and the Nature of Change in Terms of Deforestation in China since 1949

Since 1949, China was developing at the sacrifices of human abuse and environmental degradation with Mao's central government-controlled planned economy. Today, China has universally been hailed for its economic growth at an average rate of 9% during the past three decades. Similarly, China has made its economic achievements at a high cost of severe environmental deterioration. In fact, China has already replaced the United States as the world's largest emitter of carbon dioxide (Chang & Hao, 2007, p. 1).

China's environmental plight and subsequent social and natural catastrophes have attracted extensive and growing academic concern. Some scholars (Cui, 2007; Fang et al, 2001; Lang, 2002; Wang, 2004) discussed the environmental consequences as a result of the one-sided emphasis on economic development and population growth in China. Other scholars (Economy, 1998; Harris, 2006; Li, 1998; Smil, 1996; Zhang et al, 1999) explored the internal underlying forces of environmentally-related behaviors and the overwhelming forces of anti-environmental values as a result of the globalization of capitalism and consumerism. Finally, there are also scholars (Lang & Chan, 2006; Liu & Diamond, 2005; Shapiro, 2001) who studied the impact of China's environmental issues upon the neighboring countries in the globalized world.

From the above, we can see that few scholars have touched upon China's environmental issues, especially the organizational change in the Chinese government regarding deforestation from the communication perspective. This study aims to explicate the communication model the Chinese government has been adopting and the nature of change in its forestry management from 1949 to 1978 and from 1979 to the present. Meanwhile, the implications for academics and practitioners in the fields of environmental education and communication will also be discussed.

Theoretical Frameworks and Research Methods

Communication in this study refers to the social interactions between the ordinary Chinese people and the Central Government together with its affiliated agencies at different levels, which is more organizational rather than interpersonal. Organizational communication refers to "communication within and among large, extended environments" (West & Turner 2007, p. 37). Thus, Lasswell's (1948) communication model of "who says

Chapter 15

The Communication Model and the Nature of Change in Terms of Deforestation in China since 1949

what in which channel to whom with what effect" can serve as the theoretical framework as it clarifies the communication act "as a whole in relation to the entire social process" (p. 216). This model predominantly reveals a one-way communication but sometimes a two-way interaction as well. When the dominant party is afraid of the internal and external environment, the "communication process reveals special characteristics" (p. 228). For the purposes of the present study, we will focus on seeking answers to "who says what", "in which channel", and "with what effect" in the model during the two periods in China.

As for the theory of change, Timmerman (2003) stated, "planned organizational change is characterized as a set of activities and processes designed to change individuals, groups, and organizational structure and/or organizational processes" (p. 304). There are four major types of administrative, technological, product, and human resource change. The implementation of such change is usually the conversion of a technology, product, or idea from conceptual knowledge to certain types of organizational practice (pp. 303 – 304). In this study, we intend to interpret the "conversion of a technology, product, or idea from conceptual knowledge to certain types of organizational practice" by the Chinese government and the impact on the change in its administration, technology, product, and human resources.

To this end, we will adopt the research methods of historical analysis and extended literature review. As Zhao (2005) pointed out, historical analysis will illuminate on how our present has come about by providing us with a sense of the past while scholarly research findings may help uncovering those significant aspects hidden from view. Specifically, we will critically analyze the primary data such as the government's relevant policies, campaigns, and statistics from sources like *China Forest Resources Inventories*.

Deforestation and Communication in China from 1949 to 1978

Although ancient China had approximately half of its land covered with forests, China has experienced a cycle of deforestation, mild recovery, and more severe deforestation (Liao, 1987). By 1949, the estimated forest coverage in China remained "13% – 15% using today's definition" (Zhang, 1999, p. 372). Since then, the remaining forests in China have been facing further challenges due to population expansion, construction needs, and misguided administrative policies. For instance, facing both external isolation and internal population growth from 541.7 million in 1949 to 975.2 million in 1978 (State Statistics Bureau, 1949 – 1978), the Chinese government propagated that "China would pick itself up after its long history of humiliation by imperialist powers, become self-reliant in the face of international isolation, and regain strength in the world" (Shapiro, 2001, p. 6). To feed its increasing population, the Chinese government mobilized the farmers, about 85% of the Chinese population then, to clear and burn forest tracts in order to enlarge the cultivated land area. Furthermore, to realize his romantic ideal of vaulting China into the forefront of the world economy and clear away any ideological obstacles in his political control, Mao launched the "Great Leap Forward" from 1958 to 1961 and the "Cultural Revolution" from 1966 to 1976. During both nationwide campaigns, devastating deforestation took place. Just as Li (1990) remarked, "a vicious cycle appears to characterize the relationship between population growth and deforestation in China" (p. 255). The question here is what type of a communication model was prevalent then for Mao to turn his fancy ideas into national policies and make almost the whole nation follow him blindly?

The Top-down communication model with Chinese characteristics. For leapfrogs of development in the 1950s and 60s, Mao's government was practicing a top-down communication model. This model was composed of the Chinese Central Government led by the Chinese Communist Party (CCP) at the top sending its commanding policies via a network of sound broadcasting, loudspeaker system, newspapers, bulletin boards, and folk media to all the Chinese people. Due to the low cost and easy control, the CCP laid great emphasis on the implementation of a nationwide web of sound broadcasting and loudspeaker systems, which became "fully fledged in 1976" (Zhao, 2005, p. 13). While the sound broadcasting system entered each household to ensure voluntary listening from household to household, the system of loudspeakers on the top of tall trees in the countryside and high buildings in cities was operated by full-time personnel to guarantee regular reception of the CCP policies by the general public.

According to research statistics, broadcasting units increased from 835 in 1955 to 11,124 in 1959, and loud speakers increased from 90,500 in 1955 to 106 million in 1976 (Bishop, 1989; Chang, 1989). Besides, *People's Daily*, which was fully sponsored by the CCP and set the tone for all other media in China, has been the most important newspaper, with a circulation of three million. Until 2003, subscriptions to this newspaper were mandatory for all state-owned enterprises and government agencies (Yin, 2006). Bulletin boards were blackboards cemented in walls standing in conspicuous locations in villages and hard boards in obvious positions in urban areas, which carried new announcements or official instructions from Mao and a few other top CCP leaders almost on a daily basis. Finally, the CCP also transformed the traditional modes of Chinese mass media like theater, story-telling, ballad singing, and poetry reciting as effective channels of oral communication to bypass the widespread illiteracy (Liu, 1964).

Thus, a top-down communication model with special Chinese characteristics was established. To guarantee efficiency, Mao claimed four tasks for the Chinese media: to propagate the policies of the Communist Party, to educate the masses, to organize the masses, and to mobilize the masses (Bishop, 1989). The media technologies adopted at the time are not necessarily new or advanced, but what "was set in motion" is obviously "a one-way flow of influence-oriented messages from the change agencies at the top to the rural peasantry at the bottom" (Melkote & Steeves, 2001, p. 56). The ordinary Chinese people could just hear one type of voice from one information disseminating agent, Mao's government, which formulated environmental policies without public consultation. For

Chapter 15

The Communication Model and the Nature of Change in Terms of Deforestation in China since 1949

efficiency, the messages from the government were simplified as short slogans such as:

> Man must conquer heaven.
> Grain is the backbone for the nation.
> Create farmland by encircling the lake.
> Cultivate on the top of mountains, and plant rice at the center of lakes.
> How much courage you have, and how much yield the field will produce (Bao, 2006, p. 37).

When the Chinese people, especially those in the rural areas, received such messages in the form of offcial policies or the "highest instructions" from their sanctified CCP, they treated the messages as commands and immediately plunged into waves of mass campaigns launched by the local governments to seek grain from the lakes, grasslands, and mountain tops and development of the country through "large-scale deforestation, even on sloping, low-yielding land" (Démurger, Hou, & Yang, 2007, p. 3). However, their idealist behaviors violated the principles of nature and resulted in massive economic dislocation and immense waste of resources.

Deforestation and its impact. Deforestation refers to the conversion of forest to another land use or long-term reduction of the tree canopy cover below a 10% threshold, which is the loss or continual degradation of forest habitat due to either natural or human related causes (The Regents of the University of Michigan, 2006). According to China's *National Forest Resources Inventories*, the statistics of China's forest resources can be shown as follows:

Table 1   China's Forest Resources, 1973 – 2003

Yeas of Inventory	Forestry Land		Forest		Forest Cover
	Area $\frac{}{mill.\ ha}$	Stock $\frac{}{bill.\ M^3}$	Area $\frac{}{mill.\ ha}$	Stock $\frac{}{bill.\ M^3}$	%
1973 – 1976	257.6	10.3	121.9	9.4	12.7
1977 – 1981	267.1	10.3	115.3	9.0	12.0
1984 – 1988	267.4	10.6	124.7	9.1	12.3
1989 – 1993	262.9	11.8	133.7	10.1	13.9
1994 – 1998	263.3	12.5	153.6	11.3	16.6
1999 – 2003	282.8	13.6	174.9	12.5	18.2

Sources: Ministry of Forestry. *China's National Forest Resources Inventories* (1973 – 2003)

As Table 1 indicates, up to 1981, forest area in China has been declining from 121.9 million hectare to 115.3 million hectare. Based on the statistics in the above table and the analysis of Zhang (2000), it is reasonable to believe that China's forest coverage dropped from about 15% in 1949 to 12% toward the end of the 1970s. Mao's campaigns of the "Great Leap Forward" (1958 – 1961) and the "Cultural Revolution" (1966 – 1976) took place during these time periods, both of which destructed China's forests with fatal consequences.

According to scholars (Joseph, 1986; Shapiro, 2001; Zhang et al., 1999), the Great Leap Forward demonstrated Mao's urgency to achieve a type of utopian socialism, which led to widespread deforestation. To fuel backyard blast furnaces for the increase of iron and steel output, roughly 10% of China's forest cover was felled. In addition, more trees were cleared from hills and mountains so as to convert the forested land into grain fields. The Cultural Revolution wrought even greater devastation. For a whole decade, most Chinese in the nation were mobilized into a frenzy campaign to remold the earth for grain production without taking regional variations and local practices into consideration. Consequently, the forest coverage shrunk from 12.7% to 12% as shown in Table 1. Just as Shapiro (2001) remarked, "the relationship between humans and nature under Mao is so transparent and extreme that it clearly indicates a link between abuse of people and abuse of the natural environment" (p. xii).

The impact of deforestation brought about a chain reaction of soil erosion and flooding in China. Zhang et al. (2000) noted, the size of eroded lands kept increasing so rapidly in China that 38% of China's total land area is considered badly eroded by 1999. Chokkalingam, Zhou, Wang, and Toma (2006) also confirmed that severe soil erosion from the topless slopes of hills and mountains led to catastrophic floods in 1959 and 1960 followed by a three-year famine from 1961 to1963. China's agriculture suffered a 30% loss in production, and over 20 million people died of starvation during the famine. Upon reflection, Mao's intention to vault China into the forefront of the world's economy made China fall farther behind other countries.

Deforestation and Change in China from 1979 to the Present

According to the State Environmental Protection Administration of China (2007), China is one of the world's most forest-deficient countries. As of 2006, China's forest coverage is 18.2%, with only 0.1 hectare of forest per person as compared with the world average of 0.6 hectare. China's growing population and economic growth continue degrading the limited forests since 1979. It was after the 1998 Yangtze River flood that the government has fully recognized the tight link between deforestation and environmental degradation. Since then, the world has been witnessing a paradigmatic shift in China's forest policies and the immediate and far-reaching impact of such change upon the global environment.

Growth of media and continued deforestation. Since its economic reform in 1979, the new and pragmatic Chinese leadership renounced mass political movements and emphasized economic development. To modernize the country, the government first made a successful experiment with the household contract and responsibility system in the rural area in 1982. In 1992, China began adopting a socialist market economy by expanding such incentives as encouraging experiments in enterprise autonomy and reducing central planning.

To attune themselves to the demands of the market, media in China began receiving "multi-channel financing" from not only the government but also advertising and paid news since the 1980s. Major media such as radio, newspaper, and television as well as the Internet went full fledge into their development. For example, the number of radio stations and newspapers increased from 99 and 69 in 1979 to 278 and 791 in 1987 respectively (Chen, 1991). Updated satellite broadcasting network had covered 90% of the country with TV by

Chapter 15

The Communication Model and the Nature of Change in Terms of Deforestation in China since 1949

the end of 2000. The number of registered Internet users grew from 8.9 million in 1999 to 79.5 million in 2003 (Lu & Wong, 2003).

It is true that the development of telecommunications has revolutionized the channel of communication in China. However, tight control of the CCP over the functions of media in China still remains. The CCP still "organizes, coordinates and supervises all forms of communication, be it traditional or modern" (Zhao, 2005, p. 27). On the one hand, access to various communication channels makes it possible for "a juxtaposition of top-down flow of information at the national level, an upward flow of information from the grassroots and a horizontal flow of information among the local units" (Zhao, 2005, p. 27). On the other hand, the Chinese government makes sure that mass media can only play a participant and collaborating instead of an adversary role in China so as to safeguard the Party's ideology and national interests.

As the goals of the Chinese government were primarily focused on production and economic output, government officials at various levels during the 1980s and 1990s prioritized the common saying of "First Development, Then Environment" (Siciliano, 2006, p. 2). China's economy has been developing dramatically, but the problem of deforestation still remained. Even though China has strengthened its afforestation campaigns since the 1980s, efforts in the campaigns turned out to be "massive planting failures" due to "poor site selection, poor species/site adaptation, poor techniques, and inadequate supervision" (Zhu, James & Hanover, 1987, p. 41). Thus, China's total forest coverage has increased from approximately 13% in 1950 to over 18% in 2003, but the volume and area of natural forests dropped dramatically, and the quality of forests in general decreased (Zhao & Shao, 2002).

Deforestation consequences and the paradigmatic shift. Due to continuous deforestation of the natural forests and the decrease of the forest quality in general, China has been challenged with a long list of environmental problems and bombarded with alternating natural disasters of droughts and floods. Droughts damage about 160,000 km^2 of cropland and destroy large quantities of vulnerable vegetation each year. The number of dust storms in China has increased from once every 31 years before 1949 to several times almost every year since 1990. The 1998 floods along the Yangtze River, Songhua River, and Nenjiang River devastated large areas, killed 3,600 people, and left 14 million people homeless with an estimated loss of U.S. $24 billion. Just as scholars (Harris, 2006; Liu & Diamond, 2005; Ma, 2008) described, China has been plagued with pervasive and widespread environmental problems of choking air pollution, water pollution and water shortages throughout much of the country, near-total deforestation, and depletion of agricultural land. Worst of all, China's environmental problems have been affecting other parts of the world as well. Weather satellites have detected that dust and aerial pollutants from China have crossed the Pacific Ocean and reached neighboring countries including even the west coast of the United States.

All this has awakened the Chinese government to take substantial measures. According to scholars (Yamane, 2001; Yamane & Lu, 2002; Zhang et al., 2000), the Chinese government has been making a paradigmatic shift in its forest management by: first, launching the Natural Forest Conservation Program (NFCP) through a set of polices to increase the efficiency of domestic timber production under sustainable forestry management; second, implementing free trade in forest products as a state policy. Designed to run from 1998 to 2010, the NFCP aims at planting trees for soil and water protection and protecting existing natural forests from excessive logging throughout the country. With an investment of 17 billion RMB for NFCP, the Chinese government expects a gradual decrease in its annual logging quota, and a determined restructuring of the logging industry. In terms of timber trade, the value of China's forest product imports rose from $6.4 billion to $16.4 billion between 1997 and 2005. By now, China has become the leading importer of industrial round-wood and the world's largest wood workshop. The main suppliers of China's imports as of 2005 are Russia, accounting for 48.8%, Malaysia, 8.3%, Indonesia, 5.7%, Thailand, 4.6%, and Papua New Guinea, 4.2% (White, 2006, pp. 4 – 12).

The nature of change. In terms of deforestation in China since 1979, there has been profound change in institutional conception and organizational practice. On the one hand, there has been a paradigmatic shift in the conception of the Chinese government regarding natural forestry from the neglect in Mao's era to awakened attention among top national leaders since Deng's economic reform in 1979, thus bringing about planned changes in forest management. The administrative change could be demonstrated by the enactment of the Forest Law of PRC in 1984, the implementation of the ban on logging, and reinforcement of the NFCP in 1998. As for the change in managing human and natural resoureces, 45,000 workers have been shifted from logging to tree planting in Sichuan Province alone since the program started (Zhang, 2000).

On the other hand, the Chinese government is maintaining its economic growth by instituting the planned change in its organizational practice by making full use of all available technology to produce whatever products needed in the world market. To meet the increasing demand for resources, China has been expanding its timber imports and wood product exports annually, thus relocating deforestation from China to other countries. Just as Sun, Katsigris, and White (2004) noted, the Chinese efforts in forest conservation have increased its forest coverage from 12% in 1981 to 18.2% in 2003, but deforestation has partially moved to the other parts of the world, like Russia, Malaysia, and Thailand.

Conclusion

The purposes of this study were to explore the communication model between the Chinese government and the Chinese people and the nature of change in the Chinese government's policies and practices regarding deforestation from 1949 to 1978 and from 1979 to the present. By adopting the research methods of historical analysis and extended literature review through the theoretical lenses of Lasswell's communication model and the

Chapter 15

The Communication Model and the Nature of Change in Terms of Deforestation in China since 1949

theory of change, we have discovered the following research findings.

First, in the relatively isolated China from 1949 to 1978, the Chinese government was issuing unrealistic policies such as reclaiming forests for arable land and using logs to fuel backyard furnaces for the increase of iron and steel output. Via an effective network of sound broadcasting, loudspeaker system, newspapers, bulletin boards, and folk media, Mao's government extensively mobilized the whole nation to plunge into campaigns like the three-year "Great Leap Forward" and the 10-year "Cultural Revolution." As a result, China almost collapsed economically and suffered from natural disasters of flooding and famines partially due to the massive deforestation during the campaigns.

Second, since its economic reform in 1979, China has experienced a gradual paradigmatic shift in the conception of the government regarding forest management. A planned change has been witnessed with the enactment of the Forest Law of PRC in 1984, the implementation of the ban on logging, and reinforcement of the NFCP in 1998. Although the development of telecommunications makes it possible for some sort of horizontal and even upward flow of information, the Chinese government still tightly controls the mainstream media, which effectively assists the government with its reorientation of the workforce from loggers to tree growers and furniture makers using timber from foreign lands.

Finally, despite of the above change in the Chinese government, one thing that remains unchanged is that China has been developing at the great costs of degrading the environment, especially in terms of deforestation within China yesterday and outside China today and tomorrow. Due to China's sharp annual increase of timber imports and wood product exports, deforestation has been relocated from China to other countries. This has actually overshadowed China's achievements in expanding the forest coverage and already drawn international attention to the potential impact upon global environmental protection. When we think of the connectivity and the potential chain reactions in the process of globalization, it is not just the academics but all practitioners in the field of environmental education and communication that should communicate the urgent message to all the people of the world including the Chinese to seek sustainable development globally instead of in one area or just one country.

(Tian, D. X., & Chao, C. C. (2010). Communication model and the nature of change in terms of deforestation in China since 1949. *Applied Environmental Education and Communication*, 9(2), 122 – 130.)

References

[1] Bao, M. H. (2006). The evolution of environmental policy and its impact in the People's Republic of China. Conservation and society, 4(1), 36 – 54.

[2] Bishop, R. L. (1989). Qi lai! Mobilizing one billion Chinese: The Chinese

communication system. Ames, IA: Iowa State University Press.

[3] Chang, W. H. (1989). Mass media in China: The history and the future. Ames, IA: Iowa State University Press.

[4] Chang, L, & Hao, Y. (2007, June 21). China will responsibly participate in jointly formulating the international community's proposal to counteract climate change. Xinhua News Agency.

[5] Chen, L. (1991). Culture, politics, communication and development: A tentative study on the case of China. Gazette, 48(3), 1-16.

[6] Chokkalingam et al. (2006). Learning lessons from China's forest rehabilitation efforts: National level review and special focus on Guangdong Province. Jakarta, Indonesia: Center for International Forestry Research.

[7] Cui, X. (2007). Hydrological impacts of deforestation on the southeast Tibetan plateau. Earth Interactions, 11(15), 1-18.

[8] Démurger, S., Hou, Y. Z., & Yang, W. Y. (2007). Forest management policies and resource balance in China: An assessment of the current situation. Unpublished paper. Retreived Oct. 2, 2009, from ftp://ftp.gate.cnrs.fr/RePEc/2007/0712.pdf.

[9] Economy, E. E. (1998). China's environmental diplomacy. In S. S. Kim, (Ed.), China and the world: Chinese foreign policy faced the new millennium. Boulder: Westview Press.

[10] Fang et al. (2001). Changes in forest biomass carbon storage in China between 1949 and 1998. Science Magazine, 292, 2320-2322.

[11] Harkness, J. (2007). Recent trends in forestry and conservation of biodiversity in China. The China Quarterly, 156, 911-934.

[12] Harris, P. G. (2006). Environmental perspectives and behavior in China: Synopsis and bibliography. Environment and Behavior, 38(5), 5-21.

[13] Joseph, W. A. (1986). A tragedy of good intentions: Post-Mao views of the Great Leap Forward. Modern China, 12(4), 419-457.

[14] Lang, G. (2002). Forests, floods, and the environmental state in China. Organization and Environment, 15(2), 109-130.

[15] Lang, G., & Chan, C. H. W. (2006). China's impact on forests in Southeast Asia. Journal of Contemporary Asia, 36(2), 167-194.

[16] Lasswell, H. (1948). The structure and function of communication insociety. In L. Bryson (Ed.), The Communication of Ideas. New York, NY: Harper & Brothers.

[17] Li, H. (1998). Some thoughts on Confucianism and eco-feminism. In M. E. Tucker & J. Berthrong, (Ed.), Confucianism and ecology: The interrelation of heaven, earth, and humans. Cambridge, MA: Harvard University Press.

[18] Li, J. N. (1990). Population effects on deforestation and soil erosion in China. Population and Development Review, 16, 254-258.

[19] Liao, S. (1987). Introduction to forestry economics. Beijing: China Forestry

Publishing House.

[20] Liu, A. P. L. (1964). Radio broadcasting in Communist China. Cambridge, MA: Massachusetts Institute of Technology Press.

[21] Lu, D. , & Wong, C. K. (2003). China's telecommunicas market: Entering a new competitive age. UK: Edward Elgar Publishing Limited.

[22] Ma, T. J. (2008). Interconnected forests: Global and domestic impacts of China's forestry conservation. Unpublished paper. Retrieved Nov. 16, 2008, from http://www.wilsoncenter.org/topics/docs/forestry_aug08.pdf.

[23] Melkote, S. R. & Steeves, H. L. (2001). Communication for development in the Third World: Theory and practice for empowerment (2nd ed.). Thousand Oaks, CA: Sage.

[24] Ministry of Forestry. Various years. China's National Forest Resources Statistics (1973 – 1976, 1977 – 1981, 1984 – 1988, 1989 – 1993, 1994 – 1998, 1999 – 2003). Beijing: China's Forestry Publishing House.

[25] Shapiro, J. (2001). Mao's war against nature: Politics and the environment in revolutionary China. Cambridge, MA: Cambridge University Press.

[26] Siciliano, M. (2006). Policy and management: Development first, then environment. The Heinz School Review, Spring, 1 – 14.

[27] Smil, V. (1996). Barriers to a sustainable China. In D. C. Pirages, (Ed.), Building sustainable societies: A blueprint for a post – industrial world. Armonk, NY: M. E. Sharpe.

[28] State Environmental Protection Administration of China. (2007). China's biodiversity: A country study. Chinagate. Retrieved Oct. 19, 2008, from http://us.tom.com/english/2036.html.

[29] State Statistical Bureau. Various years. Statistical Yearbook of China. Beijing: China Statistical Publishing House.

[30] Sun, X., Katsigris, E., & White, A. (2004). Meeting China's demand for forest products: An overview of important trends, ports of entry, and supplying countries with emphasis on the Asia-Pacific region, International Forestry Review, 6 (3 – 4), 227 – 236.

[31] The Regents of the University of Michigan. (2006). Global deforestation. Retrieved July 11, 2006, from http://www.globalchange.edu/globalchange2/current/lectures/deforest.html.

[32] Timmerman, C. E. (2003). Media selection during the implementation of planned organizational change: A predictive framework based on implementation approach and phase. Management Communication Quarterly, 16(3), 301 – 340.

[33] Wang, Y. (2004). Environmental degradation and environmental threats in China. Environmental Monitoring and Assessment, 90, 161 – 169.

[34] West, R., & Turner, L. H. (2007). Introducing communication theory: Analysis

and application. New York, NY: McGraw‑Hill.

[35] White et al. (2006). China and the global market for forest products: Transforming trade to benefit forests and livelihoods. Forest Trends, 1 – 31.

[36] Yamane, M. (2001). China's recent forest-related policies: Overview and background— from the perspective of economic growth and forest conservation. Policy Trend Report, 1 – 12.

[37] Yamane, M., & Lu, W. (2002). Trends in China's forest-related policies—from the perspective of the growing timber trade. Policy Trend Report, 1 – 11.

[38] Yin, J. (2006). China's second long march: A review of Chinese media discourse on globalization. The Review of Communication, 6(1 – 2), 32 – 51.

[39] Zhang, Y. Q. (2000). Deforestation and forest transition: Theory and evidence in China. In M. Palo and H. Vanhanen (Eds.). World forests from deforestation to transition? Dordrecht: Kluwer Academic Publishers.

[40] Zhang et al. (1999). The forest sector in China: Towards a market economy. World Forestry, society and Environment, Special Theme, 371 – 393.

[41] Zhang et al. (2000, June 23). China's forest policy for the 21st century. Science, 288, 2135 – 2136.

[42] Zhang et al. (2007). Land use change and land degradation in China from 1991 to 2001. Land Degradation & Development, 18, 209 – 219.

[43] Zhao, J. Q. (2005). Communication and rural development in China: A historical review. Unpublished paper, 1 – 33. Retrieved Oct. 12, 2009, from http://web.ebscohost.com/ehost/detail? vid = 6&hid = 6&sid = a5d0bebf-9a03-466e – ade8 – 23d7.

[44] Zhao, G., & Shao, G. F. (2002). Logging restrictions in China: A turning point for forest sustainability. Journal of Forest, 6, 34 – 37.

[45] Zhu, X. T., James, L. M., & Hanover, J. W. (1987). Land-cover change analysis of China using global-scale pathfinder. Journal of Forestry, 1, 41 – 43.

Chapter 16
Like Tiger Mother, Like Tiger Daughter: A Content Analysis of the Impact of Cultural Differences on Eastern and Western Parenting Styles

The 2011 publication of *Battle Hymn of the Tiger Mother* by Amy Chua, a Yale University professor, and the ensuing publicity have triggered extensive attention to and heated discussions about the "tough-love" parenting style. When her prepublication excerpt entitled "Why Chinese Mothers Are Superior" (Chua, January, 2011) was published in the *Wall Street Journal*, the topic of "the" Chinese parenting style not only stirred up a controversy in the U. S. but also evoked heated international debates. So far, the online article has been read more than one million times and has attracted more than 8,800 comments that critique Amy Chua's "Tiger Mom" parenting style and compare and contrast the advantages and disadvantages of Eastern and Western parenting styles (All the comments are available at http://online.wsj.com/article/SB10001424052748704111504576059713528698754.html#articleTabs%3Dcomments).

Amy Chua was born in an academic family as the eldest of four daughters. Her father has been a successful scientist and educator, who grew up in a Chinese immigrant family from the Philippines and came to the U. S. where he earned a Ph. D. degree from the University of Illinois at Urbana-Champaign. He was extremely strict with his children. For instance, "our report cards had to be perfect; while our friends were rewarded for Bs, for us getting an A-minus was unthinkable" (Chua, 2011, p. 16). Amy's husband is a law professor at Yale University, and he "always took my side in front of the girls" (Chua, 2011, p. 171). Thus, Amy's daughters were brought up in an extraordinarily academic environment. According to Wilson and Wilson (1992), the educational level of parents is one of the indicators of a family's social status. In addition, the children whose parents have high educational levels will have high expectations of their education as well. The ideas here echo those of Chua, and that is why she made the following list that her daughters, Sophia and Louisa, were never allowed to do: "attend a sleepover; have a playdate; be in a school play; complain about not being in a school play; watch TV or play computer games; choose their own extracurricular activities; get any grade less than an A; not be the No. 1 student in every subject except gym and drama; play any instrument other than the piano or violin; not play the piano or violin" (Chua, 2011, para. 2).

However, raising children, or parenting, is not a one-dimensional job, either with purely strict disciplines or utter permissiveness. Parenting is situated in a multi-dimensional matrix under the influence of social and cultural changes (Spera, 2005). With the mindset of integrating the seemingly different perspectives of education and parenting styles between the U.S. and the China, this chapter analyzes the online comments posted to Chua's article and explores the representative themes relating to Eastern and Western styles of parenting. Specifically, by quantitatively examining the selected online forum responses, this chapter aims to explore the anticipated cultural perceptions of success in children as a result of different parenting styles and reveal the Eastern and Western preferences to and differences in parenting approaches.

Literature Review

Parenting plays an important role in a person's growth. It is from families that children first receive warmth, nutrition, support, and education. Parents provide the first essential environment in which children grow up and learn to socialize with others. Socialization is seen as the process by which children become familiar with the set of social standards of the adults in a particular culture (Parke & Buriel, 1998). Other scholars (Grusec, 1997; Parke & Buriel, 1998; Spera, 2005) also claimed that socialization is the process through which parents convey their values, goals, and attitudes to their children. Thus, parents in different cultures exert a great deal of impact on the growth of their children with different parenting styles.

Parenting styles have been studied for decades and have been categorized into single-dimension, two-dimension, and multi-dimension models (Ang, 2006; Baumrind, 1971; Becker, 1964; Chao, 2001; Darling & Steinberg, 1993; Maccoby & Martin, 1983; Tam & Lam, 2003). Based on warmth, demandingness, and autonomy granting, Baumrind (1966) proposed three major types of the single-dimensional parenting style: authoritarian, authoritative, and permissive. Maccoby and Martin (1983) added a conceptual fourth style, neglectful. According to Karavasilis, Doyle, and Markiewicz (2003), it is characteristic for the authoritarian parenting style to reveal low responsiveness, high demandingness, and low levels of autonomy granting while the authoritative parenting style to demonstrate high responsiveness, high demandingness, and high autonomy granting. Whereas a permissive parent manifests high levels of responsiveness, autonomy granting, and low levels of demandingness, a neglectful parent is disengaged, showing low levels of responsiveness, demandingness, and autonomy granting.

Based on Baumrind's (1966, 1971) initial model, Maccoby and Martin (1983) proposed a two-dimensional framework of parental socialization in which the dimensions of responsiveness and demandingness were mirrored with the traditional parenting dimensions of warmth and strictness. From the combination of the two dimensions—responsiveness (warmth) and demandingness (strictness), they further defined four types of parenting styles: authoritative-responsive and demanding, neglectful-neither responsive nor demanding, indulgent-responsive but not demanding, and authoritarian-demanding but not

Chapter 16

Like Tiger Mother, Like Tiger Daughter: A Content Analysis of the Impact of Cultural Differences on Eastern and Western Parenting Styles

responsive. This two-dimensional framework reveals a continuum in parenting styles, first, with warmth/responsiveness on one end and hostility/rejection on the other, and, second, with control/restrictiveness on one end and autonomy/permissiveness on the other.

With regard to multi-dimensional parenting style, Becker (1964) classified parenting styles into three dimensions: restrictiveness-permissive indulgence, warmth-hostility, and anxious emotion involvement-calm detachment. These dimensions are subdivided into eight types, which are permissive, democratic, anxious neurotic, neglecting, strict control, authoritative, organized effective, and overprotective. Although the classification of multi-dimensions is comparatively more complete, it is less practicable due to complexity.

Having reviewed the three dimensions of parenting styles, we now connect children's achievements and parenting styles to cultural influence. In fact, parenting styles have been used as predictors in correlational studies of a wide variety of children characteristics, including self-concept, psychosocial maturity, moral development, independence, social skills, cooperation with adults and peers, cognitive competence, and academic success (Johnson, 1998). In addition, more research attention has been paid to examine the influence of parenting styles across ethnicity, socioeconomic status, and family structure (Steinberg et al., 1992). In terms of ethnicity, quite a few studies (Bingham & Okagaki, 2004; Chao, 2001; Pearce, 2006) have identified academic achievements with specific racial or cultural factors.

For instance, Bingham and Okagaki (2004) found parents' cultural values have been tied to their social cognitions, which include parenting beliefs, goals, and attitudes. Chao (2001) reaffirmed that since the typical ways in which family members relate to each other are culturally bound, "the parenting style then can also be seen as a reflection of culture" (p. 1833). In his study of cultural effects on educational achievements, Pearce (2006) remarked, "cultural explanations tie outcomes to the beliefs and values taught and leaned at the fine unit of family" (p. 78). Although cultural generalizations and stereotyping "may appear dangerous, they are nevertheless necessary if a study's results are to have any application beyond the study's immediate participants" (Pearce, 2006, p. 77).

To extend the above research and achieve the purposes of this study described above, we developed the following research questions:

RQ1: Is there a difference between Eastern and Western parenting styles?

RQ2: What are the main factors that affect Eastern or Western parenting style adoption?

RQ3: Is there a difference between Eastern and Western parenting toward their anticipated children's achievements?

Method

To find answers to our research questions, we used the research method of content analysis which is defined as a process of "systematic, objective, quantitative analysis of message characteristics" (Naccarato & Neuendorf, 1998, p. 20). In this study, we used this research method to analyze online responses to Amy Chua's prepublication excerpt entitled "Why Chinese Mothers Are Superior" released in the *Wall Street Journal* on January 31, 2011.

From the date of its publication to August 15, 2012, the online article has been read more than one million times and has attracted more than 8,859 comments. In order to ensure a meaningful generalization from the sample, a systematic random sample consisting of every 20th comment (Wrench et al., 2008) was coded and analyzed. For the purposes of this study, our analysis only focused on those responses regarding parenting perspectives and parenting styles. Unrelated responses on issues such as racism, communism, history, economy, criticism or duplicated comments were excluded. The starting point was chosen using the random integer calculator from the website random.org. Thus, 440 responses were randomly selected, but only 312 in total, which met our coding standards, were coded for analysis.

As mentioned in our literature review, we applied Maccoby and Martin's (1983) parenting approach, which includes authoritarian, authoritative, indulgent/permissive, and neglecting dimensions. We also took into account such potentially important variables as gender, ethnicity, socioeconomic status, and parents' anticipations of their children's abilities and traits, and respondents' tones to Amy Chua's parenting style. To avoid inconsistent coding, we operationalized the independent and dependent variables, as well as the unit of analysis based on the parenting approach of Maccoby and Martin (1983).

Results

As mentioned above, we randomly selected a total of 440 responses to the article "Why Chinese Mothers Are Superior", and 312 responses that met our coding standards were coded for analysis. Through an analysis of the variables that were identified as influencing the parenting styles, we managed to objectively investigate the factors that affect Western and Eastern parenting styles and perspectives. The examined variables included the gender of respondents, ethnicity of respondents, parenting involvement, parenting styles, anticipated child's abilities, anticipated child's traits, and the tone of Amy Chua's parenting style. Sample frequencies were also calculated by SPSS from the 312 responses in the sample. After each variable was analyzed, difference testing was conducted. The overall sample frequencies and differential percentages were reported first, and then the results of the difference testing in relation to the research questions were provided. Following are the research results of or answers to the three research questions.

RQ1: Is there a difference between Eastern and Western parenting styles?

A chi-square was conducted to assess whether Eastern and Western parents perform different parenting styles. The result for this test was significant: $\chi 2\ (10, N=308) = 89.530, p<0.0005$. That means that a statistically significant difference occurs between

Chapter 16

Like Tiger Mother, Like Tiger Daughter: A Content Analysis of the Impact of Cultural Differences on Eastern and Western Parenting Styles

Eastern and Western in their perceptions of adopted parenting approaches. As a post hoc analysis, 10 pairwise comparisons were calculated to determine where the actual differences are. To avoid Type 1 error in this procedure, a Dunn-Sidak procedure was conducted to correct possible compounded error due to the 10 pairwise comparisons. The new calculated alpha value is $p<0.005$. Based on the new alpha value, only one pairwise comparison was found to be statistically significant: Authoritative Style and Indulgent Style, $\chi2(1, N=238)=28.756$, $p<0.0005$. Therefore, the answer to RQ1 is positive.

RQ2: What are the main factors that affect Eastern or Western parenting style adoption?

As discussed earlier, many variables have been examined as factors that might affect the applied parenting styles such as developmental level, gender, environmental or cultural factors (Johnson, 1998). Steinberg et al. (1991) and Baumrind (1989) also examined the influence of parenting styles across ethnicity, socioeconomic status, family structure, age, and involvement. We did take these variables into consideration at first, but only 3%-5% of the respondents revealed their education, age, child age, or socioeconomic status. Since these factors were too scarce for analysis, this study did not count them as significantly potential factors. Instead, we focused on environmental or cultural factors of gender and parenting involvement.

Chi-square tests were used to examine the differences between the adopted parenting styles to the categorical variables of gender and involvement. While gender was not significant to parenting styles ($\chi2=13.554$; $p=0.094$), involvement was found to be statistically significant, $\chi2(8, N=244)=75.380$, $p<0.0005$. This means that, among the examined factors of the respondents' gender and ethnicity, parenting involvement, parenting styles, and anticipated children's abilities and traits, and the tone of Amy Chua's parenting style, parenting involvement is a major factor that affects Eastern or Western parenting style adoption.

RQ3: Is there a difference between Eastern and Western parenting toward their anticipated children's achievements?

A chi-square was conducted to assess the differences between parenting styles to the nominal variables of anticipated abilities and anticipated traits. This study found that the anticipated traits were not significant ($\chi2=10.838$; $p=0.543$), but the anticipated abilities were found to be statistically significant, $\chi2(20, N=298)=131.394$, $p<0.0005$. That means that a statistically significant difference occurs between the adopted parenting styles and their anticipations toward their children's abilities. Therefore, the answer to RQ 3 is also positive.

As a post hoc analysis revealed, only one pairwise comparison was found to be statistically significant: Authoritative Style and Indulgent Style, $\chi2(1, N=230)=43.169$, $p<0.0005$. Apart from the above, this study found that the number of male respondents is

2.45 times (69.2%) that of female respondents (28.2%), while the number of Western respondents (67.9%) is 2.4 times that of Eastern respondents (28.2%). Only 15.3% of the respondents commented on the overall parenting involvement, with 14.7% mentioning high involvement in children's learning, 0.6% mentioning intermediate involvement, and the rest providing a "Don't know." As for the parenting styles, the majority of the samples tend to prefer a liberal/indulgent approach (39.1%), followed by the authoritative style (37.2%), authoritarian (7.7%), and neglecting (1.3%). This situation shows that overall Western and Eastern respondents are either pro-permissive or pro-authoritative.

Discussion

The overarching goal of the present study was to better understand the difference between Eastern and Western parenting styles and the factors that may influence the adopted parenting styles. The findings of this investigative study revealed that the respondents' gender did not make a difference in the selection of parenting styles. However, their ethnicity did influence parenting perspectives. Western parents tended to apply the indulgent style most (50%), followed by authoritative style (30%), authoritarian style (8%), and neglecting style (2%). In contrast, Eastern parents tended to use the authoritative style most (61%), followed by indulgent (21%) and authoritarian (9%).

In addition to parenting involvement, there are also many other factors that may affect parenting approaches. For instance, Teachman and Paasch (1998) posited that, with higher income, parents can provide their children with more learning resources and create a better environment to facilitate their academic performance. According to Johnson (1998), children of authoritative parents tend to be more competent and self-confident. These extant findings are reconfirmed by Chua's case, in which both parents are professors at a prestigious university, and their two daughters have both demonstrated excellent academic achievement.

Furthermore, parenting styles also have been examined as the predictor variables in correlational studies of a wide range of children's abilities or traits, including self-concept, maturity, moral development, independence, social skills, and cooperation, competence (Putallaz & Heflin, 1990). The answer to RQ3 in the present study confirmed part of the aforesaid research findings. In our study, indulgent parents tend to value creativity most (47%), followed by confidence (29%), hard-working (18%), and competence (5%). However, authoritative parents would focus on children's competence first (43%) for a better future, followed by hard-working (24%), confidence (21%), and creativity (12%). The findings imply that authoritative parents will require their children to have a top-grade education with marketable skills in order to succeed in the future while indulgent parents focus more on children's personality and happiness.

It is also worth pointing out here that almost half of the respondents revealed a negative tone toward Chua's parenting style (48.1%), followed by a positive tone (28.8%), partial agreement with (10.3%), and a neutral voice (8.3%). On the one hand, many Western

Chapter 16

Like Tiger Mother, Like Tiger Daughter: A Content Analysis of the Impact of Cultural Differences on Eastern and Western Parenting Styles

respondents do not want to admit that Chinese parenting style is superior; instead, they found Chua's article in the *Wall Street Journal* "stupid, arrogant, and obviously provocative" (Respondent 382). On the other hand, even the Eastern respondents do not think Chua's parenting style is typically Chinese. For instance, as a Chinese immigrant and father of a 7-year-old, "I feel sorry about Ms. Chua, for she apparently did not have the connection with Chinese culture, and she misunderstood many aspects of Chinese parenting. In her family, Chinese tradition has long lost" (Respondent 371).

Many other respondents even claimed that this is not the debate between Chinese or Eastern and Western parenting styles. Instead, it is a conflict between an *Asian American* parenting approach and the dominant U.S. perspective on parenting. Amy Chua is a Filipino of Chinese descent. Her parents immigrated to the U.S. and underwent an intense struggle to plant their roots in a foreign land that inevitably led them to adopt a more utilitarian outlook in raising their children. As she said to her daughters in her book "We struggled to get you this new citizenship status, the best way to repay us as our children is to succeed in life" (Chua, 2011, p. 58). The Chinese, especially those Chinese Americans like the Jewish and Indian immigrants to the U.S. have had to fight for themselves and survive in the new U.S. culture. To guarantee success for their children in the U.S., these parents have been obliged to direct their children toward high standards of achievement in order to succeed in their lives beyond childhood. Chua (2011) argued:

> What Chinese parents understand is that nothing is fun until you're good at it. To get good at anything you have to work, and children on their own never want to work, which is why it is crucial to override their preferences. This often requires fortitude on the part of the parents because the child will resist; things are always hardest at the beginning, which is where Western parents tend to give up. But if done properly, the Chinese strategy produces a virtuous circle. Tenacious practice, practice, practice is crucial for excellence; rote repetition is underrated in America. Once a child starts to excel at something—whether it's math, piano, pitching or ballet—he or she gets praise, admiration and satisfaction. This builds confidence and makes the once not-fun activity fun. This in turn makes it easier for the parent to get the child to work even more. (para. 6)

In this quote, Chua made clear the difference between Eastern and Western parents regarding involvement with their children. Facing the ignorance and resistance of children, many Western parents might give up under the excuse of respecting their children's free choice and independence while most Eastern parents will tenaciously encourage, guide, and push their children to learn more and better. Here, let us share the critical remarks of two representative responses:

> I am a Chinese mother. I agree with you that Chinese often produce good engineers, but not inventors, excellent piano players but not once-in-a-life time musicians. The Chinese way of parenting described by Ms. Chua tends to destroy the creativeness in a child because the parents tend to overlook the true talent and feelings of their

child.... (Respondent 220)

and

I agree with you somewhat. Although I'm Caucasian, my parents raised me very similar to that of the Japanese/Chinese culture. Academics were always placed above anything else, and anything but #1 was not an option. Anything less than straight A's prior to college was unacceptable. Math was stressed very highly at a young age. With the biggest weakness of networking and social skills, I'd not consider myself more intelligent than the others. In my short time working I have found that intelligence alone is not enough to advance. A more balanced approach seems to be better not only for future careers, but for relationships as well. (Respondent 260)

The two responses acknowledge the rationale of the strict parenting approach Chua advocated. However, they also point out the weaknesses of such an approach, which "tends to destroy the creativeness in a child because the parents tend to overlook the true talent and feelings of their child," (Respondent 220) and produces academically strong students with "the biggest weakness of networking and social skills" (Respondent 260). Therefore, a balanced approach combining the merits of both Eastern and Western parenting styles might be the final answer. Just as Chua (2011) put it at the end of her book, *Battle Hymn of Tiger Mother*, "I've decided to favor a hybrid approach of the best of both worlds," with the "Chinese way until the child is eighteen, to develop confidence and the value of excellence, and then the Western way after that" (pp. 225–226).

Conclusion

The purposes of the present study were to explore the anticipated cultural perceptions of success in children in Eastern and Western parenting styles and reveal the Eastern and Western preferences to and differences in parenting approaches. To this end, we have raised three research questions. As for RQ 1: "Is there a difference between Eastern and Western parenting styles?" the present study found that there is a significant difference between adopted parenting style between Eastern and Western parents. While Eastern parents would prefer authoritative practice because they wanted to cultivate their children to become competent and talented, Western parents tended to use the indulgent style with a focus on creativity. In addition, Eastern or authoritative parents tended to get highly involved in their children's lives and learning, which can be supported by Chua's parenting stories as well as the data in our study.

Regarding RQ2: "What are the main factors that affect Eastern or Western parenting style adoption?" this study found that, among the examined factors of the respondents' gender and ethnicity, parenting involvement, parenting styles, anticipated children's abilities and traits, and the tone of Chua's parenting style, parenting involvement is the most important factor that affects Eastern or Western parenting style adoption. Although other examined factors have attracted too few responses (only 3%–5%) to be counted as valid determining factors, we can say that, based on previous research findings and the respondents' experiences, there must be many factors that may have an impact on adopted parenting styles, such as culture, world view, gender, socioeconomic, intelligence, maturity, development, skills, to name a few. Moreover, parenting success can be measured in many other ways than simply the narrow scopes of Scholastic Aptitude Test (SAT) scores, Grade Point Average (GPA) records, places of piano competitions, or Harvard acceptance letters.

Finally, with regard to RQ3: "Is there a difference between Eastern and Western parenting toward their anticipated children's achievements?" this study found that there is a statistically significant difference between the adopted parenting styles and the parents' anticipations toward their children's abilities, but the difference between the adopted parenting styles and the parents' anticipations toward their children's anticipated traits is not significant. Therefore, there is neither a better nor definitive parenting style for the family education of children; what is expected of parents in both the East and West is flexibility for life-long learning. As many responses suggested, among lax, authoritative, or even authoritarian parenting styles, no one is absolutely superior to the other.

What does this imply for intercultural parenting? First, be equifinality-centered. That is, parenting can reach the same final state from differing initial conditions and via a variety of paths. Second, strive to exploit the Western/lax and the Eastern/tough-love polarity by taking advantage of both. Finally, sometimes replace the word "parenting" with "coaching" in the parent and children relationship may actually help. The significance of our study lies in its void-filling contribution to the existent literature on Eastern and Western parenting styles from the perspective of leadership with data from online forums.

(Chao, C. C., & Tian, D. X. (2013). Like tiger mother, like tiger daughter: A content analysis of Eastern and Western parenting styles. In A. González, & T. M. Harris (Eds.), *Mediating cultures: Parenting in intercultural contexts*. New York, NY: Lexington Books.)

References

[1] Baldwin, A. L., Kalhorn J., & Breese, F. H. (1945). Patterns of parent behavior: Its description and measurement. Psychological Monographs, 58, 1–85.

[2] Baumrind, D. (1971). Harmonious parents and their preschool children. Developmental Psychology, 4, 99–102.

[3] Baumrind, D. (1989). Rearing competent children. In W. Damon (Ed.), Child development today and tomorrow (pp. 349–378). San Francisco: Jossey-Bass.

[4] Becker, G. S. (1964). Human capital: A theoretical and empirical analysis with special reference to education. New York: Columbia University Press.

[5] Blanchard, K. H. (1985). SLII: A situational approach to managing people. Escondido, CA: Blanchard Training and Development, Inc.

[6] Chavkin, N. F., & Williams, Jr. D. L. (1989). Parent involvement in education project. Executive summary of the final report. Austin, TX: Southwest Education. Development Lab. (ERIC Document Reproduction Service No. ED2668740.

[7] Comer, J. (1984). School power: Implications of an intervention project. New York: Free Press.

[8] Darling, N., & Steinberg, L. (1993). Parenting style as context: An integrative model. Psychological Bulletin, 113(3), 487-496.

[9] Dornbusch, S. M., Ritter, P. L., Leiderman, P. H., Roberts, D. F., & Fraleigh, M. J. (1987). The relation of parenting style to adolescent school performance. Child Development. 58(5), 1244-1257.

[10] Durkin, K. (1995). Developmental social psychology: From infancy to old age. Oxford: Blackwell.

[11] Elder, G. H., Jr. (1982). Structural variations on the child-rearing relationship. Sociometry, 25, 241-246.

[12] Epstein, J. L. (1990). School and family connection: Theory, research, and implications for interpreting sociologies of education and family. Marriage and Family Review, 15, 99-126.

[13] Ginsberg, G. S., & Bronstein, P. (1993). Family factors related to children' intrinsic/extrinsic motivational orientation and academic performance. Child Development, 64, 1461-1474.

[14] Grusec, J. E. (1997). A history of research on parenting strategies and children's internalization of values. In Grusec, J. E. & Kuczynski, L. (eds.), Parenting and children's internalization of values: A handbook of contemporary theory (pp. 3-22). New York: Wiley.

[15] Grolnick, W., & Ryan, R. M. (1989). Parent styles associated with children's self-regulation and competence in school. Journal of Educational Psychology, 81, 143-152.

[16] Herman, J. L., & Yen, J. P. (1980, April). Some effects of parent involvement in schools. Paper presented at the annual meeting of the American Educational Research Association, Boston, MA.

[17] Ho, D. Y. F. (1989). Continuity and variation in Chinese patterns of socialization. Journal of Marriage and the Family, 51, 149-163.

[18] Johnson M. M. (1998). Applying a modified situational leadership model to residential group care settings. Child & Youth Care Forum, 27(6), 383-398.

[19] Krippendorf, K. (2004). Content Analysis: An Introduction to Its Methodology. Thousand Oaks: CA: Sage.

[20] Luster, T., & McAdoo, H. (1996). Family and child influence on educational attainment: A secondary analysis of the high/Scope Perry Preschool data. Developmental Psychology, 32(1), 26-39.

[21] Maccoby, E. E., & Martin, J. A. (1983). Socialization in the context of the family: Parent-child interaction. In P. H. Mussen & E. M. Heatherington (Eds.), Handbook of child psychology: Socialization, personality, and social development (pp. 535 – 585). New York: Wiley.

[22] Naccarato, J., & Neuendorf, K. (1998). Content analysis as a predictive methodology: Recall, readership, and evaluations of business-to-business print advertising. Journal of Advertising Research, 38(3), 19 – 31.

[23] Parke, R. D., & Buriel, R. (1998). Socialization in the family: Ethnic and ecological perspectives. In, N. Eisenberg & W. Damon (Eds.), Handbook of child psychology: Social, emotional, and personality development (pp. 463 – 532). New York: Wiley.

[24] Putallaz, M., & Heflin, A. H. (1990). Parent-child interaction. In S. Asher & J. Coie (Eds.), Peer rejection in childhood (pp. 189 – 216). New York: Cambridge University Press.

[25] Spera, C. (2005). A review of the relationship among parenting Practices, parenting Styles, and adolescent school achievement. Educational Psychology Review, 17(2), 125 – 146.

[26] Steinberg, L., Lamborn, S., Dornbusch, S., & Darling, N. (1992). Impact of parenting practices on adolescent achievement: Authoritative parenting, school involvement, and encouragement to succeed. Child Development, 63, 1266 – 1281.

[27] Steinberg, L., Mounts, N. S., Lamborn, S. D., & Dornbush, S. M. (1991). Authoritative parenting and adolescent adjustment across varied ecological niches. Journal of Research on Adolescence, 1, 19 – 36.

[28] Teachman, J. D., & Paasch, Kathleen. (1998). The family and educational aspirations. Journal of Marriage & Family, 60 (3), 704 – 715.

[29] Weinberg, B. A. (2001). An incentive model of the effect of parental income on children. Journal of Political Economy, 109(2), 266 – 280.

[30] Wentzel, K., Feldman, S., & Weinberger, D. (1991). Parental child rearing and academic achievement in boys: The mediational role of social-emotional adjustment. Journal of Early Adolescence. 11, 321 – 339.

[31] Wislon, P. M., & Wilson, J. R. (1992). Environmental influences on adolescent educational aspirations: A logistic transform model. Youth & Society, 24, 52 – 70.

[32] Wrench, J., Thomas-Maddox, C., Richmond, V., & McCroskey, J. (2008). Qualitative research methods for communication: A hands-on approach. New York: Oxford University Press.

Chapter 17
Keeping Relationships Positive or Doing Things Right: Bridging Women Leaders' Conflict Management Strategies in Non-profit Organizations in Taiwan and the United States

The global economy has been flourishing, information technology has kept pace with the world growth, and people around the world have gained more and more rights. Because of these factors, rapid changes are taking place in today's society and economy, as well as in people's social attitudes toward diverse needs. More and more non-profit organizations are adjusting themselves to meet these social needs, which cannot be met by challenging goals for business organizations or governmental institutions. According to Solamon (1987), non-profit organizations are sprouting up successfully just like bamboo shoots after a spring rain, many of which are organized by people with noble aspirations to fulfill lofty ideals and solve social problems. Indeed, at present, non-profit organizations are rapidly developing at an unprecedented speed, have won the world's admiration, and are collaborating with governments and business organizations to satisfy numerous social needs and accomplish a great number of needed tasks. Therefore, there is a must to understand the management practice in all areas of voluntary non-profit organizations, particularly related to social conflicts and conflict management strategies.

Although research on the topic of non-profit organizations is one of the newest and hottest research areas, many researchers still apply the models and theories of for-profit business organizations when they are investigating the management of non-profit organizations (Solamon, 1987). The assumptions of such applications imply an unrevealed and disguised presupposition that the management and engagement of non-profit organizations is similar to that of business organizations, with only the content of their services being different. Therefore, there is a need to understand the management practice in all areas of non-profit organizations, especially those related to social conflicts and conflict management strategies.

In addition, research results also indicated that today's organizations need more talented leaders and managers, and "these are increasingly found to be women" (Jogulu and Wood, 2006, p. 246). Gladwin and Walter (1980) further noted, research findings have long indicated that conflicts are more pervasive in international non-profit organizations where communicative adaptation must take place. However, "for a variety of reasons, including methodological hindrances, a predominance of male researchers are largely uninterested in the topic" (Northhouse, 2012, p. 301), and few researchers have conducted research studies related to gender and leadership (Chemers, 1997). Actually, previous studies have seldom touched upon the specific volunteering characteristics of non-profit organizations and female leadership styles in conflict management from a cross-cultural perspective. We therefore aim to fill this void by exploring women leaders' conflict management strategies in non-profit organizations of Rotary Clubs in Taiwan and the USA. With Taiwan as a representative of oriental culture and the USA representing the Western culture, the research findings of the present study will shed light on understanding women leaders' leadership styles and conflict management strategies in the international non-profit organizational settings. To this end, we will first clarify our theoretical framework and propose two research questions through an extensive and thorough review of the relevant literature, and then we will provide a detailed description of the methodology for collecting and analyzing our data followed by the presentation and explanation of our research results. Finally, this paper will end with a critical discussion about our present study and some caveats for properly interpreting our research findings.

Literature Review

Definition of Conflict. The definition of conflict is diverse due to different researchers' viewpoints and relevant contexts. Frequently, many scholars see conflict as a natural process of our lives. For instance, Robbins (2001) believed that conflict is a process in which one notices that antagonistic sides are bringing bad influences upon a person or a thing that the person cares about. Accordingly, Luthans (2002) defined conflict as a process of communication and interaction, and once dependent individuals realize that irreconcilability, inconsistence, and tension are beneficial, conflict usually erupts.

Besides, some other scholars view conflict as a contingency or a situation. Nelson and Quick (2000) indicated that conflict represents any kind of contingency, in which irreconcilable aims, attitudes, emotions, or behaviors lead both sides to antagonism (Nelson & Quick, 2000). Robbins (2001) also clearly defined conflict as a discordant situation caused by the interaction of more than two related subjects. Since this research aims to explore the conflict coping strategies of female leaders in non-profit organizations, we'd like to combine the above-mentioned definitions in order to examine how a female president coordinates, communicates with other people, and relays a difference in opinion about the goal of a project or view on service significance in her Rotary Club. Following is our review of the existing literature on various conflicts in organizations.

Conflicts Resolution Strategies. According to Mead (1998), conflicts may explode over almost any aspects of the organization process. Contemporary management literature holds the view that conflicts should be not only accepted but also encouraged. This is because conflicts, as positive forces in a group, provide a prerequisite for group efficiency. One of the primary topics in conflict studies is conflict management behavior, which focuses on situational impacts and corresponding strategies. According to Rahim (2001), the model of five styles, i. e. , integrating, obliging, dominating, avoiding, and compromising, is the most frequently used conflict management strategy.

To be specific, among the five styles in the model, the integrating style works best at solving conflicts because leaders will think highly about the needs and desires of both parties in a conflict and try to satisfy the needs of both parties by solving the problem itself, thus creating a win-win situation (Rahim, 2001). Obliging style is used when the leaders will not insist on their positions but instead accept other people's viewpoints to maintain a harmonious relation. Dominating leaders will typically use their positions or power to force their followers to accomplish the leaders' own will or preference, which is an aggressive conflict strategy. An avoidance style is used when neither the need of the leader nor the need of the other party is satisfied. The leaders using this style habitually withdraw or make excuses when facing a conflict. The result of avoiding a conflict, however, is that the conflict still exists. The compromising style meets the needs of both parties by their sacrifice (yield), and, by adopting this style, both parties will try to find an alternative choice which can be accepted by both sides (Gross & Guerrero, 2000; Rahim & Magner, 1995; Rahim et al. , 2000; Rahim, 2001).

In actuality, as Ohbuchi and Fukushima (1997) noted, many factors such as the essence of conflicts, face-work, and gender may also be influencing the personal reactions to conflicts in organizations. In a similar vein, Conrad and Poole (2001) believed still other different elements, like the relationship between members, the structure of the organization, and environment will also bring profound influences on the adoption of strategies. It is clear that conflict strategies that are used vary with different situations.

Meanwhile, interference of a third party also plays a very important role. When both interested parties are unable to solve their differences through formal or informal communication, a third party may be needed to get the conflict resolved. As Rahim (2001) indicated, a third party plays eight kinds of roles (neutral witness, alley, constituent, rewarded agent, professional interventionists, mediator, judge, and authority). In brief, a third party mainly plays the roles of mediator and professional interventionist. The mediator makes a decision that both parties must follow, while the professional interventionist encourages interactions between both parties so as to reach a decision. Harris (2002) confirmed that the interference of a third party is generally welcomed at every level. In order to maintain harmony, an effective leader always prefers such interference and thus turns a dominating kind of conflict into an integrating, compromising, or avoiding type. This is because interference can frequently satisfy the needs of both parties to different degrees.

Hierarchical Positions, Gender Role, and Conflict Management. Apart from the above, one's position in a hierarchical system (power relation) is also an important factor in settling conflicts. Brewer, Mitchell, and Weber (2002) noted that contingency elements, such as the power relation between two interested parties, are more influential on the application of conflict strategy than one's personality. One's behavior varies with one's position or level in an organization, and the relative positions of the two interested parties determine the conflict solution. In general, one would solve the conflict with a subordinate with the dominating style, while that with an associate through compromising, and that with a superior through obliging (Lee, 2002; Rahim, 2001). Chen (2002) found that when subordinates encounter a conflict with their superior, the priority of choice for solving the conflict is from integrating, obliging, avoiding, compromising to dominating. In contrast, the person of higher status tends to start choosing from the other end, i. e. the compromising style first.

It is also worth mentioning that many prior studies have also focused on gender roles and conflict strategies, applying conflict strategies other than personality, conflict contingency, and their results. These studies have developed two different views. Some studies indicate that gender does not influence the method used to solve a conflict. Renwick (1977), Schokley-Zalabak (1981), Pritchard (1985), and Guill (1991), for instance, all claimed that gender difference does not reveal any difference in the style of coping with conflicts (cited in Rahim, 2001).

However, other scholars believed that gender is a potential influence on solving conflicts (Munduate et al. , 1999). Chen (2002) found that women frequently adopt the avoiding style when facing a conflict. Cupach and Canary (1995) argued that women prefer integrating, compromising, avoiding, and obliging conflict management strategies. Conrad and Poole (2002) also added that in a conflict, women would tend to focus more on the relationship and thus apply the integrating style more than men. Rahim (2001) seconded these findings and further indicated that female supervisors tend to use integrating, compromising, and avoiding styles more than their male counterparts, but not the obliging style. In general, women prefer to use the indirect strategies more, and thus demonstrating a belief that it is more important women leaders to maintain a good relationship than to achieve the goal (Harris, 2002).

From the discussion above, we can see that when choosing strategies for solving conflicts, women prefer a mild strategy (integrating, obliging, avoiding, or compromising) to a strong one (dominating). These results partly confirm the gender stereotypes of the general public. Moreover, Eagly and Karau (2002) found that social environment also influences the behaviors of both men and women. For example, in a mainly male working environment, a female worker might also adapt a male behavior, and vice versa. Accordingly, the present study assumes that female presidents might use different conflict management strategies to deal with their members in the voluntary, male-dominated Rotary Clubs. Since this is also an intercultural study, below is the discussion about the relationship between cultural differences and conflict management.

Cultural Differences and Conflict Management. Cultural differences are an important factor in solving conflicts (Chao, 2009). A study of supervisors in Japan, Germany, and the United States shows the different preferences for solving conflicts between the supervisors in different countries. Supervisors in the United States prefer integrating more than supervisors in Japan and Germany, while Japanese supervisors prefer to solve a conflict with a mediator (the intervention of the third party), and the supervisors in Germany prefer following rules and regulations (Lee, 2002). Additionally, Tinsley and Brett (2001) echoed that cultural difference does influence a manager's style of solving conflicts. Their research showed that American managers prefer the integrating style, while a Hong Kong manager, influenced by traditional Chinese belief in emphasizing the collective interests and authority, prefers to receive aid from a superior (the third party) to solve the conflict. Thus, it can be said that different cultural preferences will become an important reference for conflict studies (Kreitner & Kinicki, 2002).

Rahim (2001) reconfirmed Ting-Toomey's (1999) study and summarized that Americans prefer dominating more than Japanese and Koreans, while Chinese and Taiwanese prefer obliging or avoiding more than Americans do. This is because high emphasis on social relations in the Chinese society sees a conflict as a major problem that may jeopardize interpersonal relations and thus demands the prevention of any conflicts. According to Conrad and Poole (2002), many scholars also found that collectivism focuses more on the achievement of the collective's goal and maintaining the relationships between individuals, and thus its typical conflict management strategy demands not only the satisfaction of an individual's need, but also the maintenance of the relationship between an individual and a group.

To summarize, conflict management strategies vary with different factors such as gender role, face-work, social environment, referent roles, and culture. Although, previous studies have examined many different situations, almost none of the available researches address how female leaders cope with conflicts in non-profit organizations in different countries. This study thus focuses on the relevant research on influencing variables to construct the argument for reference and comparison as a basis for exploring the conflict management strategies of female leaders in Rotary Clubs in Taiwan and the United States, with the following two research questions:

RQ1: What are the conflict management strategies performed by the female presidents in Rotary Clubs in Taiwan and the United States?

RQ2: What are the main factors that influence the female presidents' conflict handling strategies in Rotary Clubs in Taiwan and the United States?

Method

Rotary Clubs. Unlike Lion's Clubs or other international non-profit organizations, Rotary Clubs have their own styles such as holding regular meetings once a week, nicknaming members (no business titles in clubs), and allowing only one person per vocation to be a member in each local chapter of the club. These characteristics and behaviors distinguish Rotary Clubs and their members, Rotarians.

Today's Rotary is adapting to the rapid cultural and economic changes of the shrinking middle class. At present, there are around 1.2 million male Rotarians worldwide but only 90,000 female Rotarians around the world (Rotary, 2008). In addition, there has never been a woman who served as the president of Rotary International (RI). Even the 19-member board of RI does not have any female members. Therefore, the emphasis on female membership and leadership is the key to potential success and prosperity for Rotary. Female leaders ought to play an increasingly significant role globally in the twenty-first century because many of the feminine leadership qualities fit in with urgent demands of leadership in this century (Adler, 1999).

Therefore, RI is expected to focus more on female leadership and make all efforts to bring the feminine leadership styles, particularly women leaders' conflict management strategies into full play so as to face the changes and meet the members' needs. The present study addresses these concerns. Since the senior author of this study has been actively involved in the Rotary Clubs of both District 3510 in Taiwan and District 6600 in the USA, the two districts have been selected for convenience as the study settings.

Participants and Procedures. For the present study, we decided to conduct participant observations in the two target districts of 3510 and 6600 in addition to applying in-depth interviews for data collection. By triangulating the data, the present study injected depth in revealing the female presidents' conflict management strategies as performed in both Taiwan and the United States. To guarantee validity or trustworthiness in our findings, we have taken the following steps:

Field Observation. Participant observation is a meeting place, where different voices through the practice of interactive context gather together (Denzin, 1994). As it is taking place in the real setting of the activities being observed, field observation allows multiple perspectives of reality and alternative interpretations of data and is deemed a suitable method for a study pertaining to conflict management.

The selected samples from both Rotary districts were based on the criteria of functional equivalence and representativeness. They are functionally equivalent since all of the participants are Rotarians in both countries. Since Rotary is an international organization, Rotarians around the world all share similar missions and goals, provide similar objectives of services, and implement the same criteria for membership. In addition, the two districts are similar in size (71 clubs in District 3510 and 67 clubs in District 6600). As stated previously, the senior author has been an active member in both Rotary districts for many years and thus had access to the research sites.

Observation sites. District 3510. District 3510 is located in Kaohsiung, Taiwan. The district is composed of 71 clubs (42 male clubs, 8 female clubs, and 21 mixed gender clubs) with approximately 2,067 Rotarians, including 1763 male Rotarians (85%) and 304 female Rotarians (15%). Among these clubs, there are 15 female presidents (21%) and 3 District Governor Assistants (15%) in the year from 2007 to 2008 (Rotary, 2008). The other site, District 6600, is located in Ohio of the United States. There are 4201 members in total who belong to 67 mixed gender clubs. There are no single sex clubs. In this district, there are 50 male presidents (75%) and 17 female presidents (25%). However, there are 15 male District Governor Assistants but no female Governor Assistants in the year from 2007 to 2008.

Interview. Since survey questionnaire is unable to specifically describe if the personal uniqueness of a female leader would influence her conflict management strategies, this research has also applied in-depth interviews as a method for collecting insightful and profound information. In total, the researchers have conducted 15 in-depth interviews with female presidents in both Rotary districts. The interviews lasted from 60 to 90 minutes in length.

The interviewees in this research were not limited to only current presidents in Rotary Clubs, but they included all past or current female presidents, who completed their presidency out of their voluntariness and willingness. In addition, the choice of the interview respondents must be female leaders working in business organizations as well.

To find answers to the research questions, the researchers have designed the interview questions for this study based on the model of five conflict management styles with reference to the existing relevant literature. For example, one of our open-ended interview questions goes like:

> [...] please briefly talk about your duty, task, and styles for being a female president in the Rotary Club, and give an example of a conflict between you and your members as well as how you coped with the issue.

Interviewees were asked to freely tell their stories of their experienced conflicts. Through the interviewees' description of the conflicts as well as how she coped with them, the researchers are able to deduce the strategies used in dealing with the conflicts. In addition, the interviews were also videotaped for detailed records and exact quotes.

The conflict strategies noted in this research consists of the methods applied by female leaders to cope with and solve a conflict within Rotary Club. The category applied in this research is based on the model of five-styles proposed by Rahim (2001): integrating, dominating, compromising, avoiding, and obliging. Furthermore, the interviewees were also probed to supply many other adopted strategies while certain conflicts developed. In this way, we found that the interviewees often used more than one strategy to solve a conflict. However, to prevent any contradictory situations during the data analysis, we just focused on the first strategy used by the interviewees or the one that they found the most effective when resolving conflicts as the presidents of their Rotary Clubs.

Analysis

All data were examined on the female presidents' conflict management strategies and influencing factors of their strategies. Theme analysis of the interpretive method was used in this research. To do so, we repeatedly read the gathered information from the field observation notes and in-depth interview transcripts first to develop a structure for data analysis and then to determine the emerging themes as answers to the research questions. We also constantly compared the themes with the theoretical model and other relevant literature as discussed earlier to derive the conclusion of this research. To be specific, a theme is a relevant issue, concept, opinion, understanding, knowledge, experience, or question. To become a theme for this research, according to Owen (1984) and Glesne and Peshkin (1992), three criteria are required. As the first criterion, occurrence means that the same thread of meaning must appear at least twice in the analyzed data. The second criterion is the repetition of key words, phrases, or sentences in the selected artifacts. Finally, as the third criterion, forcefulness refers to the emphasis of words or phrases in the data concerned. While generating the themes, the two authors separately and thoroughly finished reading the field observation notes and in-depth interview transcripts and checked each other repeatedly to decide on common themes and achieve validated evidence for the whole data analysis process.

To sum up, we analyzed and compared the data collected from two methods: field observation and interview. Since triangulation emphasizes the value of examining research questions with different methods that do not share the same methodological weaknesses, the researchers in this study have built confidence through the triangulation of research methods in our assertions about the social world.

Findings

Field Observation

Conflict strategies of Taiwanese female presidents. Observation of two conflict cases showed that female presidents would employ different conflict management strategies when interacting with their members.

In Case 1, the president, Grace, has mostly applied the harmony approach to her members. Then when her presidency is approaching, she requested a meeting to discuss the issue of president-elect because nobody wanted to be the candidate. When some senior members and several past presidents who are very close to Grace proposed the idea that every past president could rotate the president position again, Grace at first disagreed about this idea, but then accepted this proposal. However, one of the past presidents, Nancy, was strongly against this idea. Therefore, the meeting failed to come up with any solutions. Grace later invited a third party, the district governor, to persuade Nancy, but Nancy was persistent that Grace caused the situation and she needed to take the whole responsibility. In the end, this Rotary club had to be dismissed, and Grace said the following words at the last meeting, "I lost face, but the club lost face as well. This was not my own responsibility only. This was all of the club's responsibility." Grace later has transferred to another club, and Nancy has tried to initiate a new club.

In Case 2, the president, Sally, was holding a regular meeting. She started with jokes to create a pleasant atmosphere. When Lisa, one of the past presidents, inquired about the poor service of an activity the club had just held, Sally at first tried to avoid discussing this issue by proposing that the issue would be submitted to an upcoming board meeting. Yet, Lisa was still arguing, and Sally then obliged to allow a discussion about the issue in the current meeting. She also invited the opinion of another senior past president, Teresa, who has good relationship with her. Teresa tried to support the president by telling Lisa that she did not participate much in the activity, so she could not judge if the activity was of a good or poor service. In the end, Sally was aware of the tense atmosphere in the meeting and tried to ease up the situation by inviting the members to go to her house. Unsatisfied, Lisa left the club later.

From the observations, we found that the strategy pattern from Case 1 and Case 2 was consistent. The female presidents of Rotary Clubs in Taiwan usually began with efforts for harmony or courtesy. However, when they encountered issues about which they had no solutions, they would avoid the issue or oblige the other party. If they were challenged further or had to save their faces, they would invite a third party who is usually a senior member or has a higher status to help them resolving the conflicts without really confronting their members. Findings here somewhat echo some past findings that Chinese leaders will use the benevolent approach due to the culture of collectivist values and tend to maintain personal relationships and smooth over conflicts for harmony in the setting (Ting-Toomey & Oetzel, 2001).

Conflict strategies of American female presidents. In Case 3, Cindy, an American female president, was chairing a regular meeting. Mark, a senior club member, was complaining about the members' poor attendance recently. He even asked the president to cancel either the lunch meeting or dinner meeting. Cindy explained to him that she needed to take many factors into consideration when holding one meeting, including the overall stability of the club for the long run. She also told him that she would work out the issue with him or other board members later, but that the ultimate decision would be made by all the Rotarians' joint efforts. Mark agreed.

In Case 4, a female president, Ana, proposed to empower a new female member, Tina, to chair and plan a large fund-raising activity in a board meeting. During the discussion, the majority of the board members strongly agreed with this idea because Tina is not only energetic and active in participating in the club meetings but also experienced in dealing with such activities. However, three members, who were in charge of the previous fund-raising activities, disagreed with this proposal. They felt that a new, especially a female member was not able to conduct such a large activity yet. Ana explained that it was at the board meeting that the decision was made, and the club needed new ideas and new approaches for activities and services. When the three members still could not accept this decision, they left the club at last.

The above findings also correspond somewhat to Tinsley's (2001) research results that American female leaders consistently focused on the integrating approach, choosing direct, confrontational, and problem-solving strategies. They perceived that avoiding conflicts is a weak strategy, so they would directly articulate their conflict concerns and bring the problem or issue to the table. For them, doing the right thing is more important than keeping the harmonious relationships in the club.

Main Factors Impacting upon the Conflict Management Strategies

The analysis of the above observations has also revealed several main factors that influenced the conflict management strategies of the female presidents, including face, relationship and the role of a third party.

Face. According to Gao (1998) and Ting-Toomey (1988; 2005), people in individualistic (Western) and collectivistic (Eastern) cultures assign different meanings to the content notions of face. In individual cultures, face is mostly associated with self-worth, self-presentation, and self-value, whereas in collectivist cultures face is concerned more about what others think of one's worth. Therefore, the face factor was obviously seen in Case 1, where Grace at first tried to protect the club face by accepting the idea of re-rotating the president position, but when they failed to reach an agreement, she felt the whole club lost face as the club was to be dismissed. In Case 2, Sally also tried to protect Lisa's face by obliging her to discuss the held activity. In Case 3 and Case 4, however, the face work of the presidents was more related to self-presentation.

Relationship/Guanxi. It was found that guanxi was playing an important role in dealing with conflicts as well. According to Chang and Holt (1991) and Chung (1996), guanxi is not only a tool used to avoid conflicts, but can resolve conflicts among people as a potential power source for persuasion, influence, and control. Findings of this study indicated in Case 1 that Grace was influenced by some senior members and past presidents who are close to her so that she supported their proposed idea that each past president would rotate the presidency position again. In Case 2, when Sally encountered the difficult member, Lisa, she invited the opinion of Teresa, who has a good relationship with her, and Teresa tried to protect Sally's face by criticizing Lisa in the meeting. In Case 4, Ana was trying to build an in-group relationship with a new female member, Tina, by proposing her to chair a fund-raising activity. Even three senior group members threatened her that they would quit the membership if the decision was made, she did not change the proposal.

The third party. In Case 1, when the meeting failed to come up with any solutions, Grace invited a third party, the district governor, to resolve the disagreement. Similarly, in Case 2, when Sally was dealing with Lisa's inquiry, she invited the third party's support to avoid the confrontation. In Case 3 and Case 4, by contrast, the American female leaders would follow the structure and procedure of clubs to handle things instead of inviting a third party to interrupt the conflict management. The above analysis echoes our interview data that female leaders in Taiwan are more likely to solve a conflict with a mediator than female presidents in the United States. All together, face, relationship/guanxi, and the role of third party were observed as active influencing factors in the management of these conflicts, particularly on the part of the Taiwanese leaders.

Interviews

Conflict strategy analysis. The first research question of the present study examines the conflict management strategies of the female leaders. To collect data, each of the 15 female leaders was asked to describe at least one case about the conflict background, as well as the management strategy she used to deal with the conflict. Among them, there were only two cases that used dominating strategies (Interviewees TF8 [Taiwan Female No. 8; Ibid] and AF11 [American Female No. 11; Ibid]). Five cases employed integrating strategies (Interviewees TF6, TF10, TF14, AF6, and AF8), and six cases applied obliging strategies (Interviewees TF9, TF12, TF13, AF7, AF9, and AF10). One case utilized compromising strategies (Interviewees TF7), and one case exercised avoiding strategies (Interviewee TF11). From the above, it is clear that the 15 female leaders mainly employed the obliging strategy (40%) and integrating strategy (33%) to deal with various conflicts in their respective Rotary Clubs.

Interestingly, among the 15 cases, ten had solicitation of third parties, including all of the nine Taiwanese female leaders and only one American female leader (Interviewees TF6, TF7, TF8, TF9, TF10, TF11, TF12, TF13, TF14, and AF7). Furthermore, we can also divide the 15 cases into two major types. The first belongs to conflicts purely over the projects or decision-making, such as the conflict between the leaders and the members in terms of the perspective of decision-making, as well as dealing with certain projects. Twelve cases were of this first type (80%). The second type of conflicts was mainly related to their leadership styles or their personal issues. There were only three cases of this type in this study (20%).

Obliging strategy. Among the six conflicts using the obliging strategy (TF9, TF12, TF13, AF7, AF9, and AF10), the data have revealed that obliging is the most often used strategy to face the conflicts with members. Five of the six cases belong to the work-related or decision-making conflicts. According to the five interviewees, they usually tried to conform to the members because Rotarians are volunteers, and if they do not get personal satisfaction, they may not stay in the clubs. However, there were still some complaints about these conflicts, and some female presidents in Taiwan even emphasized that they did not insist on their ideas because some of the past presidents tried to influence the decision results, and they wanted to keep a harmonious atmosphere in the club:

> At first, I was very active to propose some creative ideas about projects or services that we could do or needed to do. However, some senior members, especially senior past presidents always disagreed with my ideas. I felt that they were too traditional and always want current presidents to do things in old ways. Unless you can do

creative services by your own and do not need to get the financial support from the club, otherwise you just need to follow their ways to do things in order to keep a positive and harmonious atmosphere in the club. (Interviewee TF13)

In addition, one conflict in this study that used obliging strategy took place. One American female president obliged herself over a personal issue so as to bring all members into harmony. However, she faced other conflicts directly, and she would apply different strategies handling the conflicts according to various situations:

> In our club, although I am the president, I view myself as having the lowest status. My job is to provide good services not only for my members, but also for our society. Therefore, I tend to use the obliging strategy to cope with any conflicts that may arise. (Interviewee AF10)

To deal with the conflicts with the members in Rotary Clubs, this study has found that most female leaders will adopt the obliging strategy (40%) due to the volunteer nature of the clubs and necessity to keep a harmonious relationship with members. However, several Taiwanese female presidents viewed some past presidents too traditional and tried to influence the current presidents to do things in their old ways while the American female presidents were direct to face conflicts and would see situations to determine which management strategy to employ.

Integrating strategy. Besides using the obliging strategy, the interviewees often adopt the cooperative strategy (Interviewees TF6, TF10, TF14, AF6, AF8; 33%). One American interviewee remarked:

> In voluntary work, the purpose of dealing with the conflicts is to solve the conflict instead of making your stance outstanding. Therefore, if an argument cannot solve the problem, why do you still keep on using it? All the methods can be used to solve the problem and get the things done well. (Interviewee AF8)

Because most of the presidents had experience in holding different positions in Rotary Clubs, they have established extensive networks and profound professional experiences. Particularly for Taiwanese female presidents, when facing unexpected incidents or conflicts, they often integrate multiple sources or the relationships of networks to get the problem solved so as to create a win-win situation, which is demonstrated in the following:

> In a board meeting, one of our members promised to plan a project. But after a while, she told me that it was impossible with such short notice. I was upset at first, and then asked her about the difficult point. She told me that it was hard to rent a place. I contacted with some Rotary friends and then I rent a great place for our plan, but I still asked her to plan and organize the project. (Interviewee TF10)

> Once when we wanted to release a piece of news to get the public to participate in a service. The chair of that committee tried to use 'the first in the nation' in his writing. After arguing, we changed it and made it sound more reasonable. (Interviewee AF6)

The cases above prove again the significance of the leaders' capability. Coupled with their professional capabilities, the female Rotary club presidents would create a win-win situation by integrating the ideas of both sides of the conflicting parties. Nevertheless, Taiwanese female presidents would make full use of their networks and sources, including their natural sources of loving maternal roles to help club members whereas American female presidents would apply different strategies to solve problems or get things done.

Dominating strategy. Among the 25 conflict cases, the dominating strategy was used in only two cases (Interviewees TF8, AF11; 13%). This strategy was used mostly on occasions when the interviewees and their members had differences in the club agenda or club policies. As for the two conflict cases, the interviewees insisted on their opinions and used the dominating strategy to make the members agree with their ideas:

> Once there was a project about fund-raising so that our Rotary Club could accomplish more. I put forward my opinion, which was different from that of another female member. As a past president, she did not like the idea of using new tasks to get for more funds. Instead, she would like the current president to follow the traditional projects, services and rules. However, to fulfill the goal of the club, I managed to gain support of most of the club members, and finally my idea was realized. (Interviewee TF 9)

> We had a member who wanted to plan and organize our annual club celebration, and she wanted to be empowered to make her own choices regarding everything. I couldn't let her do that because that's a big project and she was asking too much. (Interviewee AF11)

From the above, we see that the female leaders in both Taiwan and the United States felt that if their ideas were right and the issues were task-related, they would adopt the dominating strategy to protect the majority rights and focus on the issue under discussion rather than the persons involved.

Besides, there was one case in which the compromising strategy was used, in which Interviewee TF7 and one of her members had some different perspectives of a certain project. After making compromises, both sides stepped back to coordinate and communicate till a compromised agreement was reached. Meanwhile, the avoiding strategy was also adopted in another case (Interviewee TF11), which occurred when both sides were excited. To avoid further face-to-face confrontation, the Taiwanese female president used the avoiding strategy as she described below:

> Once at a board meeting, a member stood up and scolded at me. I felt that she was anxious, and I did not want to confront her face to face. I tolerated it, but I felt that I was very much humiliated. However, I felt that so long I did not quarrel with her, I would win the upper hand. (Interviewee TF11)

To sum up, the conflicts between the female leaders and their members mostly came from disagreement about some projects or clubs' policies. To solve the conflicts and to keep a harmonious atmosphere in their clubs, they mostly used obliging strategy (40%), but some also adopted integrating strategy (33%) for a win-win result.

Among the 15 cases, there were 10 cases in which the third party was invited to solve the problem (67%). In the ten cases, the obliging strategy was used in four cases (Interviewees TF9, TF12, TF13, AF7), the integrating strategy was employed in three cases (Interviewees TF6, TF10, TF14), the dominating strategy was exercised in one case (Interviewee TF8), the compromising strategy was applied in one case (Interviewee TF7), and the avoiding strategy was also utilized in one case (Interviewee TF11). Interestingly, nine out of ten cases in which the third party was invited to solve the conflicts happened in Taiwan. The third party roles were either senior Rotarians or past Rotary presidents. With regard to the case in District 6600 of the United States, the third party was ordinary Rotarian. Thus, country difference is clear here.

In the four cases in which obliging strategy was adopted, the interviewees mostly had more interactions with the person she had conflicts with due to different understanding or perspectives of the projects. To avoid a worsening situation from happening in the future that might affect the relationships of the whole club, the interviewees first used the obliging strategy and then asked a third party to mediate so as to avoid face-to-face conflicts.

Similarly, the interviewees who utilized integrating strategy had conflicts with their members mostly due to the understanding of the work. To avoid face-to-face confrontation, the mediators were invited to discuss plans and help both sides to reach a win-win situation. As for the dominating strategy, the conflict case took place between the interviewee and her member. The member was not satisfied with the leader's behavior, and they did not reach an agreement. The leader went to a senior past president of the club for help and gain the member's understanding. Finally, in the application of the avoiding strategy, the interviewee was facing an unreasonable member's verbal attack. To avoid face-to-face confrontation, she first used the avoiding strategy to calm down both sides' emotions and then invited a past president to help solving the conflict.

In conclusion, among the ten cases in which a third party was invited, the motivation was either to purely solve the work problem or to seek preventive measures so as to avoid possible conflicts and maintain the harmonious relationship. Generally speaking, Taiwanese Rotarians would frequently ask for a mediator to help with both parties' negotiation, while American Rotarians rarely invited a third party to solve conflicts. One reason is that in the Chinese culture, some Confucian values such as conformity, submission, and respect for one's parents and elders are still very much in practice. Therefore, in order to avoid confrontation and keep harmonious relationships, Taiwanese female leaders were more likely to invite senior past presidents to play the role of the third party to get conflicts resolved.

Discussion and Conclusion

The purposes of this study were to examine the conflict management strategies and the factors that exert impacts upon the application of these strategies between Taiwanese female presidents and their American counterparts of Rotary Clubs as an international non-profit organization. To this end, we raised two research questions: RQ1: What are the conflict management strategies performed by the female presidents in Rotary Clubs in Taiwan and the United States? RQ2: What are the main factors that influence the female presidents' conflict handling strategies in Rotary Clubs in Taiwan and the United States?

Through the theoretical lens of Rahim's (2001) model of five-styles of conflict management and theoretical guidance of other relevant literature, we adopted the research methods of field observation and in-depth interview for data collection and theme analysis to analyze the observation cases and interview transcripts. The research findings are twofold. On the one hand, as the answer to RQ1, the female presidents of the Rotary Clubs in both Taiwan and the United States applied obliging and integrating of the five styles or strategies to handle management conflicts. However, due to the interference of past presidents, the female presidents in Taiwan are more likely to follow the traditional norms whereas American women leaders tend to employ new approaches and adopt new conflict management strategies in different situations.

On the other hand, as the answer to RQ2, the application of conflict management strategies are usually influenced by the factors of face, in-group relationships, and roles of the invited third party for Taiwanese subjects whereas American subjects oftentimes adopt appropriate strategies according to the nature of the conflicts. In terms of face, while the Taiwanese female presidents who grow up in the collectivistic culture show more concern about what other club members think of their worth, the American female presidents who bear the gradual individualistic cultural influence pay more attention to self-worth and self-expression. Regarding in-group relations, the former make the greatest efforts to maintain harmony by making repeated compromises and even at the cost of keeping the issue under discussion unresolved. Oppositely, the latter usually appear decisive by keeping a working relationship with most club members and, more importantly, by demonstrating their professional capabilities. Finally, seeking extra help from a third and usually senior party has been regarded normal, necessary, and respectful to the former, but it is in discord with the American pursuit of independence, innovation, and youth-power.

In addition, our research findings have indicated both theoretical and practical implications. Theoretically, quite a number of previous researches have overestimated the functions of culture or cultural values in their cross-cultural studies, such as Hofstede's (1997) five dimensions of culture and Hall's (1976) high- and low-context cultures. To be more specific, according to several previous studies (Brewer et al., 2002, Lee, 2002; Rahim, 2001; Daniel et al., 1997), when facing conflicts, leaders of the organizations generally tend to employ the dominating or integrating strategy with subordinates, compromising strategy with colleagues, and conforming or obliging strategies with superiors. However, by focusing on the voluntary nature of the Rotary Clubs, this study found that the female leaders in both Taiwan and the United States would adopt the obliging or integrating strategies during the daily conflict management in their respective Rotary Clubs. In fact, some relevant literature (Conrad & Poole, 2002) already revealed that females are highly relation-oriented, and they tend to adopt non-confrontational strategies to deal with conflicts. Also, just as Interviewee TF6 explained, "In our club, although I am the president, I view myself at the lowest status. My job is to provide good services not only for my members, but also for our society. Therefore, I tend to use the obliging strategy to cope with conflicts."

Practically, this study shows that the factors of face, guanxi, and the third party played more critical roles for the Taiwanese female leaders than their American counterparts in their application of conflict management strategies. For instance, in Case 1 and Case 2, when the female presidents employed avoiding or obliging strategies and when they invited the senior third parties, they were trying to not only maintain the harmonious relationships among the club members but also save the face of each one. As Yuqin (2001) remarked, face in the Chinese society is more a concern to the in-group than to the person and therefore, one's failure threatens the face of the group, and one's accomplishment gains face for the group. Moreover, this study revealed that without good quanxi, face protection and the third party's support, the Taiwanese female presidents could not have obtained their expected achievements.

Besides, this study found that, to emphasize harmony, female leaders in Taiwan tended to invite the third party to resolve conflicts and use the integrating or obliging strategies to bring some conflicts to an end. To illustrate, in the Chinese culture, Confucianism is an authoritarian value that focuses on conformity, submission, and respect for one's parents and elders. To avoid face-to-face confrontation and keep a harmonious relationship, the Chinese leaders are more likely to invite a third party who is senior or respected by both parties to resolve the conflicts. In the case of this study, when the third party appeared as an arbiter with higher authority, the conflicts would be solved soon, and when the third party was objective, he/she was able to pacify the emotion and to save face for both parties. In fact, most of the conflicts in the Rotary Clubs in Taiwan were settled due to the important existence of the third party. Thus, in cultures like Taiwan, the factors of face, quanxi, and the third party need to be guaranteed for group or organizational harmony and, possibly, prosperity or productivity.

In conclusion, this study presents a new approach and is among the first to compare and contrast the female leaders' conflict management strategies in Rotary Clubs in Taiwan and the United States. Hopefully, the triangulated research findings and implications will serve as a bridge for those in both cultures to understand and apply the right conflict management strategies in various, especially culturally different, contexts.

Nevertheless, readers are cautioned to see the limitations of this study and interpret the research findings with full awareness to the caveats. First, this study has focused on exploring the conflict management strategies of only the female presidents in the Rotary

Clubs in Taiwan and the United States. Thus, readers may not see the whole picture of the gender differences. Second, the factors influencing the application of the conflict management strategies are mainly oriental in nature. Therefore, we suggest that appropriate application of the strategies should depend on not only the factors of face, human networks or connections, and the third party, but also other factors like the characteristics of the conflicts, the impact of the personalities of the conflicting parties, the relative positions of the conflicting parties as well as the interaction of the factors themselves. All this shows that we need to interpret the application of the relevant strategies from a more comprehensive and macro perspective rather than a single angle.

(Chao, C. C., & Tian, D. X. (2013). Keep things positive or do things right: Bridging women leaders' conflict management strategies in Taiwan and the US. *Chinese Management Studies*, 7(1), 94 – 110.)

References

[1] Adler, N. J. (1999). Global leadership: Women leaders. In W. H. Mobley, M. J. Gessner, & V. Arnold (Eds,), Advances in Global Leadership, 1, 127 – 161.

[2] Brewer, N., Mitchell, P., & Weber, N. (2002). Gender role, organizational status, and conflict management style. International Journal of Conflict Management, 13(1), 78 – 94.

[3] Chang, H., & Holt, R. (1991). More than relationship: Chinese interaction and the principle of guan-his. Communication Quarterly, 39, 251 – 271.

[4] Chao, C. (2009). Cultural values and anticipations of female leadership styles in non-profit organizations: A study of Rotary Clubs in Taiwan and the United States. Saarbrücken, Germany: VDM Verlag Dr. Müller Aktiengesellschaft & Co. KG.

[5] Chemers, M. M. (1997). An integrative theory of leadership. Lawrence Erlbaum, NJ: Mahwah.

[6] Chen, T. L. (2002). Leadership behavior for solution of conflict as perceived by physical education chair persons and faculty members in the USA. Hung-Guang Learning Newspaper, 39, 149 – 157.

[7] Chung, J. (1996). Avoiding a "Bull Moose" rebelling: Particularistic ties, seniority, and third-party mediation. International and Intercultural Communication Annual, 20, 166 – 185.

[8] Conrad, C., & Poole, M. S. (2002). Strategic organizational communication: In a global economy (5th). Fort Worth: Harcourt College Publishers.

[9] Cupach, W. R., & Canary, D. J. (1995). Managing conflict and anger: Investigating the sex stereotype hypothesis. In P. J. Kalabfleisch & M. J. Cody (Eds.), Gender, power, and communication in human relationships (pp. 233 – 252). Hillsdale, NJ: Erlbaum.

[10] Daniels, T. D., Spiker, B. K., & Papa, M. J. (1997). Perspectives on organizational communication(4th ed.). Madison, WI: Brown & Benchmark.

[11] Denzin, N. K. (1994). The art and politics of interpretation. In N. K. Denzin & Y. S. Lincoln (Eds.), Handbook of Qualitative Research. Thousand Oaks, CA: Sage.

[12] Eagly, A. H., & Karau, S. J. (2002). Role congruity theory of prejudice toward female leaders. Psychological Review, 109(3), 573-598.

[13] Gao, G. (1998). "Don't take my word for it." - Understanding Chinese speaking practices. International Journal of Intercultural Relations, 22, 163-186.

[14] Gladwin, T. N., & Walter, I. (1980). Multinationals under fire. New York: John Wiley & Sons.

[15] Glesne, C., & Peshkin, A. (1992). Becoming qualitative researchers: An introduction. White Plains: NY: Longman.

[16] Gross, M. A., & Guerrero, L. K. (2000). Managing conflict appropriately and effectively: An application of the competence model to Rahim's organizational conflict style. International Journal of Conflict Management, 11(3), 200-226.

[17] Hall, E. T. (1976). Beyond Culture. Garden City, NY: Anchor Press.

[18] Harris, T. E. (2002). Applied organizational communication: Principles and pragmatics for future practice (2nd ed.), Wahwah, NJ: Lawrence Erlbaum Associates.

[19] Hofstede, G. (1997). Cultural and organizations: Software of the mind. New York, NY: McGraw Hill.

[20] Jogulu, U. D., & Wood, G. J. (2006). The role of leadership theory in raising the profile of women in management. Equal Opportunities International, 25(4), 236-250.

[21] Kreitner, A., & Kinicki, R. (2002). Organizational behavior: Key concepts, skills & practices. Burr Ridge: Illinois: McGraw-Hill.

[22] Lee, C. W. (2002). Referent role and styles of handing interpersonal conflict: Evidence from a national sample of Korean local government employees. International Journal of Conflict Management, 13(2), 127-141.

[23] Luthans, F. (2002). Organizational behavior (9th ed.). New York: McGraw-Hill.

[24] Mead, R. (1998). International management. London: Blackwell Business.

[25] Mundate, L., Ganaza, J., Peiro, J. M., & Euwema, M. (1999). Patterns of styles in conflict management and effectiveness. International Journal of Conflict Management, 10(1). 5-24.

[26] Nelson, D. L., & Quick, J. C. (2000). Organizational behavior: Foundations, realities, and challenge. Cincinnati, OH: South-Western College Publishing.

[27] Northhouse, P. G. (2012). Leadership: Theory and practice, 6th ed. Thousand Oaks, CA: Sage.

[28] Ohbuchi, K., & Fukushima, O. (1997). Personality and interpersonal conflict:

Aggressiveness, self-monitoring, and situational variables. International Journal of Conflict Management, 8(2), 99-113.

[29] Owen, W. F. (1984). Interpretative themes in relational communication. Quarterly Journal of Speech, 70, 274-287.

[30] Rahim, M. A. (2001). Managing conflict in organizations (3rd). Westport, Conn: Quorum Books.

[31] Rahim, M. A., & Magner, N. R. (1995). Confirmatory factor analysis of the style of handling interpersonal conflict: First-order factor model and its invariance across groups. Journal of Applied Psychology, 80(1), 122-131.

[32] Rahim, M. A., Magner, N. R., & Shapiro, D. L. (2000). Do justice perceptions influence styles of handling conflict with supervisors? What justice perceptions, precisely. International Journal of Conflict Management, 11(1), 9-31.

[33] Robbins, S. P. (2001). Organizational behavior (9th ed.). Upper Saddle River, NJ: Prentice Hall.

[34] Rotary (2009), Members. Retrieved July 2, 2008, from http://www.rotary.org/en/Members/Pages/ridefault.aspx.

[35] Solamon, L. M. (1987). Partners in public services: The scope and theory of government. In W. W. Powell (Ed.), The nonprofit sector: A research handbook. (pp. 99-117). New Haven, CT: Yale University Press.

[36] Thomas, K. (1992). Conflict and conflict management. In M. D. Dunnette (Ed.), Handbook of Industrial and Organizational Psychology (pp. 889-935). Chicago: Rand McNally College Publishing Company.

[37] Ting-Toomey, S. (1988). Intercultural conflict styles. In Y. Y. Kim & W. B. Gudykunst (Eds.), Theories in intercultural communication (pp. 213-235). Beverly Hills, CA: Sage.

[38] Ting-Toomey, S., & Oetzel, J. (2001). Managing intercultural conflict effectively. Thousand Oaks, CA: Sage.

[39] Ting-Toomey, S. (2005). The matrix of face: An updated face-negotiation theory. In W. B. Gudykunst (Ed.), Theorizing about intercultural communication (pp. 211-234). Thousand Oaks, CA: Sage.

[40] Tinsley, C. H., & Brett, J. M. (2001). Managing workplace conflict in the United States and Hong Kong. Organizational Behavior and Human Processes, 85(2), 360-381.

Chapter 18
Culturally Universal or Culturally Specific: A Comparative Study of Anticipated Female Leadership Styles in Taiwan and the United States

In the past several decades, great progress has been witnessed in the empowerment of women in the business world and in the political arena. In the business world, according to Wu and Hsieh (2006), Indian-born Indra Nooyi was promoted to chief executive officer (CEO) of PepsiCo in 2006, and Irene Rosenfeld became the CEO of Kraft Foods, the world's second largest food producer. The famous CEO of Hewlett-Packard, Carly Fiorina, is another example of top female business executives. She was elected as the most powerful woman in business in 1998 and 1999 by Fortune magazine. Scot and Brown (2006) also noted that women hold 30% of the managerial positions in Europe, 36% in Canada, and 37% in the United States. In comparison, women in Taiwan own 33.87% of the enterprises and run 10% of the large-sized companies, and they "are as good as their counterparts in the developed societies such as the United States and Canada" (Wang, 2007, p.1). With each passing year, there are more and more well-known female representatives, not only in the fields of business but in politics as well.

For instance, there are six female prime ministers and nine female presidents worldwide. Specifically, Germany elected its first female chancellor, Angela Merkel, in 2005; South Korea gained its first female prime minister, Han Myeong-sook, in 2006; and in the same year, the United States elected its first female speaker of the House, Nancy Pelosi. As for Taiwan, Lu Hsiu-lien was elected as vice president in 2000 and 2004, which "marked the beginning of a new era of party change, and rule shared by both men and women in Taiwan" (Government Information Office, 2007, p.1). In terms of female parliamentarians, Taiwan's ratio was 22.2% or 31st in the world. Taiwan's Gender Related Development Index in 2000 was .888, ranking 23rd in the world and at the top of Asia's "four little dragons" (Taiwan, South Korea, Hong Kong, and Singapore; I. Wu & Hsieh, 2006).

However, there is still a long way to go to achieve gender equality. Equality here does not necessarily mean that women and men must be the same in all circumstances. What should be emphasized is the realization of the full potential of men and women and the full consideration of their interests, needs, and priorities. In other words, the opportunities, rights, and responsibilities of women and men do not depend on whether they are born female or male. In actuality, the progress for women "while steady, has been painfully slow" (Chen, Vanek, Lund, & Heintz, 2005, p. 1).

In the United States, as Mather (2007) reported, although women currently account for nearly one half of the total U.S. labor force, only one fourth of them are in the science and engineering labor force. Pynes (2000) also noted that women made up just 16% of the chief executives in the nation, and their median salary was almost $30,000 less than that of the average male executives in one survey of 188 of the United States' largest nonprofit organizations. The results of another study involving 100 nonprofit organizations showed that female board members accounted for 23% of the board, and nine of the boards examined had no female members. According to Falk and Grizard (2005), in American *Fortune 500* companies, females occupied just 13.6% of managerial positions. In other corporations, only 16% of the managers were women, and they held just 4% of senior managerial positions. Obviously, "men were disproportionately represented in upper-level management and earn higher salaries than women at all levels of the organization" (Pynes, 2000, p. 35).

In Taiwan, the rate of female participation in business and politics also lags behind that of men and that of other developed areas around the world. Within Taiwan proper, the number of females accounts for just 16% of managerial and administrative positions. The ratio of female to male administrators and managers is relatively low (I. Wu & Hsieh, 2006). To sum up, it is true that female political and economic status have been promoted because of equal rights efforts and education. However, female participation rates in public affairs and decision-making positions are still quite low.

Therefore, we undertook a comparative quantitative study specifically on female leadership in nonprofit organizations in the diverse cultural contexts of the United States and Taiwan. Although Dorfman and House (2004) emphasized the importance of conducting leadership studies in different cultures, we kept fully aware of Denmark's (1993) caveat that "by ignoring gender as a variable in studying leadership, researchers created many blanks in theoretical and research design" (p. 345). House (1995) also remarked that about 98% of leadership theory emanates from the United States; therefore, Bass (1995) urged that there has been a need for research in more culturally diverse settings as most leadership research has used samples merely from Western cultures. Since there have been very few studies comparing female leadership in nonprofit organizations in different countries or cultures in communication studies, we aimed to fill in this void by conducting a comparative and cross-cultural study of the impact of cultural values on the anticipated female leadership styles in nonprofit organizations in Taiwan and the United States. To this end, the following research question guides this study:

Research Question: What are the cultural values that affect Rotary Club members' anticipated female leadership styles? And what are the best predictors of leadership style anticipations?

In the following sections, we first present the literature review, theoretical framework, and the developed hypotheses. We then describe the data used to test these hypotheses and report our research results. Finally, we discuss how cultural dimensions are associated with anticipated female leadership styles and the implications behind the numbers.

Literature Review

The study of leadership has a long history with abundant scholarship both in China and the United States. According to Chang (2008), the study of different leadership styles in China began to be recorded in historical documents 2,500 years ago. In the United States, however, there have been more profound and comprehensive scholarships on leadership in the past several decades. For instance, there have been more than 7,500 studies relevant to leadership in the social and science literature in the United States (Aldoory & Toth, 2004). For the purpose of this study, we will briefly review the Chinese and American scholarships on leadership in terms of cultural values, gender, and leadership styles in the following section.

Cultural Values

Cultural values guide people's behavior, and leadership styles reflect cultural values Research has also shown that cultural values influence leadership behaviors (Booysen, 1999, 2000; Hofstede, 1980a, 1980b, 1991, 1998; House et al., 1999; House, Wright, & Aditya, 1997). Kluckhohn (1951) defined value as "a conception, explicit or implicit, distinctive of an individual or characteristic of a group, of the desirable which influences the selection from available modes, means, and ends of action" (p. 395). Hofstede (1980a) added that a value is "a broad tendency to prefer to certain states of affairs over others" (p. 19). Martin and Nakayama (2007) further indicated that cultural values are the worldview of a cultural group or the core symbols of a particular identity. For example, individualism is often cited as one of the most important Euro-American values, as reflected in the emphasis on participative leadership. In the case of Taiwan, although studies show that the current generation is more individualistic than older generations, the traditional value of collectivism is still the core symbol of the Taiwanese culture and social structure, as reflected in the preference in authoritarian leadership (M. Wu & Stewart, 2005). In summary, all of the above scholars agreed that values form the core of culture, and cultural values exert impact on leadership styles.

Leadership Styles

Leadership can be described as processes that not only influence members to recognize and agree with what needs to be done and how it can be done effectively but also facilitate individual and collective efforts to accomplish the shared goals and visions (Yukl, 2002). In addition, according to Eagly, Johannesen-Schmidt, and Engen (2003), leadership styles are the relatively appropriate patterns of behavior applied by leaders. Based on their multifactor leadership questionnaire, Eagly et al. further summarized and described three major leadership styles. First, transformational leaders tend to bring about change in organizations and establish oneself as a role model by gaining the followers' trust. Transactional leaders, however, usually appeal to subordinates' self-interest through establishing exchange relationships with them. Finally, leaders following the laissez-faire style are often found failing to take responsibility for what they are managing.

As for the Chinese leadership styles in Taiwan, according to scholars (Chang, 2008; Chen, Beck, & Amos, 2005), they not only had their basis in the philosophies of Legalism, Taoism, and Confucianism, but they also integrated contemporary Western theories of leadership into actual practice. As a result, leadership styles in Taiwan demonstrate three frame orientations: director, parent, and mentor. Originated from Legalism, the features of the director leadership style are legality, strategy, and position. Parent leadership style is based on Taoism, so leaders and followers form emotional relationships that function like a family to a great extent. Finally, the mentor leadership style reflects the influence of Confucianism, and leader-led relationships are similar to mentor-learner dynamics with features such as guiding, sharing, and inspiring.

It is not hard to see from the above that differences in cultural values in Taiwan and the United States shape different leadership styles. Although frequent exchanges in all social sectors between the two peoples have brought about more and more commonalities, there still exist substantial discrepancies in leadership styles in the two societies. As this study specifically addresses female leadership styles, it is crucial to examine the relevant scholarships on gender and leadership styles.

Gender and Leadership Styles

With regard to the relationship between gender and leadership styles, many studies (Aldoory & Toth, 2004; Bass & Avolio, 1997; Eagly, 2007; Eagly et al., 2003; Morgan, 2006) indicated that there is a significant difference between male and female leadership styles. In 1991, the International Women's Forum conducted a survey and discovered that male supervisors tend to adopt a transactional leadership style, which means that men would give nominal rewards when subordinates do something right and punish them if they do something wrong. Female supervisors, by contrast, tend to use a transformational leadership style, which means that the leader will achieve the company's major goals by actively interacting with subordinates, encouraging employee involvement in decision making, sharing authority and information, respecting employee self-value, and encouraging employees to love their jobs.

Bass and Avolio (1997) indicated that the development tendency of U.S. organizations may contribute to the exhibition and emphasis of female leadership styles. Female leaders may use more transformational leadership skills than male leaders, which make a positive impact on the performance of an individual, group, and organization. Morgan (2006) also remarked that organizations shaped by male value systems emphasize logical, linear modes of thought and action, and drive for productivity at the cost of network and community building. In contrast, organizations that are shaped by female value systems tend to "balance and integrate the rational-analytic mode with values that emphasize more empathic, intuitive, organic forms of behavior" (p. 131). Chao and Ha (2007) reconfirmed the above study results in their qualitative study that examined top female leaders in the U.S. cable industry and found that these female leaders demonstrated a common use of the transformational leadership style and integrating conflict management strategy.

Based on their meta-analysis of 45 studies of transformational, transactional, and laissez-faire leadership styles, Eagly et al. (2003) added that female leadership styles are more transformational and women leaders are more likely to use rewards for appropriate performance from subordinates. Thus, compared with their male counterparts, female leaders are "more focused on those aspects of leadership that predict effectiveness" (p. 586). However, women and men do not enjoy equal access to opportunities of leadership, and they may be treated differently even if they are in leadership positions. Just as Eagly (2007) described, women "are still portrayed as suffering disadvantages in access to leadership positions as well as prejudice and resistance when they occupy these roles" (p. 1). The fact is that in the United States today, women are often considered secondary in competitions to obtain leadership positions though research findings prove that women have "the right combination of skills for leadership, yielding superior leadership styles and outstanding effectiveness" (p. 1).

From the above, it can be inferred that the issues concerning gender and leadership styles are very extensive; one single factor is not sufficient to make a thorough study. Besides gender, factors affecting leadership styles may include management level, organizational style, work ambiance (such as departmental heterogeneity and team members' gender), industrial type, size, and company policy (Van Engen & Willemsen, 2001). It is also clear that the bulk of the leadership literature reflects Western industrialized culture; even Hofstede's study (1980a) used subjects from a large U.S. multinational corporation with a strong American culture. It is likely that most leadership scholarships are culture bound, reflecting U.S. values and beliefs.

Therefore, putting a cross-cultural study of female leadership styles on the agenda has become all the more necessary. The review of relevant scholarships in the above sections also shows that the leadership style of female supervisors is turning to the trend of transformational leadership. Because of the development and the popularity of nonprofit organizations, competition among similar organizations has become more severe, and the pressure resulting from such competition inevitably creates conflicts among members. As the number of females who are either involved in or lead nonprofit organizations is rapidly increasing, how females cope with challenges, especially in male-dominated organizations, is an issue worth studying.

Theoretical Frameworks and Hypotheses

To search for the answers to our research question, we modified Hofstede's (1984,

1994, 2001a) cultural dimensions and adopted Bass and Avolio's (1997) leadership notions as the theoretical frameworks.

Cultural Dimensions and Hypothesis 1

We used Hofstede's cultural theory not only because he was one of the major researchers who studied more than 100,000 employees in more than 40 countries to increase intercultural understanding and has been linked most clearly to communication behavior, but also because his cultural dimensions are still widely used for analyses of phenomena pertaining to different cultures (Arrindell, Steptoe, & Wardle, 2003). However, Hofstede's theory of cultural dimensions has sparked criticism over the years. For instance, according to Soendergaard (1994), the use of employees of one company as a foundation for conclusions about national dimensions was questionable. Baskerville (2003) also questioned the use of countries as a unit of cultural analysis.

To minimize cultural bias, we, therefore, modified Hofstede's cultural dimensions and developed more culturally specific scale items. Two of Hofstede's dimensions (Power Distance and Uncertainty Avoidance) are not adopted for this study for a couple of reasons. First, there is less power distance in nonprofit organizations, since nonprofit organization members tend to follow self-governing and voluntary models, and everyone is supposed to be equal in such settings. Second, according to Howell (1992), the items of uncertainty avoidance index reflect three different constructs. Wu and Stewart (2005) added that the dimension of uncertainty avoidance is not statistically reliable. Apart from this, we also expanded Hofstede's cultural dimension of Long-Term Orientation (or Confucian Work Dynamics) by operationalizing it as "Customs/Value Priorities" and "Lifelong/Work-Related Relationships". The essential dimensions that serve as the focus of the study are defined below.

Collectivism/individualism. This dimension, collectivism versus individualism, investigates how people value themselves and their groups/organizations. For instance, organizational goals are more important than individual goals in collectivistic cultures. According to Hofstede (1980a), differences between Eastern and Western cultures regarding individualism/collectivism have been found. Many Eastern cultures (e.g., China and Korea) tend to have high scores in collectivism, whereas numerous Western cultures (e.g., the United States and Canada) are more oriented to individualism.

Masculinity/femininity. The second dimension, masculinity versus femininity, refers to the gender roles in cultures. In high feminine cultures, men and women are treated equally; in highly masculine organizations, however, there may be a "labyrinth" for females to pass through a tortuous, demanding, and exhausting path in order to move upward (Eagly & Carli, 2007).

Customs and value priorities. Hofstede and Bond (1988) proposed the dimension of long-term orientation or Confucian work dynamics. As we mentioned previously, this dimension has been expanded to the dimensions of "Customs/Value Priorities" and "Lifelong

Relationships". Smith and Schwartz (1997) claimed that the customs and value priorities that are prevalent in a society are key elements in its culture to relate to all aspects of an individual's behavior. It is well known that Confucianism, which represents the essential Chinese value priorities such as the concepts of face and *ren qing*, has played an important role in Asian countries over many thousands of years. Thus, customs and values are well suited for examining the ongoing process of cultural changes in the dynamic social context of the world.

According to Hu and Grove (1991), there are two basic categories of face in the Chinese culture: *lian* and *mianzi*. A person's lian can be preserved by faithful compliance with ritual and social norms. One gains *lian* by displaying moral character, but when one loses *lian*, he or she cannot function properly in the community because respect is lost. However, *mianzi* represents a more Western concept of face, reputation, or respect achieved through success in life. Thus, although Americans may prefer not to embarrass themselves or others in public, they will not generally go as far as Chinese do to avoid embarrassment. As a Chinese saying goes, a person needs face like a tree needs bark (*ren yao lian*; *shu yao pi*). The saying expresses the meaning that a person's self-esteem is often formed on the basis of others' remarks.

In the Chinese culture, *ren qing* coupled with *bao* is managed in different types of interpersonal transactions. A person who understands *ren qing* knows how to reciprocate (*bao*). Therefore, the receiver of *ren qing* will not reject the provider's requests because a person who is indebted to *ren qing* needs to pay back. A well-known Chinese saying, "You honor me a plum, and I will in return honor you a peach," attests to this principle of reciprocity. To illustrate, if one were given a favor or a gift, one would immediately be in a double bind situation: rejecting it would be rude and disruptive to the harmony of the relationship; accepting it, however, would put one in an only "yes" situation (i.e., unable to decline a request from the gift provider for a favor). Also, if one fails to reciprocate, one is perceived as heartless. Americans, by contrast, do not view give-and-take as a relationship-building or social investment (Zhu, 1990).

Life-long/work-related relationships. Since social interactions in Chinese cultures involve dynamic relationships, this important Chinese value is one of the cultural dimensions of the present study. Friendship/support relationships (or *guanxi* in Chinese) are increasingly complex relationships, which expand day by day, throughout the entire lives of the Chinese. To the Chinese, it is essential to create connections (or *la guanxi*) between people who have a mutually dependent relationship in their daily life. To do so, the Chinese may use some strategies such as showing care, giving a gift, or offering a favor (Hwang, 1991). In contrast to the social patterns in Western societies, especially the United States, these relationships continue long after the groups dissolve. Except within some families, Americans generally avoid relationships of mutual dependence. Even though Americans have the notion of "networking," it involves more limited obligations than "*guanxi*." Networking may require getting acquainted with people who are in a position to give information and perhaps help in areas related to gaining employment or promotion in a job and to carry out work-related responsibilities (Hwang, 1990). Thus, people in one's network are not expected to provide assistance in a wide range of aspects of life as in *guanxi*; they are expected to take care of themselves (Bond & Hwang, 1993). Therefore, the different concepts of relationship are worthy of examination in this study.

In addition to the above rationale, Hofstede (2001a) further revealed that the American business culture is characterized by very low long-term orientation (score: 29) but high masculinity (score: 62) and individualism (score: 91). In contrast, Taiwan has very high long-term orientation (score: 87), moderate masculine (score: 45), and low individualism (score: 17).

Given the above rationale and previous research findings, our first hypothesis was the following:

Hypothesis 1: Cultural value dimensions significantly differ between Taiwan and the United States as represented by Rotary Club members.

Leadership Framework: Hypotheses 2 and 3

Apart from Hofstede's cultural dimensions, we also adopted Bass and Avolio's (1997) full-range leadership notions, including transformational, transactional, and laissez-faire leadership styles, as our theoretical frameworks. Transformational and transactional leadership styles were first developed by Burns (1978) and expanded by Bass (1985) and Sadler (2003). According to Burns (1978), traditional leadership emphasizes transactions and is thus called transactional leadership. This type of leadership relationship is based on an exchange process; a leader offers a reward in exchange for the employees' efforts. Transactional leadership is represented by four behavioral elements: Contingent Rewards, Active Management by Exception, Passive Management by Exception, and Laissez-Faire. In Contingent Rewards, leaders reinforce the loyalty of subordinates for accomplishing job goals by using contingent rewards. As for Active Management by Exception, leaders are vigilant for any variations beyond regulations and standards and are ready to take action. In Passive Management by Exception, in contrast, leaders intervene only when standards are not fulfilled. In Laissez-Faire style, however, leaders will give up their authority and avoid making decisions (Robbins, 2001; Yukl, 2002).

Transformational leadership builds on transactional leadership (Bass & Avolio, 1994). Transformational leadership can be considered as a process where leaders and followers influence each other to enhance morale and motivation. According to Burns (1978), transformational leadership is more effective than transactional leadership, where the appeal is to more self-centered concerns. He also views transformational leadership as a continuing process rather than the discrete exchanges of the transactional approach. Bass and Avolio

(1994) proposed that transformational leadership contains four types of characteristics, also known as the four Is, including Charisma/Idealized Influence, Inspirational Motivation, Intellectual Stimulation, and Individualized Consideration.

Albritton (1998) applied a Multifactor Leadership Questionnaire to test transactional and transformational models in academic libraries and found that transformational leadership was perceived as having more effect on leadership outcomes and dimensions of organization effectiveness than did transactional leadership. Bass and Avolio (1989) supported the distinction between transformational and transactional leadership. They also pointed out that although laissez-faire leadership is revealed infrequently in U.S. businesses, leaders still exhibit it in varying amounts (as cited in Bass, 1990). Previous studies have also found that laissez-faire leadership has an adverse impact on work-related performance of subordinates (Bass, 1990).

According to Engen, Leeden, and Willemsen (2001), since the transformational leadership style emphasizes the leader's intellectual stimulation and the individual consideration given to employees, this style can be depicted as a feminine leadership style. As mentioned above, some studies discovered female leaders displaying more transformational behaviors and fewer transactional styles than male leaders. In addition, transactional and transformational leadership have also been examined in various cultures. For example, Yokochi (1989) reported that the top leaders in several large Japanese firms rated by followers as more transformational also had higher ratings on their followers' level of effectiveness.

Furthermore, according to Earley and Gibson (1998), a number of cross-cultural studies have shown that collectivists tend to have a stronger attachment to their organizations and tend to subordinate their individual goals to group goals. Indeed, many leaders in collectivist cultures highlight the importance of maintaining long-term relationships as well as in-group solidarity (Elenkov, 1998). The aforementioned central values of collectivist cultures are some of the main orientations associated with transformational leadership. That is, a transformational leader is anticipated to build followers' identification with a collective vision, as well as to enhance motivation and performance among followers (Jung, Bass, & Sosik, 1995).

By contrast, to satisfy their own self-interests, people with high individualism place higher priority on individual achievement, as well as on personal rewards based on satisfying transactional agreements. The person or self is defined as an independent entity. These characteristics match the transactional leadership model since they are typically more focused on short-term results. Given the previous rationale and literature review, we proposed two more hypotheses:

Hypothesis 2: Anticipated female leadership styles significantly differ between Taiwan and the United States as represented by Rotary Club members.

Hypothesis 3: Cultural values and anticipated female leadership styles in Taiwan and the

United States are significantly correlated with each other

Method

As we mentioned previously, the present study was conducted in Rotary Clubs. Briefly, Rotary is an international organization of business and professional leaders who provide humanitarian service, encourage high ethical standards in all vocations, and help build goodwill and peace in the world. More than 160 countries worldwide have Rotary Clubs. Approximately 1.2 million Rotarians belong to more than 30,000 Rotary Clubs (Rotary International, 2007).

However, constrained by the shortage of time, resources, and funds, only two independent samples are selected, for this study, from the population of Rotary District 3510 in Taiwan and Rotary District 6600 in the United States. We used the mail survey method to collect data so as to explore the causal relationship between the cultural values of the Rotary Club members and their general anticipation of female leadership styles in Taiwan and the United States. According to Singleton and Straits (2005), the survey method is an appropriate way to generalize an accurate picture of behaviors or ideas, and mail questionnaires have been found to be one of the most frequently used methods to conduct an accurate survey. The survey instrument in this study was developed by using some existing, field-tested leadership measures, including Bass and Avolio's (1997) Multifactor Leadership Questionnaire Form 6S, and Hofstede's (1994) Value Survey Module. However, since the Value Survey Module was initially designed for American culture, and this study was conducted in both Taiwan and the United States, some scale items were changed to include culturally specific items.

The questionnaire contains three parts. Part A comprises 20 declarative statements to measure four cultural dimensions (Collectivism, Masculinity, Customs, and Lifelong Relationships). On all subscales, a high score indicates a high degree of the characteristic concerned. For instance, a high score on the collectivism dimension displays a high degree of collectivism. An example of the statements on collectivism is "Harmony and consensus in our club are ultimate goals." Part B assesses Rotarians' anticipated female leadership style. The 21 items in Part B are adapted from the Multifactor Leadership Questionnaire Form 6S, including transformational leadership style, transactional leadership styles, and laissez-faire style. A sample item of idealized influence in transformational leadership style is "I anticipate female leaders to let members feel good to be around them." Part C asks for the demographic information of the participants.

For cross-cultural research, it is imperative to create equivalent bases on which such comparisons could be made, and the equivalence can only be assured through the use of rigorous procedures such as back-translation (Lonner, 1979). Thus, the questionnaire were designed in English and translated into Chinese. A Chinese doctoral student back-translated the Chinese version of the questionnaire to English. An American English professor compared the original English questionnaire and the back-translated version to identify the questions that could cause differences between them. The translation was revised to deal with the differences. All participants were invited to complete the questionnaire in their native languages.

A pilot survey was conducted with a sample of 50 in both Taiwan and the United States to identify potential problems with the interpretation of terms and concepts. To ensure the internal consistency of the scales that measure members' cultural values and their anticipated female leadership styles, reliability tests based on Cronbach's coefficient alpha were conducted. The reliability scores were from .932 to .587. Although the scales reached the acceptable standard (Reinard, 2001), we still fixed the wording of some items in Part A based on some comments of two quantitative professors.

Formal Study

The two independent samples for this study are Rotary Club members drawn from the population of Rotary District 3510 in Taiwan and Rotary District 6600 in the United States, since the senior researcher has been a Rotary member in both districts. The samples for this study were selected based on the criteria of functional equivalence and representativeness. The samples are functionally equivalent since all the participants are Rotary Club members in both locations. Since Rotary is an international organization, all its members around the world share similar missions and goals, provide similar objectives of services, and observe the same criteria. In addition, the two districts are similar in size with 71 clubs in District 3510 and 67 clubs in District 6600. To be representative of the targeted Rotary Club members, the samples were randomly chosen.

Instrumentation. Similar to the pilot study, the questionnaire contains three parts, which ask for responses on the four cultural dimensions (Part A), anticipated female leadership styles (Part B), and demographic information (Part C). The items in the first two parts ask the respondents to indicate how much they disagree or agree with each of the statements on a 5-point Likert-type scale (1=*strongly disagree* to 5=*strongly agree*).

Procedure and participants. Although the senior author had been an active Rotarian for both districts, we still had to conduct the surveys for each sample at different times because we needed time to get the members' list of both Rotary districts and the governors' endorsement from each district. By so doing, we actually increased the response rate. In total, 550 questionnaires were sent out to Rotary Club members in District 3510, Taiwan, from June 15 to July 15, 2007, and 550 questionnaires were sent out to Rotary Club members in District 6600, the United States, from September 15 to October 15, 2007. The survey instruments were distributed by mailing to the randomly chosen subjects with an enclosed preaddressed and postage-paid return envelope, district governors' endorsement, and a consent letter explaining the purpose of the study. The consent letter stated plainly that their response would be treated as confidential, and there were no right or wrong answers to the questions. Also, it is stated clearly in the questionnaire instruction that participation was completely voluntary. Respondents were asked to return the completed surveys via the enclosed preaddressed and postage-paid envelope and informed that completion of the surveys equated to granting their consent to partake in the study.

The total number of the participants was 307, and the overall response rates of the questionnaires were 27.3% ($n=150$) in Taiwan and 28.5% ($n=157$) in the United States. The data show that the number of male respondents is 2.5 times (60.7%) that of female respondents (24%) in Taiwan, whereas the number of male respondents (84.1%) is 5 times that of female respondents (16.7%) in the United States. The overall distribution of formal educational attainment is slightly skewed to higher education with the majority of the sample earning a bachelor's degree (43.3%) in Taiwan. The majority of the U.S. samples even have master's or Ph.D. degrees (45.9%). This means that, overall, both samples are well educated in the two districts, and most of the respondents are married (76.7% in Taiwan and 86.5% in the United States).

In Taiwan, most respondents are between 51 and 65 years (43.3%) with a mean age of 55 years, whereas in the United States, most respondents are similarly between 51 and 65 years (41.7%) with a mean age of 57 years. As for the years of membership, most respondents have 11 to 20 years of membership (35.4%) in Taiwan, but most respondents have just 4 to 10 years of membership (37.8%) in the United States. Whereas nearly half of the samples are past presidents (46.7%), more than half of the respondents are regular members (52.9%) in the United States. In terms of their work positions, most respondents are in managerial positions in both countries, with the United States slightly higher in proportion of respondents holding managerial positions (48% in Taiwan and 66.9% in the United States). Finally, most Taiwanese respondents believe in Buddhism (58.7%), whereas most U.S. respondents' religious beliefs are either Christianity or Catholicism (93%).

Validity and reliability. Similar to the pilot study, the formal questionnaire had four parts, which measure the participants' cultural values and anticipated leadership styles. Hofstede's (1994) cultural dimensions were modified as the theoretical basis for the questions. As previously stated, the wording of some items in Part A was fixed based on the results of the pilot study and two experts' comments. However, after running the Cronbach's coefficient alpha tests for the formal questionnaire, we still encountered low reliability scores for some items. To achieve acceptable reliability scores, we canceled three items in Part A. As for the leadership items in Part B, all the three leadership clusters performed adequately, ranging from $\alpha=0.917$ to $\alpha=0.681$ in the present study. Just as Clark and Watson (1995) indicated, reliabilities in the 0.6 to 0.7 range have been characterized as good or adequate. The factors of customs and lifelong relationships fell below the recommended value but were included in the analyses because they approximated the cut-off scores. Nevertheless, the low reliability coefficients were viewed as a limitation to the study. The internal consistency coefficients of the items in the questionnaire are presented in Table 1.

Table 1 Reliability for Subscale Variables

Variables	α
Part A: Cultural dimensions	
Collectivism/Individualism	0.662
Masculinity/Femininity	0.625
Customs and Value Priorities	0.574
Lifelong/Work-Related Relationships	0.575
Part B: Leadership styles	
Transformational Leadership	0.917
Transactional Leadership	0.681
Laissez-Faire Leadership	0.781

Results

In our analysis, demographic variables such as gender, age, marital status, length of membership, education, religious beliefs, and business position have been statistically controlled to rule out their influence on the results. Frequencies were run for all cultural dimensions, leadership styles, demographic information, and control variables to examine data distribution and data entry errors. Statistical significance tests were also run to compare the differences between Taiwan and the United States. To answer the research question, three hypotheses were formulated.

Hypothesis 1: Country Differences on Cultural Value Dimensions

Hypothesis 1 proposed that cultural value dimensions significantly differ between Taiwan and the United States as represented by Rotary Club members. The independent sample t test was applied to test the differences in dimension scores, the results of which are shown in Table 2.

Table 2 T-Test Results of Cultural Values

Variable	Taiwan of China (n=150)		United States (n=157)		t	df	p
	Mean	SD	Mean	SD			
Collectivism	3.85	0.53	3.68	0.59	2.629	305	0.009
Masculinity	2.73	0.55	2.34	0.72	5.295	305	0.001
Customs/Value Priorities	3.92	0.46	3.21	0.47	13.321	305	0.001
Lifelong relationships	3.97	0.46	3.42	0.53	9.688	305	0.001

Based on a sample of 307 Rotarians and a 95% confidence level, we can conclude that the research findings verify the assumption that there is a significant difference in the Rotary Club members' cultural values between Taiwan and the United States (collectivism: $t=$

2.629, $df=305$, $p=0.009$; masculinity: $t=5.295$, $df=305$, $p=0.001$; customs: $t=13.321$, $df=305$, $p=0.001$; and lifelong relationships: $t=9.688$, $df=305$, $p=0.001$). Rotary Club members in Taiwan demonstrated higher means in all four cultural dimensions than those in the United States: collectivism (Taiwan mean = 3.85, U.S. mean = 3.68), masculinity (Taiwan mean = 2.73, U.S. mean = 2.34), customs (Taiwan mean = 3.92, U.S. mean = 3.21), and lifelong relationships (Taiwan mean = 3.97, U.S. mean = 3.42). Hence, the assumption of this study that the two countries exhibit different cultural dimensions is validated.

Hypothesis 2: Country Difference on Anticipated Female Leadership Styles

Hypothesis 2 proposed that anticipated female leadership styles significantly differ between Taiwan and the United States as represented by Rotary Club members. The results of the independent sample t test revealed that there is a significant difference in the anticipations of female leaders demonstrating transformational ($t=-2.287$, $df=305$, $p=0.023$) and laissez-faire ($t=12.616$, $df=305$, $p=0.001$) leadership styles in Taiwan and the United States, but there is no significant difference in the anticipation of female leaders displaying transactional leadership style ($t=0.917$, $df=305$, $p=0.360$) in Taiwan and the United States (as shown in Table 3).

Table 3 T-Test Results of Leadership Styles

Variable	Taiwan of China ($n=150$)		United States ($n=157$)				
	Mean	SD	Mean	SD	t	df	p
Transformational Leadership	3.63	0.57	3.76	0.47	−2.287	305	0.023
Transactional Leadership	3.54	0.49	3.49	0.48	0.917	305	0.36
Laissez-Faire Leadership	2.94	0.67	2.05	0.57	12.616	305	0.001

In addition, after comparing their means, the data show that Rotary Club members in the United States have a higher anticipation that female leaders will demonstrate transformational leadership styles than their Taiwanese counterparts (Taiwan mean = 3.63, U.S. mean = 3.76). Rotary Club members in Taiwan have a slightly higher anticipation that female leaders will demonstrate transactional leadership styles (Taiwan mean = 3.54, U.S. mean = 3.49) and much higher anticipation of laissez-faire style (Taiwan mean = 2.94, U.S. mean = 2.05) than their American counterparts.

Hypothesis 3: The Correlated Relationship between Cultural Values and Anticipated Female Leadership Styles

Hypothesis 3 proposed that cultural values and anticipated female leadership styles in Taiwan and the United States are significantly correlated with each other. To compare the country differences between cultural values and anticipated female leadership styles and determine how different variables affect each other, a series of regression analyses were run via Statistical Package for the Social Sciences. To find the best equations in predicting each anticipated leadership style, we examined three models as shown in Tables 4 to 6.

Table 4 Regression Models for the Relationship Between Cultural Dimensions and Anticipations of Female Leaders to Use Transformational Leadership Style in Taiwan of China and the United States

Regressor	Model 1		Model 2		Model 2	
	B	β	B	β	B	β
Intercept	1.826***	0.000	1.279***	0.000	1.044*	0.000
Collectivism	0.105*	0.113*	0.171**	0.184**	0.157*	0.169*
Masculinity	−0.009	−0.012	0.036	0.047	0.097	0.127
Customs	0.097	0.108	0.051	0.057	0.090	0.101
Lifelong relationships	0.369***	0.397***	0.354***	0.385***	0.349***	0.380***
Taiwan(Taiwan of China=1, United States=0)	−0.423***	−0.402***	−0.324*	−0.311*	0.235	0.226
Age			0.003	0.070	0.002	0.053
Female			0.153	0.121	0.168	0.133
Education(less than a college degree is the reference group)						
Bachelor			−0.021	−0.020	−0.031	−0.030
MA, PhD			−0.063	−0.059	−0.081	−0.075
Married			0.025	0.016	0.015	0.015
President			0.038	0.036	0.041	0.041
Managerial			0.078	0.073	0.094	0.094
Religion(neither Christian nor Buddhist is the reference group)						
Christianity			0.103	0.099	0.124	0.119
Buddhism			−0.015	−0.014	−0.016	−0.015
Interaction terms						
Taiwan × Collectivism					0.008	0.029
Taiwan × Masculinity					−0.201*	−0.551*
Taiwan × Customs					−0.050	−0.189
Taiwan × Long-Term Relationship					0.036	0.138
RSS	17.317		20.81		21.773	
MSE	0.226		0.206		0.206	
F	15.294***		6.302***		5.288***	
R^2	0.203		0.275		0.288	
Adjusted R^2	0.189		0.231		0.233	

NOTE: RSS = regression sum of squares; MSE = mean square error
* $p<0.05$. ** $p<0.01$. *** $p<0.001$.

Table 5 Regression Models for the Relationship Between Cultural Dimensions and Anticipations of Female Leaders to Use Transactional Leadership Style in Taiwan of China and the United States

Regressor	Model 1		Model 2		Model 2	
	B	β	B	β	B	β
Intercept	2.114***	0.000	1.729***	0.000	1.801*	0.000
Collectivism	0.087*	0.103*	0.088	0.103	0.040	0.047
Masculinity	−0.099*	−0.139*	−0.089*	−0.128*	−0.077	−0.110
Customs	0.240***	0.291***	0.221***	0.272***	0.245**	0.301**
Lifelong relationships	0.151**	0.177**	0.156**	0.186**	0.147*	0.176*
Taiwan (Taiwan of China=1, United States=0)	−0.178**	−0.185**	0.010	0.11	−0.307	0.012
Age			0.000	0.011	0.000	−0.324
Female			0.132	0.114	0.145	0.125
Education (less than a college degree is the reference group)						
Bachelor			−0.122	−0.129	−0.108	−0.115
MA, PhD			−0.084	−0.086	−0.074	−0.075
Married			0.031	0.022	0.023	0.016
President			0.040	0.042	0.041	0.043
Managerial			0.005	0.005	0.010	0.010
Religion (neither Christian nor Buddhist is the reference group)						
Christianity			0.226*	0.238*	0.235*	0.247*
Buddhism			0.090	0.089	0.073	0.072
Interaction terms						
Taiwan×Collectivism					0.134	0.555
Taiwan×Masculinity					−0.011	−0.034
Taiwan×Customs					−0.096	−0.402
Taiwan×Long-Term Relationship					0.055	0.229
RSS	9.259		10.638		11.035	
MSE	0.206		0.197		0.198	
F	8.994***		3.381***		2.785***	
R^2	0.103		0.169		0.175	
Adjusted R^2	0.116		0.119		0.112	

NOTE: RSS = regression sum of squares; MSE = mean square error

* $p<0.05$. ** $p<0.01$. *** $p<0.001$.

Chapter 18

Culturally Universal or Culturally Specific: A Comparative Study of Anticipated Female Leadership Styles in Taiwan and the United States

Table 6 Regression Models for the Relationship Between Cultural Dimensions and Anticipations of Female Leaders to Use Laissez-Faire Leadership Style in Taiwan of China and the United States

Regressor	Model 1		Model 2		Model 2	
	B	β	B	β	B	β
Intercept	1.013**	0.000	1.686***	0.000	2.203*	0.000
Collectivism	0.100*	0.074	0.094	0.068	−0.015	−0.011
Masculinity	0.147*	0.129**	0.122*	0.107*	0.062	0.054
Customs	0.169*	0.129*	0.120	0.090	0.042	0.032
Lifelong relationships	−0.064	−0.047**	−0.069	−0.050	0.052	0.038
Taiwan (Taiwan of China=1, United States=0)	0.739***	0.483***	0.717***	0.463***	−0.373	−0.241
Age			−0.001	−0.015	0.000	−0.006
Female			−0.144	−0.76	−0.162	−0.086
Education (less than a college degree is the reference group)						
Bachelor			−0.059	−0.038	−0.025	−0.016
MA, PhD			0.046	0.029	0.080	0.050
Married			−0.027	−0.011	−0.025	−0.011
President			−0.036	−0.023	−0.048	−0.031
Managerial			−0.153	−0.097	−0.179*	−0.113*
Religion (neither Christian nor Buddhist is the reference group)						
Christianity			0.070	−0.045	−0.122	−0.079
Buddhism			0.035	0.021	0.013	0.008
Interaction terms						
Taiwan×Collectivism					0.290	0.739
Taiwan×Masculinity					0.229	0.421
Taiwan×Customs					0.171	0.437
Taiwan×Long-Term Relationship					−0.345*	−0.889*
RSS	68.865		68.447		72.485	
MSE	0.367		0.372		0.362	
F	37.522***		11.497***		10.002***	
R^2	0.384		0.409		0.433	
Adjusted R^2	0.374		0.373		0.390	

NOTE: RSS=regression sum of squares; MSE=mean square error
* $p<0.05$. ** $p<0.01$. *** $p<0.001$.

Before looking at the exact results concerning the anticipated leadership styles, it is necessary to point out that Model 1 included the focus independent variables: four cultural dimensions and the variable *country*. In Model 2, all control variables such as gender, age, marital status, length of membership, education, religious beliefs, club's position, and business position were added. In Model 3, four cross-products were created to examine the interactions between country and each cultural dimension. Following are the research findings of the anticipated leadership styles:

Transformational leadership. In this regression analysis as seen in Table 4, the variable of *lifelong relationships* is the best predictor of transformational leadership style anticipation among the variables in the study ($\beta = 0.385$, $p < 0.001$). In other words, people who treasure lifelong relationships are likely to anticipate their female leaders to display transformational leadership style. In addition, the cultural variables of collectivism ($\beta = 0.184$, $p < 0.01$) and Taiwan ($\beta = -0.311$, $p < 0.05$) also have significant effects on the variable of anticipating female leaders to display transformational leadership style.

Transactional leadership. Based on the data analysis in Table 5, the variable *customs* in the regression analysis is the best predictor of transactional leadership style anticipation among the variables in this regression analysis ($\beta = 0.272$, $p < 0.001$). In addition, the variables of *Christianity* ($\beta = 0.238$), *lifelong relationships* ($\beta = 0.186$), and *masculinity* ($\beta = -0.128$) also have significant impact on anticipation of female leaders using transactional leadership style. The predictive power of cultural dimensions and cross products for the transaction leadership style anticipation is low.

Laissez-faire leadership. In this regression analysis in Table 6, the interaction variable of *Taiwan × lifelong relationships* is the strongest predictor variable among all variables. Its high standardized coefficient has statistically significant effect on the response variable: anticipation of female leaders using laissez-faire leadership style ($\beta = -0.889$, $p < 0.001$). In addition, the variable managerial also has negative significant effects on the variable of anticipating female leaders to demonstrate laissez-faire leadership style ($\beta = -0.113$).

In conclusion, comparing the results, the cultural dimensions discussed above and the country variables best predict the respondents' anticipations of laissez-faire and transformational leadership styles, but they are much weaker in predicting the respondents' transactional leadership style in anticipations.

Discussion

With regard to the findings of the first hypothesis, we found that Rotary Club members in Taiwan have higher scores in the cultural dimensions of collectivism, masculinity, customs, and lifelong relationships than their counterparts in the United States. Moreover, the Rotary Club members in Taiwan reveal the highest score in lifelong relationships and the lowest score in masculinity, whereas those in the United States have the highest score in collectivism and lowest score in masculinity. Nonetheless, Taiwan's score in masculinity is still much higher than that of the United States. The results are contradictory to Hofstede's study (2001a) that the American culture is characterized by high masculinity and low collectivism.

Before addressing the research findings different from those of Hofstede's (2001a) study, we find it necessary to use cultural dimensions to explain the different mentality of the respondents from Taiwan and the United States. For instance, there are two major differences between the American and Taiwanese respondents regarding lifelong relationships and customs. Taiwanese respondents have much longer tenure and are more likely to reveal former leadership positions in Rotary Clubs, which can be explained by the dimensions of lifelong relationships and value priorities. As explained above, the Chinese tend to form rich, life-long networks of mutual relations. Since personal relationships often take a long time to develop, the Chinese tend to stay solid once the relationships have been established. In contrast, Americans generally do not build long-term relationships outside of their families. Chinese relationships last for a long time, even after the groups dissolve or there are no more work-related relationships. This is less likely the case for Americans. As for revealing former leadership positions, the Chinese attach importance to "face need" just as a tree needs bark to cover it. Therefore, the Taiwanese respondents are more likely to feel honored and respected with the title of a past president, whereas American respondents feel that taking a turn to be the president of a Rotary Club is a duty for each member. When the duty is fulfilled, they behave like the other ordinary members again.

As for the research findings different from those of Hofstede's (2001b) study in collectivism and masculinity, we argue that, based on previous scholarships (Ardichvili & Kuchinke, 2002; Kuchinke, 1999), Hofstede's (2001b) cultural dimensions might not be stable over time. In addition, when specific samples are collected, they do not necessarily correspond with Hofstede's cultural-dimension scores. For instance, Gudykunst, Nishida, Chung, and Sudweeks (1992) did a cross-cultural study and found that when college students were sampled in Japan and the United States, the Japanese students appeared more individualistic than their American counterparts. Gudykunst and Nishida (1986) also explained that both collectivism and individualism existed in all cultures, but one pattern was likely to predominate. Moreover, one of the comments in our survey provides further proof: "Leaders in Rotary Clubs have to be careful so as not to be too aggressive and demanding because every project in the club is voluntary teamwork." Therefore, it is less likely for a leader to show high masculinity and individualism in Rotary Clubs because of the nature of the voluntary, teamwork-based projects.

Concerning leadership styles, there is significant difference between the Taiwanese and American Rotary Club members' anticipations of female leaders to display transformational and laissez-faire. To be specific, Rotary Club members in both locations reveal the highest scores in their anticipations of female leaders to display transformational leadership and the lowest scores in the anticipations of female leaders to demonstrate the laissez-faire style. The U.S. Rotary Club members, however, are somewhat more expectant of female leaders to display the transformational leadership style than those in Taiwan. With a statistically significant difference, the Taiwanese Rotary Club members have a much higher anticipation of laissez-faire style than their American counterparts. Specifically, among the four features of transformational leadership, the data of this study reveal that American respondents have the highest anticipation of female leaders to demonstrate Intellectual Stimulation, followed by Idealized Influence, Inspirational Motivation, and Individualized Consideration. Taiwanese respondents, in contrast, put the highest anticipation on female leaders to perform Individualized Consideration, followed by Inspirational Motivation, Intellectual Stimulation, and Idealized Influence. The reasons are that most American respondents anticipated female leaders to focus more on creativity and leading by example, whereas Taiwanese female leaders were highly anticipated to take good care of each member and assign tasks on an individual basis.

The results of the third hypothesis reveal that there is a significant relationship between cultural dimensions and Rotary Club members' anticipated female leadership styles in both places. Based on the adjusted R2s of the three multiple regression analyses, the data show that the laissez-faire leadership style can be best explained by the factors of the cultural dimensions and countries, followed by transformational leadership style. Transactional leadership style, however, can be explained little by the factors of the cultural values and countries. Why little? The reason lies in that Rotary Club members are mostly from top positions of various organizations and are motivated by voluntarism or willingness rather than exchanging rewards for services rendered. Thus, they do anticipate female leaders to demonstrate transformational leadership style rather than transactional leadership style.

Meanwhile, the Rotary Club members' lowest scores in anticipating female leaders to demonstrate the laissez-faire style in both countries can be explained by the voluntary and teamwork features of the Rotary Club. As shown in the study, Rotary Club members have high collectivist values and tend to collaborate with their leaders and other members, so they are unlikely to fulfill projects based on the self-directed ways in a laissez-faire style. As for the results that the Taiwanese Rotary Club members have higher masculinity and much higher anticipations of female leaders to demonstrate laissez-faire leadership than their American counterparts, we argue that organizations in highly masculine cultures often have goals that agree with the achieving role of the male and, as such, are almost always led by males with a setting established by men (Hofstede, 1980a). This trend leads to prejudice against female leaders and supports the general way of male dominance in most societies that men have a higher status than females. Consequently, men are not anticipated to be led by females. According to traditional Chinese cultural norms, the elderly males should be treated as natural rulers, and people at the lower rank, including females, should demonstrate obedience and submission (MacCormack, 1991). Therefore, for the Rotary Clubs in Taiwan, the more masculinity the members reveal, the more laissez-faire leadership they anticipate their female leaders to demonstrate, because it is against the cultural norms for masculine members to be led by females. However, we are also aware that in cross-cultural studies, it is often difficult to attribute observed mean differences between country scores to national cultural differences, because these differences may be products of methodological problems, such as lack of equivalence of meaning for measure and response bias (Yukl, 2010).

In this study, although the significant differences between Taiwan and the United States seem to support that the major variables of cultural dimensions can explain the anticipated female leadership styles, they are not sufficient to fully explain the anticipated female leadership styles. Only 38% of the variance can be explained by these cultural factors in the anticipated laissez-faire leadership style, 19% of the variance in the anticipated transformational leadership style, and only 12% of the variance in the anticipated transactional leadership style. The results could suggest two possibilities. First, the four cultural dimensions used in this study may not cover the whole national-level cultural dimensions relevant to leadership. For instance, according to Ralston, Van Thang, and Napier (1999), individualism and collectivism are unique constructs and should be split into individual continua. Second, some other factors such as language, political system, organizational culture, and past experience working under female leaders might have stronger impacts on female leadership than national culture. These factors, however, are beyond the scope of this study.

Conclusion

Through the theoretical lenses of Bass and Avolio's leadership notions and Hofstede's modified cultural dimensions, this survey-based study examined and compared cultural values and anticipated female leadership styles of 307 members in 138 Rotary Clubs between Taiwan and the United States, which differ very dramatically in terms of their cultural, social, political, and economic histories. The research findings are twofold. First, in terms of cultural dimensions, Rotary Club members in Taiwan demonstrated higher scores in all of the cultural dimensions of collectivism, masculinity, customs, and lifelong relationships than their American counterparts. Second, with regard to leadership styles, Rotary Club members in both Taiwan and the United States anticipated female leaders to display transformational leadership. The significance of this study lies in that, besides confirming some previous research findings concerning the correlations between cultural values and female leadership, we have modified Hofstede's cultural dimensions so as to adjust certain dimension bias in cross-cultural studies, and we have also found that national culture alone could not account for the anticipated female leadership styles. It is hoped that the results of the study will not only build an understanding of the cultural values of Rotary Clubs and the Rotary Club members' anticipated styles of female leadership but also contribute to the body of knowledge related to the research on nonprofit organizations and cross-cultural comparison of leadership styles. We further hope that as a result of some heightened awareness, because of this study, the Rotary Clubs and other nonprofit organizations may move toward more equality between men and women, especially with regard to leadership in senior or executive positions.

With the rapid changes and uncertainty in the new century, new types of leaders with new styles and skills are demanded (Adler, 1997, 1999; Bennis, 1996, 1997, 1998; House, 1995; Kanter, 2000). This study shows that people anticipate female leaders who bring different perspectives to the table as leaders. Their transformational leadership style can foster innovation and development in organizations. As Adler (1999) claimed, feminine characteristics or styles are more suitable for both transformational leadership and the 21st-century leadership perspectives. She predicted that the 21st century is a century for women to bring their talents into full play. In the knowledge-based economic system, the demand for physical labor in the past has turned to the emphasis on brainpower. Since the new century is in urgent need of female leaders, the unique feminine qualities have become the leadership styles that are greatly advocated in the new era. Therefore, we believe that the topic of female leadership will continue to be emphasized. The development of women's positions and roles will gradually proceed toward an optimistic and positive direction, even though advancing to the top positions for female leaders is like passing "through a labyrinth that requires persistence, awareness of one's progress, and a careful analysis of the puzzles that lie ahead" (Eagly & Carli, 2007, p. x).

Limitations

Apart from the strengths in this study, there are some limitations that readers are cautioned in interpreting the findings and conclusions in this study. First, although there are quite a number of research studies on cultural values and leadership styles, there are few studies on the topic of female leadership in international nonprofit organizations. Therefore, lacking existing categories, this study can only analyze data based on general inferences or constructions about cultural values and female leadership in nonprofit organizations. Second, some survey items in this study have shown minor problems. For instance, we have encountered low reliability scores for several items in the survey questionnaire; we, therefore, had to delete these items from the questionnaire and used only three items in the survey to measure each cultural dimension. Finally, because of the lack of financial support and pressed for time, this study is mainly based on probability samples from the two accessible Rotary Districts, 3510 in Taiwan and 6600 in the United States. After conveniently choosing the two Rotary Districts, we have randomly chosen a probability sample of 550 subjects from each district according to their respective membership list.

Suggestions for the Future Research

As previously mentioned, in the survey of this study, the reliability scores of some items are low in both Taiwanese and American cultural groups, especially in Part A's life-long relationships dimension. Technically, this dimension is somewhat related to Confucianism, a complicated philosophical system and cultural value. Hence, the items used to measure this cultural dimension in this study are somewhat insufficient. Thus, we suggest adding more effective items to this cultural dimension in future studies.

In addition, although the laissez-faire leadership style is less prevalent in the two places than the other two styles, the Taiwanese Rotary Club members have shown much higher anticipations of female leaders to demonstrate laissez-faire leadership than their American counterparts. This suggests that the laissez-faire leadership style is worth more attention for future research.

Moreover, this research is actually inquiring whether leadership style is a culturally universal or culturally specific concept. Researchers such as Hofstede (1984, 1994, 2001a) proposed a culture-specific approach, which assumes that leadership concepts and styles should be different among cultures. On the other hand, researchers like Bass (1997) contended that leadership is culture free and transcends cultural boundaries. From the findings of this study, we suggest a combination of both approaches. That is, national culture is not the only factor to account for the anticipated female leadership styles as shown in the research results of this study. Finally, the study of leadership concepts and styles should include more variables such as organizational culture, political system, language, and feminine or masculine characteristics to provide more sufficient explanations for female leadership styles in nonprofit organizations.

(Chao, C. C., & Tian, D. X. (2010). Culturally universal or culturally specific: A comparative study of the anticipated female leadership styles in Taiwan and the United States. *Journal of Leadership and Organizational Studies*, 18(1), 64-79.)

References

[1] Aldoory, L., & Toth, E. (2004). Leadership and gender in public relations: Perceived effectiveness of transformational and transactional leadership styles. Journal of Public Relations Research, 2004(16): 157-183.

[2] Adler, N. J. (1999). Global leadership: Women leaders. In W. H. Mobley, M. J. Gessner, & V. Arnold (Eds.), Advances in global leadership (Vol. 1, pp. 127-161). Stamford, CT: JAI Press.

[3] Albritton, R. A. (1998). New paradigm of leader effectiveness in academic libraries: An empirical study of the Bass model of transformational leadership. In T. Mech & G. B. McCabe (Eds.), Leadership and academic libraries (pp. 66-82). Westport, CT: Greenwood Press.

[4] Ardichvili, A., & Kuchinke, P. (2002). Leadership styles and cultural values among managers and subordinates: A comparative study of four countries of the former Soviet Union, Germany, and the US. Human Resource Development International, 5, 99-117.

[5] Arrindell, W. A., Steptoe, A., & Wardle, J. (2003). Higher levels of state depression in masculine than in feminine nations. Behavior Research and Therapy, 41, 809-817.

[6] Baskerville, R. F. (2003). Hofstede never studied culture. Accounting, Organizations and Society, 28, 1-14.

[7] Bass, B. M. (1985). Leadership and performance beyond expectations. New York, NY: Free Press.

[8] Bass, B. M. (1990). Bass and Stogdill's handbook of leadership: Theory, research,

and managerial applications. New York, NY: Free Press.
[9] Bass, B. M. (1995). Comment: Transformational leadership. Journal of Management Inquiry, 4, 293-297.
[10] Bass, B. M. (1997). Does the transactional-transformational paradigm transcend organizational and national boundaries? American Psychologist, 52, 130-142.
[11] Bass, B. M., & Avolio, B. J. (1994). Improving organizational effectiveness through transformational leadership. Thousand Oaks, CA: Sage.
[12] Bass, B. M., & Avolio, B. J. (1997). Full range leader development: Manual for the Multifactor Leadership Questionnaire. Palo Alto, CA: Mind Garden.
[13] Bennis, W. (1996). Leader as transformer. Executive Excellence, 13, 15-16.
[14] Bennis, W. (1997). Leaders of leaders. Executive Excellence, 14, 3-4.
[15] Bennis, W. (1998). Rethinking leadership. Executive Excellence, 15, 7-8.
[16] Bond, M. H., & Hwang, K. (1993). The social psychology of Chinese people. In M. H. Bond (Ed.), The psychology of the Chinese people (pp. 213-266). Oxford, England: Oxford University Press.
[17] Booysen, A. E. (1999). An examination of race and gender influences on the leadership attributes of South African managers (Unpublished DBL dissertation). University of South Africa, Pretoria.
[18] Booysen, A. E. (2000, October). Cultural differences between African black and white managers in South Africa. Paper presented at 12th Annual Conference of Southern African Institute for Management Scientists, Midrand, South Africa.
[19] Burns, J. M. (1978). Leadership. New York, NY: Harper & Row.
[20] Chang, Y. (2008). The impact of Chinese cultural values on Taiwan nursing leadership styles: Comparing the self-assessments of staff nurses and head nurses. Journal of Nursing Research, 16, 109-119.
[21] Chao, C., & Ha, L. (2008, November). Breaking the glass ceiling: Leadership styles and conflict management strategies of prominent female cable industry leaders. Paper presented at the 94th National Communication Association Annual Convention, San Diego, CA.
[22] Chen, H. C., Beck, S. L., & Amos, L. K. (2005). Leadership styles and nursing faculty job satisfaction in Taiwan. Journal of Nursing Scholarship, 37(4), 374-380.
[23] Chen, M., Vanek, J., Lund, F., & Heintz, J. (with Jhabvala, R., & Bonner, C.). (2005). Progress of the world's women 2005: Women, work, and poverty. New York, NY: United Nations Publications.
[24] Clark, L. A., & Watson, D. (1995). Constructing validity: Basic issues in objective scale development. Psychological Assessment, 7, 309-319.
[25] Denmark, F. L. (1993). Women, leadership, and empowerment. Psychology of Women Quarterly, 17, 343-356.
[26] Dorfman, P. W., & House, R. J. (2004). Cultural influence on organizational leadership: Literature review, theoretical rationale, and GLOBE project goals. In R.

J. House, P. J. Hanges, M. Javidan, P. W. Dorfman, & V. Gupta (Eds.), Culture, leadership, and organizations: The GLOBE study of 62 societies (pp. 51 – 73). Thousand Oaks, CA: Sage.

[27] Eagly, A. H. (2007). Female leadership advantage and disadvantage: Resolving the contradictions. Psychology of Women Quarterly, 31, 1 – 12.

[28] Eagly, A. H., & Carli, L. (2007). Through the labyrinth: The truth about how women become leaders. Boston, MA: Harvard Business School Press.

[29] Eagly, A. H., Johannesen – Schmidt, & Engen, M. L. (2003). Transformational, transactional, and laissez – faire leadership styles: A meta – analysis comparing women and men. Psychological Bulletin, 129, 569 – 591.

[30] Earley, P. C., & Gibson, C. B. (1998). Taking stock in our progress on individualism/collectivism: 100 years of solidarity and community. Journal of Management, 24, 265 – 304.

[31] Elenkov, D. (1998). Can American management concepts work in Russia? A cross-cultural comparative study. California Management Review, 40(4), 133 – 156.

[32] Engen, M. L., Leeden, R., & Willemsen, T. M. (2001). Gender; context and leadership styles: A field study [Electronic version]. Journal of Occupational and Organizational Psychology, 74, 581 – 600.

[33] Falk, E., & Grizard, E. (2005). The "glass ceiling" persists: Women leaders in communication companies. Journal of Media Business Studies, 2(1), 23 – 49.

[34] Government Information Office, Republic of China. (2007). Lu Hsiu – lien: The eleventh-term vice president of the Republic of China. Retrieved from http://www.gio.gov.tw/taiwanwebsite/5-gp/yearbook/2006/Biographies-2.htm.

[35] Gudykunst, W. B., & Nishida, T. (1986). Attributional confidence in low-and high-context cultures. Human Communication Research, 12, 525 – 549.

[36] Gudykunst, W. B., Nishida, T., Chung, L., & Sudweeks, S. (1992, January). The influence of strength of cultural identity and perceived typicality on individualistic and collectivistic values in Japan and the United States. Paper presented at the Asian Regional Congress of the International Association for Cross-Cultural Psychology, Katmandu, Nepal.

[37] Hofstede, G. (1980a). Culture's consequences: International differences in work-related values. Newbury Park, CA: Sage.

[38] Hofstede, G. (1980b). Motivation, leadership, and organization: Do American theories apply abroad? Organizational Dynamics, 9, 42 – 63.

[39] Hofstede, G. (1984). Culture's consequences: International differences in work-related values (2nd). Newbury Park, CA: Sage.

[40] Hofstede, G. (1991). Cultures and organizations: software of the mind. London, England: McGraw – Hill.

[41] Hofstede, G. (1994). Values Survey Module 1994 [Manual]. Maastricht, Netherlands: University of Limburg, Institute for Research on Intercultural

Cooperation.

[42] Hofstede, G. (1998). A case for comparing apples with oranges. International Journal of Comparative Sociology, 39, 16 – 31.

[43] Hofstede, G. (2001a). Culture's consequences: Comparing values, behaviors, institutions, and organizations across nations (2nd ed.). Thousand Oaks, CA: Sage.

[44] Hofstede, G. (2001b). Culture's consequences: International differences in work-related values (3rd ed.). Newbury Park, CA: Sage.

[45] Hofstede, G., & Bond, M. (1988). The Confucian connection: From cultural roots to economic growth. Organizational Dynamics, 16, 4 – 21.

[46] House, R. J. (1995). Leadership in the 21st century: A speculative inquiry. In A. Howard (Ed.), The changing nature of work (pp. 411 – 450). San Francisco, CA: Jossey – Bass.

[47] House, R. J., Hanges, P. J., Ruiz-Quintanilla, S. A., Dorfman, P. W., Javidan, M., Dickson, M., & Gupta, V. (1999). Cultural influences on leadership and organizations: Project GLOBE. In W. H. Mobley, M. J. Gessner, & V. Arnold (Eds.), Advances in global leadership (pp. 171 – 233). Stamford, CT: JAI Press.

[48] House, R. J., Wright, N. S., & Aditya, R. N. (1997). Cross- cultural research on organizational leadership: A critical analysis and a proposed theory. In P. C. Earley & M. Erez (Eds.), New perspectives on international industrial/organizational psychology (pp. 535 – 625). San Francisco, CA: New Lexington Press.

[49] Howell, D. (1992). Statistical methods for psychology. Belmont, CA: Duxbury Press.

[50] Hu, W., & Grove, C. L. (1991). Encountering the Chinese: A guide for Americans. Yarmouth, ME: Intercultural Press.

[51] Hwang, K. K. (1990). Modernization of the Chinese family business. International Journal of Psychology, 25, 593 – 618.

[52] Hwang, K. K. (1991). Dao and the transformation of power of Confucianism: A theory of East Asian modernization. In W. M. Tu (Ed.), The triadic chord, the Institute of East Asian philosophies (pp. 229 – 278). Singapore: Institute of East Asian Philosophies.

[53] Jung, D. I., Bass, B. M., & Sosik, J. J. (1995). Bridging leadership and culture: A theoretical consideration of transformational leadership and collectivistic cultures. Journal of Leadership Studies, 2(4), 3 – 18.

[54] Kanter, R. M. (2000). A culture of innovation. Executive Excellence, 17, 10 – 12.

[55] Kluckhohn, C. (1951). Values and value-orientations in the theory of action. In T. Parsons & E. A. Shils (Eds.), Toward a general theory of action (pp. 388 – 433). Cambridge, MA: Harvard University Press.

[56] Kuchinke, K. P. (1999). Leadership and culture: Work-related values and

[57] Lonner, W. J. (1979). Issues in cross-cultural psychology. In A. J. Marsella, R. G. Tharp & T. P. Ciborowski (Eds.), Perspectives on cross-cultural psychology (pp. 17-45). New York, NY: Academic Press.

[58] MacCormack, G. (1991). Cultural values in traditional Chinese law. Chinese Culture, 32(4), 1-11.

[59] Martin, J. N., & Nakayama, T. K. (2007). Intercultural communication in contexts (4th ed.). Boston, MA: McGraw-Hill.

[60] Mather, M. (2007). Closing the male-female labor force gap. Washington, DC: Population Reference Bureau. Retrieved from http://www.prb.org/Articles/2007/ClosingtheMaleFemaleLaborForceGap.aspx.

[61] Morgan, G. (2006). Images of organization. Thousand Oaks, CA: Sage.

[62] Pynes, J. E. (2000). Are women underrepresented as leaders of non-profit organizations? Review of Public Personal Administration, 20, 35-49.

[63] Ralston, D. A., Van Thang, N., & Napier, N. (1999). A comparative study of the work values of North and South Vietnamese managers. Journal of International Business Studies, 30, 655-672.

[64] Reinard, J. (2001). Introduction to communication research (3rd ed.). New York, NY: McGraw-Hill.

[65] Robbins, S. P. (2001). Organizational behavior (9th ed.). Upper Saddle River, NJ: Prentice Hall.

[66] Rotary International. (2007). Members. Retrieved from http://www.rotary.org/en/Members/Pages/ridefault.aspx.

[67] Sadler, P. (2003). Leadership (2nd ed.). London, England: Kogan Page.

[68] Singleton, R. A., & Straits, B. C. (2005). Approaches to social research (4th ed.). New York, Oxford University Press.

[69] Scot, K. A., & Brown, D. J. (2006). Female first, leader second? Gender bias in the encoding of leadership behavior. Organizational Behavior and Human Decision Progress, 101, 230-242.

[70] Smith, P. B., & Schwartz, S. H. (1997). Values. In J. W. Berry, M. H. Segall, & C. Kagitcibasi (Eds.), Handbook of cross-cultural psychology: Vol. 3. Social behavior and applications (2nd ed.). Needham Heights, MA: Allyn & Bacon.

[71] Soendergaard, M. (1994). Hofstede's consequences: A study of reviews, citations and replications. Organization Studies, 15, 447-456.

[72] Van Engen, R., & Willemsen, T. (2001). Gender, context, and leadership styles: A field study. Journal of Occupational and Organizational Psychology, 74, 581-598.

[73] Wang, S. (2007). Women's status in Taiwan. CACCI Journal, 1, 1-3.

[74] Wu, I., & Hsieh, M. (2006). Female leaders: Breaking the 2% curse. Common

Wealth Magazine, 12(20), 1-7.

[75] Wu, M., & Stewart, L. (2005). Work-related cultural values and subordinates' expected leadership styles: A study of university employees in Taiwan and the United States. Journal of Intercultural Communication Research, 34, 195-212.

[76] Yokochi, N. (1989). Leadership styles of Japanese business executives and managers: transformational and transactional. San Diego, CA: United States International University.

[77] Yukl, G. (2002). Leadership in organizations (5th ed.). Upper Saddle River, NJ: Prentice Hall.

[78] Yukl, G. (2010). Leadership in organizations (7th ed.). Upper Saddle River, NJ: Pearson Education.

[79] Zhu, R. L. (1990). Expressive and instrumental ren qing. In The Chinese social game: Ren qing and shi gu (Chinese Psychology Series, Vol. 8., pp. 120-127). Taipei, Taiwan: Professor Zhang's Press. (In Chinese)

Chapter 19
Chimerica: US-China Communication in the 21st Century

With the collapse of the Berlin Wall in 1989 and the dissolution of the former Soviet Union in 1991, the US found itself the only one superpower in the world at the start of the 21st century. Meanwhile, China characterized by Napoleon as "a sleeping giant", has been making big strides as a rising economic power since the launch of its market-oriented policy in 1979. While the U. S. and China's bilateral relationship has become increasingly interdependent in a variety of aspects within the context of globalization, the two countries have been examining each other closely and cautiously from the opposite sides of the Pacific Ocean. By globalization, we refer to the transformative process of global integration in terms of transnational flows of people, trade, finance, technologies, ideas, and communication (Shome & Hegde, 2002). In our globalized world, Koh (2004) remarked: "The United States cannot succeed by acting as a lone ranger" due to the paradoxical situation where it "has never been so powerful and, at the same time, so dependent on the rest of the world" (p. 35). Similarly, Fenby (2008) noted: "In the 30 years since Deng Xiaoping launched China on the path to the market, no country has benefited more from globalization" than China; however, "to maintain its economic growth and development, China must continue to borrow from, sell to, and learn from the U. S." (pp. 1 - 2).

To describe the integration phenomenon of the U. S. and Chinese economies, Ferguson and Schularick (2007) coined the term "Chimerica" to refer to "the sum of China, the world's most rapidly growing emerging market, and America, the world's most financially advanced developed economy" (p. 1). Specifically, Chimerica accounts for 13 percent of the world's land surface, a one-fourth of the world's population, a third of its gross domestic product (GDP), and over half of the global economic growth over the past six years. This symbiotic relationship between the U. S. as the big spender and China as the big saver is likened to "a marriage made in heaven" and regarded as "the defining feature of the current world economy" (p. 1). To a great extent, Ferguson and Schularick are right because, different as they are, the U. S. and China are not only economically complementary but also interdependent in their concerted efforts in programs in the pursuit of agendas to find solutions to problems such as anti-terrorism and non-proliferation, global warming and poverty reduction, transnational crime and HIV/AIDS; mitigation of energy shortages; and cultural exchanges, to name just a few.

As the two countries are brought closer through intensified contacts and broadened exchanges due to their economic complementariness and potential areas of cooperation, we find it worthwhile to explore the prospects of the U. S.-China communication in the 21st century. To this end, this chapter will begin with the description of the current status of the interdependence between the U. S. and China. Then, we will provide a discussion about the ways to deepen and broaden the understanding between the two nations. What follows is an introduction to some of the existing programs and approaches implemented in both the U. S. and China and an evaluation of them from the intercultural communication perspective in light of pragmatism or social constructionism. Finally, we end the chapter with suggestions on how to improve U. S.-China intercultural communication so as to maximize mutual benefit, and global peace and harmony.

The Current Interdependence between the U. S. and China

There are three things that are worth mentioning before we embark on our discussions about the interdependence and mutual understanding between the U. S. and China. First, from a historical point of view, the U. S. and China were allies during World War II, and, President Roosevelt had hoped that Sino-American cooperation would continue, as the U. S. had intended to transform China into the biggest democratic country in Asia (Kissinger, 1994). However, what followed was a three-decade absence of communication—a result of the severance of the diplomatic relation between the two countries due to the takeover of power in China by the Chinese Communist Party in 1949. But the circumstances before the breakup can still serve as a foundational basis or reference for our present discussion. Second, by "current", we refer to the time period since the end of the Cold War in 1991 till the present. It is from this point on that the U. S. has begun reconsidering the strategic role of China as a rising power rather than China's instrumental function as a card against the former Soviet Union. Finally, and most importantly, we need to clarify the grand strategies of the two countries because they are the determining factors for the nature, scope and degree of the U. S.-China interdependent relationship.

Since the end of the Cold War, the position of China with respects to the U. S. has been rotating between a strategic partner and a strategic competitor depending on the changing focus of the U. S.' grand strategy. Historically, both liberals and conservatives strongly believe that the U. S. is a revolutionary country, founded on the principles of freedom, equality, and progress, which have universal applicability. After emerging as the only winner from the Cold War bipolarity, and experiencing a short period of post Cold-War multi-polarity, the U. S. has become what the French Foreign Minister Hubert Védrine referred to as a "hyper-power" (Ikenberry, 2001, p. 1). As a hyper-power, the U. S. considers it its destined obligation to guard American interests worldwide. As a result, the China policies established by all U. S. post-Cold War administrations have been shifting from either to "countenance China's emergence as a peer competitor" or to "give China the opportunity to integrate itself into the American-led international order on Washington's terms" (Layne & Thayer, 2007, p. 70). Seeing China as a rising power in East Asia and a strategic competitor, the Bush Administration, in its early period, adopted the containment policy towards China as an alternative to engagement and strategic partnership as advocated in the second term of the Clinton Administration. Since the containment policy dramatically increased tensions between U. S. and China such as the Spy Plane Incident and due to the war on terror, the Bush Administration had to shift to the policy of congagement (Khalilzad, 1999)—consisting of both containment and engagement towards China. Some realist pessimists, who argued that rising powers tended to be troublemakers in history, even compared rising China to Germany and Japan during the two world wars. However, there have been signs today that the Obama Administration emphasizes the U. S. commitment to, if not a strategic partnership yet, a stronger cooperative relationship with China. For example, when they met at the G-20 summit in London on April 1, 2009, Hu Jintao and Barack Obama "agreed to work together to build a positive, cooperative, and comprehensive relationship in the 21st century" (Xinhua, 2009, p. 1). Thus, the realist-pessimistic voice for U. S. containment of China is gradually drowned by the liberal-optimistic voice for U. S. engagement and cooperation with China, a manifestation of the Obama Administration's smart power model of strategic thinking.

What is the grand strategy of China then? With an annual economic growth rate of 9 percent on average over the past decades, China has been emerging or reemerging as a rising power in Asia. The velocity and impact of the growth of China's comprehensive national capability and lack of knowledge about the direction of her development and future intentions caused China's neighboring countries and other big powers such as the U. S. to view Chinese intentions with caution, suspicion, and even fear. China announced that she has been pursuing a goal of "peaceful rise." As one government-affiliated think tank noted: "China aims to grow and advance without upsetting existing orders, and we are trying to rise in a way that benefits our neighbors" (Funabashi, 2003, p. 2). While taking a series of confidence-building measures to offset the regional concerns, Beijing even officially adjusted the description of China's emergence from "peaceful rise" to "peaceful development" (Gries, 2007, p. 46). This line of thought has directly come from the development targets of the Chinese leadership. Former Chinese leader Deng Xiaoping's target was to "increase China's per capita GDP fourfold by 2020 to attain a state of relatively comfortable livelihood," and Hu Jintao's "'big idea' is to create a 'harmonious and prosperous society' via 'peaceful development'" (Dorn, 2008, p. 13). As for its relationship with the U. S., China has been faithfully following Deng's maxim to never act haughtily towards the U. S. while "hiding our capacities and biding our time" (Gompert, et al., 2005, p. 36). Thus, China has been concentrating on her domestic construction and refraining from demonstrating her power externally. On one hand, China intends to learn a lesson from the collapse of the Soviet Union and avoid confronting the U. S. so as to maintain security and stability for a prosperous state and a harmonious society. On the other hand, China will not jump on the bandwagon and accept the U. S. -version of the universal value system without considering the degree of her compatibility with the Chinese cultural heritage.

Having clarified the grand strategies of the two countries, we find it easier to understand and describe the complex and multi-faceted U. S. -China relation and the interdependence between the two countries. As was reported about the meeting between the two presidents at the G-20 London Summit, the U. S. and China share common interests in tackling the global financial crisis, striving to recover global economic growth, dealing with international and regional issues, and safeguarding world peace and security. Viewing each other from a positive perspective, the two countries expect to deepen exchanges and cooperation in economy, counter-terrorism, non-proliferation, law enforcement, energy, climate change, science and technology, education, culture, healthcare, and military affairs. More importantly, both the presidents recognize that a positive relationship between the U. S. and China extends far beyond the interests and benefits of the two countries. For instance, Hu Jintao said: "Good relations with the United States are not only in the interests of the two peoples, but also beneficial to peace, stability and prosperity of the Asia-Pacific region, and the world at large" (Xinhua, 2009, p. 2). Similarly, President Obama reiterated: "I said publicly that our relations are not only important for citizens of the two countries, but also help set the stage for how the world deals with a host of challenges" (Xinhua, 2009, p. 2). To calculate roughly, the two presidents agree that the U. S. and China share common interests in four main fields and look forward to expanding exchanges and cooperation in 12 major aspects. This means that the two countries are interdependent in at least a dozen areas.

According to Ching (2009), when U. S. President-elect Barack Obama asked about his foreign priorities, he was provided with a list consisting of nuclear proliferation, climate change and global poverty, Iraq, Afghanistan, Iran, the trans-Atlantic alliance, Russia, the Israeli-Palestinian conflict, and managing the United States' relationship with China and the entire Pacific Rim as an afterthought. Although the afterthought reflects a relatively calm state of relationship, with no crisis that needs immediate presidential attention, the author emphasized that China "is not just a relationship to be managed — but perhaps the key relationship that the United States sustains if Obama is to achieve success in virtually all his other foreign policy priority areas" (p. 1).

Ways to Deepen and Broaden the Understanding between the Two Nations

As you can see from the above discussion, a good U. S. -China relationship not only benefits the American and Chinese people but will also bring about world peace and prosperity. It is now important for both the U. S. and China to readjust their foreign policies toward a "more positive and constructive" relationship and implement the "positive, cooperative, and comprehensive" programs of exchanges and cooperation (Xinhua, 2009, p.

2). To meet these goals, first of all, the decision-makers of the two countries should be so well-informed via regular and smooth communication that they will make neither misjudgment of each other's development intentions nor overestimation of their own strength. By starting with their joint efforts in tackling the global financial crisis and striving to spur global economic growth, the U.S. and China can then gradually deepen and broaden their understanding and appreciation of each other's sincerity and contributions to their cooperation projects and exchange programs one after another. The significance of regular and smooth communication can never be emphasized enough, especially in the management of a crisis. According to Yang Jiechi (Yang, 2009), Chinese foreign minister then, the leaders of the two countries have maintained close communication on major issues concerning bilateral relations "through mutual visits, meetings, telephone calls, and correspondence," which "have given a strong boost to the sustained, sound, and steady growth of our relations" (p. 4). Yet Lampton (2004) listed three examples of deficient communication cases in the U.S.-China relations in recent years. First: On the tragic June 4th incident of 1989, Deng Xiaoping repeatedly refused to pick up the telephone when U.S. President George Herbert Walker Bush called. In return, the U.S. Congress suspended all minister-level exchanges between the two countries for a considerable period of time during 1989 and 1990. Second: In 1999, after the Chinese Embassy in Belgrade was bombed, it took Jiang Zemin a long time to respond to President Clinton's initiatives to talk and the Chinese military curtailed bilateral exchanges. Third: Immediately after the U.S. EP-3 collided with the Chinese J-8 fighter above China's Hainan Island on April 1, 2001, the U.S. Ambassador to China could not make contact with any member of the Chinese government to talk about the incident. Moreover, the U.S. Department of Defense curtailed military-to-military exchanges with China. According to David Lampton, Director of China Studies at John Hopkis-SAIS and the Nixon Center, "when we are angry at each other our reflex has been to cut communications at the highest levels and between the militaries. This is the wrong impulse!" (p. 6).

Beijing must have drawn lessons from the above when it took a series of confidence-building measures to offset the concerns of the neighboring countries regarding her rising power. For instance, she strengthened bilateral security dialogues with Australia, India, Japan, Mongolia, and South Korea and invited some of them to observe or participate in joint military exercises. Meanwhile, China actively participated in the ASEAN Regional Forum with the intention to establish a regional cooperative security community (Shambaugh, 2005). In contrast, the U.S. took the risk of creating an impression that it is "a dangerous, trigger-happy military power interested only in its own safety by elevating the concept of 'preemption'" after 9/11 (Kim, 2004, pp. 18-19). To many people in Asia, the causes of terrorism are multiple and complex, and the U.S. policy of trying to eradicate it through the use of force alone is ineffective.

According to Suettinger (2003), American and Chinese policy-makers have made many mistakes about each other such as factual inaccuracies, poor intelligence, errors of judgment, sins of commission and omission, misperceptions, mistranslations, over-estimates of knowledge, under-estimates of sensitivity, misplaced confidence, misread intentions, unintended consequences, unfulfilled rewards, missed signals, ineffective bluffs, and violations of confidence. In many ways, the above mistakes are attributable to groupthink pervasive among both the decision-making groups, a phenomenon characterized by over-estimation of their own power or moral superiority, close-mindedness toward the out-group, and pressure for in-group uniformity. Thus, to minimize such mistakes, we see the necessity and urgency to not only ensure that the U.S.-China communication channels are open and smooth but also to improve the quality of communications through periodic top-level contacts and regular exchanges in as many aspects and levels as possible.

Both the U.S. and China have been serious in their commitment to tackling the global financial crisis through intensified cooperation and exchanges. For example, during her recent visit to Beijing, Secretary Clinton (2009) remarked that, facing the global economic crisis that hit both the U.S. and China, "we have to look inward for solutions, but we must also look to each other to take a leadership role in designing and implementing a coordinated global response to stabilize the world's economy, and begin recovery" (p. 2). Actually, Nail Ferguson (2008), a professor of history at Harvard University and one of the inventors of the term "Chimerica", noted that at the heart of this financial crisis is the huge imbalance between the United States with her current account deficit in more than one percent of the world GDP, and the surplus countries that finance her such as the oil exporters, Japan, and other emerging Asian countries. Of course, "the relationship between China and the U.S. has become the crucial one," and "an alternative for the Chinese is to turn inward to increase its domestic consumption" (p. A19). One point that needs clarification here is: "the reality that the growth in U.S. government spending and borrowing, not the trade deficit with China, is the key reason for concern" (Dorn, 2008, p. 153).

Although China "only accounts for about 25 percent of the U.S. overall current account deficit of around $800 billion" (Dorn, 2008, p. 153), the government of China made it her top priority to combat the financial crisis in 2009. In his speech entitled "Broaden China-U.S. Cooperation in the 21st Century," Chinese Foreign Minister Yang Jiechi (2009) reported that, while closely following the measures taken by the U.S. government to stabilize financial markets and stimulate economic recovery, the Chinese government launched a four trillion RMB ($585 billion) investment program to jump-start growth by boosting domestic demand, reinvigorating industries, developing science and technology, and improving the social safety net. Yang remarked: "Some of the measures have already produced initial results, as evidenced by the recent signs of economic recovery" (p. 4). Besides, the Chinese government has also applied conventional tools such as large interest rate cuts and a massive fiscal stimulus plan of $5880 billion for 2009 and 2010. To restore consumer confidence, local governments in China have issued various consumption coupons as a response to the recent call of Wen Jiabao, who stated: "Confidence is more valuable than gold" (Xu, 2009, p. 3). Although it is still too early to hear the U.S. comments on the Chinese efforts, we strongly believe that timely and responsible commitment to the areas of mutual and global interests is key to the success of collaboration between the two countries.

To sum up, any deepened or broadened understanding between the U.S. and China results from regular and smooth communication at various levels and in a variety of ways. The showcase of China's serious commitment to the most acute and immediate area of collaboration— tackling bilateral trade imbalance and global financial crisis, definitely invites more confidence and greater success in other areas of mutual and global interests like clean energy and climate change, safeguarding world peace and security, as well as counter-terrorism and nuclear non-proliferation. However, there are two caveats here. First, genuine cooperation between the U.S. and China can result only from quality communication between the two countries, each with a different culture, a different social system and a different ideology. Thus, quality communication will have to be based on mutual understanding, mutual adjustment, and mutual respect, seeking harmony amid differences, and cooperation for win-win results. Second, in the globalized world situation, true understanding between the two nations needs to take such new elements as economic globalization, domestic politics, and geopolitical strategy into consideration. Economic globalization makes the U.S.-China relationship go beyond national boundaries with a network of dynamic relations. Due to the difference in the distribution of profits from the interdependence between the U.S. and China, different interest groups will exert their influence and pressure on the national policies of their respective countries. In terms of geopolitical strategies, the U.S. needs China's cooperation in regional and global affairs while China needs the support of the U.S. to sustain a stable global environment for her peaceful development.

Institutionalized Efforts Promoting U.S.-China Communication

Since the Nixon-Mao Summit in the early 1970s, various institutionalized efforts have been made by both the governments, businesses educational institutions and NGOs (non-governmental organizations). While China created U.S.-China Friendship Association, the U.S. established her own counterpart. In addition, some leading American scholars of China studies such as Lucian Pye, Robert Scalapino, and others founded the National Committee on U.S.-China Relations which aims to promote Track-II diplomacy.[1] The East-West Center, founded and funded by the State Department of the United States in the early 1960s, has also been playing a vital intellectual role in promoting intercultural understanding between the West and the East, particularly between the U.S. and China. The Institute of Intercultural Communication of East-West Center, which has been unjustifiably closed, was created to specifically address the issues of intercultural miscommunication. Some leading scholars such as Harvard-Yenching Professor Tu Weiming acted as its director. Similarly,

美国梦——教育因·学术果
The American Dream — From Education Commitment to Academic Excellence

John King Fairbank Center for China Studies, the Harvard-Yenching Institute and the Asia Center, all at Harvard University, have been instrumental in deepening an intellectual understanding between China and the United States. With a mission to build new bridges between the U. S. and China, it consists of distinguished members such as the world-renowned cellist Yo-Yo Ma and Steven Chen, co-founder and chief technology officer of YouTube. Since China's economic rise in the beginning of the 21st century, many American institutions of education have been investing more and more on Chinese language and cultural education venues. Some 80 Confucian academies funded by the Chinese Government have already been established in the United States with the co-sponsorship of American universities such as University of Maryland at College Park and University of California at Los Angeles. The College Board has recently included Chinese as an Advanced Placement subject in American high schools. Multiple elementary schools and middle schools on the East and West Coasts of the U. S. have begun to provide Chinese language classes to their students. The growth of East Asian Studies, American and China Studies, and Asian Studies programs have been explosive, due in large part to the growing demand to learn everything about China. New centers of China studies have been mushrooming and exchange programs between American and Chinese universities have been multiplying. For example, the Institute for International Education of Students headquartered in Chicago, founded in 1950, has recently expanded into China with the addition of two centers.

Compared with the U. S., China seems to have studied the U. S. on a larger scale. China has been conducting a massive campaign of English language learning on Chinese university campuses as well as on some high school and even elementary school campuses since Deng Xiaoping's visit to the United States in 1978. Today, about 300 million Chinese are fluent English speakers with considerable knowledge of the U. S. and the American culture. These Chinese, especially China's newly emerging youth, are ferociously consuming American culture, news and goods in English in China simultaneously with Americans on the American soil. One million Chinese have studied overseas since 1978. Almost half of them have studied or are studying in the United States. More than 300,000 Chinese students have already returned to China after studying abroad in various countries around the world. Some of them, especially returnees from the U. S., are assuming leadership positions. Zhili Chen, who was a visiting scholar at Pennsylvania State University at University Park in the 1980s, was Minister of Education and now Vice-Chairwoman of China People's Congress. Both the current Chinese Communist Party Secretary, Weifang Min, and President of Peking University, Fengqi Zhou, received their Ph. D. degrees in the U. S. in the 1980s. In addition, thousands of Chinese government leaders of younger generations have received or are receiving training from Kennedy School of Government, Harvard University and Yale University has been offering training to groups of Chinese university presidents. Yuanchao Li, Director of Department of Personnel of Chinese Communist Party, was one of the first groups of China's young leaders who received training at Harvard University in 1998.

Even though so much has been done to promote mutual understanding by the respective countries, neither side thinks that it is enough. Both sides feel the need to do more U.S.-China exchanges. On the American side, in November 2009, during Obama's state visit to China, the Obama Administration announced to increase the number of American students who study in China five fold in the next few years. This means that in a few years, the number of American students who study in China each year will reach about 200,000. On the Chinese side, in March 2010, Chinese Ministry of Education announced that it plans to send every principal of K-12 education in China to the U.S. and European countries to receive training in the next few years. The U.S. has also become one of the hottest tourist destinations for Chinese tourists. Even when the U.S. and China were exchanging hostile words against each other with regard to the White House's decision to sell arms to Taiwan, New Yorkers welcomed the arrival of 1,000 Chinese tourists in New York City on February 19, 2010 and Hong Kong welcomed the port call of an American aircraft carrier Nimitz on the Eve of Chinese Spring Festival on February 17, 2010.

Such frequent educational, cultural and military exchanges between the two countries are occurring simultaneously with frequent high-level intergovernmental visits and dialogues; obviously these concerted efforts are exerting a positive impact on U.S.-China relations. Collectively, they are personalizing the impersonal and contentious trade relations between the U.S. and China and expanding Ferguson's economic concept of Chimerica into an intercultural one. As a result, Chimerica not only means economic interdependence between the U.S. and China, but also is increasingly characterized by an intercultural identity drawing upon and emerging from the deepened interaction between the American culture and Chinese culture which are unique in its own ways and are complementary in nature. This is because such persistent and prolonged communicative efforts, from the perspective of pragmatism (i.e., Jia, 2005), a U.S. home-grown philosophy, contribute to the creation of more shared knowledge, more shared experience, more common ground, and ultimately a shared destiny and a shared identity between two cultures, in this case, between the American culture and Chinese culture.

Becoming a Functional Chimerican

As we have shown above, Chimerica is a new phenomenon created by globalization at the second half of the 20th century. It is challenging the traditional concept of nation-state and redefining the economic, cultural and economic contour of the human race in the 21st century. As an individual, whether you are a Chinese or an American, whether you like it or not, you are drawn into a transnational entity called Chimerica and become a willing or unwilling member of Chimerica called Chimerican. A functional Chimerican would be someone who is proficient in both English and Chinese, competent in communicating between Chinese and Americans, have a working knowledge about the geography, history, economy, politics, culture, media and so on of both the countries, have a working knowledge of the history of the relationship between the two nations and two cultures as well as a working knowledge about the current status and future prospect of Chimerica.

If you are not from Chimerica, this does not mean that you do not have to know about Chimerica and do not need to learn how to communicate with Chimericans. Since Chimerica is the marriage of the world's most advanced country and the world's largest developing country, this marriage will only continue to make an undeniably large impact on the future global ecommunity. To learn to get along with Chimerica and Chimericans means to grasp the meanings, functions and the global implications of an intricate and complex system of hybridized world views, mixed political models, diversified cultures and synergized economies called Chimerica. While Chimericans are responsible for improving Chimerica for more peace, unity and harmony between the U. S. and China internally, non-Chimericans are advised to check against the ethics of Chimerica's global behavior externally to ensure balance and a diversity of opinions. Such conjoint internal and external efforts are expected to sustain Chimerica from deteriorating into Chimera—a fire-breathing monster with no harmony on the inside and positing a threat to harmony on the outside. But in order to ensure this monster does not emerge, let's start to do our own homework today.

Note

Track II diplomacy is a diplomatic action taken by individuals or agencies other than politicians and government representatives. For instance, the U. S. academic or business representatives engaging in discussions with their Chinese counterparts on how to resolve U. S. -China trade imbalances would be conducting Track II diplomacy.

References

[1] Ching, F. (2009, Jan. 3) China: Key to U. S. foreign policy success. The Japan Times, 1-3.

[2] Clinton, H. R. (2009, Feb. 21). Toward a deeper and broader relationship with China: Remarks with Chinese Foreign Minister Yang Jiechi. Retrieved from http://www.state.gov/secretary/rm/2009a/02/119432.htm.

[3] Dorn, J. A. (2008, June 13). The danger of economic nationalism. Beijing Review, 13-14.

[4] Dorn, J. A. (2008). The debt threat: A risk to US-China relationships? The Brown Journal of World Affairs, 14(2), 151-164.

[5] Fenby, J. (2008, July 24). China's rumble with globalization, Part II. YaleGlobal, 1-4.

[6] Ferguson, N. (2008, Nov. 17). Team "Chimerica."The Washington Post, A19.

[7] Ferguson, N., & Schularick, M. (2007, Feb. 5). Chimerical? Think again. The Wall Street Journal, 1-4.

[8] Funabashi, Y. (2003, Dec. 19). China's "peaceful ascendancy." YaleGlobal, 1-4.

[9] Gompert, D. C., Godement, F., Medeiros, E. S., & Mulvenon, J. D. (2005). China onthe move, RAND: National defense research institute, Santa Monica, CA: Retrieved from http://www.rand.org/pubs/conf _ proceedings/2005/RAND _ CF199.pdf.

[10] Ikenberry, G. J. (2001). Getting hegemony right. The National Interest, 63, 1-2.

[11] Jia, W. S. (2005). The Deweyan pragmatism: Its implications for the study of intercultural communication. Heisey Festchrift, a special issue Intercultural Communication Studies, XIV (1), 101-107.

[12] Khalilzad, Z. M. (1999). Congage China. Santa Monica, CA: Rand/IP-187.

[13] Kim, K. (2004). Northeast Asia. In In K. Kim, T. Koh & F. Sobhan, America's role in Asia: Asian views. San Francisco, CA: The Asian Foundation.

[14] Kissinger, H. (1994). Diplomacy. New York, NY: Simon & Schuster.

[15] Koh, T. (2004). Southeast Asia. In K. Kim, T. Koh & F. Sobhan, America's role in Asia: Asian views. San Francisco, CA: The Asian Foundation.

[16] Lampton, D. M. (2004). The United States and China: Competitors, Partners, or Both? A speech delivered at the US Foreign Policy Colloquium, George Washington University. Retrieved from http://www.nixoncenter.org/publications/ElliotSchoolspeech.pdf.

[17] Layne, C., & Thayer, B. A. (2007). American empire: A debate. New York: Routledge.

[18] Shambaugh, D. (2005, April 20). Rising dragon and the American eagle, Part I. YaleGlobal, 1-4.

[19] Shome, R., & Hedge, R. S. (2002). Culture, communication, and the challenge of globalization. Critical Studies in Media Communication, 19(2), 172-189.

[20] Suettinger, R. L. (2003). Beyond Tiananmen: The politics of the US-China relations 1989-2000. Washington, D. C. : Brookings Institution Press.

[21] Xinhua. (2009). China, U. S. to build positive, cooperative and comprehensive relationship in 21st century. Retrieved from http://china-embassy.org/eng/zmgx/t555667.htm

[22] Xu, S. T. (2009, Jan. 30). US and China: Grappling over economic rescue, Part I. YaleGlobal, 1-4.

[23] Yang, J. C. (2009, March 12). Broaden China-US cooperation in the 21st century: Remarks by Foreign Minister Yang Jiechi at the Center for Strategic and International Studies, Washington, D. C. Retrieved from http://www.china-embassy.org/eng/zmgx/t542231.htm

[24] Zhang, C. (2007). Harmony, hegemony, & US-China relations. World Literature Today, 45-47.

Chapter 20
Prominent Chinese Terms and Their Profound Cultural Roots

In his book *Language and Culture*, Kramsch (1998) noted:

> Linguistic signs do not signify in a social vacuum. Sign-making and sign-interpreting practices are motivated by the need and desire of language users to influence people, act upon them or even only to make sense of the world around them. (p. 21)

To understand the need and desire of Chinese language users in their creation and application of signs in Chinese, this chapter offers a systematic elaboration of the Chinese conceptualizations of communication by examining a rich variety of Chinese terms for talk and practice as an inseparable, hybridized, and evolving dimension of the living Chinese cultural system. Since the Chinese culture is so substantial in content, so comprehensive in variety, and so long in history that herein we take great cautions so as to avoid the fallacy of taking the part for the whole.

Specifically, we aim to explore answers to three research questions:

RQ 1: What is the cultural backdrop for the configurations of the Chinese conceptualizations of communication?

RQ 2: How can we make a selection of the prominent Chinese terms for talk and practice in the living Chinese cultural system?

RQ 3: What are the Chinese cultural roots that are associated with the prominent Chinese vocabulary on talk and practice?

In the remainder of the paper, we provide a detailed introduction to the backdrop of the cultural impact of the three Chinese religio-philosophical traditions of Confucianism, Daoism, and Buddhism, and the three dominant ideologies of Marxism-Leninism, Maoism as well as Dengism. Then we explicate the dialectical approach of Yin and Yang, followed by a description of the research methods of ethnography and hermeneutics. Finally, we analyze and discuss the selected prominent Chinese terms for communication practices during significant periods of Chinese history. Where necessary, we also compare the Chinese value system on talk and practice with the Euro-American cultural values.

Literature Review: Religio-Philosophical Bases for the Chinese Communication

It is widely acknowledged (e. g. : Bond & Hofstede, 1989; Chan, 2008; Chen, 2008; Fang & Faure, 2011; Hansen, 1985; Hsu, 1963; Jia, 2001; Nisbett, Peng, Choi &

Chapter 20

Prominent Chinese Terms and Their Profound Cultural Roots

Norenzayan, 2001) that the configurations of Chinese conceptualizations of communication are deeply rooted in the Chinese ideas both ancient and modern. The predominant Chinese ideas include Confucianism, Daoism, and Buddhism as well as Marxism-Leninism, Maoism, and Deng Xiaoping's theories concerning market economy. The following sections elaborate such connections:

Impact of Confucianism, Daoism, and Buddhism. After comparing the Greek civilization with the Chinese civilization, Nisbett, Peng, Choi and Norenzayan (2001) concluded that "from the location of the power in the individual, ordinary people in the then Greece and later Euro-American cultures" developed "a sense of personal agency", "a sense of personal freedom", "a sense of curiosity", and "a tradition of debate" (p. 292). In contrast, the Chinese civilization boasts of a long history of centralized control of power. It has nurtured "a sense of reciprocal social obligation or collective agency," "Confucian obligations between emperor and subject, parent and child, husband and wife, older brother and younger brother, and between friend and friend," and "prescribed ethical conducts of considering individuals part of a closely-knit collectivity, sharing with the community as a whole, and valuing in-group harmony" (p. 192). Many scholars (e.g.: Bond & Hofstede, 1989; Chan, 2008; Chen, 2008; Fang & Faure, 2011; Hansen, 1985; Hsu, 1963; Jia, 2001; Jia, in press) have explored the impact of traditional Chinese philosophies and religions on the style of Chinese communication. The three great teachings have been research topics of top priority in their studies.

According to Chan (2008), the Confucian ethics has laid a solid foundation for Chinese communication practices. Confucian ethics, which includes five constant virtues such as 仁 [rén] benevolence, 义 [yì] righteousness, 礼 [lǐ] propriety, 智 [zhì] wisdom, and 信 [xìn] fidelity, emphasizes the significance of human virtues and the adoption of proper behaviors. Hwang (1997) identified the first three of the five constant virtues as the Confucian ethical system of Ren-Yi-Li (benevolence-righteousness-propriety), with the expressive components of 关系 [guān xi] (human connections) representing Ren, 人情 [rén qíng] (favor) Yi, and 面子 [miàn zi] (face or positive image) Li. Here we just elucidate the three expressive components of the Confucian ethical system.

Scholars (e.g.: Chan, 2008; Chen, 2008; Fei, 1985; Jia, 1997 – 1998, 2008, 2006, in press) have extensively discussed the three expressive components. First, 关系 [guān xi] means personal connections and contacts as a Chinese networking system. It is a system of concentric social circles with oneself and his or her family members at the innermost circle followed by subsequent circles of relatives, friends, and colleagues. Reciprocity is the key to managing the network of personal connections without which one could not survive. Second, 人情 [rén qíng] refers to the exchange of favors and sympathy or humanized feelings. In other words, the exchange of favors is the way in which 人情 is practiced (Yen & Barnes, 2011). Regarded as a kind of social investment, favors can take place in a variety of social contexts. There are two connotations with 人情, with one being the humanized feelings as mentioned earlier, and the second the sympathetic give-and-take in the social exchange of the Chinese networking system. Finally, 面子 [miàn zi] refers to the positive image of oneself. It requires that all parties involved in a communication transaction save each other's dignity and the sacred social attribute. According to Gao and Ting-Toomey (1998), the Chinese concept of face is similar to the concept of face in the Euro-American cultures in that it emphasizes the positive image of the individual. However, it is different in that it is tied to the reputation and face of the group. Just as Jia (1997-1998) noted, 面子 has been emphasized in Chinese culture for both the goal and the means to express and strengthen the Confucian value of maintaining harmonious human relationships.

In addition, both Daoism and Buddhism have greatly influenced the use of language in the expression of thoughts and feelings in China. Daoism is a Chinese philosophical and religious tradition emphasizing living in harmony with the Dao. The term Tao means "way," "path" or "principle," which refers to something "that is both the source and the driving force behind everything that exists" (Hong, 2015, p, 1). The Chinese language and communication practice are enriched with such Daoist terms as 风水 [fēng shuǐ]: geomantic omen, 黄道吉日 [huáng dào jí rì]: an auspicious day, and 命相不合 [mìng xiàng bù hé]: The horoscopes of the couple don't match.

In her Master's thesis, Ruan (2008) gave a detailed discussion about the influence of Buddhism on Chinese language and culture. Besides the large number of terms, thousands of Buddhist teachings and concepts have become popular Chinese daily expressions and communication practices such as 不看僧面看佛面 [bù kàn sēng miàn kàn fó miàn]: do something out of consideration for somebody else; If not for the monk's sake, please consider that of the Buddha and 人不为己，天诛地灭 [rén bù wèi jǐ, tiān zhū dì miè]: Everyone for himself and the devil takes the hindmost.

Impact of Marxism-Leninism, Maoism and Dengism. According to Hanson (2001), Marxism-Leninism refers to the "official state ideology adopted by the Union of Soviet Socialist Republics (USSR), its satellite states in Eastern Europe, the Asian communist regimes, and various 'scientific socialist' regimes" (p. 1). The three identifiable and dogmatic principles held in the Soviet-type regimes are: (1) dialectical materialism as the only basis for philosophy, (2) the political leadership of the Communist party, and (3) planned economy with state-owned property. All these principles were influential in China with major revisions and development by Mao first and then Deng.

According to Wertz (1998-2004), instead of Maoism, Mao Zedong Thought has been used within China. Unlike the Soviet and other socialist revolutions, usually based in big cities, Mao first focused on the peasantry as a revolutionary force, then made all-round rural development the priority, and finally explicitly connected its political ideology with military strategy. Mao's line of thoughts proved valid and led the Chinese Communist revolution to ultimate victory in 1949. Mao died in 1976, and Deng Xiaoping succeeded him with strategic policies of economic reform and opening up to the outside world in 1979. As a result, China is now in direct contact with foreign concepts, technologies, cultures and lifestyles. What is more important is that "globalization, foreign direct investment and the Internet are exposing China, for the first time in its history, to unprecedented global knowledge transfer, information sharing, and cultural learning" (Faure & Fang, 2008, p. 194).

Theoretical Frameworks

For the present study, we follow the dialectical approach of Yin and Yang as Fang and Faure (2011) explained, "Yin-Yang permeates the Chinese culture and impacts the Chinese communication characteristics" (p. 330). Martin and Nakayama (2010) defined the dialectical approach as a "method of logic based on the principle that an idea generates its opposite, leading to a reconciliation of the opposites" (p. 73). By the dialectical approach of Yin and Yang, we emphasize an optimal balance in-between two extremes in our selection and analysis of the prominent Chinese terms and discussion about the cultural roots in their Chinese communication practices.

As Wang explained in the Internet Encyclopedia of Philosophy, the Yin-Yang is a Chinese philosophy with the conception that everything in the universe is created by the dual yet mutually complimentary cosmic energies. While the former stands for the feminine energy such as the moon, water, dark, passivity, and femininity, the latter stands for the masculine energy like the sun, fire, light, activity, and masculinity. With no borderline between them, Yin and Yang together form an evolving unity while containing within them the seed of each other. In brief, Yin and Yang are exhibited in all existence as the coherent fabric of nature and mind. Connecting the cosmic realm with the human world, Yin and Yang harmonize and balance all things in the world. With Yin and Yang offering a holistic and dialectic worldview, it is easier to explain many seemingly contradictory communication concepts in Chinese.

Plenty of examples are available in everyday life such as 危机 [wēi jī]: crisis, 祸福相依 [huò fú xiāng yī]: having the upside traced in your downside, and 一国两制 [yī guó liǎng zhì]: one country, two systems. In the first two examples, 危 [wēi] means danger and 机 [jī] means opportunity, 祸 [huò] means woe and 福 [fú] means weal. The last example 一国两制 [yī guó liǎng zhì] shows that two systems of socialism and capitalism can co-exist in one country of P. R. China. These Chinese terms which may look inconsistent and contradictory to English-speaking people are actually natural and routine Chinese conceptions about their communication practices because there is "internal consistency and coherence" (Faure & Fang, 2008, p. 196).

In their study, Nisbett, et al. (2001) found that, unlike Westerners who "are more analytic, paying attention primarily to the object and the categories to which it belongs," East Asians are "more holistic, attending to the entire field and assigning causality to it..., and relying on 'dialectical' reasoning" (p. 291). Faure and Fang (2008) seconded, "a constant reality of China has been its outstanding capability for keeping up with paradoxical values throughout its history including the current period" (p. 194). By "paradoxical values," the authors meant "the seemingly contradictory value orientations both of which can nonetheless be true within the same society" (p. 195). They also emphasized that it is crucial to understand the nature of the Chinese culture in terms of the Chinese philosophical conception of Yin and Yang. By the same token, many other scholars (e. g.: Chen, 2008; Faure & Fang, 2008; Peng & Nisbett, 1999) agreed that we need to draw inspirations from the dialectical and dialogical interactions between Yin and Yang to genuinely understand the essence of the Chinese culture and styles of Chinese communication. Thus, we follow the dialectical approach of Yin and Yang in the categorization of and discussion about the selected prominent Chinese terms in this study.

Research Methods

In this section, we explicate the parameters and criteria for selecting the prominent Chinese terms and hermeneutics for analyzing the selected terms.

Parameters. As a member of the Sino-Tibetan language family, Mandarin is the native language of the Chinese and the official language of P. R. China. It is also one of the six official languages of the United Nations. Spoken Chinese is a tonal language, and it is common for the Chinese to be able to speak several variations of it. The Chinese written language employs characters, which are mostly phonetically-based. While there are at least seven dialects in China, including Mandarin, Wu, Xiang, Gan, Hakka, Cantonese, and Min, there exists only one uniform written language. Different from the Western conceptions of language, the Chinese makes a sharper distinction between spoken vernacular 语 [yǔ] and written vernacular 文 [wén] and written word 字 [zì] and spoken word 话 [huà] (Beijing Normal University). Although all the ethnic groups in China are free to use and develop their own spoken and written languages, the *Law of the People's Republic of China on the Standard Spoken and Written Language* (2001) aims at popularizing "the standard spoken and written Chinese language which means Putonghua, a common speech with the pronunciation based on the Beijing dialect, and the standardized Chinese characters" (p. 1). In this paper, we focus on the Chinese conceptualizations of communication based on Mandarin mostly used by the Han majority.

Criteria. We observe three criteria to select the prominent Chinese terms about communication. First, our selection is from three types of Mandarin, i. e., 文言 [wén yán], 白话 [bái huà], and e-language in two periods with 1919 as the demarcation line and two kinds of co-existing space- real and virtual. Specifically, two major changes have taken place in modern Chinese history. On one hand, the Chinese language experienced a dramatic transformation from 文言 [wén yán] to 白话 [bái huà] or from Classical to Vernacular initially in the writing system and then in the spoken version as well. On the other hand, there has appeared an equally dramatic change in the Chinese language from the traditional version to the electronic version due to globalization and information revolution. While traditional language here refers to the "non-electronically mediated linguistic communication in the old-style speech and writing," e-language means the "ubiquitous form of the computer-mediated communication, the language people use on Bulletin Board Systems" (Crystal, 2001, p. 160). Today's Chinese Internet users are already more than 600 million (China Internet Network Information Center, 2014), twice as much as the American population. Thus, the three body of resources for our selection of the cultural terms about communication are 文言 [wén yán] before 1919, 白话 [bái huà] since 1919, and the e-language during the past two decades.

Second, we select the prominent Chinese cultural terms about communication according to their predominance in use and research based on our ethnographic engagement, field notes, and extensive literature review. As a method, ethnography typically refers to fieldwork conducted by a single investigator who lives with and lives like those who are studied, usually for a year or more (Van Maanen, 1996, pp. 263-165). As ethnographic engagement in the Chinese culture, the authors were born in China and have become familiar with the Chinese culture by living in it since childhood, studying in it from kindergarten to graduate school, and working in it as university professors for decades. We certainly brought the resources of our personal backgrounds and experiences into full play. In addition, we also consulted quite a number of native Chinese scholars and authoritative English-speaking experts in Chinese language and culture. In terms of literature review, we find that there has been extensively published scholarship on Chinese culture and communication via 文言 [wén yán] or Classical Chinese before 1919 (e.g., Cheng; 1986; Greenholtz, 2003; Xiao, 2001), Chinese culture and communication via 白话 [bái huà] or Vernacular Chinese in its simplified writing and spoken systems since 1919 (e.g., Bond & Wang, 1983; Gao, Ting-Toomey, & Gudykunst, 1996; Pye, 1982), and Chinese culture and communication via e-language or computer-mediated linguistic form (e.g., Bond & Hwang, 1986; Chan, 1963; Confucius, 1990; Faure & Fang, 2008). In addition, we also make our selection of the prominent Chinese terms by observing the authoritative *Glossary of Frequently-Used Contemporary Chinese Characters* published by the Commercial Press in 2008.

The final selection criterion is that such terms should have significant Chinese philosophical, religious, and ideological foundations as well as sufficient importance in school education and academic research. To examine the meanings of the selected cultural terms and identify their associations with the Chinese philosophical, religious, and ideological roots, we have also checked some key reference sources (Chan, 1963; Yu, 2001b; Fang & Liu, 2006).

Hermeneutics. For data analysis, we adopted hermeneutics to interpret the selected Chinese terms. Byrne (2001) explains that hermeneutics is usually used for the interpretation and understanding of texts derived from stories, interviews, participant observations, letters, speeches, or other relevant written documents and personal experiences. Girish (2008) further clarifies that, as an art of interpreting, hermeneutics developed into a theory of human understanding through the works of Scheleiermacher, Dilthey, Heideggar, Gadamar, and Derrida. The essence of hermeneutics is that "the concealed import of a text cannot be understood without uncovering the historical contact and the socio-cultural milieu of the community on which it is based" (p. 2). This means that, to thoroughly and appropriately analyze a text, it is essential to understand the origin of the text along with its historical and cultural backgrounds. Thus, the selected Chinese terms in this study are closely examined in connection to their relevant historical and socio-cultural contexts.

Research Findings: Prominent Chinese Terms

The following six dialectic pairs of categories of Chinese terms for talk and practice with a couple or several illustrations of each side of each pair have been identified. In the process, we transcend the dichotomous thinking (e. g., Hofstede, 2001) and follow a dialectical framework based on previous researches (e. g.: Fang & Faure, 2011; Gao, Ting-Toomey, & Gudykunst, 1996; Kluckhohn & Strodtbeck, 1961).

Implicit vs. Explicit. While the Chinese have been brought up not to utter any words unless being called upon to do so especially when elders or strangers are present, they are encouraged to speak up their minds in-between close friends and among family members. This is why many Chinese are reserved and cherish their words like gold. Even if they have to make comments in public, especially critical remarks in cases like class discussions or public debates, they tend to beat about the bush for fear that they may hurt the feelings of their classmates or people they do not know well. Thus, there are implicit terms such as 1) 含蓄 [hán xù]: reserved or indirect communication and 2) 委婉 [wěi wǎn]: euphemistic.

However, the Chinese are expected to be frank with their friends and hide nothing significant from their closed ones in the family. Actually, close friends and family members in China are so open and straightforward that something vulgar like "son-of-bitch" may be applied in their exchange of greetings or other daily interactions. Examples are 3) 直率 [zhí shuài]: straightforward and 4) 畅所欲言 [chàng suǒ yù yán]: speak directly from one's heart.

Polite vs. Impolite Terms. The Chinese regard themselves as a nation emphasizing etiquette, and they strongly believe that people are born virtuous. Since it is regarded as one of the fundamental virtues to be polite to others, there are plenty of polite terms in the Chinese language such as 5) 礼貌 [lǐ mào]: politeness, 6) 谦让 [qiān ràng]: politely compromising, and 7) 良言一句三冬暖,恶语伤人六月寒 [liáng yán yí jù sān dōng nuǎn, è yǔ shāng rén liù yuè hán]: A kind word is remembered for a long time, but an abusive one hurts the feelings at once. Meanwhile, to avoid impolite behaviors and rude terms, the Chinese strategically follow the suggestions of 8) 先小人,后君子。[xiān xiǎo rén, hòu jūn zǐ]: Be mean first in order to become gentle later and 9) "非礼勿视,非礼勿听,非礼勿言,非礼勿动" [fēi lǐ wù shì, fēi lǐ wù tīng, fēi lǐ wù yán, fēi lǐ wù dòng] (Confucius, 1990): See no evil, hear no evil, speak no evil, and do no evil. Although both 8) and 9) are ancient adages, they are frequently observed even today when the Chinese are involved in business transactions and when they intend to lead a socially-expected, normal way of life.

In-Group vs. Out-Group. The Chinese culture is a typical high-context culture, which attaches great significance to in-groups and out-groups. In a high-context culture, "most of the information is either in the physical context or is internalized in the person, while very little is in the coded, explicit, transmitted part of the message" (Hall, 1976, p. 79). Introductions should be made in China if an out-group member intends to do anything successful with an in-group member. Even so, in-group and out-group members are treated differently. This is why there are in-group terms such as 10) 圈内人士 [quān nèi rén shì]: an insider or in-group member and 11) 内外有别 [nèi wài yǒu bié]: Treat insiders and outsiders differently. Whenever the Chinese are together with out-group members, an inner voice keeps telling them: 12) 逢人且说三分话，未可全抛一片心 [féng rén qiě shuō sān fēn huà, wèi kě quán pāo yī piàn xīn]: Never pour out your heart to strangers. Certainly, since the Chinese understand the theory of Yin and Yang, they may also observe the advice of 13) 兼听则明，偏听则暗。[jiān tīng zé míng, piān tīng zé àn]: Listen to both sides and you will be enlightened; heed only one side and you will be benighted.

Positive vs. Negative. There are two main schools of thought that dominate the Chinese patterns of thinking. While Confucianism focuses on the present world, Daoism advocates inaction and seeks harmony between humanity and nature. Thus, when the Chinese are making achievements, they tend to use terms such as 14) 正能量 [zhèng néng liàng]: having positive energy, 15) "天行健，君子以自强不息。" [tiān xíng jiàn, jūn zǐ yǐ zì qiáng bù xī] (Zhang, 2008): As Heaven's movement is ever vigorous, so must a gentleman ceaselessly strive along, and 16) "己欲立而立人，己欲达而达人。" [jǐ yù lì ér lì rén, jǐ yù dá ér dá rén] (Confucius, 1990): Establish oneself, and seek also to establish others; develop oneself, and seek also to develop others. Nevertheless, when one is going downhill, one can be described in negative terms like 17) 748 [去死吧 qù sǐ ba]: go to hell, 18) 今朝有酒今朝醉 [jīn zhāo yǒu jiǔ jīn zhāo zuì]: Enjoy while one can, 19) 人不为己，天诛地灭 [rén bù wèi jǐ, tiān zhū dì miè]: Everyone is for himself and the devil takes the hindmost.

Superstitious vs. Rational. Superstitious terms are still widely used especially among elderly Chinese people. For important decisions like choosing the location for a house or tomb and selecting the lucky date for marriage or even birthday of babies, some Chinese are still very superstitious, and they frequently use terms like 20) 风水 [fēng shuǐ]: belief in the influence on one's fortune as a result of the location of one's house or family members' tombs, 21) 黄道吉日 [huáng dào jí rì]: an auspicious day, and 22) 命相不合 [mìng xiàng bù hé]: The horoscopes of the couple do not match.

Definitely, there are much more Chinese who believe in modern science, and they are rationally-minded in their decision-making. With China's economy booming for decades, many Chinese hold true the following expressions: 23) 实事求是 [shí shì qiú shì]: seek truth from facts, 24) "未知生,焉知死?" [wèi zhī shēng, yān zhī sǐ] (Confucius, 1990): Without knowing sufficiently about life, how can I know anything about death? and 25) "科学技术是第一生产力。"[kē xué jì shù shì dì yī shēng chǎn lì] (Hui, 1997): Science and technology are the primary productive forces.

Guanxi-Motivated（Relational）vs. Utilitarian. Guanxi-motivated or relational terms are Chinese words or expressions about the complex human networks in the collectivistic Chinese society. In such a society, collective identities in the form of first family, then institutions, and finally country precede those of individuals. For survival, each individual must squeeze himself or herself into a variety of relational networks, so countless Guanxi-motivated terms have come into being, such as 26) 拉关系 [lā guān xi]: tuft-hunt, 27), 裙带关系 [qún dài guān xi]: nepotism, 28) 一个篱笆三个桩,一个好汉三个帮。[yī gè lí ba sān gè zhuāng, yī gè hǎo hàn sān gè bāng]: Just as a fence needs the support of three stakes, an able fellow needs the help of three other people.

Meanwhile, China has been practicing market economy for decades, and the whole nation is practically-minded nowadays. On the lips of many Chinese are such utilitarian terms as 29) 打破铁饭碗 [dǎ pò tiě fàn wǎn]: break the iron rice bowl, 30) 优化组合 [yōu huà zǔ hé]: maximization of benefits, 31) 优胜劣汰 [yōu shèng liè tài]: survival of the fittest, and 32)不管白猫黑猫,抓住老鼠就是好猫 [bù guǎn bái māo hēi māo, zhuā zhù lǎo shǔ jiù shì hǎo māo]: Never mind if a cat is white or black, as long as it catches mice it's a good cat, which was coined by Deng Xiaoping.

Discussion

In the above, we have discussed the cultural impacts of the three Chinese religio-philosophical traditions of Confucianism, Daoism, and Buddhism, and the three dominant ideologies of Marxism-Leninism, Maoism as well as Dengism upon the Chinese communication practice. We have also explicated the dialectical approach of Yin and Yang and the three criteria for selecting, categorizing, and analyzing over 30 terms subsumed under 6 paradoxical pairs. To apply the above cultural values for the appropriate usage of Chinese language in various social contexts, Confucian ethics, Daoism and Buddhism all advocate for the observation of three criteria: "sincerity, expressiveness, and elegance" (Yang, 1990, p. 28). In other words, writers and speakers are supposed to convey their genuine feelings and true ideas clearly and smoothly by making appropriate and skillful use of rhetorical devices.

A Confucian example reads "巧言令色,鲜矣仁!" [qiǎo yán lìng sè, xiǎn yǐ rén] (Confucius, 1990): The Master says those who are glib in their speech and wear an ingratiating expression have little benevolence in them. It emphasizes sincerity in the expression and practice of benevolence instead of the exaggerated use of verbal expressions or speaking techniques. However, this does not mean that skills, styles, or ornamentation of language should be absolutely abolished. Another Confucian example backs it up here, which goes "言之无文,行而不远。"[yán zhī wú wén, xíng ér bù yuǎn](Confucius, 2012): Inelegant words will not become popular.

There are examples from Daoism like 真心 [zhēn xīn] sincere heart, 借花献佛 [jiè huā xiàn fó] present Buddha with borrowed flowers, and 人不为己,天诛地灭 [rén bú wèi jǐ, tiān zhū dì miè] Heaven destroys those who don't look out for themselves are all from Buddhism. In one way or another, they indicate sincerity, the exchange of favors, and the concern for oneself. As for Daoism, according to Yang (1990), the classical text of 《道德经》(Tao Te Ching) well exemplifies the three principles of sincerity, expressiveness, and elegance. One example is "道可道,非常道。名可名,非常名。"[dào kě dào, fēi cháng dào. míng kě míng, fēi cháng míng](Lao Tzu, Tao Te Ching): The Dao that can be told is not the eternal Dao, and the name that can be named is not the eternal name. It is clear that Dao, the most important doctrine of Daoism is impressively conveyed in the adoption of terse diction and parallel sentence structures. Just as the balance of things in the universe is achieved via Yin and Yang, the balance of appropriate use of language is achieved through the three Chinese rhetorical principles of sincerity, expressiveness, and elegance.

As reflections of the dramatic ideological changes in the use of language, first the introduction of Marxism-Leninism at the beginning of the 20th century brought quite a few special terminologies into China such as 共产主义 [gòng chǎn zhǔ yì]: communism, 社会主义 [shè huì zhǔ yì]: socialism, and 人民公社 [rén mín gōng shè]: people's commune. The implementation of Maoism since 1949 has produced 农民运动 [nóng mín yùn dòng]: peasant campaigns, 农村包围城市 [nóng cūn bāo wéi chéng shì]: taking over the rural areas first and then the urban ones, 大跃进 [dà yuè jìn]: great leap forward, and 文化大革命 [wén huà dà gé mìng]: the Cultural Revolution. Finally, with Deng's reform and opening up to the outside world policy in 1979, the Chinese language is enriched with such popular terms as 改革开放 [gǎi gé kāi fàng]: reform and opening up to the outside world, 思想解放 [sī xiǎng jiě fàng]: ideological emancipation, and 发展是硬道理 [fā zhǎn shì yìng dào lǐ]: Development is of overriding importance, and 打破铁饭碗 [dǎ pò tiě fàn wǎn]: break the iron rice bowl. These terms have quickly become household phrases of the Chinese people. Due to such impacts, modern Western conceptualizations of communication like professional communication, rational commumication and polite communication rooted in the Renaissance tradition and the American culture have been integrated into the modern and contemporary, Chinese communication and cultural system, differentiating from, yet intermixing with the indigenous Chinese cultural and communication system during the past six decades since the founding of P. R. China in 1949.

Conclusion

Possessing the biggest number of speakers, Chinese or Mandarin serves as the communication tool of 56 ethnic groups or 1.3 billion people within P. R. China, and it is widely used by millions of Chinese or Chinese communities all over the world. For the 30 terms under 6 paradoxical pairs, each is illustrated with real-life examples. It reveals that the Chinese conceptualizations of communication are predominantly interpersonal and relational, inclusive and dialectical, conflictual yet harmony-oriented, rational and utilitarian, adaptive and integrative. Such apparent paradoxes belie a Chinese view of communication deriving from a vigorous inclusion and harmonization of differences among both the ancient Chinese tradition and modern Western culture of various inclinations. It is part and parcel of the hybridized and evolving living Chinese cultural system energized by the synergy of both the three ancient teachings of Confucianism, Daoism, and Buddhism and the new three teachings consisting of Marxism-Leninism, Maoism and Dengism.

References

[1] Bond, M. H., & Hofstede, G. (1989). The cash value of Confucian values. Human Systems Management, 8, 195-200.

[2] Bond, M. H., & Hwang, K. (1986). The social psychology of Chinese people. In M. H. Bond (Ed.), The psychology of Chinese people (pp. 213-226). Hong Kong: Oxford University Press.

[3] Bond, M. H., & Wang, S. H. (1983). Aggressive behavior in Chinese society: The problem of maintaining order and social harmony. In A. P. Goldstein and M. Segall (Eds.), Global perspectives on aggression (pp. 58-74). New York, NY: Pergamon.

[4] Byrne, M. (2001). Hermeneutics as a methodology for textual analysis: Nursing application. AORN Journal 5: 1-4.

[5] Chan, G. K. Y. (2008). The relevance and value of Confucianism in contemporary business ethics. Journal of Business Ethics 77, 347-360.

[6] Chan, W. T. (1963). A sourcebook in Chinese philosophy. Princeton, NY: Princeton University Press.

[7] Chang, D. Q. (2003). Teaching Chinese to foreigners and the Chinese culture. Xiamen, Guangzhou: Xiamen University Press.

[8] Chen, G.-M. (2008). Towards transcultural understanding: A harmony theory of Chinese communication. China Media Research, 4(4), 1-13.

[9] Cheng, C. Y. (1986). The concept of face and its Confucian root. Journal of Chinese Philosophy, 13, 329-348.

[10] China Internet Network Information Center. (2014). Statistical reports on Internet development in China. Available at http://www1.cnnic.cn/IDR/ReportDownloads/201411/P020141102574314897888.pdf. V[11] Confucius. (2012). The twenty-fifth year of Duke Xiang. In H. Zhentao (Ed.), Guwenguanzhi. Shanghai University Press.

[12] Confucius. (1990). The analects of Confucius (translated by A. Charles Muller). Available at: http://www.acmuller.net/con-dao/analects.html.

[13] Crystal, D. (2001). Language and the Internet. Cambridge: Cambridge University Press.

[14] Fang, T., & Faure, G. O. (2011). Chinese communication characteristics: A Yin Yang perspective. International Journal of Intercultural Relations, 35, 320–333.

[15] Fang, D., & Liu, L. X. (2006). Handbook of Chinese idioms. Beijing: Beijing University Press.

[16] Faure, G. O., & Fang, T. (2008). Changing Chinese values: Keeping up with paradoxes. International Business Review, 17, 194–207.

[17] Fei, X. (1985). Shihui diaocha zibai (Statement Regarding Social Investigations). Shanghai, Knowledge Press.

[18] Gao, G., Ting-Toomey, S., & Gudykunst, W. B. (1996). Chinese communication processes. In M. H. Bond (Ed.), The handbook of Chinese psychology (pp. 280–293). Hong Kong: Oxford University Press.

[19] Glossary of Frequently-Used Contemporary Chinese Characters. (2008). Beijing: Commercial Press in 2008

[20] Greenholtz, J. (2003). Socratic teachers and Confucian learners: Examining the benefits and pitfalls of a year abroad. Language and Intercultural Communication, 3 (2), 122–130.

[21] Girish, P. M. (2008) Text and reading: Exercises in hermeneutics. Language in India, 8(3): 2–8.

[22] Hall, E. T. (1976). Beyond culture. Garden City, NY: Anchor Press/Doubleday.

[23] Hall, E. T. (1959). The silent language. New York, NY: Doubleday & Company, Inc.

[24] Hansen, C. (1985). Chinese language, Chinese philosophy, and "truth." Journal of Asian Studies XLIV(3), 491–519.

[25] Hanson, S. E. (2001). Marxism and Leninism. International Encyclopedia of the Social & Behavioral Sciences, 1, 9298–9302.

[26] Hofstede, G. (2001). Culture's consequences: Comparing values, behaviors, institutions, and organizations across nations (2nd ed.). Thousand Oaks, CA: Sage.

[27] Hong, X. P. (2015). Impact of Confucianism, Taoism and Buddhism. Chinese Social Sciences Today. Available at: http://www.csstoday.com/Item/1573.aspx.

[28] Hwang, K. K. (1997). Guanxi and mientze: Conflict resolution in Chinese society. Intercultural Communication Studies, 7(1), 17–38.

[29] Jia, W. (1997–1998). Facework as conflict-preventive mechanism: A cultural/discourse analysis. Intercultural Communication Studies, 7, 43–61.

[30] Jia, W. S. (2008). Chinese perspectives on harmony: An evaluation of the harmony and peace paradigms. China Media Research, 4(4), 25–30.

[31] Jia, W. (2006). Wei (positioning)-ming (naming)-lianmian (face)-guanxi (relationship)-renqing (humanized feelings). In Peter Hershock & Roger Ames

(Eds.) Cultures of Authority: China (pp. 49 – 64). Albany, NY: SUNY Press.

[32] Jia, W. (2001). Remaking the Chinese character and identity in the 21st Century: The Chinese face practices. Westport, CT: Ablex/ Greenwood.

[33] Kluckhohn, F. , & Strodtbeck, F. (1961). Variations in value orientations. Evanston, IL: Row, Peterson.

[34] Kramsch, C. (1998). Language and culture. Oxford, London: Oxford University Press. Law of the People's Republic of China on the Standard Spoken and Written Chinese Language (Order of the President No. 37). Available at http://www. gov. cn/english/laws/2005 – 09/19/content_64906. htm.

[35] Martin, J. N. , Nakayama, T. K. (Eds.) (2010). Intercultural communication in contexts, (5th ed.). New York, NY: McGraw-Hill Higher Education.

[36] Nisbett, R. E. , Peng, K. P. , Choi, I. , & Norenzayan, A. (2001). Culture and systems of thought: Holistic versus analytic cognition. Psychological Review, 108 (2), 291 – 310.

[37] Pye, L. W. (1982). Chinese commercial negotiating style. Cambridge, MA: Oelgeschlager, Gunn & Hain.

[38] Ruan, Y. X. (2008). The Buddhism terms in the Chinese language. Master's thesis. Available at:http://www. docin. com/p – 125941090. html.

[39] Van Maanen, J. (1996). Ethnography. In A. Kuper and J. Kuper (Eds.), The social science encyclopedia, (2nd ed.), pp. 263 – 265. London: Routledge.

[40] Wang, R. R. (n. d.). Yinyang. Internet Encyclopedia of Philosophy. Available at: http://www. iep. utm. edu/yinyang/.

[41] Wertz, R. R. (1998 – 2014). Maoism. Available at: http://www. ibiblio. org/ chinesehistory/contents/02cul/c04s07. html.

[42] Yang, H. R. (1990). A short history of Chinese rhetoric studies. Journal of Chengdu University, 1, 27 – 32.

[43] Yen, D. A. , & Barnes, B. R. (2011). Analyzing stage and duration of Anglo-Chinese business-to-business relationships. Industrial Marketing Management, 40(3), 346 – 357.

[44] Yu, G. Y. (2001). An introduction to e-language. Beijing: China Economic Press.

[45] Yu, G. Y. (2001b). Dictionary of Chinese e-language. Beijing: China Economic Press.

[46] Xiao, X. (2001). Li: A dynamic cultural mechanism of social interaction and conflict management. In G. M. Chen & R. Ma (Eds.), Chinese conflict management and resolution (pp. 39 – 50). Westport, CT: Abex.

[47] Zhang, C. (2008). Understanding the book of changes. Beijing: Zhonghua Book Company.

Chapter 21
Border Institutions—What Is Lacking in the Diaoyu/Senkaku Islands Dispute

Lying in the East China Sea, an island group consisting of five uninhabited islands and three rocks (known as the Senkaku in Japan, Diaoyu in China, and Diaoyutai in Taiwan) has been causing waves of sensation of the whole world. For instance, Kristof (2010) asked the global audience to stay tuned because "this is a boundary dispute that could get ugly and some day have far-reaching consequences for Mainland China, Japan, Taiwan and the United States" (p. 1). Most recently, Harner (2013) began his blog article in the online Forbes magazine with "second only to nuclear weapon development on North Korea and Iran, it is the most dangerous potential *casus belli* [sic] in the world today, and it is likely to remain so indefinitely" (p. 2). Thus, we can clearly sense the intensity and severity of the conflict under discussion.

On the one hand, Japan declares full sovereignty and rejects any territorial dispute over these islands arguing that it discovered the islands *terra nullius* or land of no human beings and incorporated them into Japan as a cabinet decision in 1895 and exercised effective control over the islands with no Chinese protest until 1971. On the other, both Mainland China and Taiwan claim that China, not Japan, discovered and exercised sovereignty over the islands since the 14th century, and Japan seized them from Taiwan under Article Two of the *Treaty of Shimonoseki of 1895* after Japan won the first Sino-Japanese War from 1894 to 1895.

Although disputes over the Diaoyu/Senkaku islands have been recurring for many decades, what flared up the most recent conflict involving Japan, China, Taiwan, and the US is Tokyo Governor Shintaro Ishihara's proposal of purchasing these islands by the Tokyo Metropolitan Government in April 2012 and the subsequent nationalization of three of the islands by the Japanese government in September 2012. For months, China has been regularly sending out surveillance ships and planes towards the disputed areas. To confront the aggressive Chinese patrol missions each time, war ships of Japanese Coast Guards and jet fighters from the Japanese Maritime Self-Defense Force would come to intercept the approaching Chinese ships and planes. The non-compromise positions of the two governments have not only put their bilateral relationship into a stand-off but also filled the whole world with increasing worries about unexpected face-off or more catastrophic consequences.

To complicate the conflict, Liang Ying-ping, Taiwan's top representative to Seoul,

South Korea announced to the media: "Our stance is clear. The Diaoyutai Islands are the territory of the Republic of China (ROC). The dispute is a three-party concern, not just confined to Japan and China" (Kim, 2012, p. 1). Just as Ma Yingjiu of Taiwan remarked, "we will not make any concessions on national sovereignty.... There could be more serious confrontations or wars if we do not resolve the dispute peacefully" (Mo, 2012, p. 7). Ma Yingjiu called for a trilateral dialogue between Taiwan, Japan and China to resolve the sovereignty dispute. In fact, there is also a fourth party, the US, which has been directly and indirectly involved in the Senkaku/Diaoyu Islands dispute.

From the above, we can see that there are actually two sides of four parties deeply involved in the Senkaku/Diaoyu Islands dispute: Japan and the US as the accused on the defensive side; China and Taiwan as the accusers on the challenging side. This does not mean that there are no conflicts between Japan and the US and China and Taiwan. However, for the purpose of this study and based on the existing literature, we just focus on exploring what is lacking in the available interactions between the two sides and among the four parties in this multi-lateral international conflict.

Literature Review

The backdrop and influence of the Senkaku/Diaoyu Islands dispute. The Senkaku/Diaoyu Islands are located northeast of Taiwan, east of China, and southwest of Okinawa, the southern-most prefecture of Japan. In his Congressional Research Service Report, Manyin (2013) reported, the Senkaku/Diaoyu Islands consist of five islets and three rocky outcroppings with a total landmass of less than seven square kilometers or three square miles. The largest island is about two miles in length and less than one mile in width. None of the islands are inhabited and unlikely to support any human life or economic activities from indigenous resources. Despite the unfavorable natural features, Japan, China, and Taiwan all claim sovereignty over the islands. Periodic tensions and conflicts have been occurring among the claimants and, fueled by rising nationalism in all parties, waves of nation-wide campaigns have been witnessed, all claiming the sovereignty over theses islands due to their strategic significance in terms of economy, security, and political implications.

Economically, sovereignty over the Senkaku/Diaoyu Islands could "convey exclusive economic rights to nearly 20,000 square nautical miles of undersea resources" (Ramos-Mrosovsky, 2008, pp. 903-904). It means that control of the islands would confer ownership of natural resources such as fishery and potential oil and gas reserves in their vicinity. In terms of security, the Senkaku/Diaoyu Islands lie close to key shipping lanes in the region. As Pan (2007) said, the location of the islands on the eastern edge of the continental margin in the East China Sea exerts strategic impact upon "both China and Japan's increasingly voracious appetite for energy, natural resources, and extension into the high seas" (p. 72) and the sovereignty over the islands "can be a factor that significantly influences the location of a maritime boundary between China and Japan" (p. 84). This is

Chapter 21

Border Institutions—What Is Lacking in the Diaoyu/Senkaku Islands Dispute

why Suganuma (2000) remarked: "If there is a flash point to ignite a third Sino-Japanese War, it will be the ownership of the Diaoyu Islands in the East China Sea" (p. 151). Finally, since both China and Japan have maritime territorial disputes with their neighboring countries, both have been making the greatest efforts avoiding any potential negative domino effect in the handling of the Senkaku/Diaoyu Islands dispute. Just as Koo (2009) noted, any concessions in the dispute "could possibly jeopardize their respective claims to the other disputed islands" (p. 206). Thus, the Senkaku/Diaoyu Islands dispute is not just territorial. It bears more chain-effect significance in politics, economics, and national, even international security.

At least, how the dispute will be resolved will definitely affect the Asia-Pacific region directly and indirectly. The Asia-Pacific region, which covers 70% of the earth's surface and 50% of the world's ocean surface, provides many export-oriented economies around the Pacific Rim with the most dynamic and strategic trade routes and energy resources. As a "key engine for the global economy" (VOC, 2013, p. 1), the region has half of the world's population, with a combined gross domestic product (GDP) of $39 trillion, accounting for 56% of the world economic output. The region is home to quite a number of the world's largest militaries and the majority of the world's nuclear power.

Therefore, in his remarks to the Australian Parliament, President Obama (2011) predicted that this region will "largely determine whether the century ahead will be marked by conflict or cooperation, needless suffering or human progress" (p. 15). In her article entitled "America's Pacific Century," Secretary Clinton (2011) emphasized a smart and systematic US effort over the next decade by "locking in a substantially increased investment diplomatic, economic, strategic, and otherwise in the Asia-Pacific region" (p. 1). It is clear that the year 2011 became a pivot point for the United States to complete its withdrawal of soldiers from Iraq and Afghanistan and began reasserting itself in the Asia-Pacific region. Although the reassertion of the Asia-Pacific region is a continuation of the US policies undertaken by previous administrations, the Obama Administration intends to achieve some larger purposes and make the US "play a larger and long-term role in shaping this region and its future, by upholding core principles and in close partnership with our allies and friends" (Obama, 2011, p. 16).

Scholarship on territorial conflict. Among all kinds of conflict, territorial conflict is next to none in its frequency, severity, and consequences. Holsti (1991) noted, among interstate wars between 1648 and 1989, "territorial issues were by far the most important single issue category" (p. 307). Vasquez (1995) found, "a minimum of 79% of wars were fought over territory-related issues in five historical periods from 1648 to 1990" (p. 284). Hensel (2000) also found that, between 1816 and 1992, more than half of the wars were related to issues of disputed territory, and disputes over territory tended to result in conflicts with much more fatalities than disputes of other categories. Gleditsch (1998) provided reasons for the territorial conflict by saying, "the territory itself might be seen as important to the identity of a people and the symbolic function might be more important than any material value" (p. 385). Similarly, Knight (1982) remarked, "territory is not; it becomes, for territory itself is passive, and it is human beliefs and actions that give territory meaning" (p. 517). Murphy (1990) also stressed, as a social construct, "territory is fundamentally embedded in social processes," which is "at the heart of national identity and cohesion and of supreme importance to the state" (p. 531).

To comprehend international disputes or conflicts, there are two main camps of scholars. While liberals argue that territorial disputes lose their salience as a result of increasing economic interdependence, realists counter-argue that economic interdependence not only fails to promote peace but also increases conflicts due to asymmetric dependence and inequality between economic partners. Nevertheless, Simmons (2005) found, while scholars of realist thought regard territory as the object of zero-sum state competition for power, prestige, or an imagined national identity, liberal scholars of globalization stress that in this increasingly borderless world, human capital matters more than territorial matters and national power. In reality, less than one third of the international borders have been disputed since World War II. Even in the Middle East, 80% of the borders remain peaceful through mutually accepted formal treaties. Take China for example, it has settled 17 of its 23 territorial disputes since 1949. Moreover, China has made substantial compromises in most of these settlements, "usually receiving less than 50% of the contested land" (Fravel, 2005, p. 46). In contrast, it is also argued, "national boundaries continue to have significant influences on international economic relations" (Simmons, 2005, p. 826). An empirical study of bilateral trade between the US and Canada revealed that "trade between Canadian provinces was 22 times that of Canada-US trade, all other factors being held equal" (McCallum, 1995, p. 617).

As a summary, Mowle (2003) commented, realism and liberalism "are as much quality as they are of action. A comparison of the two approaches must somehow pry open the intent behind the action" (p. 562). It means that there must be a shift of the analysis from the state to the individuals within the state who make decisive decisions and implement purposive actions. Chiozza and Choi (2003) concurred with Mowle in their empirical study, "leaders, who have the political interest and ability to lead their countries onto a different road, do matter in explaining decisions to settle territorial disputes" (p. 275). Thus, territorial disputes may lead to military confrontations, but wise leadership guided by domestic needs and international norms may set the interactions between or among claimants and bilateral or trilateral relationships onto peaceful paths.

Literature on the Senkaku/Diaoyu Islands dispute. Existing literature concerning the Senkaku/Diaoyu Islands dispute falls into three major categories. The first category of literature explains the continuity and escalation of the dispute. Scholars (e.g., Bush III, 2010; International Institute for Strategic Studies, 2010; Kenny, 2004; Park, 1973; Valencia, 2000) predicted that the Senkaku/Diaoyu Islands dispute would continue and escalate so long historical and legal issues among the claimants remain unresolved and the dispute involves material and symbolic significance. For example, Bush III (2010) predicted, "there was a danger that the dispute might become militarized," (p. 6) as strategists in both Japan and China "cited with concern the old Chinese expression, 'two tigers cannot coexist on the same mountain'" (p. 8). However, all the flare-ups over the Senkaku/Diaoyu Islands have been eventually calmed down.

The second category of literature provides explanations for the mutual restraint from all parties involved in the Senkaku/Diaoyu Islands dispute. Some scholars (e.g., Blanchard, 2000; Bush III, 2010; Fravel, 2010; Ito, 2008; Hara, 2001; Lind, 2004) remarked, due to the US factor, the Sino-Japanese dispute over the Senkaku/Diaoyu Islands was taking place within certain limits. For example, Blanchard (2000) noted, "it [the US] currently has the authority, at a minimum, to press both sides to explicate their real interests and to promote alternatives for a settlement of the controversy" (p. 121). Fravel (2010) seconded, "the United States is an important actor in the China-Japan disputes, especially the conflict over the Senkaku Islands" (p. 144). Some other scholars (e.g., Christensen, 2006; Friedberg, 2005; Goldstein, 2005; Niksch, 1996; Wiegand, 2009) showed their worries that a more capable China might become a nascent China threat. Wiegand (2009) claimed, as the second largest consumer of oil after the US, China "continues to claim sovereignty over the islands and the dispute is nowhere close to being resolved" (p.170). Nevertheless, it has been found that China has been cooperative and peaceful in its territorial disputes since 1949 (Fravel, 2005, 2008, 2010; Nie, 2009).

The final category of literature accounts for the repeated ups and downs in the Senkaku/Diaoyu Islands dispute. On the one hand, many scholars (e.g., Chung, 2004; Fravel 2005; Hagström, 2005; Pan, 2007) associated the ups and downs of the dispute with the desires and power struggles of the state elites among all sides of the claimants in their domestic decision-making processes. Pan (2007) remarked that the handling of Senkaku/Diaoyu Islands dispute "is seen as a factor impacting on the legitimacy of Chinese and Japanese central governments in domestic politics and on their foreign relations in the international arena" (p. 72). Meanwhile, many other scholars (e.g., Blanchard, 2000; Fravel, 2010; Koo, 2009; Manyin, 2013; Tanaka, 2010) emphasized the international nature of the dispute, especially the US factor. Blanchard (2000) noted, the US "has been deeply involved" in the Senkaku/Diaoyu Islands dispute, and it "should become more actively involved in trying to encourage a resolution of the dispute, or at a minimum, serious discussion between the Chinese and the Japanese" (p. 121).

It can be seen from the above that the Senkaku/Diaoyu Islands dispute is not simply a conflict between Japan/US and China/Taiwan, it is a complicated and multi-sided conflict of international nature. So far, much ink has been spilled about the Senkaku/Diaoyu Islands dispute from various perspectives as described, little has been done from the perspective of communication in terms of argumentation. We attempt to fill this void by exploring how the involved parties have been communicating to the public to seek answers to the following three research questions:

RQ1: What are the conflicting points in the claimants' claims?

RQ2: What are the pieces of supporting evidence and counterevidence?

RQ3: What is lacking for a genuinely peaceful and win-win solution to the Senkaku/Diaoyu Islands dispute?

The research findings of this study are expected to enrich the existing body of literature on conflict communication in general and the dispute over the Senkaku/Diaoyu Islands in the East China Sea in particular while shedding light on similar disputes over islands in the South China Sea at the same time.

Theoretical Framework of Institutions

The application of international borders as institutions "neither falls prey to claims that borders do not matter nor is prisoner to realism's zero-sum assumptions" (Simmons, 2005, p. 827). Simmons is a Harvard scholar of international affairs, and he defined institutions as "sets of rules, compliance procedures, and moral and ethical behavioral norms designed to constrain behavior" (p. 827). Giordano, Giordano, and Wolf (2005) specified that, in the international resource arena, "institutions range from customary practices among neighboring states to multilateral resource conventions and treaties" (p. 53). As a summary, Slaughter (1995) clarified, the theory of institutions posits that rules, norms, and decision-making procedures define international regimes, which reduce transaction costs consistent with regime principles through cooperation. Simultaneously, they facilitate connections within and between regimes over issues by creating conditions for orderly, multilateral negotiations.

Amenta and Ramsey (2010) noted further that there are three types of theoretical claims in institutions: sociological, historical, and political. The first holds that cultural and ideational causes in a society exert influence on the state policies. Focusing on macro-political or macro-economic determinants, the second asks big questions and highlights the importance of institutions. The third argues that the process of formation of states, political systems, and political party systems have strong impact upon political processes and outcomes. Nie (2009) specified two major forms of institutional explanations over territorial disputes. The first argues that "border territories are extraordinary spaces embodying a defined legal order within international relations," therefore; "border issues influence the attitudes of policymakers" (p. 491). Jean-Marc Blanchard and Paul K. Huth are representative scholars here, and they predict democratic countries tend towards peaceful means, and non-democratic states towards non-peaceful means of resolving territorial issues. The second emphasizes: "International institutions are an important guarantee of conflict prevention" (Nie, 2009, p. 492). Stephen A. Kocs and Mark W. Zacher are representatives in this regard. To them, without clear and legally demarcated boundaries, wars will probably break out between involved states.

Furthermore, Giordano, Giordano, and Wolf (2005) summarized three causes for potential territorial conflicts and four conditions for successful institutions. The most likely locations for territorial conflicts are "those in which (1) institutional development is hindered; (2) previously functioning institutions collapse; or (3) change in resource conditions outpace the ability for institutional adaptation" (p. 48). Critical factors for long-term institutional success include: (1) clear language concerning resource allocation and quality control; (2) high degree of institutional adaptability; (3) allocating benefits considered more productive than allocating the resource; and (4) clearly defined conflict resolution mechanism in place.

Research Method

For the purpose of this study, we collected our primary data from relevant wartime declarations[1], bilateral treaties[2], government statements[3], and dozens of news briefs from the governments of the above three governments plus the government of the US. The supporting evidence and counterevidence of the claimants' claims are composed of historical records of Chinese missions and official decrees during the Ming and Qing dynasties and Japanese survey and Cabinet decision to annex the Senkaku/Diaoyu Islands; letters between the Chinese and Japanese and among the Japanese, relevant maps of Japan, China, and the US, and experts' interview transcripts with Professor Susumu Yabuki and Kurt Campbell, former assistant secretary of state for East Asian and Pacific affairs. Besides, we made a purposive selection of artifacts in terms of the relevant media reports and readers' online responses concerning the Senkaku/Diaoyu Islands dispute, from both the LexisNexis news database and Google News website. In total, we have printed over 100 pages of singled-lined news reports. For the discussion about the role of the US in the Senkaku/Diaoyu Islands dispute, we focused on the online Forbes Magazine blog article entitled "The U. S. Could Have Prevented the Senkaku/Diaoyu Crisis. Why Did It Not?" in February 2011 by Stephen Harner, who has worked in both Japan and China for dozens of years, and the 60- some responses to his blog.

For data analysis, we adopted hermeneutics to interpret the interactions in the above-mentioned communication artifacts of Japan, China, Taiwan and the US. Byrne (2001) explained, hermeneutics is usually used for the interpretation and understanding of texts derived from stories, interviews, participant observations, letters, speeches, or other relevant written documents and personal experiences. Girish (2008) further clarified, as an art of interpreting, hermeneutics developed into a theory of human understanding through the works of Scheleiermacher, Dilthey, Heideggar, Gadamar, and Derrida. The essence of hermeneutics is that "the concealed import of a text cannot be understood without uncovering the historical contact and the sociocultural milieu of the community on which it is based" (p. 2). This means that, to thoroughly and appropriately analyze a text, it is essential to understand the origin of the text along with its historical and cultural background. To this end, the texts are usually closely examined in connection to their relevant historical and socio-cultural contexts for the generation of themes or patterns as research findings, which reflect the knowledge of the phenomenon under study.

Research Findings and Critical Analysis

As mentioned earlier, there are two sides and four parties in the Senkaku/Diaoyu Islands dispute, namely Japan and the US on one side and China and Taiwan on the other. Among the four parties, Japan, China, and Taiwan are claimants of the sovereignty over the Senkaku/Diaoyu Islands while the US is a deeply-involved participant and important factor in the Senkaku/Diaoyu Islands dispute. In addition to the literature review, our analysis of the selected raw data results in the following three interrelated aspects as the conflicting points in the claimant's claims: (1) the ownership of the Senkaku/Diaoyu Islands; (2) the change of hands of these islands; and (3) the US role in the dispute. Below are the provided supporting evidence and counterevidence of Japan, China, and Taiwan regarding the above conflicting points, our critical analysis of the conflicting points and evidence, and our conclusion of the US role in the dispute.

Evidence and counterevidence regarding the ownership of the Senkaku/Diaoyu Islands. With the Senkaku/Diaoyu Islands under administrative control, Japan rejects the existence of any dispute over the sovereignty of these islands. According to its official statements of "The Basic View on the Sovereignty over the Senkaku Islands (The Basic View)" and "Q&A on the Senkaku Islands" (Q&A) by the Ministry of Foreign Affairs (MOFA) of Japan, the Japanese government began a series of thorough surveys of the Senkaku Islands from 1885, which proved the islands uninhabited. Then, a Cabinet Decision (Appendix 1) was made on Jan. 14, 1895, and the islands were incorporated into Japan as *terra nullius* with markers erected (Fact Sheet of MOFA, 2012, para. 9).

Even during the US administration of the islands, the US Navy "established firing ranges on the islets and paid an annual rent of $11,000 to Zenji Koga, the son of the first Japanese settlers of the islets" (Manyin, 2013, p. 4). A copy of the lease contract is provided in Appendix 2. Besides, the Japanese government also lists the following as examples of valid control of the Senkaku/Diaoyu Islands: (1) Patrol and law enforcement; (2) Levying taxes on the owners of the islands; (3) Management as state-owned land; (4) Implementing researches for utilization and development (Q&A, p. 4).

However, the Chinese side counter-argued that when the Japanese Cabinet decided to annex the islands to the territory of Japan in 1985, Japan was fully aware that "the islands have already been well-known to Qing envoy ships dispatched to crown the former Zhongshan King and already given fixed Chinese names and used as navigation aids en route to the Ryukyu Islands" (MOFA of Japan, 1950). The citation is from a report of the Magistrate of Okinawa, Nishimura Sutezo to the Japanese Home Secretary Yamagata

Chapter 21

Border Institutions—What Is Lacking in the Diaoyu/Senkaku Islands Dispute

Aritomo on September 22, 1885. In less than a month on October 21, 1885, the Japanese Foreign Minister announced: "Most recently Chinese newspapers have been reporting rumors of our government's intention of occupying certain islands owned by China located next to Taiwan," and he warned, "the investigations of the above-mentioned islands should not be published in the Official Gazette or newspaper. Please pay attention to this" (MOFA of Japan, 1950).

In its "Statement of the Ministry of Foreign Affairs of P. R. China" (Statement) on Sept. 10, 2012 and "Diaoyu Dao, an Inherent Territory of China" White Paper (White Paper) on Sept. 28, 2012 by the State Council Information Office of P. R. China, the Chinese government held that it was China, instead of Japan, that discovered and peacefully used the Diaoyu Islands since its Ming Dynasty in the 14th century. According to the White Paper, 24 mission voyages were made from China to the Ryukyu Kingdom, a tributary nation of China, from 1732 to 1866. There were ample records from these voyages about the Diaoyu Islands. Envoy Chen Kan from the Ming Court recorded in the *Envoys to Ryukyu* in 1534, "the ship has passed Diaoyu Dao, Huangmao Yu, Chi Yu…. Then, Gumi Mountain comes into sight, which is where the land of Ryukyu begins" (White Paper, 2012, p. 3). For another example, to guard against Japanese pirates along the southeast coast, Zheng Ruozeng compiled the Illustrated Compendium on Maritime Security (Zhouhai Tubian) in 1556 under the auspices of Hu Songxian, who is the supreme commander of the southeast coastal defense of the Ming Court. The Diaoyu Islands were included in the *Compendium* (Appendix 3).

Geographically, China posits that the Diaoyu Islands sit on the edge of the Asian continental shelf and are separated from the Ryukyu Islands by a deep underwater trench called the Okinawa Trough (Appendix 4). China holds that the distance between Taiwan and the Diaoyu Islands is 120 nautical miles, which is shorter than the 200 nautical miles between the Diaoyu Islands and Okinawa of Japan. Moreover, the surrounding waters of the Diaoyu Islands have been traditionally Chinese fishing grounds (White Paper, 2012, pp. 3-5). In one of the envoy missions, Envoy Xu Baoguang also recorded in his *Records of Messages from Chong-Shan* in 1719: "After sailing 10 geng[4], our ships passed Diaoyu Islands…. After sailing another 6 geng, our ships will arrive at Kume Hill, which is the southwest boundary between the Ryukyu Kingdom and China" (Inoue, para. 8). Envoy Xu Baoguang also described "the Senkaku/Diaoyu Islands are the same color as other Chinese territories on Fuzu" (Appendix 5) (Inoue, para. 9).

By the same token, in its official statement of "The Diaoyutai Islands: An Inherent Part of the Territory of Republic of China" (Diaoyutai Islands) by the Ministry of Foreign Affairs of Republic of China, Taiwan claims, "The Diaoyutai Islands, an island group of Taiwan, are under the jurisdiction of Yilan County" (Diaoyutai Islands, para. 1). Historically, it is the Chinese that discovered and named the Diaoyutai Islands and put it under the jurisdiction of Yilan County of Taiwan. Chinese fishermen frequently sought shelter on the islands and knew that there were no *terra nullius* between China and the Ryukyu Kingdom (The Diaoyutai Islands, para. 6).

Geographically and geologically, the Diaoyutai Islands share the same monsoon zone with Taiwan, thus making it favorable for sail from Taiwan to the islands than from the Ryukyu Islands. Geologically, the Okinawa Trough separates the Diaoyutai Islands and the Ryukyu Islands, making them reside on different tectonic plates in the East China Sea (The Diaoyutai Islands, para. 2-5). Thus, to the Chinese in China and Taiwan, these historical records demonstrate that the Senkaku/Diaoyu Islands and Chiwei Island belong to China and Kume Island belongs to Ryukyu. The dividing line between China and Ryukyu is Hei Shui Gou, which is today's Okinawa Trough between Chiwei Island and Kume Island. However, it is "an established principle in international law that neither discovery nor use by itself is sufficient to establish sovereignty over land territory" (Su, 2005, p. 49).

Evidence and counterevidence regarding the change of hands of the Senkaku/Diaoyu Islands. The Japanese government held that the Senkaku/Diaoyu Islands were not part of "the Island of Formosa together with all islands appertaining or belonging to the said Island of Formosa," (*Treaty of Shimonoseki*, 1895, (b) of Article 2), which were ceded to Japan in May 1985 at the end of the First Sino-Japanese War (Fact Sheet of MOFA, 2012, para. 11). Whether the Senkaku Islands were included in the islands of the above treaty article, "there was no mutual recognition between the two countries" (About the Senkaku Islands of MOFA, 2013, p. 11).

Furthermore, Under the *San Francisco Peace Treaty* of 1951, Japan renounced Taiwan but maintained territorial sovereignty over the Senkaku/Diaoyu Islands (The Basic View, 2013, para. 2). The *San Francisco Peace Treaty* stipulates the US "as the sole administering authority" over "Nansei Shoto south of 29 degree north latitude (including the Ryukyu Islands and the Daito Islands)" (1951, Article 3). The Ryukyu Islands and the Daito Islands were reverted to Japan with "all and any powers of administration, legislation, and jurisdiction" under Article 2 of the *Agreement between Japan and the United States of America Concerning the Ryukyu Islands and the Daito Islands* of 1971 (also known as the *Okinawa Reversion Agreement*). The Senkaku Islands were included in this agreement as can be seen in Appendix 6.

The Japanese government also pointed out that neither China nor Taiwan made any objections to the stipulations in the *San Francisco Peace Treaty* of 1951 and the *Okinawa Reversion Agreement* of 1971 (About the Senkaku Islands of MOFA, 2013, p. 7). Instead, both China and Taiwan actually recognized the Senkaku/Diaoyu Islands as Japanese territory. For example, it was mentioned in a letter of appreciation from a Chinese consul in Nagasaki in 1919 that the Senkaku/Diaoyu Islands were within the "Yaeyama District, Okinawa Prefecture, Empire of Japan" (Appendix 7). For another example, an article in the *People's Daily* dated January 8, 1953 reported that the Senkaku/Diaoyu Islands are one of the seven island groups belonging to the Ryukyu Islands (Appendix 8). Finally, the

Chapter 21

Border Institutions—What Is Lacking in the Diaoyu/Senkaku Islands Dispute

Republic of China New Atlas published in 1933 (Appendix 9) and *World Atlas* published in 1958 (Appendix 10) identified the Senkaku Islands as part of Japan (Fact Sheet of MOFA, 2012, para. 13).

In response, the Chinese government argued that the Diaoyu Islands were grabbed from China by Japan in the first Sino-Japanese War from 1894 – 1895 (White Paper, 2012, pp. 5 – 8). Early in 1884, a Japanese businessman by the name of Tatsushiro Koga applied to lease the Diaoyu Islands, but both the Okinawa Prefecture Government and the Home Ministry in Tokyo turned down his applications because "it was not clear at that time whether the islands belonged to the Japanese empire" (White Paper, 2012, p. 5). Nevertheless, in response to a report of the Magistrate of Okinawa, the Japanese National Home Secretary wrote on Sept. 22, 1885: "In regard to the matter of placing national markers and developing the islands, it should await a more appropriate time" (MOFA of Japan, 1950). The appropriate time came when China was defeated in the First Sino-Japanese War and had to sign the *Treaty of Shimonoseki* on April 17, 1985. In the *Treaty of Shimonoseki*, China was made to "cede to Japan in perpetuity and full sovereignty... the island of Formosa, together with all islands appertaining or belonging to the said island of Formosa" (*Treaty of Shimonoseki*, 1895, (b) of Article 2).

Legally, China argues that the Diaoyu Islands were returned to China after World War II. However, it is the US that had made backroom deals with Japan by arbitrarily including the Diaoyu Islands under the US trusteeship in the 1950s and returned the power of administration over the islands to Japan in the 1970s (White Paper, 2012, pp. 7 – 9). On Sept. 2, 1045, Japan solemnly "undertakes for the Emperor, the Japanese Government and their successors to carry out the provisions of the *Potsdam Declaration* in good faith" (*First Instrument of Surrender*, 1945, para. 6), which stipulates that "Japanese sovereignty shall be limited to the islands of Honshu, Hokkaido, Kyushu, Shikoku and such minor islands as we determine" (*Potsdam Declaration*, 1945, (8), (b), Annex II). Nonetheless, when Taiwan and its appertaining islands were returned to the Republic of China in 1945, Japan did not give back the Diaoyu/Diaoyutai Islands, whose name had been changed to Senkaku Islands since 1900. Thus, the Chinese were left "unaware that the uninhabited 'Senkaku Islands' were in fact the former Diaoyu Islands" (Shaw, 2012, para. 15). To make matters more complicated, the US extended the Ryukyu to include the Diaoyu Islands during its administration from 1953 to 1971 and returned Ryukyu Islands including the Diaoyu Islands to Japan under the *Okinawa Reversion Treaty* in 1971, which was signed without the presence and agreement of China (White Paper, 2012, pp. 2, 5 & 7). All this not only supports the Chinese arguments but also explains the belated protests from the Chinese people in China and Taiwan over Japan's theft of Chinese territory, Chinese maps incorrectly identifying the Senkaku/Diaoyu Islands as Japanese territory, and the US manipulation of its hegemonic power.

From the perspective of the government of Taiwan, Japan annexed the Daioyutai Islands as a direct consequence of the first Sino-Japanese War and never made any public announcement in order to avoid arousing China's objection. The islands should have been returned to Taiwan after World War II (The Diaoyutai Islands, para. 16 – 17), but the US gave the Diaoyutai and Ryukyu Islands to Japan against the strong will of the Chinese. According to declassified documents of the *Foreign Relations of the United States* (FRUS), the embassy of Republic of China (ROC) sent a note to the US State Department on March 15, 1971, making clear that "the U. S. is requested to respect the ROC's sovereign rights over the Senkaku Islets and restore them to the ROC" (FRUS, Vol. XVII, China, 1969 – 1976, Document 115, para. 7). Although Kissinger's hand-written comment "but that is nonsense since it gives islands to Japan. How can we get a more neutral position?" (FRUS, Vol. XVII, China, 1969 – 1976, Document 115, footnote 3) on the US position of the sovereignty over the Senkaku Islands, the US finally did implement such a nonsensical policy till this very day.

The US role in the Senkaku/Diaoyu Islands dispute. Although the US is not a claimant, it is still necessary to demonstrate the US position in the Senkaku/Diaoyu Islands dispute due to its alliance with Japan and its deep involvement. The US began administrating the Senkaku/Diaoyu Islands from 1953 and returned them to Japanese administration in 1971. According to Fravel (2010), since World War II, the US "has been a direct participant in the dispute over the Senkaku Islands" (p. 147). The US policy towards the Senkaku territorial dispute is based on: "(1) neutrality in terms of the ultimate sovereignty of contested areas and (2) peaceful resolution without resort to coercion or armed force" (p. 147). In other words, "the United States took a neutral position with regard to the competing claims of Japan, China, and Taiwan, despite the return of the islets to Japanese administration" (Manyin, 2013, p. 4). Upon stepping down as the Secretary of State, Hillary Clinton reiterated the US neutral position over the sovereignty of the Senkaku/ Diaoyu Islands. She further stated: "We oppose any unilateral actions that would seek to undermine Japanese administration and we urge all parties to take steps to prevent incidents and manage disagreements through peaceful means" (Quinn, 2013, para. 5 – 6). Furthermore, the US Senate unanimously approved an amendment to the 2013 *National Defense Authorization Act*, announcing: "While the United States takes no position on the ultimate sovereignty of the Senkaku Islands, the United States acknowledges the administration of Japan over the Senkaku Islands" (Johnston, 2012, para. 2). Clearly, the US stance in the Senkaku/Diaoyu Islands dispute is officially neutral but actually pro-Japan.

Just as Blanchard (2000) noted, "the historical record clearly shows that the United States favored in both word and deed Japanese claims to the islands" (p. 97). On January 19, 1946, the commander of the Okinawa Naval Base was instructed to "extend Military Government operations so as to include the Northern Ryukyus south of the 30th parallel north and to include Sakishima Gunto, [which includes the Senkaku/Diaoyu Islands included]" (p. 103). On August 6, 1948, a report from the US Central Intelligence Agency

(CIA) emphasized, "if the Communists won control of China, the return of the Ryukyus to China would give the Soviet Union access to these islands and thereby endanger the entire US Pacific base system as well as Japan" (p. 105). In January 1951, the Prime Minister of Japan sent a message to the US State Department, agreeing to "give the US all required military rights there" for "transferring title to the Ryukyus and Bonins" (p. 107). As a result, former US Secretary of State Dulles claimed that Japan had "residual sovereignty" in the Ryukyu Islands, which means: "The United States will not transfer its sovereign powers [administrative, legislative, and jurisdiction] over the Ryukyu Islands to any nation other than Japan" (p. 109). Therefore, it is questionable for the US, which has been so deeply involved in the Senkaku/Diaoyu Islands dispute, to "insist on remaining on the sidelines" (p. 120).

This is why China responded by saying, "the United States and Japan conducted backroom deals concerning the 'power of administration' over the Diaoyu Dao" (White Paper. China, 2012, p. 8). Harner (2011) seconded in his blog article, "it was the US acquiescence in (if not encouragement of) the Noda government's decision to nationalize the disputed islands ... that enabled this crisis" (para. 5). There is also supporting voice in the media, "indeed, the ambiguity of maintaining US neutrality on sovereignty yet giving Japan administrative power over the islands, backed by a mutual defense treaty, has emboldened Tokyo to nationalize the islands" (Cheong, 2012, para. 2).

Discussion

As mentioned before, territorial conflict is next to none in its frequency, severity, and consequences among all kinds of conflict. To guard against potential territorial conflict and strive for mutually beneficial resolutions, the theory of border institutions has been proposed, which refers to "sets of rules, compliance procedures, and moral and ethical behavioral norms designed to constra in behavior" (Simmons, 2005, p. 827). In the case of the Senkaku/Diaoyu Islands dispute, unwritten rules, compliance procedures, and ethical norms did exist since China's Ming Dynasty in the 14th century till 1885. Thus, the Chinese envoys could use the islands as navigation aids during many mission voyages to the Ryukyu Kingdom, and the ocean areas around the islands could remain peaceful for so long. There were also common understandings and restrained behaviors on all sides of Japan, China, and Taiwan even after Japan secretly annexed the islands to its territory in 1885 and changed the name of the islands from Diaoyu to Senkaku. For instance, the Japanese government has done a good job for many years to keep not only foreigners but also its own nationals from approaching and developing the islands. It is when such status quo was violated that waves of dispute and conflict arose consequently.

In our theoretical framework, both positive and negative prospective scenarios have also been depicted with or without border institutions. As Giordano, Giordano, and Wolf (2005) noted, the most likely locations for territorial conflicts are "those in which (1) institutional development is hindered; (2) previously functioning institutions collapse; or (3) change in resource conditions outpace the ability for institutional adaptation" (p. 48). With regard to the Senkaku/Diaoyu Islands dispute, all these three conditions were met. Change in resource conditions resulted in the hindrance to and collapse of existing institutions. For example, the Japanese government declared that it was in the 1970s that China and Taiwan began arguing for the sovereignty over the islands only after the United Nations' report of potential oil and gas reserves of 200,000 square kilometers in the East China Sea in 1968 (About the Senkaku Islands, 2013, p. 7). Taiwan was even caught to have changed the terminology of the "Senkaku Group of Islands" to "Diaoyutai Islets" in its middle school geography textbook (Appendix 11).

The Japanese government also insisted that there was no agreement to shelve the Senkaku/Diaoyu Islands issue when Japan and China normalized their diplomatic relations in 1972 and when they were negotiating for the *Treaty of Peace and Friendship* in 1978. Former Japanese Foreign Minister Maehara officially confirmed that at the Japan-China summit meeting on Sept. 27, 1972, "they [the Chinese] did not mention the words 'shelving the issue,' therefore; it cannot be judged that there existed any agreement of 'shelving the issue' from the meeting." Maehara continued that, at the Japan-China summit meeting on Oct. 25, 1978, "'shelving the issue' was the remark made by Mr. Deng Xiaoping unilaterally" (About the Senkaku, 2013, pp. 9 – 10).

However, the Chinese government remarked that the Japanese Government, besides changing the name of Diaoyu to Senkaku to mislead the Chinese people, is also attempting to "write off with one stroke the consensus between the two nations" (Statement, 2012, para. 6). According to the Statement of China, the leaders of the two countries, during their summit meetings in 1972 and 1978 "reached important understanding and common ground on 'leaving the issue of the Diaoyu Island to be resolved later'" (para. 6). This consensus "opened the door to normalization of China-Japan relations and was followed by tremendous progress in China-Japan relations and stability and tranquility in East Asia in the following 40 years" (para. 6).

It is even recorded in "About the Senkaku Islands" by MOFA of Japan, "Vice Premier Deng: 'We refer to the Senkaku Islands as the Diaoyu.... At this time of negotiations on the *Treaty of Peace and Friendship*, we agreed to leave the issue aside in much the same way'" (p. 9). Deng's remark of "we agreed to leave the issue aside" is written in black and white, but MOFA of Japan still denies there is no agreement to shelve the Senkaku issue. Professor Susumu of Yokohama City University further clarified, the exchange of Japanese apology in all sincerity and shelving of the Senkaku issue between former Prime Minister Tanaka Kakue and Chinese Premier Zhou Enlai were "removed in the MOFA-prepared transcripts," which became "the source of mistrust between China and Japan" (Harner, 2012, pp. 1 – 2).

When we reread Giordano, Giordano, and Wolfa's (2005) four critical factors for long-term institutional success, which include: (1) clear language concerning resource allocation and quality control; (2) high degree of institutional adaptability; (3) allocating benefits considered more productive than allocating the resource; and (4) clearly defined conflict resolution mechanism in place (pp. 58 - 59), we cannot but emphasize President Ma Yingjiu's peace initiative over the Senkaku/Diaoyu, which proposed that "all parties concerned hold conflicting standpoints, and that this is the cause of the long-standing disputes and the recent rise of tensions in the region" (East China Sea Peace Initiative by the Ministry of Foreign Affairs of the Republic of China, para. 4). In line with the critical factors for and as the first step towards long-term institutional success, Taiwan calls on all the involved parties to "resolve disputes peacefully based on the UN Charter and relevant provisions in international law" (para. 5).

Conclusion

The purpose of this study was to explore the interactions between the two sides and among the four parties over the Senkaku/Diaoyu Islands dispute with the intention to find out what is lacking in their communication for a genuinely peaceful and mutually beneficial solution to the multilateral international conflict. To this end, we raised three research questions and searched for the answers under the theoretical guidance of border institutions and the research methods of hermeneutics.

We found that, as the answer to RQ1, the three conflicting points in the claimants' claims are: (1) the ownership of the Senkaku/Diaoyu Islands; (2) the change of hands of these islands; and (3) the US role in the dispute. As the answer to the RQ2, we found that in terms of the ownership of the Senkaku/Diaoyu Islands, Japan provided evidence that the islands were *terra nullius* after repeated survey when it annexed them with a Cabinet Decision in 1895. In response, both China and Taiwan supplied geographical and geological evidence, historical envoy mission records, maritime defense system, and letters between high-ranking officials of Japan as well as international conference declarations and the instrument of Japanese surrender. It is really hard to provide a universally accepted warrant as to which side the Senkaku/Diaoyu Islands belongs. Each side has vulnerable points in its claims. It appears that Japan is legally stronger in its evidence, but such legal evidence has been overshadowed by its secretive annexation of the islands without public notice and backroom deals with the US. Both China and Taiwan have provided rich historical, geographical, and ethical evidence; however, more legal evidence may be required for international law court resolution.

As the answer to RQ3, we found that what is lacking in the Senkaku/Diaoyu dispute is threefold: First, among the claimants, each claimant may need to study its own claims in relation to the mingled history and the positive future prospects. To avoid the worst in history from repeating itself and maintain stability and prosperity in bi-lateral or tri-lateral relations, Japan, China, and Taiwan ought to seek consensus again by calming down and sitting down for open dialogues and better understanding. Second, since it has been so deeply involved in the Senkaku/Diaoyu Islands dispute and anxious to "play a larger and long-term role in shaping this region and its future" (Obama, 2011, para. 16), the US should play a more active, more responsible, and more impartial role. In other words, the US is expected to take the lead to establishing and maintaining international rules and norms, not just US core principles, and nurture mutually-beneficial partners with all claimants instead of just its allies. Just as Campbell, a renowned US diplomat for Asian affairs, stressed in an interview: "So we're going to push hard for more diplomacy, more dialogue, and more caution, in both Beijing and Tokyo" (Kato, 2013, p. 6).

Last but not least, all the three claimants are advised to seek commonalities by putting aside differences and begin working out constructive border institutions. As mentioned before, border institutions can maintain peace between neighboring countries; whereas, catastrophic consequences may occur as a result of increasing conflicts when the existing institutions collapsed. In other words, territorial disputes may lead to military confrontations, but wise leadership guided by domestic needs and international norms may set the interactions between or among claimants and bilateral or trilateral relationships onto peaceful paths. Hopefully, by recognizing and appreciating the existing border institutions in the form of customary practices since the 14th century, all the three claimants, possibly under the influence or leadership of the US, start working together towards acceptable and legal resource conventions and treaties in the East China Sea today and South China Sea tomorrow.

Notes:

1. The Cairo Declaration on Dec. 1, 1943, The Yalta Agreement on March 24, 1945, The Potsdam Proclamation on Aug. 2, 1945, and Japan Instrument of Surrender of Sept. 2, 1945

2. Treaty of Shimonoseki on April 17, 1895, San Francisco Peace Treaty with Japan on Sept. 8, 1951, and the Okinawa Reversion Treaty on June 17, 1971

3. "The Basic View on the Sovereignty over the Senkaku Islands" in February, 2013 and "About the Senkaku Islands" in February 2013 of the Ministry of Foreign Affairs of Japan, "Statement of the Ministry of Foreign Affairs of P. R. China" on Sept. 10, 2012 and "The Diaoyu Dao, an Inherent Territory of China" of Sept. 28, 2012 of China, "The Diaoyutai Islands: An Inherent Part of the Territory" of the Republic of China and the official announcement of "Our Clear Stance" on Dec. 30, 2012 of Taiwan

4. One geng equals 18.6 miles.

(Tian, D. X., & Chao, C. C. (2013). Border institutions: What is lacking in the Diaoyu/Senkaku Islands Dispute. *China Media Research*, 9(4), 27-44.)

References

[1] Amenta, E., & Ramsey, K. M. (2010). Institutional theory. In K. T. Leicht, & J. C. Jenkins (Eds.), Handbook of politics: State and civil society in global perspective. New York, NY: Springer.

[2] Blanchard, J. F. (2000). The U.S. role in the Sino-Japanese dispute over the Diaoyu (Senkaku) Islands, 1945 – 1971. The China Quarterly, 161, 95 – 123.

[3] Bush III, R. C. (2010). China-Japan security relations. Brookings Policy Brief Series, #117. Retrieved from http://www.brookings.edu/research/papers/2010/10/china-japan-bush

[4] Byrne, M. (2001). Hermeneutics as a methodology for textual analysis: Nursing application. AORN Journal, 5, 1 – 4.

[5] Cheong, C. (2012, Oct. 23). Isles dispute rooted in US policy. The Straits Times. Retrieved from http://www.stasiareport.com/the-big-story/asia-report/china/story/isles-dispute-rooted-us-policy-20121023.

[6] Christensen, T. J. (2006). Fostering stability or creating a monster? The rise of China and U.S. policy toward East Asia. International Security, 31(1), 81 – 126.

[7] Chung, C. (2004). Domestic politics: International bargaining and China's territorial disputes. New York, NY: Routledge.

[8] Clinton, H. (2011, November). America's Pacific century. Foreign Policy. Retrieved from http://www.foreignpolicy.com/articles/2011/10/11/americas_pacific_century

[9] First Instrument of Surrender. (1945). Retrieved from http://www.taiwandocuments.org/surrender01.htm.

[10] Foreign Relations of the United States, 1969 – 1976, Vol. XVII, China, 1969 – 1972, Document 115. Retrieved from http://history.state.gov/historicaldocuments/frus1969 – 76v17/d115#fnref2

[11] Fravel, M. T. (2005). Regime insecurity and international cooperation: Explaining China's compromises in territorial disputes. International Security, 30(2), 46 – 83.

[12] Fravel, M. T. (2008). Strong borders, secure nation: Cooperation and conflict in China's territorial disputes. Princeton, Princeton University Press.

[13] Fravel, M. T. (2010), Explaining stability in the Senkaku (Diaoyu) Islands dispute. In G. Curtis, R. Kokubun, & J. Wang (eds.), Getting the triangle straight: Managing China-Japan-US Relations. Tokyo: Japan Center for International Exchange.

[14] Friedberg. A. L. (2005). The future of U.S.-China relations: Is conflict inevitable? International Security, 30(2), 7 – 45.

[15] FRUS, Vol. XVII, China 1969-1976 Document 115. (1971). Retrieved from http://history.state.gov/historicaldocuments/frus1969-76v17/d115.

[16] Giordano, M. F., Girodano, M. A., & Wolf, A. T. (2005). International resource

[17] conflict and mitigation. Journal of Peace Research, 42(1), 47 – 65.

[17] Girish, P. M. (2008). Text and reading: Exercises in hermeneutics. Language in India, 8(3), 2 – 8.

[18] Gleditsch, N. P. (1998). Armed conflict and the environment: A critique of the literature. Journal of Peace Research, 35(3), 381 – 400.

[19] Goldstein, A. (2005). Rising to the challenge: China's grand strategy and international security. Standford, CA: Standford University Press.

[20] Hagström, L. (2005). Quiet power: Japan's China policy in regard to the Pinnacle Islands. The Pacific Review, 18(2), 159 – 188.

[21] Harlan, C. (2013, Feb. 20). Japan's Prime Minister Shinzo Abe: Chinese need conflict is 'deeply ingrained.' The Washington Post. Retrieved from http://articles. washingtonpost. com/2013 – 02 – 20/world/37196937_1_prime-minister-shinzo-abe-south-china-sea-chinese-education

[22] Harner, S. (2012, March 10). Interview with Professor Yabuki on the Senkaku/Diaoyu crisis and U. S.-China-Japan relations. Forbes. Retrieved from http://www. forbes. com/sites/stephenharner/2012/10/03/interview-with-professor-yabuki-on-the-senkakudiaoyu-crisis-and-u-s-china-japan-relations/.

[23] Harner, S. (2011, Feb. 14). The US could have prevented the Senkaku/Diaoyu crisis. Why did it not? Forbes. Retrieved from http://www. forbes. com/sites/stephenharner/2013/02/14/the-u-s-could-have-prevented-the-senkakudiaoyu-crisis-why-did-it-not/.

[24] Hensel, P. R. (2000). Territory: Theory and evidence on geography and conflict. In J. Vasquez, (Ed.), What do we know about war? Lanham, MD: Rowman and Littlefield.

[25] Hara, K. (2001). 50 years from San Francisco: Re-examining the peace treaty and Japan's territorial problems. Pacific Affairs, 74(3), 361 – 382.

[26] Harner, S. (2013, Feb. 14). The U. S. could have prevented the Senkaku/Diaoyu crisis. Why did it not? Forbes. Retrieved from http://www. forbes. com/sites/stephenharner/2013/02/14/the-u-s-could-have-prevented-the-senkakudiaoyu-crisis-why-did-it-not/.

[27] Holsti, K. J. (1991). Peace and war: Armed conflicts and international order 1648 – 1989. Cambridge, MA: Cambridge University Press.

[28] Inoue, K. (n. d.). Japanese Militarism & Diaoyutai (Senkaku) Island- A Japanese Historian's View. Retrieved from http://www. skycitygallery. com/japan/diaohist. html.

[29] International Institute for Strategic Studies. (2010). Chinese navy's new strategy in action. Strategic Comments, 4, 1 – 3.

[30] Ito, G. (2008). Politics and regionalism in the Asia-Pacific and U. S. Nanzan Review of American Studies, 30, 167 – 174.

[31] Johnston, E. (2012, Dec. 1). US Senate passes Senkaku backing. Retrieved from

http://www. japantimes. co. jp/news/2012/12/01/national/u-s-senate-passes-senkaku-backing/#.UTzDuuPZ9-E.

[32] Kato, Y. (2013, Feb. 9). Interview with Kurt Campbell: China should accept U. S. enduring leadership in Asia. Retrieved from http://ajw. asahi. com/article/views/opinion/AJ201302090016.

[33] Kenny, H. J. (2004). China and the competition for oil and gas in Asia. Asia Pacific Review, 11(2), 36–47.

[34] Kim, S. J. (2012, Dec. 30). Taiwanese envoy speaks up on Diaoyutai. The Korea Times. Retrieved from http://www. koreatimes. co. kr/www/news/nation/2013/02/176_127993. html.

[35] Knight, D. B. (1982). Identity and territory: Geographical perspective on nationalism and regionalism. Annals of the Association of American Geographers, 72, 512–531.

[36] Koo, M. G. (2009). The Senkaku/Diaoyu dispute and Sino-Japanese political-economic relations: Cold politics and hot economics? The Pacific Review, 22(2), 205–232.

[37] Kristof, N. D. (2010, Sept. 10). Look out for the Diaoyu Islands. NYT. com. Retrieved from http://kristof. blogs. nytimes. com/2010/09/10/look-out-for-the-diaoyu-islands/.

[38] Lind, J. (2004). Pacifism or passing the buck? Testing theories of Japanese security policy. Intercultural Security, 29(1), 92–121.

[39] Manyin, M. E. (2013). Senkaku (Diaoyu/Diaoyutai) Islands dispute: U. S. treaty obligations. Congressional Research Service, R42761. Retrieved from http://www. fas. org/sgp/crs/row/R42761. pdf.

[40] McCallum, J. (1995). National borders matter: Canada-U. S. regional trade partners. American Economic Review, 85(3), 615–623.

[41] Ministry of Foreign Affairs of Japan. (1950). Nihon Gaiko Bunsho (Japan Foreign Affairs Documents), 18(573). Tokyo.

[42] Ministry of Foreign Affairs of Japan. (2012, Nov.). Fact sheet on the Senkaku Islands. Retrieved from http://www. mofa. go. jp/region/asia-paci/senkaku/fact_sheet. html.

[43] Ministry of Foreign Affairs of Japan. (2013, Feb.). The basic view on the sovereignty over the Senkaku Islands. Retrieved from http://www. mofa. go. jp/region/asia-paci/senkaku/basic_view. html.

[44] Ministry of Foreign Affairs of Japan. (2013, March). About the Senkaku Islands. Retrieved from http://www. mofa. go. jp/region/asia-paci/senkaku/pdfs/senkaku_en. pdf.

[45] Ministry of Foreign Affairs of Japan. (2013). Q&A on the Senkaku Islands. Retrieved from http://www. mofa. go. jp/region/asia-paci/senkaku/fact_sheet. html.

[46] Ministry of Foreign Affairs of the Republic of China. (n. d.). East China Sea peace

initiative. Retrieved from http://www.mofa.gov.tw/EnOfficial/Topics/TopicsIndex/? opno=cc7f748f-f55f-4eeb-91b4-cf4a28bbb86f.

[47] Ministry of Foreign Affairs of Republic of China (Taiwan). (n. d.). The Diaoyutai Islands: An inherent part of the territory of the Republic of China. Retrieved from http://www.mofa.gov.tw/EnOfficial/Topics/TopicsArticleDetail/fd8c3459-b3ec-4ca6-9231-403f2920090a.

[48] Mo, Y. C. (2012, Sept. 8). Ma urges trilateral talks on Diaoyutais. Taipei Times. Retrieved from http://www.taipeitimes.com/News/front/archives/2012/09/08/2003542234.

[49] Mowle, T. S. (2003). Worldviews in foreign policy: Realism, liberalism, and external conflict. Political Psychology, 24(3), 561–592.

[50] Murphy, A. B. (1990). Historical justification for territorial claims. Annals of the Association of American Geographers, 80(4), 531–548.

[51] Nie, H. Y. (2009). Explaining Chinese solutions to territorial disputes with neighboring states. Chinese Journal of International Politics, 2, 487–523.

[52] Niksch, L. A. (1996). Senkaku (Diaoyu) Islands dispute: The U. S. legal relationship and obligations. Washington, Library of Congress.

[53] Obama, B. (2011). Remarks by the president to the Australian Parliament. Parliament House, Canberra, Australia. Retrieved from http://www.whitehouse.gov/the-pressoffice/2011/11/17/remarks-president-obama-australian-parliament.

[54] Okinawa Reversion Treaty. (1971). Retrieved from http://www.niraikanai.wwma.net/pages/archive/rev71.html.

[55] Pan, Z. Q. (2007). Sino-Japanese dispute over the Diaoyu/Senkaku Islands: The pending controversy from the Chinese perspective. Journal of Chinese Political Science, 12(1), 71–92.

[56] Park, C. (1973). Oil under troubled waters: The northeast Asia sea-bed controversy. Harvard International Law Journal, 14(2), 212–260.

[57] Potsdam Declaration. (1945). Retrieved from http://www.taiwandocuments.org/potsdam.htm.

[58] Quinn, A. (2013, Jan. 18). Clinton assures Japan on islands, invites Abe to U. S. in February. Reuters. Retrieved from http://www.reuters.com/article/2013/01/18/us-japan-usa-idUSBRE90H1AX20130118.

[59] Ramos-Mrosovsky, C. (2008). International law's unhelpful role in the Senkaku islands. University of Pennsylvania Journal of International Law, 29(4), 903–946.

[60] Richardson, M. (2013, Feb. 4). Securing allies amid China's rise. The Straits Times. Retrieved from http://www.iseas.edu.sg/documents/publication/mr4feb13.pdf.

[61] San Francisco Peace Treaty with Japan. (1951). Retrieved from http://www.taiwandocuments.org/sanfrancisco01.htm.

[62] Shaw, H. Y. (2012, Sept. 19). The inconvenient truth behind the Diaoyu/Senkaku

Islands. The New York Times. Retrieved from http://kristof.blogs.nytimes.com/2012/09/19/the-inconvenient-truth-behind-the-diaoyusenkaku-islands/? smid = tw-share.

[63] Simmons, B. A. (2005). Rules over real estate: Territorial conflict and international borders as institution. The Journal of Conflict Resolution, 49(6), 823–848.

[64] Slaughter, A. (1995). Liberal international relations theory and international economic law. American University International Law Review, 10(2), 717–743.

[65] State Council Information Office of P. R. China. (2012, September). Diaoyu Dao, an inherent territory of China (White Paper). Retrieved from http://www.china-embassy.org/eng/zt/bps/t974694.htm.

[66] Statement of the Ministry of the Foreign Affairs of P. R. China. (2012, Sept. 10). Retrieved from http://www.fmprc.gov.cn/eng/zxxx/t968188.htm.

[67] Su, S. W. (2005). The territorial dispute over the Tiaoyu/Senkaku Islands: An update. Ocean Development & International Law, 36, 45–61.

[68] Suganuma, U. (2000). Sovereign rights and territorial space in Sino-Japanese relations: Irredentism and the Diaoyu/Senkaku Islands. Honolulu, HI: Association for Asian Studies and University of Hawaii Press.

[69] Tanaka, H. (2010). The Senkaku Islands and mending Japan-China relations. East Asia Insights 5, 1–4.

[70] Treaty of Shimonoseki. (1895). Retrieved from http://www.taiwandocuments.org/shimonoseki01.htm.

[71] US Central Intelligence Agency. (1948, Aug. 6). The Ryukyu Islands and their significance. Retrieved from http://www.faqs.org/cia/docs/131/0000259203/THE-RYUKYU-ISLANDS.html.

[72] Valencia, M. J. (2000). Regional maritime regime building: Prospects in Northeast and Southeast Asia. Ocean Development and International Law, 31(3), 223–247.

[73] Valencia, M. J. (2007). The East China Sea dispute: Context, claims, issues, and possible solutions. Asian Perspective, 31(1), 127–167.

[74] Vasquez, J. A. (1995). Why do neighbors fight? Proximity, interaction, or territoriality. Journal of Pace Research, 32(3), 277–293.

[75] VOC. (2013). The importance of the Asia-Pacific region. Retrieved from http://editorials.voa.gov/content/the-importance-of-the-asia-pacific-region/1514099.html.

[76] Wachman, A. M. (2008). Why Taiwan? Geostrategic rationales for China's territorial integrity. Singapore: National University of Singapore Press.

[77] Wiegand, K. E. (2009). China's strategy in the Senkaku/Diaoyu Islands dispute: Issue linkage and coercive diplomacy. Asian Security, 5(2), 170–193.

Appendix 1: Japanese Cabinet Decision on Jan. 14, 1895

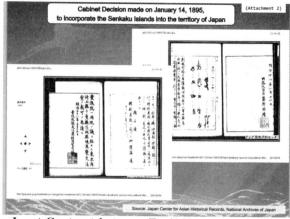

Appendix 2: Least Contract between Zenji Koga and the US Navy in 1958

Appendix 3: Illustrated Compendium on Maritime Security of 1556

Map of Fujian's Coastal Mountains and Sands (Fu Jian Yan Hai Shan Sha Tu)

In 1562 (the 41st year of the reign of Emperor Jiajing of the Ming Dynasty), the map was drawn and printed in the book An Illustrated Compendium on Maritime Security (Chou Hai Tu Bian). This map also included Diaoyu Dao, Huangwei Yu and Chi Yu within the scope of China's maritime defense.

Appendix 4: The Geographical Position and Bird's Eye View of the Diaoyu Islands

Chapter 21

Border Institutions—What Is Lacking in the Diaoyu/Senkaku Islands Dispute

Appendix 5: The Zhongshan Chuan Xin Lu by Xu Baoguang

Navigation Map (Zhen Lu Tu)

The map was included in Records of Messages from Chong-shan (Zhong Shan Chuan Xin Lu), a book by Xu Baoguang, a deputy title-conferring envoy to Ryukyu in 1721 (the 60th year of the reign of Emperor Kangxi of the Qing Dynasty). Showing the sailing route between China and Ryukyu, the map clearly demonstrates that Diaoyu Dao and its affiliated islands must be passed on the way from China to Ryukyu.

Appendix 6: Geographical Boudaries of the Ryukyu Islands

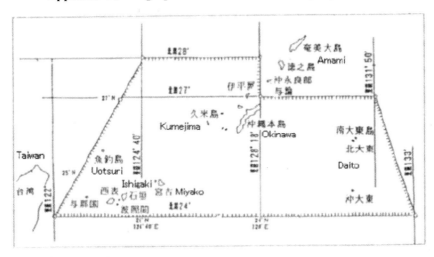

Geographical boundaries of the Ryukyu Islands (Source: U.S. Civil Administration Proclamation NO. 27, 1953)

Appendix 7: Letter of Appreciation from the Consul of the ROC in Nagasaki

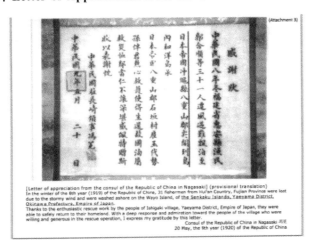

[Letter of appreciation from the consul of the Republic of China in Nagasaki] (provisional translation)
In the winter of the 8th year (1919) of the Republic of China, 31 fishermen from Hui'an Country, Fujian Province were lost due to the stormy wind and were washed ashore on the Wayo Island, of the Senkaku Islands, Yaeyama District, Okinawa Prefecture, Empire of Japan.
Thanks to the enthusiastic rescue work by the people of Ishigaki village, Yaeyama District, Empire of Japan, they were able to safely return to their homeland. With a deep response and admiration toward the people of the village who were willing and generous in the rescue operation, I express my gratitude by this letter.
Consul of the Republic of China in Nagasaki 馮冕
20 May, the 9th year (1920) of the Republic of China.

Appendix 8: Article on the People's Daily dated Jan. 8, 1953

[The article on the People's Daily titled "Battle of people in the Ryukyu Islands against the U.S. occupation", dated 8 January 1953] (Excerpt, provisional translation)

"The Ryukyu Islands lie scattered on the sea between the Northeast of Taiwan of our State (note: China; same in the following text) and the Southwest of Kyushu, Japan. They consist of 7 groups of islands: the Senkaku Islands, the Sakishima Islands, the Daito Islands, the Okinawa Islands, the Oshima Islands, the Tokara Islands and the Osumi Islands. Each of them consists of a lot of small and large islands and there are more than 50 islands with names and about 400 islands without names. Overall they cover 4,670 square kilometers. The largest of them is the Okinawa Island in the Okinawa Islands, which covers 1,211 square kilometers. The second largest is the Amami Oshima Island in the Oshima Islands (the Amami Islands), which covers 730 square kilometers. The Ryukyu Islands stretch over 1,000 kilometers, inside of which is our East China Sea (the East Sea in Chinese) and outside of which is the high seas of the Pacific Ocean."

Appendix 9: Republic of China New Atlas published in 1933

Chapter 21

Border Institutions—What Is Lacking in the Diaoyu/Senkaku Islands Dispute

Appendix 10: World Atlas published in 1958

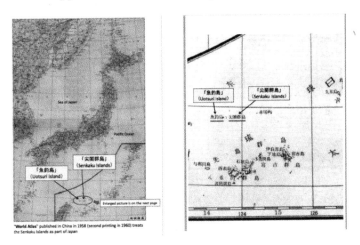

Appendix 11: Change of Terminology in the Middle School Geography Textbook

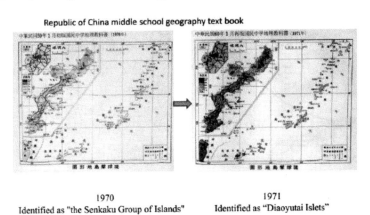

1970
Identified as "the Senkaku Group of Islands"

1971
Identified as "Diaoyutai Islets"

Chapter 22
Laying the Cornerstone: Transforming the Public Speaking Course with Themed Classics

A report from the Independent Task Force of the Council on Foreign Relations (2012) found that "far too many U. S. schools are failing to teach students the academic skills and knowledge they need to compete and succeed," and "many are also neglecting to teach civics, the glue that holds our society together" (p. 3). In addition, a survey of employers in a wide variety of professions shows that most of the employers are hardly satisfied with the communication skills of their new graduate recruits even though "the ability to verbally communicate with persons inside and outside the organization" (National Association of Colleges and Employers, 2013, p. 31) tops the list of important candidate qualifications. Such awakening finding about the quality of college graduates reverberates the debate between the skills-based approach and the contextual approach in the teaching of public speaking. For instance, Lucas (1999) posited, the public speaking course "can at best provide an exposure to the basic principles of speechmaking and some opportunity for students to begin to develop their own skills" (p. 76). Oppositely, Gayle, Martin, Mann, and Chouser (2002) argued, students in an in-context public speaking course can "grapple with larger, theoretically-complex issues while improving their public speaking skills" (p. 21). To realize the dual goals of teaching students to master public speaking skills and educating them to appreciate the construct of civil public discourse for active participation in a democratic society, a semester-long class activity has been adopted to transform the basic public speaking course at a university in the southeastern part of the United States since the beginning of 2013. Besides the required textbook, classic readings regarding a certain theme are selected and integrated into the public speaking course. "Classic readings" mean readings that are "judged over a period of time to be of the highest quality and outstanding of its kind" (Oxford Dictionaries Online, 2015). "Theme" refers to the main subject or topic which the selected readings are about. So far, the author and his colleagues have introduced such themes as "Appreciating Culture and Cultural Differences," "Great Ideas of the World," "Food and American Culture," "Afternoon Tea and British Culture," "Federalist Papers," "Founding Fathers on the Second Amendment," "New Media and Communication," "Social Media and Communication," "Innovation in the 21st Century," and "Leadership and the U. S. Role in the 21 Century" into their public speaking courses.

Chapter 22

Laying the Cornerstone: Transforming the Public Speaking Course with Themed Classics

The Objectives

The objectives of this semester-long activity in the public speaking course are three-fold. First, the activity is meant for meaningful class discussions, during which all students are able to share their independent and critical opinions on a certain topic based on pre-class readings and personal experiences. This does not mean that class discussions in a public speaking class with one textbook cannot be meaningful. In the author's two public speaking classes, *The Art of Public Speaking* (11th ed.) by Stephen Lucas has been adopted. Before the introduction of the themed readings, class discussions were mainly focused on the basic principles and suggested skills with mostly student sample speeches. However, classic readings regarding a chosen theme enrich the class content and make the discussion topics focused, thus motivating the students to complete their pre-class reading and participate in class discussions actively. Second, through the semester-long activity, students are expected to make quality speech presentations in terms of language use, overall structure of the speech, and balanced viewpoints of the issue under discussion. Public speaking instructors have suffered from too many cliché speeches like "The Story of My Mum," "How to Make Mixed Fruit Juice," and "Why a PC Is Better than a Mac" from their students for narrative, informative, and persuasive speeches. Themed classic readings stimulate ideas for the students' presentations and provide students with appropriate language, helpful organization, and various perspectives of thinking. Finally, in their class discussions and speech presentations, students are asked to relate their speech topics to the themed readings and significant issues in the society. Thus, the students are no longer shut off in ivory towers of books nor glued to cell phone screens all the time. Gradually, they are sure to realize that careful reading of great thoughts before class and lively class discussions with different viewpoints from classmates first make them reflect upon what is reported in the media and then help them connecting what they are learning at school with what is happening in the real world.

Initial successes in this activity have already made the above-mentioned university transform its public speaking course from the former Speech and Public Speaking to the now Speaking of Ideas: Plus Theme. The course description of the former public speaking course reads:

> The course introduces students to the fundamental principles and practices of public speaking. Topics include organization and communication skills that focus on audience analysis, topic selection, delivery styles, listening skills, argumentation, verbal and nonverbal skills, and the acquisition of academic resources. (2013, p. 307)

Now, the new course description of Speaking of Ideas goes:

> In this course, students study classic and contemporary theories and techniques of oral communication to design, develop, and deliver presentations to a live audience. Through a series of oral presentation assignments, students will engage with, and marshal arguments in response to, important historical, cultural, and intellectual ideas through works of literature, scholarship, journalism, and criticism. (Proposed

Course Description of Speaking of Ideas)

A comparison of the above course descriptions reveals two different approaches to the basic course of public speaking. While the former stresses the training of mere public presentation skills, the latter emphasizes the teaching of both presentation skills and civil public discourse capabilities via the content of both the chosen textbook and the relevant themed readings.

The Activity

The activity consists of three components: criteria for selecting appropriate readings, steps of integrating the readings into the class teaching, and rubrics for assessing class discussions and speech presentations. The criteria for selecting the themed readings are: (1) the expertise of the faculty member who teaches public speaking; (2) the necessity of expanding certain parts of the chosen textbook; and (3) the real needs of the students and the society. In the case of the author, since he has a rich cross-cultural background as an international faculty member and former diplomat with a series of publications on intercultural issues, he has chosen two themes of "appreciating culture and cultural differences," and "great ideas of the world" for his two classes. Based on his experience in teaching the course and analysis of the textbook, he has selected such additional readings as "The Allegory of the Cave" by Plato, "Dimensionalizing Culture: The Hofstede Model in Context" by Geert Hofstede, and "The Clash of Civilization" by Samuel Huntington for the first theme and "Rhetoric" by Aristotle, "Thinking in Education" by John Dewey, and "Civil Disobedience" by Henry D. Thoreau for the second theme. The list of the supplementary readings may be prolonged or changed according to the necessities of the class and the needs of the students.

To integrate the themed readings into the class teaching, grading rubrics are used for five in-class quizzes (10%), five group discussions (10%), three speech presentations (50%), and the mid-term exam (10%) and final examination (20%). The five in-class quizzes are conducted throughout the semester, with essay questions specifically on the additional readings so as to make sure that all students complete the pre-class readings. The five group discussions are held to discuss the highlights in the additional readings and textbook chapters. The groups are formed with students meeting new peers each time to discuss the most impressive points in the assigned readings. A different representative from each group will report the highlights of the group discussion to the whole class each time. In this way, students become motivated to complete the assigned pre-class readings and obtain more opportunities to present their ideas in groups and to the whole class. Here is an example of the essay questions on the themed readings: John Dewey advocated progressive education, and its two tenets are questioning of authority and independence of thought on the part of the students. Please elaborate on one of the tenets in relation to yourself. All the quizzes are graded, and students can earn 20 points or 2% in each quiz. As groups, students also earn 20 points or 2% according to their performance during the class discussions. Since all group members get the same grade, they usually compete with other groups for better performance. Thus, each student is experiencing the very essential training in public speaking by first talking about the assigned readings in groups and then presenting their ideas about the readings in front of the class.

Meanwhile, three major presentations of narrative, informative, and persuasive speeches are held throughout the semester, and students are given clear instructions that each of their speech presentations needs to be related to the theme of the class by drawing inspirations from or shedding light on the selected readings. In other words, students need to make sure that their speeches either indicate cultural implications if the theme of their class is "appreciating culture and cultural differences," or have something to do with the creation and/or distribution of ideas if their class theme is "great ideas of the world." To grade the three speeches of the narrative speech (10%), informative speech (10%), and persuasive speech (30%), two steps are taken. First, students turn in a detailed outline according to the instructions for each type of speech in terms of structure, content, and style of citations. Second, students prepare and present their speeches based on the graded and revised outline. Outlines account for half of the points of each speech, and they are turned in for grading and revisions before the presentations to ensure that students really make careful preparations related to the themed readings. For example, one student made a narrative speech about his dad who had frequently been transferred in his job from country to country. Together with other family members, the student had to move with his father now and then. At first, he really hated it because he could hardly maintain any steady relationships with the people in his new homes. When he was preparing for the narrative speech about his dad and his influence on the family, the student began to realize the benefits of his rich cultural experiences and the genuine appreciation of cultural differences. Another student made a persuasive speech on why people should keep an open and critical mind while perceiving the world around them. His argument was mainly based on Plato's The Allegory of the Cave, and he was able to flesh out the ancient idea with sufficient supporting details from the present-day society. It is clear that students have successfully integrated what they have got from their readings into their public speech presentations.

Finally, written examination answers are expected to demonstrate a clear connection with the additional readings. In the mid-term examination (10%) and final examination (20%), there are multiple-choice questions, true or false statements, and essay questions, which test the students on specific knowledge of basic public speaking principles, critical thinking of what they take in in the readings and class discussions, and creative application of the key concepts in the selected readings. For example, a typical multiple-choice question looks like: The five canons of rhetoric were synthesized by: A. Plato; B. Cicero; C. Aristotle; D. Quintilian. A true or false statement goes: John Dewey is famous for his proposition of civil disobedience. One of the essay questions for the examinations is: Please comment on "that government is best which governs least" (p. 305) in "Civil Disobedience" by Henry David Thoreau based on your life experiences at home, at school, and the society.

Debriefing

At the author's university, over three semesters have passed since the introduction of themes into the basic public speaking course. Overall students' performance indicates that this semester-long effort is worthwhile and meaningful in three major aspects. First, the class teaching content is enriched and the quality of class discussions is guaranteed with the integration of stories, figures of speech, and valuable concepts from the additional readings. For example, metaphors and other figures of speech in "Rhetoric" by Aristotle, "The Japanese Gardens," and "American Football" provide sufficient examples for the class discussion about the discussion topic of "Using Words Effectively for Speech Presentations." Besides, students have made adept and extensive use of concepts like questioning of authority, independence of thought, and learning through doing from "Thinking in Education" by John Dewey, and "the bounds of one's experience" and "the power of one's imagination" as the two restrictions of free thought in *A History of Freedom of Thought* by John B. Bury, to name just a few.

Second, as required and expected, all the major speech presentations do demonstrate clear influences and guidance of the textbook chapters and additional readings. Students in the author's classes get inspired for creative ideas they are genuinely interested in and follow academic criteria in their speech outlines and speech presentations. Some students framed their narrative speeches with the help of Geert Hofsted's individualism and collectivism cultural dimension and Mark Orbe's co-cultural communication strategies and preferred outcomes. Other students are enlightened by the morals in Plato's "The Allegory of the Cave" and insights from Huntington's "The Clash of Civilizations" and presented on controversial issues like same-sex marriage and gender equality, school-shooting and gun control, democracy versus meritocracy either from more than one perspectives or a dialectic, balanced point of view. Most students have learned to enrich and empower their speech presentations with at least three required citations from the assigned readings, statistics from reliable sources, and study results from other scholars and give credit to each citation in the outline and presentation by following either MLA or APA.

Finally, and most importantly, students themselves have become motivated to finish reading both the textbook chapters and the additional readings before class, and they get genuinely interested in participating in class discussions and speech presentations closely related to themselves. They find it necessary and helpful to peruse rigorous, provocative, and classic texts first before making well-organized and flesh-out public speeches of different types on various occasions. In addition, they find it important and meaningful to relate the expressions and presentations of their original and creative thoughts to some real issues in both their daily lives and the civil affairs in the real world. For example, to the examination

Chapter 22

Laying the Cornerstone: Transforming the Public Speaking Course with Themed Classics

essay question on the role of government in "Civil Disobedience" by Henry David Thoreau, one student wrote:

> Although I am familiar with the concept of civil disobedience, I have never actually finished reading the article by Henry David Thoreau. A thorough reading of the original enlightens me a great deal, especially Thoreau's idea on the role of the government. The statement "that government is best which governs least" echoes a truth many continue to believe today. In a world where the government threatens to listen to our phone calls, monitor our Internet usage, seize our weapons, and regulate the amount of fast food we can eat, we forget that the government is a tool not a fence made to control and guide us. In a successful and efficient society, government plays a minimal role to aid the people it serves. It is a hammer, not a carpenter. It is a pen, not a writer. It should never take control of an issue, but instead make it easier for the people to process.
>
> There are many forms of "government" throughout one's life. Parents, teachers, and bosses are all examples of daily governments that exercise control over us, but that control is never absolute as they do not dictate all what we do. Parents will hold a child's hand until that child can stand on its own. Teachers will lecture their students until they understand the materials. Bosses manage their workers until they become proficient to do their work on their own. For any one of these governments to continue performing their actions beyond the point of necessity, they gradually become more of a burden than a useful tool. Imagine if your mother still held your hand to cross the street when you were 37 years old. Such an act is no longer needed. Likewise, our nation's government should assist us where we fall short until we are able to act on our own. (Courtesy from Gary Fink)

When reading this student essay, I cannot help uttering out loud, "Great!" The student did enjoy the reading and was impressed by the author's idea of the role of a government. More importantly, he conveys his deep and insightful understanding with real-life examples of parents at home, teachers at school, and bosses at work before arriving at the logical and convincing conclusion that the government should function in a similar manner.

Limitations

Nevertheless, those instructors who intend to follow suit in their courses need to address the following questions. First, am I really an expert in the introduced theme? Sufficient expertise in the theme guarantees first of all passion in the instructor and then the expected teaching effects. For young teachers of introductory public speaking, an alternative may be readings on a certain popular topic mutually interesting and meaningful to both the teachers and their students. Second, are the selected readings representative and classic enough? Surprisingly, the author has found that no matter how occupied students may be with the subject matter of their various majors, they usually show genuine interest in classic and representative readings on a chosen theme in liberal arts. The reason is that these carefully selected classics not only provide them with profound ideas, useful theoretical lenses, and rich rhetorical devices, but also help them laying an essential foundation for the success of their future careers and growth into qualified citizens in the global village. Third, how can I effectively allocate the in-class time to allow for quizzes, group discussions, speech presentations, and examinations? A key point for the effective adjustment of the themed public speaking course is that the assigned readings, both textbook chapters and the readings on the theme, must be completed before class. During class lectures, themed readings become ready sources for examples to replace those less relevant ones in the textbook. During class discussions, examinations, and presentations, the author found it a better use of time when themed readings enrich class discussions, motivate students for more class participation, and inspire them for potential topics of speech presentations. Finally, do I have the effective measures to check and motivate the students to complete the selected readings before class, meaningful participation in class quizzes and discussions, and creative applications of the theme in the readings in their major speech presentations? So far in the author's classes, the in-class quizzes, group discussions, examinations, and presentations related to the chosen themes prove to be workable and effective. Moreover, there is a growing number of the "credible, logical, and passionate speech that is grounded in the past experiences of a speaker who is oriented toward making an impact on the future," which is defined as "transformational presentation" (Ivic & Green, 2012, p. 65).

References

[1] Gayle, B. M., Martin, D., Mann, S., & Chouser, L. (2002). Transforming the public speaking classroom: A scholarship of teaching and learning project on civil public discourse. Journal of the Northwest Communication Association, 31, 1 - 26. doi: 10.1080/03634520410001682438.

[2] Independent Task Force of the Council on Foreign Relations. (2012). U.S. education reform and national security. Available at: http://www.cfr.org/united-states/us-education-reform-national-security/p27618.

[3] Ivc, R. K., & Green, R. J. (2012). Developing charismatic delivery through transformational presentations: Modeling the persona of Steve Jobs. Communication Teacher, 26(2), 65-68. doi: 10.1080/17404622.2011.643808.

[4] Lucas, S. E. (1999). Teaching public speaking. In A. L. Vangelisti, J. A. Daly, & G. W. Friedrich (Eds.), Teaching communication: Theory, research and methods (2nd ed.). Mahwah, NJ: Lawrence Erlbaum, 75 - 84.

[5] National Association of Colleges and Employers. (2013). Job outlook 2013. Available at: http://cbe.calstatela.edu/is/pdfs/NACEJobOutlook2013.pdf.

[6] Oxford Dictionaries Online. (2015). New York, NY: Oxford University Press. Available at: http://www.oxforddictionaries.com/definition/english/classic.

Chapter 23
Testing News Trustworthiness in an Online Public Sphere: A Case Study of *The Economist*'s News Report Covering the Riots in Xinjiang, China

On July 5, 2009, deadly riots suddenly occurred in Urumqi, the capital of Xinjiang Uighur Autonomous Region in China's western frontier. After reporting consecutively on the riots in Xinjiang for two days with titles such as "Unrest in China: Unrest on the Western Front" (2009) on July 6 and "Riots in China: Rumbling On" (2009) on July 7, the British online weekly newspaper *The Economist* published "The Riots in Xinjiang: Is China Fraying?" (2009) on July 9, 2009, a six-page news report of about 3,000 words. Below the article on July 9, the newspaper opened a "Readers' Comments" forum to attract responses from readers regarding the article and the riots in Xinjiang. During the 15 days the forum was open from July 9 to July 24, 2009, the forum attracted 1,098 responses from readers all over the world. Impressed by the quantity, quality, and variety of the responses and the voluntary, interactive, and meaningful interactions in the forum, we looked into *The Economist*'s July 9, 2009, news report under the theoretical guidance of news translation and cultural resistance and the communicative roles of online responses against Dahlberg's (2001) six conditions for an ideal online public sphere. Although media credibility and the roles of online readers have attracted increasing attention, especially Western media coverage concerning non-Western regions (Antaki, Ardévol, Nuñez, & Vayreda, 2006; Jo, 2005; Kiousis, 2001; Lent, 2006; Leung & Huang, 2007; Steensen, 2009), few studies have critiqued a provocative news report by online mainstream Western media by comparing and contrasting the report itself with its readers' responses. The present case study aims to fill this void by searching for answers to the following research questions:

RQ1: How trustworthy is *The Economist*'s July 9, 2009, news report in its coverage of the Xinjiang riots?

RQ2: What roles do the online readers play with their forum posts as a result of the online news report?

Literature Review

In this section, we begin with the literature review to set the academic background for this study. The purposes of this study call for four major categories of existing literature:

The backdrop of and rationale for studying The Economist. According to Media UK (2011), Britain boasts 783 radio stations, 512 TV channels, 1,970 magazines, and 1,596 newspapers owned by 287 media outlets. Newspapers in Britain are generally divided into three groups: mass-market tabloids, such as *The Sun* and *Daily Mirror*; midmarket tabloids, such as *Daily Mail* and *Daily Express*; and quality newspapers, such as *The Times*, *The Guardian*, and *The Daily Telegraph*. As Cridland (2010) noted, although the first two groups are collectively regarded as the popular press, generally focusing on covering celebrity and human-interest stories, the third group is usually considered more serious, mainly covering political reporting and international news.

The Economist belongs to the third group of quality newspapers. It is categorized as a magazine and published weekly in a magazine format, but it is a newspaper because it covers news and provides opinions against a newspaper deadline. We selected *The Economist* as the primary source in this study for three reasons. First, since its founding in 1843, *The Economist* has been one of the leading sources of analysis of international business and world affairs in the Western world. *The Economist*'s traditional and online versions "offer authoritative insight and opinion on international news, politics, business, finance, science and technology" ("About *The Economist* Online," 2011, para. 1). Thus, *The Economist* can be regarded as representative of mainstream Western media covering international news. Second, The Economist operates according to the conventional principles of editorial independence and journalistic objectivity. The published articles bear no bylines because they are "written anonymously… for collective voice and personality" ("*The Economist*'s Philosophy," 2011, para. 2-3). Finally, *The Economist*'s news report on the Xinjiang riots attracted 1,098 forum responses from readers all over the world, so the newspaper provides a worthwhile phenomenon for cross-cultural media study.

News trustworthiness in relation to media bias and media credibility. According to Liu and Bates (2009), media credibility and journalistic objectivity are "the critical components in developing public trust in audiences" (p. 307). In this section, we discuss the relevant literature on these two critical components and their impact on news trustworthiness. Levi and Stoker (2000) remarked, being relational, trustworthiness assures potential trusters that the trusted party or trustees will not betray a trust. To be trustworthy, the trustees not only make a commitment but also prove able to act in the interests of the trusters by observing moral values or professional standards. In the case of news reports, trustworthiness means journalists "will not betray the trust as a consequence of either faith or bad ineptitude" (Levi & Stoker, 2000, p. 476). Such trustworthiness calls for, instead of media bias, media credibility.

Media bias, in the words of McQuail (1992), means "a consistent tendency to depart from the straight path of objective truth by deviating to the left or right," and in news, bias refers to "a systematic tendency to favor (in outcome) one side or position over another" (p. 191). Xiang and Sarvary (2007) also defined media bias as "the different impressions created from an objective event by slanting information" (p. 611). As a summary, Gunter (1997) remarked, "the key point where impartiality is concerned is that the news should not tend systematically to favor one side of an argument or dispute over another. Where this does happen, then the news can be legitimately described as 'biased'" (p. 19). With a clear understanding of media bias, we will go on discussing the major categories of bias.

According to Entman (2007), media bias falls into three categories: distortion bias, content bias, and decision-making bias. The first category of bias refers to news that "purportedly distorts or falsifies reality," the second "favors one side rather than providing equivalent treatment to both sides in a political conflict," and the third results from "motivations and mindsets of journalists and editors who allegedly produce the biased content" (p. 163). From the perspective of the causes of media bias, some scholars (Gentzkow & Shapiro, 2006; Page & Shapiro, 1992) have noted that media bias emerges from competition among media. For example, Page and Shapiro (1992) listed the procapitalist bias, minimal government bias, and nationalistic bias based on their study of the nature of the U. S. media as businesses operating in a competitive economic marketplace.

Other scholars (D'Alessio & Allen, 2000; Mullainathan & Shleifer, 2005) posited that media bias is mainly driven by consumers' socioeconomic or political demands. In the words of D'Alessio and Allen (2000), media can bias news by releasing selected news reports according to the most convenient ideological approach. Through examining possible ideological media bias in presidential elections, the authors found three types of media biases. The first is gate-keeping, which is the preference for selecting stories for one party or the other. The second is coverage bias, which considers the relative amounts of coverage each party receives. The third is statement bias, which focuses on the favorability of coverage toward one party or the other (p. 133). The three types of media biases overlap the three categories of media biases mentioned, thus facilitating our comprehension of media bias.

With regard to media credibility, Hovland, Janis, and Kelly (1953) identified that credibility comprises expertise and trustworthiness. While the former means the degree to which reporters are believed to be able to write correct news reports, the latter refers to the degree to which media audiences perceive the news stories as valid. According to Kiousis (2001), credibility has been researched in terms of source credibility and medium credibility, with the former focusing on "characteristics of message senders or individual speakers," and the latter focusing on "the channel through which content is delivered" (p. 382). For this study, we carefully consider both types of credibility as well as media bias.

Nevertheless, the ideals of media credibility may be difficult to fulfill given the constraints and various filters at work whenever organized professional journalism content is created (Shoemaker & Reese, 1996). In our case, the filters here refer to the media gatekeepers, who make decisions about whether certain news will be released. Furthermore, as scholars (Kohring & Matthes, 2005; Kovach & Rosenstiel, 2001; Singer, 2007) have noted, in today's virtual space of open and ubiquitous publication, journalism's ideals and norms have encountered new challenges. Oversight of professional standards has become a team sport, and journalists no longer control who gets to play. Such negligence makes journalism unable to fulfill its social function as a guiding instance, and readers may lose a certain amount of trust in mass media on a daily basis. Thus, news trustworthiness and media credibility have become all the more crucial between journalists as trustees and readers as trusters.

Western media coverage of developing countries such as China. By Western media, we refer to the mainstream media in the industrialized, developed countries in Western Europe and North America. Shan and Wang (2009) found freedom of the press, truth-telling, social justice, and media benefit are fundamental ethical ideas of modern Western journalism. Because of these media functions and fundamental ideas, "a free press in the Western tradition entails the risk of negative news coverage" (Peterson, 1980, p. 68). As Peterson (1980) remarked, spokespeople from the developing world regard the Western media's concentration on wars, conflict, and disasters as psychologically damaging to the development and image of their countries.

Other scholars (Chang, 1988; Graber, 1989; Huang & McAdams, 2000) also confirmed that the Western media's news coverage of developing countries has been charged with being biased, negative, crisis-oriented, and looking down upon developing countries while displaying strong Western supremacism.

For example, when riots occurred on April 14, 2008, in Lhasa, Tibet, mainstream Western media rushed to criticize the Chinese government for cracking down on protesters. According to Wang (2008), some Western media wrote fraudulent reports about Chinese police officers beating Tibetans. Even after the armed forces were revealed in the media as Nepali and Indian policemen putting down violent Tibetan protesters in Nepal and India, most Western media continued their coverage of the riots as usual. One explanation is that "Western reporters tend to dramatize problems and overplay controversy to attract readers' and viewers' attention with headline-making news" (Yu, 2003, p. 92).

Roles of the readers, especially those in the cyberspace. As for the critical academic views of the growing roles of readers, especially in online forums, in today's cyberspace of open and ubiquitous publication, some scholars (Hayes, Singer, & Ceppos, 2007; Kovach & Rosenstiel, 2001; Singer, 2007) have observed an infinite number of participants simultaneously serve as sources, audiences, and information providers. In addition to sharing information and exchanging ideas, readers set out to influence and compete for attention with cable networks and popular user-generated content. Via various online media, readers today are actually challenging journalists' exclusive right to deem a particular piece of information credible.

Other scholars (Grunig, 2009; Steensen, 2009; Wood & Smith, 2005) have noted, compared with traditional media, online media have adopted an "open media code" and "buffet style" to organize their news content. This means online media are open to all possible readers, and readers, as if they were in a buffet restaurant, can taste whichever part of a piece of news or type of media they are interested in. Via web links, readers not only choose media content but also, through uploading posts, instantly make comments publicly on what they have read and simultaneously check their opinions with those of other readers for continuous and dynamic online discussions. Thus, Grunig (2009) commented, digital media, which are "dialogical, interactive, relational, and global," seem to turn online communication "toward a two-way symmetrical model" (pp. 6-7). Meanwhile, he also cautioned that a common problem with online communication has been the unethical use of fake blogs or posts. Steensen (2009) seconded the caution by saying, "assuming different identities has become a normal practice in online discourse," and for different purposes, some online discussion participants "express themselves through transformed identities" (p. 20). We took these factors in the existent literature into careful consideration in the present study. Having completed a review of the relevant literature, we discuss the theoretical frameworks for this study below.

Theoretical Frameworks

For this study, we applied Conway's (2010) news translation and cultural resistance theory and Dahlberg's (2001) online public sphere principles as the theoretical frameworks. Based on previous studies, especially Pym's study of localization in his translation theory, Conway (2010) summarized and applied the theory of news translation and cultural resistance in his study of news stories in Canadian broadcasts. Briefly, news translation occurs when international news agencies localize foreign news in the local press for local readers. The localization process involves translating between languages and substituting local cultural references for foreign ones. In the words of Pym (2004), "the foreign news we read in the local press can legitimately be seen as a localization of foreign-language texts and transformed in ways that go beyond endemic notions of translation" (p. 4). This means that foreign news reports are usually translated and shaped according to the anticipated end-users' culturally specific needs and responses.

According to Conway (2010), news translation involves three types of people. The first are the locals with whom journalists make contact and from whom they get news. The second are the journalists who compile accounts from eyewitnesses among the locals and translate the accounts into stories for the targeted consumers. Finally, gate-keepers such as the chief editors and news media sponsors make certain the stories to be published fit the expected readers' tastes and observe the newspaper's conventions.

As a result, news translation is characterized by two forms of cultural resistance. The first form of resistance comes from the culture of reception. Briefly, this means that journalists "transform their stories" or "make their descriptions of events taking place in foreign cultural context to conform to the anticipated readers' expectations" (Conway, 2010, p. 189). Furthermore, with the increase in the cultural gap, journalists have to make a greater effort to make their reports conform to end-users' expectations. In contrast, the second form of resistance emanates from the culture being described. This is a resistance to the use of language describe the whole meaning-making mechanism of culture. When journalists try to describe an event in a foreign culture through the process of news translation, they are limited by "circumscribing the event from symbol to symbol to symbol" (p. 191). They may capture certain aspects of an event in a foreign land, but their reports are "necessarily reductive" (p. 189) because capturing culture "exhaustively will always be out of reach" (p. 191).

Having described the news translation and cultural resistance theory, we now talk about online public sphere principles. With regard to the public sphere, Jürgen Habermas proposed the concept in his book *Strukturwandel der Öffentlichkeit*, published in German in 1962. The book was translated into English as *Structural Transformation of the Public Sphere* and published in 1989 (*Stanford Encyclopedia*, 2007). Habermas (1962/1989) saw the public sphere as a domain of social life in which a body of private individuals actively assembles to freely and openly discuss and debate matters of common concern. Just as Villa (1992) remarked, the public sphere, as an institutional arena of discursive interaction, is central to democratic theory and practice. Grbeša (2003) also noted the media in traditional form and online versions facilitate public discussions by providing a technological and structural forum and by initiating public discussions and, perhaps, setting the agenda.

Although irresponsible behaviors and even false posts are criticized as a result of the anonymous nature of online forum discussions, scholars (Al-Saggaf, 2006; Antaki et al., 2006; Dahlberg, 2001; Fung & Kedl; 2000; Papacharissi, 2002) still regard online forum discussions as a new public sphere. In this virtual space, diverse participants as netizens enjoy the privilege of freedom of speech and political participation they are deprived of elsewhere and converge, interact, and converse to construct a deliberative democracy by transcending geographical, technological, social, and psychological boundaries. Based on a comprehensive review of the research results concerning online forum discussions, Dahlberg (2001) developed six conditions for an ideal online public sphere.

The first condition is autonomy from the State and economic power. Under the overwhelming threat of the State and the corporate colonization of cyberspace, a plethora of noncommercial online forums still exist through e-mail lists, Usenet groups, chat rooms, and Web publishing. Without affiliation in any political parties, interest groups, or corporate concerns, these online forums actually "facilitate the growth and coordination of a global culture of resistance to the corporate takeover of cyberspace and of public life in general" (Dahlberg, 2001, para. 8). Thematization and critique of criticizable moral-practical validity claims form the second condition. Thematization refers to the pattern of discussion in most online forums that "clearly parallels the rational, dialogic form of conversation required within the public sphere" (para. 10). Meanwhile, participants from various backgrounds follow this pattern to exchange and critique "claims on every conceivable question on a myriad of online forums," the type of dialogue that Habermas speaks of, which demands justification for each speech act and inquires into the validity and sincerity of claims (Kolb, 1996). As the third condition, reflexivity means "the process of standing back from, critically reflecting upon, and changing one's position when faced by 'the better argument'" (Dahlberg, 2001, para. 15). Aware of the self-transformative and democratic possibilities of cyber-interaction, some forum participants could transform from privately oriented individuals into publicly-oriented netizens.

As for the fourth condition of ideal role-taking, "few Internet forums presently involve any great proportion of ongoing, respectful, and meaningful exchange of ideas" (Dahlberg, 2001, para. 33). Nevertheless, participants tend to "[attempt] to put themselves in the position of the other so as to come to an understanding of the other's perspective" (para. 24) regardless of their social and cultural differences. Sincerity is the fifth condition for an ideal public sphere. To ensure genuine understanding and rational assessment of identities and positions, discursive participants are expected to "make a sincere effort to make known all relevant information and their true intentions, interests, needs, and desires" (para. 34). Aware of the problem of online postings that aim to misinform, embarrass, self-promote, provoke, gossip, and trivialize, participants have to "provide convincing support for their assertions before their positions become accepted by other participants" (para. 41). The final condition is discursive equality and inclusion. Since "social hierarchies and power relations are leveled out by the 'blindness' of cyberspace to bodily identity, it allows people to interact as if they were equals" (para. 43). However, despite the so-called bracketing of identity, the development of netiquette, and moderation, discursive inequalities and exclusions still exist in the present online discourse, which "tend to be biased in favor of those individuals and groups that dominate the offline discourse" (para. 52). Before analyzing our collected data under these two theoretical frameworks, we introduce the research methods for our study.

Research Methods

To collect data, we used field observation of online interactions. As mentioned earlier, *The Economist* news report attracted 1,098 forum posts all in English. Due to the repetition, meaningless and irrelevant messages, or provisions of mere links to other sources, we excluded 252 posts from our analysis, for a total of 846. To analyze the news report and the selected posts, we used discourse analysis to sift the emerging themes. Van Dijk (1999) defined discourse as "text and talk in context" (p. 291). According to Potter (1987), discourse analysis is a type of content analysis concerned with studying language use, texts, conversational interaction, or communicative events, used to "construct and create social interaction and diverse social worlds" (p. 158). Fairclough (1995) also noted that discourse analysis is not only a research method but also a perspective and a self-sufficient paradigm for approaching and studying the social world. To him, discourses are coherent bodies of representations that do not faithfully reflect reality like mirrors but are artifacts of language through which "a given social practice is represented from a particular point of view" (p. 56).

Applicable to all types of social texts including recorded online media reports and forum discussions, the method analyzes the selected texts by searching for patterned differences and similarities in the content and form of the dialogues and examining the function and results of the dialogues. To reduce subjectivity during our analysis, the two authors independently coded *The Economist*'s online news report and the transcripts of the 846 forum posts and analyzed them comparatively at the message level from the perspective of the writer of the messages rather than from the angle of a mere intercoder. By categorizing whether the posts were supportive, negative, or neutral to *The Economist*'s news report in terms of content and stances, we used Cohen's kappa (Cohen, 1960) to calculate the intercoder reliability for each category. We used an online kappa calculator from the website graphpad.com/quickcalcs/Kappa2 to calculate the kappa. Intercoder reliabilities were calculated based on 200 randomly selected posts (approximately 20%), and the intercoder agreement (Cohen's kappa) was .922, .895, and .852 for the three categories of posts (affirmative, negative, and neutral, respectively).

Second, against the theoretical guidance of news translation and cultural resistance, we examined how exactly the news report maintained objectivity and credibility in terms of positively providing "independent, reliable, accurate, and comprehensive information" or negatively offering "partial, unfair, and outright lies" (Kovach & Rosenstiel, 2001, p. 42). Finally, we examined the communicative roles of the forum posts against Dahlberg's (2001) six conditions of an ideal online public sphere. Since the chosen online news report and all the posts in the forum are intended for public consumption, our selection and analysis were consistent with the ethics of online human subjects research (Eysenbach & Till, 2001).

Findings and Analysis

We discuss our research findings, which concern the news trustworthiness and media credibility of *The Economist*'s news report and the communicative roles of the forum posts.

Localization of foreign news. As discussed earlier, the first major aspect of Conway's (2010) theory of news translation and cultural resistance is the localization of foreign news through translation between languages and the substitution of local cultural references for foreign ones. *The Economist*'s news report fits in with this aspect of the theory very well. On the one hand, translation between the local languages Mandarin, Uighur, or other local dialects and English was involved. According to Shan and Chen (2011), among the 21 million residents in Xinjiang Uighur Autonomous Region, there are 47 ethnic groups, with Uighurs making up 46%, Han Chinese 39%, Kazaks 7%, and others 8%. However, in Urumqi, the capital city of the autonomous region and the site of the riot on July 5, 2009, Han Chinese account for 73% while Uighurs make up 12.3% of the total population. On the other hand, localization of cultural references for the English-speaking world included at least the Chinese and Uighur cultures. Other cultural references could also be involved depending on the efforts of *The Economist*'s journalist in compiling the news report during the entire translation process.

People involved in the news translation process. According to Conway (2010), the news translation process involves the locals providing the news, the journalist covering the news, and the news media gatekeepers. How did the three types of people perform in this particular news coverage of the Xinjiang riot? To be relatively objective, we searched for answers to this question mainly by analyzing the forum posts. Of the 846 posts, 165 supported the news report (19.50%), 325 posts were neutral (38.42%), and 356 posts criticized the report (42.08%) according to the content and stances. Among the first category, we read posts expressing straightforward support such as, "Great article —probably the most nuanced description of what has been going on in Xinjiang over the past six days" (Li, July 10, 2009, 10:01). We also encountered supportive posts that reveal the posters' wishes for more information such as the following:

> Good article! Nobody hears about the atrocities unleashed against the minorities in China. Tibet has always been in the limelight, but people don't know the other ethnic groups, their rights, and religious beliefs in China. Please highlight those other groups as well, who suffer under the Communist rule. (Justice, July 14, 2009, 4: 13)

More importantly, supportive posts argued for the critical tradition of the Western media (Amused Observer, July 10, 2009, 12:09; Feelsonatural81, July 10, 2009, 4:32; Gargantual 1, July 14, 2009, 12:56; Taiwanlong, July 9, 2009, 11:34; Vischwen, July 10, 2009, 12:07). For example, in response to Happyfish (July 18, 2009, 2:08) concerning the Western media's berating of China, Goodman (July 18, 2009) wrote the following:

> Western media berates all countries, not just China. They berate even their own government. That's what freedom of [the] press means. I find articles in your *Economist* very good and impartial. If you don't like what *The Economist* says, you can always listen to your government. (4:24)

Clearly, posts in this category agree with and support *The Economist*'s news story with complimentary terms such as "good," "great," and "impartial."

Among the second category of posts, which were neutral, some posts simply clarified or added information to the news story, such as the following: "Tibet is a nation invaded by China in 1950. It is off the mark to compare the two with the riots in Xinjiang" (Nagarjuna, July 9, 2009, 8:38). Other posts expressed straightforward opinions such as the following: "The killing of innocent people, regardless by Hans or by Uighurs, is a crime! And the murderers represent themselves only, NOT [sic] those sharing the same ethnicity" (Fraser, July 10, 2009, 3:11). Most importantly, in still other posts, posters exchanged critical and constructive ideas. For example:

> *The Economist* is not like other newspapers. It doesn't disguise the fact that its news section contains mixed facts and opinions. I have been reading the newspaper for 20

years, and it has always been like this. If you want accurate reporting without a slant, you'd better off reading AP or Reuters. (Bismarck, July 10, 2009, 5:14)

I am a Chinese that grew up in the States, but I live in China now. To my fellow Chinese writing here, you guys really NEED [sic] to cool it. Reading the article, I wouldn't say that there is anything blatantly anti-China about it at all. It remains relatively neutral. Chinese are too sensitive and purposely go through every sentence written/uttered by Western media for signs that Westerners are against China. (Chelau, July 10, 2009, 11:20)

Thus, these posts neither staunchly supported nor strongly opposed *The Economist* and its news report. Nevertheless, they enriched the online discussions with additional information or personal critique from a neutral perspective.

The third category consists of posts that explicitly opposed *The Economist*'s gatekeepers and reporting of the Xinjiang riot. There is strong skepticism in quite a number of posts (Bismarck 111, July 10, 2009, 5:56; Funiushan, July 9, 2009, 23:36; Gold Phoenix, July 10, 2009, 2:18; Neptune Gao, July 10, 2009, 6:39; Toytony, July 10, 2009, 7:14) about the reliability of the news story's sources. For example:

"Overseas Uighur activists say, because the police opened fire." Is that independently confirmed truth? Did the police fire at people or did the police fire warning shots? There is no integrity in journalism these days, just partial truth. One simple thing, why did the Western media choose to ignore the fact that most of the 156 deaths are Han Chinese? (Toytony, July 10, 2009, 7:14)

Why did the journalist regard the overseas Uighur activists as a reliable source of information instead of eyewitnesses at the scene? One post provided an answer to this question: "Instead of sympathizing with the Han Chinese who had 123 lives lost among the total number of 156 in the riots, *The Economist* sees this incident as an opportunity to bash China" (Shah, July 13, 2009, 9:16). Other posts (Bismarck111, July 10, 2009, 6:03; Hidden Dragon, July 10, 2009, 7:12; EReader, July 15, 2009, 8:41; Man On Earth, July 10, 2009, 7:16; Scatologist, July 10, 2009, 4:57) criticized the journalist, with one correcting the journalist by saying, "Xinjiang is officially one of the five autonomous regions in China. It is not a province" (Scatologist, July 10, 2009 4:57). Another poster (Economistbuster, July 9, 2009, 9:39) commented on the misleading caption above Picture No. 1: "the journalist is logically chaotic and has confused the relationship between cause and effect by paralleling 'racial killing' and 'heavy-handed policing.'" The original caption reads: "Racial killings and heavy-handed policing stir up a repressed and dangerous province" ("Riots in Xinjiang," 2009, p. 1).

Finally, other posts (Deng, July 15, 2009, 7:50; Fischer, July 17, 2009, 8:27; Gold Phoenix, July 10, 2009, 2:18; NotSoBlackAndWite, July 10, 2009, 8:12; Wei, July 11, 2009, 2:42) denounced the clear bias and double standards among the gatekeepers in

Western media including *The Economist*. For example, one post observed: "*The Economist* often failed to provide a good enough report in Asia and Africa like its reports about the US or EU" (Wei, July 11, 2009, 2:42). Another post said, "No! It is bias, one-sided, and its double standards and selective reporting permeate the article. It is clearly aimed at shaping public opinion at the expense of innocent lives, journalistic ethics, and basic human conscience" (Dekoff, July 12, 2009, 3:08). This stance is reaffirmed in the following post:

> Most Western media may be very careful in reporting domestic news when their audience is relatively familiar with the facts so you seldom see blatant lies. In international news reporting, however, they may feel their latitude for truth-bending is much wider... *The Economist* just proved it didn't rank high on the truth scale.
> (Emperors Clothes Ripper, July 15, 2009, 3:18)

Two forms of cultural resistance. These posts clearly show readers did not like the double standards of *The Economist*'s gatekeepers, who released clearly biased news reporting. Coupled with the unreliable news sources and the journalist's irresponsibility, readers hesitated to accept *The Economist* as a credible media source for trustworthy news reports as can be seen in the following posts (BJren, July 20, 2009, 8:12; EmperorsClothesRipper, July 15, 2009, 3:18; Jyoshin, July 10, 2009, 9:06; Louis, July 11, 2009, 4:41; NotSoBlackAndWhite, July 10, 2009, 8:12; Universalist, July 13, 2009, 7:49). Below are two examples:

> I am disappointed that an *Economist*'s article can be filled with much speculation and biased views... It often requires good knowledge of the history and culture of a country to fully understand issues arising over that land. (NotSoBlackAndWhite, July 10, 2009, 8:12)

> It should be no surprise that *The Economist* has persisted its biased views when it covers China issues. It does so at least because in this world there are still many people loving this tone, and liking to see China through this type of colored glass. In the news coverage, I see few reliable facts, and Western readers are thus misled.
> (BJren, July 20, 2009, 8:12)

These examples expressed readers' disappointment and dissatisfaction. To them, *The Economist*'s news report was biased due to speculation and the lack of basic knowledge of local history and culture. The biased views of the Western media regarding Chinese issues were often taken for granted because this tone was conventional and popular among some targeted readers. Readers' disappointment in the culture of description and dissatisfaction with the culture of reception fit in very well with the two forms of cultural resistance described in the last aspect of Conway's (2010) theory of news translation and cultural resistance. The journalist and the gatekeepers of *The Economist* made a significant effort to "make their descriptions of events taking place in foreign cultural context to conform to the anticipated readers' expectations" (Conway, 2010, p. 189).

Having analyzed the media credibility of *The Economist*'s news story and the forum posts, we now discuss the communicative roles of the chosen posts against the six conditions of Dahlberg's (2001) ideal online public sphere.

Autonomy from the State and economic power. The first condition of Dahlberg's (2001) ideal online public sphere theory means posters in any online bulletin board such as a chatroom, message board, or online forum are not affiliated with any political parties, interest groups, or corporate concerns. Together, the posters "facilitate the growth and coordination of a global culture of resistance to the corporate takeover of cyberspace and of public life in general" (Dahlberg, 2001, para. 8). Close examination of the selected posts revealed that, except for 55 posters who clarified their origins, including China (23), India (15), Turkey (five), Canada (three), the United States (three), Germany (two), Thailand (two), Malaysia (one), and Finland (one), 791 of the 846 posters simply created nicknames such as "EmperorsClothesRipper," "Universalist," or "Gold Phoenix." Although some posters were suspicious that some Chinese posters had been brainwashed and paid by the Chinese government, the posters showed no clear evidence to prove their suspicion. In fact, one poster claimed, "I may not be able to speak on behalf of all the Chinese here, but I believe most of them are self-hired just like me" (Serene Sea, July 14, 2009, 10:36). Accordingly, we cannot say for certain there is complete autonomy from the State and economic power though we found most of the posts expressed personal opinions and the interactions between posters were genuine and meaningful.

Thematization and critique of criticizable moral-practical validity claims. Dahlberg's (2011) second condition requires forum participants follow "a rational, dialogic form of conversation" to exchange and critique "claims on every conceivable question" (para. 10) with justification. Abundant evidence supported this condition among all three categories of supportive, neutral, and opposed posts (EmperorsClothesRipper, July 15, 2009, 3:18; Feelsonatural81 July 10, 2009, 4:32; Goodman, July 18, 2009, 4:24; Gold Phoenix, July 11, 2009, 1:39; Hartog, July 12, 2009, 5:49; Moveon, July 12, 2009, 13:06; NoGo, July 10, 2009, 8:55; Wack-Intelligence, July 9, 2009, 11:27; Wei, July 11, 2009, 5:16). For example:

> @ Fahrettin Tahir,
> Can you please clarify what you meant your peoples who live in Chinese occupied territory; How many of them and the name of the occupied territory? (Small Fry, July 12, 2009, 10:30)

> Small Fry,
> Our people are the Uighurs, who speak a Turkish we in Turkey understand without much trouble. There are only about 8 million of them left because the Chinese governments in preceding centuries have killed so many and the present government prevents them from making as many children as they want. (Tahir, July 12, 2009, 10:39)

Chapter 23

Testing News Trustworthiness in an Online Public Sphere: A Case Study of The Economist's News Report Covering the Riots in Xinjiang, China

@ Fahrettin,

The Uighurs live in Xinjiang, which, under International Law, is Chinese territory, since all nations of the world recognize that China has the sovereignty over it. If the Uighurs have any complaints about their lives, they can also petition to the Central Government of China. Just because they have grievances does not mean they have the rights to claim the whole of Xinjiang. If the Chinese-Americans in California have grievances, can they have the rights to claim all the China-towns? (Gold Phoenix, July 12, 2009, 11:10)

This is a typical exchange of ideas in a rational and dialogic form of conversation. From Small Fry's question to Tahir, to Fahrettin's response, and to Gold Phoenix's response, we heard a complete and meaningful conversation about the Uighurs' complaints and the Chinese government's family planning policy for minorities in China. Moreover, the critical responses are justified with specific details such as the language and number of Uighurs and rational reasoning regarding an analogy between Uighurs in Xinjiang and Chinese Americans in California.

Reflexivity. Dahlberg's third condition calls for meditative and critical self-reflection and empathy in a heated online debate so as to think and talk as a "publicly-oriented netizen" instead of fighting for "the better argument" from the perspective of a "privately oriented individual" (Dahlberg, 2001, para. 15). There are also sufficient illustrations of this condition among the forum posts (Anti-Rob, July 20, 2009, 9:21; Aurona, July 11, 2009, 1:58; JasonP76, July 10, 2009, 7:40; Indica, July 11, 2009, 11:59; Moveon, July 12, 2009, 1:21; SeeingIsBelieving, July 17, 2009, 7:19). Below are two examples:

An inquiring mind:
You said, 'the Western civilization is not perfect, but in that system, there is always room for open debate and free elections,' and you asked, 'do you have that in China?'
I want to say we can talk freely on the Internet just as you. Maybe we are still not as free as you, but there has been big progress. We'll do better and we believe in democracy, but it takes time. (Anti-Rob, July 20, 2009, 9:21)

Aussie Louis:
Thanks for your comments. I was thinking of Western political commentators, editorials in the serious media. I have stated my view that Xinjiang and Tibet should, could, have become autonomy within the framework of one China. I want to see an economically strong China. Without some fairness in her political and economic systems, it is not possible for China to achieve the status she deserves. (Indica, July 11, 2009, 11:59)

In these examples, the two posters expressed their ideas calmly and thoughtfully. Instead of heating up the debate, they offered factual information and reasonable thoughts to other posters. The first poster was responding to another poster's question concerning freedom of speech and democratic elections. The second poster was describing his peaceful blueprint concerning the future of Xinjiang and Tibet and the efforts China needs to make in terms of political and economic fairness. The dialogic interactions between the posters demonstrate that their ideas are self-reflective and their thoughts are profound. Moreover, the posters carried on these discursive interactions as publicly-oriented netizens.

Ideal role-taking. Dahlberg's fourth condition expects posters to put themselves in others' shoes and carry out an "ongoing, respectful, and meaningful exchange of ideas" (Dahlberg, 2001, para. 33). Again, quite a few posts (Bismarck, July 11, 2009, 1:53; Chelau, July 10, 2009, 11:37; Gold Phoenix, July 11, 2009, 1:39; Goodman, July 18, 2009, 4:24; Happyfish, July 18, 2009, 2:08; John2003, July 10, 2009, 11:32) on the chosen forum met this condition. For instance:

> I think this article tries to inform those not living in China about what happened in Xinjiang. This newspaper is not meddling in anyone's affairs. If all countries prohibit other media from writing about them, then how do we know what happened in other countries? And there is nothing wrong with commenting on this issue. (Braveman, July 17, 2009, 4:00)

> I read about the religious restrictions by the Chinese government in Xinjiang . . .
> Here is a list:
> Banning boys under 18, government officials and workers in state owned companies from entering a Mosque. In some cases women.
> The same group is not being allowed to pray in public.
> Not allowing the same people to fast during the Ramadan month and not allowing children past puberty and under 18 to fast.... (Bismarck 111, July 10, 2009, 22:42).

> To Bismack 111:
> The religion restriction on Uighur government officials and workers is based on the fact that these people are Uighur Communists. As members of the Communist Party, they are atheists. For people under 18, they lack the judgment for religious affairs, especially institutionalized regions. This is similar to why they cannot vote either. (Peng, July 10, 2009, 22:51)

In the above, the first poster commented on the media's necessary function to keep readers abreast of what is going on in any country. More importantly, the poster expressed his or her rational and emotional understanding of *The Economist* to carry news with opinions. The second and third posters offered an extended example, which illustrates clearly a complete and meaningful ongoing dialogue between Bismarck111 and Luke Peng over the Chinese government's restrictions on religious belief among Uighurs in Xinjiang. Both posters showed respect to each other in their repeated questions and answers.

Sincerity. To meet Dahlberg's fifth condition, online posters ought to sincerely present all relevant information and their true intentions, interests, needs, and desires to one another and provide convincing evidence to support their argument (Dahlberg, 2001, para.

34). On the chosen online forum, posts (AusChin, July 18, 2009, 4:40; Daveycool, July 24, 2009, 6:04; Liverpool2005, July 21, 2009, 3:46; Smiter, July 15, 2009, 11:13; Tahir, July 18, 2009, 5:49; Xiong, July 15, 2009, 11:12) frequently met the fifth condition. For example:

> We happened to be travelling in Xinjiang early July . . . What we had seen gave a picture that those conflicts in Urumqi's several spots arose at the same time. We believed those were not occasional . . . This article is long enough to expose the typical adherence to subjects like this one. When talking about the dead or injured, it tries to refute 'those killed were overwhelmingly Hans.' Instead, it complained that the authorities did not provide racial breakdown and that the Uighur exiles said those killed included many Uighurs. What a signal it wants to convey? It seems that they don't care how many Hans were killed, but if there is any Uighur killed, it's a matter! Those dead are all lives vanished, no matter they were Uighurs or Hans . . . Remember the history that the British organized East Turkestan independence movement in early 20th century in Kashgar attempting to separate Xinjiang from China? Should China talk to Britain? China today is not China in 1989. Since China has been changing, though not to the extent that satisfies all democratic standards (none does in the world), we should take their achievements into account, and we in the democratic world should examine ourselves if we have changed enough to cope with the new situation. (RN, July 14, 2009, 8:26)

This lengthy post is an excellent example of sincerity with rational arguments supported by sufficient and convincing evidence. As an eyewitness tourist, the poster confirmed that the killing and burning during the Xinjiang riots "were not occasional" based on what he or she had seen on the tour bus on the night of July 5, 2009 in Urumqi. More importantly, this poster exposed the news report's biased writing style by showing concern over the lost lives of Uighurs only while neglecting those of Han Chinese. What is most praiseworthy is the poster's eye-opening statement that China today is not what it was yesterday, and countries in the developed world ought to adjust to the new situation in China.

Discursive equality and inclusion. Due to the social hierarchies and power relations, discursive inequalities and exclusions still exist in online discourse, though discursive equality and inclusion is Dahlberg's sixth condition for an ideal online public sphere (2001, para. 52). In fact, we observed posts with both features in the chosen online forum. For example:

> Hey, guys. I'm from Yining City, Xinjiang. It's our Xinjiang's [internal] affairs whether we belong to China or not. I have two points: First, why did *The Economist* delete my comments? Is it because I said we Xinjiang people are against your white bias? Don't you Western media brag about your freedom of speech? I am so disappointed at your so-called freedom of speech! (Cui, July 17, 2009, 2:14)

Azureangel's comment is so far the best and the most rational I have ever seen. Criticizing the Chinese government shouldn't be met with furious nationalism by

Chinese. It's just totally unnecessary and counter-productive. Similarly, it is worthless to be too angry about bias within the Western community regarding China's rising clout... (HikingAdam, July 23, 2009, 11:18)

In the first post, the poster complained *The Economist* might have deleted his or her post. Similar complaints were observed in four other places (Bismarck111 July 13, 2009, 14:16; Cui, July 17, 2009, 2:14; Sanmartinian, July 16, 2009, 10:50; Serene Sea July 14, 2009, 10:34). As one poster remarked, "I don't think it is the regular users who deleted the posts" (Bismarck111, July 13, 2009, 14:16); whoever deleted and supervised the posts, the issue is more human-made rather than technical. This shows that excluding some posters' voices may be a reality in online forum discussions. Discursive equality and inclusion were demonstrated in the second post, which called for fair treatment of different opinions and various criticisms from China and Western countries. Here, we heard outcries from the posters, who advocated that all media should play their roles to "foster world peace and harmony" instead of "sowing discord and miseries" by "distorting the truths and sensationalizing them to sell their publications" (AussieLouis, July 11, 2009, 4:41).

Conclusion

Answers to the research questions. The purposes of this study were to explore the news trustworthiness and media credibility of *The Economist*'s news report of the Xinjiang riots on July 9, 2009, and the communicative roles of the selected 846 readers' responses to this media source and its news report. To this end, we raised RQ1 (How trustworthy is *The Economist*'s July 9, 2009, news report in coverage of the Xinjiang riots?) and RQ2 (What roles do online readers play with their forum posts as a result of the online news report?). Through the theoretical lenses of Conway's (2010) news translation and cultural resistance theory and Dahlberg's (2001) online public sphere principles and via online field observation and discourse analysis, we achieved the following findings as answers to the research questions.

Regarding RQ1, we found that, on the one hand, the news story and *The Economist* still appealed to many readers, especially those who were accustomed to the Western media's news reporting. Therefore, *The Economist* and its July 9, 2009, news report together with two earlier reports on July 6 and 7 should be recognized for their timely and flexible coverage of the riots in Xinjiang for readers all over the world. In the case of the particular news report on July 9, the journalist compiled a variety of necessary facts and details and transformed them into a six-page, 3,000-word news story, which was quite comprehensive and attractive from the beginning to the end. More importantly, *The Economist* opened an online forum, which not only spread its news far and wide but also contributed to the online public sphere by attracting more than 1,000 posts offering responses from various cultural perspectives.

However, the news report and consequently *The Economist*, on the other hand, lost much of their trustworthiness and credibility due to a series of media biases. By relying on overseas Uighur activists as the source of information, the journalist reported that because the police opened fire, the Uighur protesters became angrier and killed Han Chinese with clubs and stones. Even when trying to cite the words of eyewitnesses, the journalist did not clarify whether the killers with clubs and stones were Uighurs or Han Chinese. No wonder some readers doubted the intentions or professionalism of *The Economist* in releasing this news report. Other forum readers also observed that clear bias and double standards existed among the gatekeepers of *The Economist*. Thus, we found all three types of media biases, gate-keeping bias, coverage bias, and statement bias, put forward by D'Alessio and Allen (2000).

Consequently, two types of dissatisfaction with the news story and rejection of *The Economist* by readers in and outside China arose. For instance, 356 of the 846 or more than 42% of the selected posts opposed *The Economist*'s news report due to its media biases. Many posters in the culture of description opposed *The Economist*'s news report because of its speculation and lack of basic knowledge of the local history and culture. Many other posters in the culture of reception lost hope in *The Economist* due to its clear biases and double standards in providing misleading reports about developing countries such as China and more carefully examined news about domestic affairs for British readers.

As for RQ2, our findings generally match Dahlberg's six conditions of an ideal online public sphere. First, although we cannot say for certain there is complete autonomy from the State and economic power, we found that most of the posters expressed personal opinions and interacted with one another genuinely and meaningfully. Second, the online forum was filled with repeated exchanges of interesting arguments. Some posters tracked one another for further dialogues about an idea or aspect in the news report until a meaningful end. Others formed two lines of active posts for or against a proposed topic in the forum. The majority of the posts along both lines were usually justified with specific supporting evidence. Third, with sufficient meditation and empathy, posters exchanged their ideas concerning the merits and demerits of *The Economist*'s news coverage with facts and opinions mixed together. These are typical examples of reflexivity from the perspective of publicly-oriented netizens.

Fourth, ideal-role taking is well illustrated by posts explaining the media's function in general and *The Economist*'s news report with opinions in particular. Quite a few posts showed sufficient empathy and carried out their exchange of ideas or argument on an ongoing, respectful, and meaningful manner. As for the fifth condition of sincerity, the extended example suffices it to say that this condition has been met. As an on-site tourist, the poster exposed the biased perspective of *The Economist*'s news report with eyewitness evidence and historical facts. Finally, the examples of the sixth condition revealed the strong possibility of an ideal public sphere, where every participant contributes mutually beneficial news and information on an equal footing though discursive inequalities and exclusions still exist in online discourse and some online media take all commercial measures available for survival.

Contributions as theoretical and practical implications. The contributions of the present study lie in its theoretical and practical implications. Theoretically, the study has enriched the existent body of literature on media bias and credibility through a specific case study of an online mainstream Western media news report of developing countries such as China. By analyzing the online news report and its forum posts representing opinions from various cultural perspectives, this study has not only added more validity to Conway's (2010) news translation and cultural resistance theory but also proved that Dahlberg's (2001) online public sphere principles are basically sound in theory.

Practically, this study demonstrates that the media credibility of online Western media such as *The Economist* is differently observed in the West and developing countries. Online readers need to be engaged in increased message scrutiny to guard against partial, unfair, and outright lies while fighting for more independent, reliable, accurate, and comprehensive news reports. Meanwhile, the present study also reveals that, although some mainstream media may still distort truths and sensationalize events to sell more publications for survival in the competitive commercial world, the ideal online public sphere for freedom of speech, political participation, and deliberative democracy is not far from reality. The ideal online public sphere is under construction right now with millions of online discussion participants as message decoders and encoders representing various cultural perspectives.

Limitations and call for future studies. This case study has at least three limitations. First, in this critical media study, we as researchers should have made our critical voices heard louder throughout the paper. Instead, we mainly depended on the existing literature by other scholars and online forum posts to convince readers of our arguments. Meanwhile, as researchers, we might have been somewhat subjective due to our cultural backgrounds and national emotions, thus affecting our critical ability in analyzing the news story and the online forum responses. Second, this is just a qualitative discourse analysis of one news report of a mainstream Western newspaper, *The Economist*. Therefore, readers are advised not to apply the findings here to other Western media or Western media as a whole. Finally, the quality of the findings of the present study may have been greatly strengthened if we had injected triangulation of either a quantitative content analysis or ethnographic in-depth interviews with some online forum participants or other ordinary readers. Future studies may either explore those areas we have not touched on or make a comparative study of the major differences in certain Western media in their coverage of similar events in different parts of the world.

(Tian, D. X., & Chao, C. C. (2012). Testing news trustworthiness in online public sphere: A case study of *The Economist*'s news report covering riots in Xinjiang, China. *Chinese Journal of Communication*, 5(4), 455-474.)

References

[1] About The Economist online. (2010). The Economist. Retrieved from http://www.economist.com/help/about-us#About_Economistcom.

[2] Al-Saggaf, Y. (2006). The online public sphere in the Arab world: The war in Iraq on the Al Arabiya website. Journal of Computer-Mediated Communication, 12, 311-334.

[3] Antaki, C., Ardévol, E., Nuñez, F., & Vayreda, A. (2006). "For she who knows who she is": Managing accountability in online forum messages. Journal of Computer-Mediated Communication, 11, 114-132.

[4] Bosch, T. (2010). Digital journalism and online public sphere in South Africa. Communicatio: South African Journal for Communication Theory and Research, 36(2), 265-275.

[5] Chang, T. K. (1988). The news and U.S./China policy: Symbols in newspapers and documents. Journalism Quarterly, 65, 320-327.

[6] Cohen, J. (1960). A coefficient of agreement for nominal scales. Educational and Psychological Measurement, 20, 37-46.

[7] Conway, K. (2010). News translation and cultural resistance. Journal and International and Intercultural Communication, 3(3), 187-205.

[8] Cridland, J. (2010). An introduction to newspapers in the UK. Retrieved from http://www.mediauk.com/article/32719/the-mid-market-tabloids.

[9] Dahlberg, L. (2001). Computer-mediated communication and the public sphere: A critical analysis. Journal of Computer-Mediated Communication, 7(1).

[10] D'Alessio, D., & Allen, M. (2000). Media bias in presidential elections: A meta-analysis. Journal of Communication, 50(4), 133-156.

[11] Entman, R. M. (2007). Framing bias: Media in the distribution of power. Journal of Communication, 57, 163-173.

[12] Eysenbach, G., & Till, J. E. (2001). Ethical issues in qualitative research on Internet communities. British Medical Journal, 323(7321), 1103-1105.

[13] Fairclough, N. (1995). Critical discourse analysis: The critical study of language. London, England: Longman.

[14] Fung, A. Y., & Kedl, K. D. (2000). Representative publics, political discourses and the Internet: A case study of a degenerated public sphere in a Chinese online community. World Communication, 29(4), 69-84.

[15] Gentzkow, M., & Shapiro, J. M. (2006). Media bias and reputation. Journal of Political Economy, 114(2), 280-316.

[16] Graber, D. A. (1989). Mass media and American politics. Washington, DC: Congressional Quarterly.

[17] Grbeša, M. (2003). Why if at all is the public sphere a useful concept? Politicka

Misao, XL(5), 110 – 121.

[18] Grunig, J. E. (2009). Paradigms of global public relations in an age of digitalization. PRism, 6(2), 1 – 19. Retrieved from http://www.prismjournal.org/fileadmin/Praxis/Files/globalPR/GRUNIG.pdf

[19] Gunter, B. (1997). Measuring bias on television. Luton, England: University of Luton Press.

[20] Habermas, J. (1989). The structural transformation of the public sphere: An inquiry into a category of bourgeois society. Cambridge, MA: MIT Press. (Original work published 1962)

[21] Hayes, A. S., Singer, J. B., & Ceppos, J. (2007). Shifting roles, enduring values: The credible journalist in a digital age. Journal of Mass Media Ethics, 22(4), 262 – 279.

[22] Hovland, C. I., Janis, I. L., & Kelly, H. H. (1953). Communication and persuasion: Political studies of opinion change. New Haven, CT: Yale University Press.

[23] Huang, L. N., & McAdams, K. C. (2000). Ideological manipulation via newspaper accounts of political conflict. In A. Malek & A. P. Kavoori (Eds.), The global dynamics of news: Studies in international news coverage and news agenda (pp. 57 – 74). Stamford, CT: Ablex.

[24] Jo, S. (2005). The effect of online media credibility on trust relationships. Journal of Website Promotion, 1(2), 57 – 78.

[25] Kiousis, S. (2001). Public trust or mistrust? Perceptions of media credibility in the information age. Mass Communication & Society, 4(4), 381 – 403.

[26] Kohring, M., & Matthes, J. (2005, May). Trust in news media: Development and validation of a multidimensional scale. Paper presented at the annual meeting of the International Communication Association, New York, NY. Retrieved from http://web.ebscohost.com/ehost/pdf?vid=2&hid=111&sid=e161b429 – 7b08 – 4892 – 8b96 – 07b81dd73af4％40sessionmgr110

[27] Kolb, D. (1996). Discourses across links. In C. Ess (Ed.), Philosophical perspectives on computer-mediated communication (pp. 15 – 26). Albany: State University of New York.

[28] Kovach, B., & Rosenstiel, T. (2001). The elements of journalism: What newspeople should know and the public should expect. New York, NY: Crown.

[29] Lent, J. A. (2006). Foreign news in American media. Journal of Communication, 27(1), 46 – 51.

[30] Leung, C. C. M., & Huang, Y. (2007). The paradox of journalistic representation of the other: The case of SARS coverage on China and Vietnam by Western-led English-language media in five countries. Journalism, 8(6), 675 – 697.

[31] Levi, M., & Stoker, L. (2000). Political trust and trustworthiness. Annual Review

of Political Science, 3(1), 475 – 507.

[32] Liu, T., & Bates, B. J. (2009). What's behind public trust in news media: A comparative study of America and China. Chinese Journal of Communication, 2(3), 307 – 329.

[33] McQuail, D. (1992). Media performance: Mass communication and the public interest. London, England: Sage.

[34] Media UK. (2011). The British media industry. Retrieved from http://www.mediauk.com.

[35] Mullainathan, S., & Shleifer, A. (2005). The market for news. American Economic Review, 95(4), 1031 – 1053.

[36] Page, B. I., & Shapiro, R. Y. (1992). The rational public: Fifty years of trends in Americans' policy preferences. Chicago, IL: University of Chicago Press.

[37] Papacharissi, Z. (2004). The virtual sphere: The Internet as public sphere. In F. Webster (Ed.), The information society reader (pp. 379 – 392). New York, NY: Routledge.

[38] Peterson, S. (1980). A case study of Third World news coverage by the Western news agencies and the Times. Studies Comparative International Development, 15(2), 62 – 98.

[39] Potter, J. W. M. (1987). Discourse and social psychology: Beyond attitudes and behavior. London, England: Sage.

[40] Pym, A. (2004). The moving text: Localization, translation, and distribution. Philadelphia, PA: Benjamins.

[41] Riots in China: Rumbling on. (2009, July 7). The Economist. Retrieved from http://www.economist.com/world/asia/displaystory.cfm?story_id=E1_TPJRDJNT.

[42] Shan, B., & Wang, J. L. (2009). On the fundamental ethical ideas of Western journalism. China Media Report Overseas, 5(4), 85 – 97.

[43] Shan, W., & Chen, G. (2011). The Urumqi riots and China's ethnic policy in Xinjiang. East Asian Policy, 1(3), 14 – 22.

[44] Shoemaker, P. J., & Reese, S. D. (1996). Mediating the message. Theories of influences on mass media content (2nd ed.). Essex, London, England: Longman.

[45] Singer, J. B. (2007). Contested autonomy: Professional and popular claims on journalistic norms. Journalism Studies, 8(1), 79 – 95.

[46] Stanford Encyclopedia of Philosophy. (2007). Jürgen Habermas. Retrieved January 10, 2010, from http://plato.stanford.edu/entries/habermas/

[47] Steensen, S. (2009). Online feature journalism: A clash of discourse. Journalism Practice, 3(1), 13 – 29.

[48] The Economist's philosophy. (2011). The Economist. Retrieved from http://www.economistgroup.com/what_we_do/editorial_philosophy.html.

[49] The riots in Xinjiang: Is China fraying? (2009, July 9). The Economist. Retrieved from http://www.economist.com/displaystory.cfm?story_id=E1_TPJRRQSJ.

[50] Unrest in China: Unrest on the Western front. (2009, July 6). The Economist. Retrieved from http://www.economist.com/world/asia/displaystory.cfm?story_id = E1_TPJSJQQD.

[51] Van Dijk, T. A. (1999). Editorial: On context. Discourse & Society, 10(3), 291-292.

[52] Villa, D. R. (1992). Postmodernism and the public sphere. American Political Science Review, 86, 712-721.

[53] Wang, J. (2008). China's missing voice rises up from the Internet. New America Media. Retrieved from http://news.newamericamedia.org/news/view_article.html?article_id=ab2892f06e32f01f066cabc48c8f2297.

[54] Wood, A. F., & Smith, M. J. (2005). Online communication: Linking technology, identity, and culture (2nd ed.). Mahwah, NJ: Erlbaum.

[55] Xiang, Y., & Sarvary, M. (2007). News consumption and media bias. Marketing Science, 26(5), 611-628.

[56] Yu, S. (2003). Lessons from SARS coverage. Nieman Reports, 4, 91-93.